WORKS of
ST. BONAVENTURE

Commentary on Ecclesiastes

Translation and Notes by Campion Murray, O.F.M.
and Robert J. Karris, O.F.M.
Introduction by Robert J. Karris, O.F.M.

Franciscan Institute Publications
The Franciscan Institute
Saint Bonaventure University
Saint Bonaventure, NY 14778
2005

Copyright © 2005
The Franciscan Institute
St. Bonaventure University
St. Bonaventure, New York

Library of Congress Card Catalogue Number: 2005921754

ISBN: 1-57659-197-2

Printed in the United States of America
        Bookmasters
        Mansfield, Ohio

CONTENTS

INTRODUCTION

THE DATE AND PURPOSE OF BONAVENTURE'S COMMENTARY ON ECCLESIASTES

The *Commentary on Ecclesiastes* by St. Bonaventure (d. 1274) was written between 1253-1257, when Bonaventure was teaching at Paris, and quickly became the dominant commentary on Ecclesiastes, displacing the commentaries of Jerome, Hugh of St. Victor, and Hugh of St. Cher as well as the *Glossa Ordinaria*.[1] Although its primary audience seems to have been the classroom, its multiple spiritual interpretations and the role that Ecclesiastes played as the second step of a three-step spiritual life suggest that this commentary may have aided preachers and spiritual directors.[2] As far as I can tell, all of Bonaventure's Latin commentary on Ecclesiastes has never been translated into a modern language.[3]

---

[1]See *Medieval Exegesis of Wisdom Literature: Essays by Beryl Smalley*, edited by Roland E. Murphy (Atlanta: Scholars Press Reprint, 1986), esp. 39-40.

[2]In a tradition going back to Origen, Proverbs was for beginners. Ecclesiastes was for those making progress in the spiritual life while The Song of Songs was for the perfect.

[3]For the Latin original see *Commentarius in librum Ecclesiastae* in *S. Bonaventurae Commentarii in Sacram Scripturam*, Tomus VI (Quaracchi: Collegium S. Bonaventurae, 1893), 1-99.

Bonaventure's Threefold Style of Exegesis in his Commentary on Ecclesiastes

Bonaventure Arrives at the Literal Sense by Interpreting Scripture by Scripture

Anyone familiar with Bonaventure's *Commentary on the Gospel of Luke* knows that the dominant style of exegesis in that commentary focuses on the literal sense.[4] Bonaventure arrives at the literal sense of a passage in Luke's Gospel by means of interpreting Scripture by Scripture. He maintains that the Spirit who ultimately wrote the Scriptures must be interpreted by the Spirit of the Scriptures and by the Spirit at work in the interpreter. As Bonaventure states in his "About the Mode of Expounding Scripture" in his *Breviloquium*: "Scripture has this special mode of proceeding and should be understood and expounded in a way that corresponds to it. Since it hides several meanings under a single text, the expositor must bring hidden things to light (Job 28:11). That is, once a meaning has been brought forth, to clarify it through another, more evident, scriptural passage. For instance, if I were expounding on the words of the Psalm, *Take hold of arms and shield, and rise up to help me* (35:2), and wanted to explain what is meant by the divine 'arms,' I would say that these are God's truth and good will. I would then use a more explicit biblical passage to prove that this is so. For it is written elsewhere: *You have crowned us, as with the shield of your good will* (Psalm 5:13), and again: *His truth will compass you with a shield* (Psalm 91:5). No one will find this kind of thing an easy task except by long practice in reading the text and committing its literal sense

---

[4]See *Bonaventure on Luke, Chapters 1-8, 9-16, 17-24* (St. Bonaventure, NY: Franciscan Institute Publications, 2001, 2003, 2004).

to memory. Otherwise, that person will never have any real capacity to expound the scriptures. The person who is too proud to learn the letters that make up a word can never understand the meaning of those words or grammatical constructions. So, too, the one who scorns the letter of sacred scripture will never rise to interpret its scriptural meanings."[5]

In Collation 19 n. 7 of his *Collations on the Six Days* Bonaventure expresses himself more succinctly: "All of scripture is like a single zither. And the lesser string does not produce the harmony by itself, but in union with others. Likewise, one passage of scripture depends upon another. Indeed, a thousand passages are related to a single passage."[6]

As readers work through Bonaventure's *Commentary on Ecclesiastes,* they will find that more than fifty percent of Bonaventure's exegesis is an interpretation of Scripture by Scripture. I give an example from his interpretation of Ecclesiastes 4:1: "'And I saw the oppressions that are done under the sun,' that is, in this world. Ezekiel 22:29 reads: 'The people of the land have used oppression and committed robbery. They afflicted the needy and poor, and they oppressed the stranger by calumny without judgment.' A violent seizing of goods is called *oppression*, when done not in justice, but in malice."

---

[5]I have modified the translation of Dominic V. Monti found in Timothy Johnson, *Bonaventure: Mystic of God's Word* (Hyde Park, NY: New City Press, 1999), 43. See also Opera Omnia 5:207 and *St. Bonaventure on Luke, chapters 1-8*, xx-xxi.

[6]This is my translation of Opera Omnia 5:421. See *Bonaventure on Luke, chapters 1-8*, xxi-xxii.

Bonaventure's spiritual interpretations derive from the literal sense

While the vast majority of Bonaventure's *Commentary on Ecclesiastes* deals with the literal sense, the literal sense often becomes the springboard for various spiritual interpretations, as is the case with his *Commentary on the Gospel of Luke*. There are twelve passages of spiritual interpretations in Bonaventure's *Commentary on Ecclesiastes*. Interestingly enough, none occurs in his interpretations of Ecclesiastes 5-8.[7] The longest is found after 12:6-7. These spiritual interpretations occur as follows: after Ecclesiastes 1:7, 2:8a, 3:8, 4:9-12, 4:15-16, 9:9-10, 9:12, 9:15, 10:15, 11:7, 12:2, 12:6-7. I provide two examples, one from the beginning of his commentary and one towards the end.

The first example comes from the three spiritual interpretations of sun, spirit/wind, and rivers that Bonaventure gives after his interpretation of the literal sense of Ecclesiastes 1:1-7. He gives a christological interpretation of "the sun" in Ecclesiastes 1:7 (#20): "Note the *spiritual* interpretation of *the sun . . . .The sun* is Christ, about whom Malachi 4:2 says: "But unto you who fear my name, the Sun of justice will arise." This sun *arose* in the nativity to enlighten. Isaiah 60:1 reads: "Arise, be enlightened, O Jerusalem." And John 1:9 has: "He was the true light that enlightens every human being." – This sun *set* in the passion for our redemption. Amos 8:9 says: "The sun shall go down at midday," that is, in a strong love of charity. – This sun *returned to its place* in the ascension. Luke 19:12 states: "A certain nobleman went into a far country," etc.[8] – This sun *makes its round by the south,*

---

[7]Could the reason be that these chapters have a preponderance of Bonaventure's *quaestiones*, that is, thirteen of thirty-four?

[8]Luke 19:12 concludes: " . . . to obtain for himself a kingdom and then return."

that is, in a fervent love of the Saints. The Song of Songs 1:6 reads: "Show me, O you whom my soul loves, where you feed, where you lie down at midday." And John 14:23 has: "If anyone loves me . . . we will come to him and will make our abode with him." – It *turns again to the north* in a final searching. Jeremiah 1:14 says: "From the north every evil will break," etc.

The second example comes from Bonaventure's spiritual interpretation of Ecclesiastes 11:1: "Cast your bread upon the running waters." In his commentary on Ecclesiastes 11:7 (#13) Bonaventure provides a tropological or moral interpretation: "These verses can also be briefly interpreted to apply to *spiritual almsgiving* that consists in instructing one's neighbor. As he did earlier, Ecclesiastes exhorts us to do this *willingly* or liberally, *abundantly*, and *without ceasing*, when he says: *Cast your bread*, etc., that is, give freely. Matthew 10:8 reads: "Freely have you received, freely give." *Give bread*, that is, the bread of *teaching*, about which Lamentations 4:4 says: "The little ones asked for bread, and there was none to break it for them." *Upon the running waters*, that is, those who despise temporal goods. To these alone should the bread of teaching be given. Matthew 7:6 states: "Do not give what is holy to dogs."

BONAVENTURE'S USE OF *QUAESTIONES*

Whereas in his *Commentary on the Gospel of Luke*[9] Bonaventure does not supplement his method of interpreting Scripture by Scripture by means of the scholastic method of the *quaestio*, his *Commentary on the Gospel of John*[10] and his *Commentary on Ecclesiastes* do. J. A. Weisheipl explains the scholastic method of the *quaestio*

---

[9]See *Bonaventure on Luke, chapters 1-8, 9-16, 17-24.*
[10]See Omnia Opera 6:237-530.

in this manner: "Generally, the lecture on a text was given in the morning, and the disputation on some significant point was held in the afternoon as a kind of seminar. The question was posed by the master; a senior student, later called a bachelor, was appointed to respond to closely argued objections (*videtur quod non*) proposed by other students. In conclusion the master summarized the state of the question. . . ."[11] In his *Commentary on Ecclesiastes* Bonaventure has adapted the scholastic method to address various thorny issues of interpretation.

I have numbered the thirty-four *quaestiones* Bonaventure employs in his commentary, so that they might be more readily accessible to my readers. Readers should be alerted to the fact that each *quaestio* may, in turn, have sub-questions. I refer to these sub-questions by numbering them within the larger *quaestio*. For example, I might be referring to question two of *quaestio* #1. Every chapter of Bonaventure's commentary except chapters 11 and 12 contains at least one *quaestio*. Chapter 7 has the most *quaestiones* (six) and the General Introduction and Chapter 6 have the least (one each). This method of exegesis comprises about one third of Bonaventure's entire exposition of Ecclesiastes and might helpfully be compared to the *excursus* in certain commentary series that allows the interpreter to delve into a particularly difficult issue or key concept at greater length. I like to compare these *quaestiones* to arias at operas such as "Give Me Some Music" in Samuel Barber's *Anthony and Cleopatra* that give pause to and interpret the movement of the opera.

Through his *quaestiones* Bonaventure shows himself to be very skilled in matters literary, moral, scientific, anthropological, and theological. Using somewhat broad categories and realizing that some categories overlap, I have

---

[11]See "Scholastic Method," *New Catholic Encyclopedia*, 2nd edition, Volume 12 (Detroit: Thomson Gale, 2003), 747.

determined that Bonaventure has eight *quaestiones* that deal with anthropological matters (#3, 6, 12, 13, 19, 20, 24, 29) and eight that deal with moral questions (#7, 21, 23, 26, 27, 31, 32, 33). Six concern questions of theology or more properly theodicy (#1, 5, 8, 15, 25, 28). Five focus on physics (#3, 4, 9, 11, 30). Four discuss literary issues (#1, 2, 10, 17), and four treat questions about riches and also religious life (#14, 16, 18, 22). Finally, one *quaestio* concerns demonology (#34). In a real sense Bonaventure's *quaestiones* are a commentary within a commentary and display Bonaventure struggling with various issues and finding answers in dependence upon philosophers such as Plato and Aristotle, theologians such as Augustine and Bernard of Clairvaux, and legal principles such as those found in the *Decretals of Pope Gregory IX*. We suggest that readers interested in pursuing Bonaventure's *quaestiones* look at the indices, primarily Index 3, which deals with philosophical sources.

In summary, the *quaestiones* deal with such issues as natural science,[12] theodicy, and the proper methodology to use in reading and studying Ecclesiastes and show Bonaventure at his creative best. In what follows I will briefly describe the nature of each one of his thirty-four *quaestiones* to whet the appetites of my readers for more leisurely enjoyment.

Quaestio #1 is one of the most important and valuable of all Bonaventure's *quaestiones*, as he discusses the problematic of Ecclesiastes from the perspective of the four Aristotelian causes. Time after time Bonaventure, especially in question one of *quaestio* #1, has to wrestle with the tradition that maintains that the purpose of

---

[12]Bonaventure treats questions of natural science, it seems, since the tradition, going back to Origen, required that teaching on physics or natural science be derived from Ecclesiastes. See Smalley, *Medieval Exegesis of Wisdom Literature*, 40-41.

Ecclesiastes is contempt of the world.[13] Much is at stake in his theological wrestling, for a main thesis of his theology is that creation is a stepping-stone to God or God's footprints.[14] Or as he himself says in question two of his *quaestio* #4: "A divine word is every creature because each creature speaks of God." His use of the traditional image of the world as a ring given by the bridegroom to the soul contributes to a solution of the problem of how Christians are to despise the world that God has created for human enjoyment and as a vehicle to knowledge of God. A further strength of this *quaestio* is Bonaventure's detailed discussion of the meaning of "vanity" in question two. Employing the philosophical category of "the true," Bonaventure argues: "Vanity is the lack of being ordered to a purpose, and thus all sins and abuses are vanities." He further argues: "To have true being a thing has unchangeable being. And in this way vanity is the opposite of the true in that it is changeable and transmutable." In the fourth question of *quaestio* #1 Bonaventure deals with an issue that exercises contemporary exegetes: How can such a pessimistic book as Ecclesiastes be canonical and generate trust?

---

[13]The tradition grouped Proverbs, Ecclesiastes, and The Song of Songs together and taught that Proverbs is for beginners in the spiritual life, Ecclesiastes for those making progress in the spiritual life, and The Song of Songs for those proficient in the spiritual life. So Ecclesiastes taught that a person made progress in the spiritual life by showing contempt for things. See Smalley, *Medieval Exegesis of Wisdom Literature*, 40-41 and also question 2 of Bonaventure's *Quaestio* #2 in his commentary on Ecclesiastes 1.

[14]See Bonaventure's *Itinerarium Mentis in Deum*, ed. Philotheus Boehner and Zachary Hayes, Works of St. Bonaventure II/Revised and Expanded (St. Bonaventure, NY: Franciscan Institute Publications, 2002). See also Ilia Delio, *Simply Bonaventure: An Introduction to His Life, Thought, and Writings* (Hyde Park, NY: New City Press, 2001), 54-66 (Creation).

Quaestio #2 devotes five individual questions to largely literary problems between the three works that Solomon wrote: Proverbs, Ecclesiastes, and The Song of Songs.

Quaestio #3 dedicates five individual questions to issues of natural science, e. g., the movements of the sun and the rivers. In this *quaestio* Bonaventure shows his dependence upon Aristotle.

Quaestio #4 revolves around four individual questions. Three of these questions deal with anthropological questions arising from specific verses in Ecclesiastes 1. For example, what is the meaning of "men and women cannot explain them in words" in Ecclesiastes 1:8? The remaining question concerns physics and stems from Ecclesiastes 1:9: "Nothing under the sun is new." Bonaventure relies on Aristotle to solve some individual questions.

Quaestio #5 considers the meaning of two very difficult verses. Ecclesiastes 1:13 reads: "This worst occupation (the search for wisdom) God has given to men and women to be exercised therein." Bonaventure answers that this is a "worst" occupation because it is God's just judgment on sin. The second verse is 1:15: "The perverse are corrected with difficulty." Bonaventure makes a threefold distinction to explain this verse. In the first distinction he borrows from Aristotle: "The answer is taken from the point of view of an *evil work*, because 'good is done in one way, but evil is done in many ways.'"

Quaestio #6 deals solely with the meaning of Ecclesiastes 1:18: "The person who adds knowledge also adds sorrow." In his response to this question Bonaventure quotes Aristotle: "All people by nature want to know."

Quaestio #7 concerns the interpretations of four verses, two of which involve Bonaventure in questions of morality, e. g., why is it sinful to delight in songs (Ecclesiastes 1:8)? In answering this question, Bonaventure relies on philosophical distinctions about various types of delight.

Quaestio #8 focuses on the exposition of four trouble-some verses. For example, question 4 asks about the meaning of Ecclesiastes 2:17: "I was weary of my life when I saw that all things under the sun are evil." Contrary to Ecclesiastes 2:17 Bonaventure quotes Genesis 1:31: "God saw all the things that God had made, and they were very good." His solution is found in Romans 7:12: "The law is holy and the commandment holy," but it is human beings who abuse these gifts and make them deadly.

Quaestio #9 questions the meaning of the two parts of Ecclesiastes 3:1: Do all things, including spiritual sub-stances, have their season? Do all things, including the four elements, pass away? While quoting some texts from Scripture, Bonaventure argues mainly from philosophical and ecclesiastical authorities.

Quaestio #10 asks about the reason for the twenty-eight times mentioned in Ecclesiastes 3:2-8: Are they ex-amples? Are they sufficient? Bonaventure's answer ulti-mately goes back to Augustine's interpretation of num-bers: "So he used numbers that include everything and its perfection. He lists twenty-eight times and fourteen dif-ferences, because twenty-eight is a perfect number and includes a seven, that is, the whole of time."

Quaestio #11 is one long question about the meaning of Ecclesiastes 3:14: "I have learned that all the works which God has made continue forever." Using Aristotle, Bonaventure answers the question by playing on the vari-ous nuances of perpetuity, changeability, and corruption.

Quaestio #12 concludes Bonaventure's exposition of Ecclesiastes 3 and concerns the fundamental anthropological questions behind Ecclesiastes 3:19 ("Human beings have nothing more than beasts") and Ecclesiastes 3:21 ("Who knows if the spirit of the children of Adam ascends upward?"). Bonaventure's reply to question two of this *quaestio* is worthy of quotation: "Our faith says and presumes that good souls go upward to be rewarded and that the souls of beasts go downward into corruption. Reason and philosophy agree with this. However, reason and philosophy are both obscure and provide many grounds for doubt."

Quaestio #13 considers four sub-questions. Two of these deal with Ecclesiastes 4:2-3 and its consideration of the non-alive as better than the living, e. g., "I praised the dead rather than the living." Bonaventure's answers to these fundamental questions about the value of existence and non-existence flow from Aristotle, Paul, Jonah, and Augustine.

Quaestio #14 deals with Ecclesiastes 4:7-12 and whether a solitary life should be preferred to communal living. In his reply Bonaventure seems to use two pre-formed pieces that describe three kinds of solitude and three kinds of communal living. Two quotations from Bernard of Clairvaux play a key role in Bonaventure's formulation of this *quaestio*.

Quaestio #15 raises two questions about what making vows means in Ecclesiastes 5:3: "If you have vowed anything to the Lord, defer not to pay it." In answering the first question, Bonaventure refers to *The Decretals of Gregory IX*. Bonaventure's second two questions focus on Ecclesiastes 5:6: "Do not say before the angel: There is no providence." Bonaventure's answers seem based on God's attributes, e. g., "Since it is characteristic of a wise person to provide for his household, this is even more so the case with the One who is most wise."

Quaestio #16 addresses one issue, based on Ecclesiastes 5:10: "What does the author mean by saying that 'riches do not profit their owner'"? In his response Bonaventure cites Scripture, Aristotle, and Bernard of Clairvaux. The latter writes: "Temporal things of themselves are neither good nor evil. Their use is good, their abuse evil. To worry over them is worse. To seek them is more shameful." Bonaventure's answer has the feeling of a preformed response.

Quaestio #17 has four questions. The first two contain one of the most profound examinations of the literary style and argument of Ecclesiastes as Bonaventure deals with the author's commendation of the enjoyment of present delight in Ecclesiastes 5:17-19. I quote at length from his second question. The author "speaks as a preacher, who weaves his argument in such a way that different persons present diverse opinions. Thus, one person speaks as a carnal person while another as a wise person. . . .But later he speaks in his own person and says in Ecclesiastes 12:13: 'Let us all hear together the conclusion of the discourse,' where he passes sentence on those whose arguments he had earlier presented: 'Fear God, and God will judge everything.' So anything read in the book that is contrary to that sentence is made void by that sentence. Such are all the things said to recommend present pleasure."

#18 is the formulation of three questions concerning the avaricious in Ecclesiastes 6:3. Bonaventure uses Albert the Great, Jerome, insightful literary analysis, and Augustine to arrive at his answers.

Quaestio #19 deals with three questions that concern the human capacities of knowledge and will, as Bonaventure fathoms the meaning of texts such as Ecclesiastes 6:9: "It is better to see what you may desire than to desire what you do not know." Bonaventure's answers are enriched by texts from Augustine and Aristotle. For example, he cites Augustine: "We are able to love what is not seen, but in no way can we love what is not known."

Quaestio #20 considers two texts. Ecclesiastes 7:2: "The day of death is better than the day of one's birth" and Ecclesiastes 7:4: "Anger is better than laughter." Aristotle and tradition help Bonaventure solve issues raised by the first text: ". . . death is preferred to life, for its dissolution, namely, death, has as its consequence rest and existence with Christ." Augustine assists Bonaventure in distinguishing between "anger over sin" and "the anger of nature."

Quaestio #21 is one of the shortest and least developed of the *quaestiones* and deals with two verses. Ecclesiastes 7:8 reads: "Oppression troubles the wise person" and Ecclesiastes 7:10 states: "Do not get angry quickly." In responding to issues raised by Ecclesiastes 7:8, Bonaventure quotes the *Glossa Ordinaria*: This text refers "to a wise person who is just and perfect." His response to the meaning of 7:10 is snappy: "It has to be said that anger has many forms."

Quaestio #22 focuses on three texts. One of them is Ecclesiastes 7:12: "Wisdom with riches is more useful." In replying to the objection that the Lord preferred the state of poverty, Bonaventure uses what seems to be a response fashioned in disputes about evangelical perfection: There is a triple poverty. He also has to deal with Aristotle's dictum: "Art and virtue are concerned about what is difficult."

Quaestio #23 is one of the longest of the *quaestiones* and has five individual questions. The first two questions revolve around the meaning of Ecclesiastes 7:17: "Do not be too just and do not be more wise than is necessary."

Bonaventure is indebted to Aristotle for his answer: "Virtue consists of the middle way and is damaged by too much and too little."

Quaestio #24 grapples with the meaning of two texts. Bonaventure employs Paul, especially 1 Thessalonians 5:21 ("Test all things. Hold fast to that which is good.") to explain Ecclesiastes 7:24: "I have tried all things in wisdom." The second text is Ecclesiastes 7:29: "One man among a thousand I have found. A woman among them all I have not found." Bonaventure appeals to grammar, Jesus' life and teaching, and tradition to argue that just men *and* *women* exist.

Quaestio #25 focuses on two verses. Ecclesiastes 8:2 reads: "I observe . . . the commandments of the oath of God." Relying on Augustine, Bonaventure handles problems such as how the all-truthful God can swear an oath. Ecclesiastes 8:5 states: "The person who keeps the commandment will find no evil." It seems that the commentaries of Salonius and Rupert of Deutz help Bonaventure to distinguish between evils that always endure and those that are transitory.

Quaestio #26 addresses two texts. I select Ecclesiastes 8:9: "Sometimes one person rules over another." Bonaventure's major question is whether one person can rule over another. After acknowledging that all people by nature are free and distinguishing between nature after and nature before the fall, Bonaventure argues that it is just that some people are servants. He comments: "Another reason for ruling over someone is to restrain the wicked." *Quaestio* #32 (the rule of the wicked over the just) corresponds to this question.

Quaestio #27 treats Ecclesiastes 8:14-15 under the general question: "Which status is better and more useful:

the condition of prosperity or adversity?" Scripture and Aristotle aid Bonaventure in distinguishing between the conditions of prosperity/adversity suffered by wicked people and those same conditions suffered by good people who are perfect or imperfect.

Quaestio #28 deals with three issues, the first of which arises from the meaning of Ecclesiastes 8:17: "I understand that a human being can find no reason for the works of God." Bonaventure uses Aristotle ("words are to be understood with reference to the topic") and Gregory ("God's judgments are not to be discussed, but venerated in an awesome silence") to argue that Ecclesiastes is not talking about God's works in general, but specifically about God's judgments.

Quaestio #29 considers four issues raised by Ecclesiastes 9:5-7. The first three issues concern life after death. For example, what does Ecclesiastes 9:5 mean: "The dead know nothing more"? Bonaventure observes that if Ecclesiastes is speaking in the person of Epicurus, his statement is clear. If he is speaking in his own name, however, these words "are to be understood of things in this world."

Quaestio #30 provides a sophisticated discussion of chance as Bonaventure asks the meaning of Ecclesiastes 9:11: "But time and chance in all." He uses Plato's understanding of causation to argue that nothing happens by chance. In turn, he uses Aristotle's understanding of causation to argue that there is chance: "In this way there is chance in everything, not because all things happen by chance, but because some element of chance is present in every changeable creature."

Quaestio #31 investigates the theological problem of the nature and power of sin raised by Ecclesiastes 9:18:

"The person who will sin in one will lose many good things." Bonaventure's answer is based on distinctions. For example, sin is to be seen from the point of view of a threefold deformity. Within the first deformity or loss there is a connection between sins: "Concerning the loss of a good freely given, there is indeed a connection between sins, because to commit one sin is to lose grace and all the virtues in so far as they are freely given."

Quaestio #32 corresponds to *Quaestio* 26 and asks about the situation where the wicked rule over the just. Since Waldensians and others claimed that the authority of wicked rulers was null and void, Bonaventure seems compelled to deal with such an issue as implied in Ecclesiastes 10:6: "A fool set in high dignity." Bonaventure distinguishes between three kinds of unjust rulers. Of the second kind he comments: "There is another ruler who acquires his office unjustly and rules without justice. Such a person can neither rule with justice nor should one be subject to this person."

Quaestio #33 comprises a long discussion about the sin of detraction that is prompted by Ecclesiastes 10:11: "If a serpent bites in secret, the person who backbites in secret is not better." After making three distinctions, Bonaventure offers this summary: "When there is neither necessity nor usefulness, even if what is said is the truth, a person is not excused by the passion of committing detraction. Further, such a person commits the sin of detraction, even if he is speaking the truth."

Quaestio #34 deals with the very strange Ecclesiastes 10:20: "Do not speak detraction against the king in your thought, and in your private chamber speak no evil of the rich person, because even the *birds of the air will carry your voice*." Bonaventure's focus is on "the birds of the air," who are the demons. Like many a medieval theologian

Bonaventure linked Luke 8:5 and 8:12, that is, the birds that eat up the seed along the wayside are demons. For their part demons know human thoughts and affections through some human sign, action, facial expression, or word.

BONAVENTURE'S SOURCES

As readers work their way through Bonaventure's Commentary on Ecclesiastes, it becomes clear that his major acknowledged ecclesiastical sources are the *Glossa Ordinaria*, the *Glossa Interlinearis*, Jerome, and Hugh of St. Victor. But as Crescentius v. d. Borne rightly contended over eighty-five years ago, Bonaventure's primary unacknowledged ecclesiastical source was his contemporary Hugh of St. Cher (d. 1263).[15] The indices at the end of this volume will direct interested readers to the numerous and detailed footnotes where I provide instances of Bonaventure's dependence upon the wisdom of his elder commentator. For our purposes I limit myself to three examples of Bonaventure's creative adaptation of Hugh of St. Cher's materials.[16]

---

[15]"De fontibus Commentarii S. Bonaventurae in Ecclesiasten," *Archivum Franciscanum Historicum* 10 (1918): 257-270. On p. 99 QuarEd mention as Bonaventure's primary ecclesiastical sources the *Glossa Ordinaria* and *Glossa Interlinearis*, Jerome, and Hugh of St. Victor, that is, they do not recognize the influence of Hugh of St. Cher. As Beryl Smalley comments: "An examination of his own sources has revealed a close dependence on Hugh of St. Cher. . . .The fact that Bonaventure had the postill (of Hugh of St. Cher) on Ecclesiastes on his table need only show that it had come to be regarded as an indispensable adjunct to the *Gloss*, as Hugh had intended it to be, in the eighteen years or so that separate the two regencies." See *Medieval Exegesis of Wisdom Literature*, 39-40.

[16]For examples of Bonaventure's creative use of Hugh of St. Cher's commentary on St. Luke's Gospel see the indices in: *St. Bonaventure's Commentary on the Gospel of Luke, Chapters 1-8, 9-16, 17-24*, With an

First, Bonaventure and Hugh of St. Cher have well over one hundred citations from Scripture in common. It may be due to pure coincidence that they have so many quotations in common, or it may be due to the way their memories were trained to retain the Scriptures during their education at Paris. But when Bonaventure and Hugh of St. Cher have the same two quotations from Scripture in sequence, then coincidence may fly out the door and dependence enter.[17] In their interpretations of Ecclesiastes 5:14-15a they both cite Job 1:21 and 1 Timothy 6:7. Ecclesiastes 5:14-15a reads: "As he came forth naked from his mother's womb, so shall he return and will take nothing away with him of his labor. A most deplorable evil: As he came, so shall he return." Job 1:21 states: "Naked I came out of my mother's womb, and naked shall I return thither." 1 Timothy 6:7 says: "We brought nothing into this world, and certainly we can carry nothing out."[18]

A second example occurs in Bonaventure's commentary on Ecclesiastes 12:11 (#58): "So he says: *Which by the counsel of the masters*, that is, a deliberate discussion and statement, *given by one shepherd*, that is, by Christ, who

---

Introduction, Translation and Notes by Robert J. Karris, Works of St. Bonaventure VIII/1, 2, 3 (St. Bonaventure, NY: Franciscan Institute Publications, 2001, 2003, 2004). See further my "A Comparison of the *Glossa Ordinaria*, Hugh of St. Cher, and St. Bonaventure on Luke 8:26-39," *Franciscan Studies* 58 (2000) 121-236, "Bonaventure's Commentary on Luke: Four Case Studies of His Creative Borrowing from Hugh of St. Cher," *Franciscan Studies* 59 (2001): 133-236, and "St. Bonaventure's Use of *Distinctiones*: His Independence of and Dependence on Hugh of St. Cher," *Franciscan Studies* 60 (2002): 209-250.

[17]In this and other instances I provide sufficient indication of dependence and direct interested readers to the specific passages where more detail will be given in the notes.

[18]More details will be found in the commentary on Ecclesiastes 5:12-15a (#19) and the notes there.

is the shepherd, according to what is said in John 10:11: 'I am the good shepherd.' Words of the wise are given to them by this shepherd, according to Augustine: 'He has the office of teacher in heaven who teaches us in our heart.' For Matthew 23:8 states: 'One is your teacher, the Christ.'" In his commentary on this passage Hugh of St. Cher also quotes John 10:11 and Matthew 23:8: "Given by one shepherd], that is, by Christ, who alone is the true shepherd of souls. For John 10 says: I am the good shepherd. And Matthew 23 states: One is your teacher, the Christ."

Second, there are a significant number of instances where Bonaventure states that he is quoting a certain author, for example, Seneca, and it can be determined by comparing Bonaventure's text, that of Hugh of St. Cher, and Seneca's text itself, that Bonaventure is actually quoting Seneca through Hugh of St. Cher. I take my first example from Bonaventure's commentary on Ecclesiastes 5:9a (#13): "A covetous person will not be satisfied with money." Bonaventure observes: "And Seneca comments: 'If you want to make yourself rich, it is not necessary to accumulate money, but to curb greed." The editors of the critical edition of Bonaventure's Commentary on Ecclesiastes scoured Seneca's writings for this citation and had to settle for this parallel: "Money never made a man rich; on the contrary, it always smites men with a greater craving for itself." In a quotation that is virtually identical with that of Bonaventure Hugh of St. Cher writes: "And Seneca says: If you want to make yourself rich, it is not necessary to accumulate riches, but to curb greed."

My second instance stems from Bonaventure's exposition of Ecclesiastes 1:13 (#33): "Note what Hugh says: 'An occupation is a distraction of the mind that turns away, distracts, and traps a soul from being able to think of what concerns salvation.' Curiosity, however, is a willful prostitution of a human mind, embracing any truth it chances on and being adulterous with it, because the first truth is the soul's only spouse."

I translate Hugh of St. Victor: "An occupation is a distraction and entanglement of minds that turns away, dissipates, and traps souls, lest they succeed in thinking of what pertains to salvation."

Hugh of St. Cher comments: "An occupation is described by Master Hugh of St. Victor in this way: An occupation is a distraction and an entanglement of the mind that turns away and dissipates and entangles it from being able to think of what concerns salvation. Curiosity, however, is nothing other than the willful prostitution of the human mind, embracing any truth it chances upon, and fornicating with it, or to speak more truthfully, being adulterous with it. For the first truth, which is God, is human mind's only spouse."[19]

I draw the conclusion: Bonaventure is not quoting Hugh of St. Victor directly, but is adapting the quotation of Hugh of St. Victor from Hugh of St. Cher.[20]

My third and final test case provides two examples that may not be probative, because there is no third text that can be used as a control. Yet the fact that both Bonaventure and Hugh of St. Cher cite the same texts virtually in the same way does not seem to be the result of sheer coincidence. In his second question of *Quaestio* #12, after his commentary on Ecclesiastes 3:22 (#42), Bonaventure addresses the issue of whether the spirit of Adam's children ascends upward and gives this first re-

---

[19]See the full commentary and notes on Ecclesiastes 1:13 (#33) below.

[20]See "De fontibus," 260-261 where Crescentius v. d. Borne also adduces this passage as proof of his contention that Bonaventure borrowed from Hugh of St. Cher.

sponse: "First, from the disposition of the body, which is arranged and organized with a view to its suitability towards what is above. If, then, 'he gave to humans an uplifted face to turn their eyes to heaven,' they also look for what is above. Therefore, the spirit goes upward." The Latin text of Bonaventure's citation is: *Os homini sublime dedit caelumque tueri*. This is a quotation from Ovid's *Metamorphoses*, whose Latin text is: *Os homini sublime dedit caelumque videre iussit et erectos ad sidera tollere vultus* ("he gave to human beings an uplifted face and bade them stand erect and turn their eyes to heaven"). Hugh of St. Cher also quotes Ovid: "*Os homini sublime dedit coelumque videre jussit*" ("He gave to humans an uplifted face and commanded them to look to heaven"). Neither Bonaventure nor Hugh of St. Cher state that they are quoting Ovid. My hypothesis is that Bonaventure is quoting Ovid from Hugh of St. Cher and not directly.[21]

In his commentary on Ecclesiastes 10:7 (#31), "Blessed is the land, whose king is noble," Bonaventure observes: "Namely, in nobility of character, for true nobility consists in having a soul adorned with virtues." The Latin is: *Quia nobilitas sola est quae animum moribus ornat*. Hugh of St. Cher uses a variant of the same dictum: "*Nobilitas animi sola est, quae moribus ornat*" ("Nobility of soul consists solely in having it adorned with virtues"). The editors of Hugh of St. Cher's commentary put this saying into italics and set it off as a quotation. It would seem to me that Bonaventure quoted this saying from Hugh of St. Cher.[22]

---

[21]For more detail see the commentary below and especially the notes.
[22]See the commentary below and the notes for more detail.

With these three instances of dependence I rest my case for Bonaventure's dependence upon Hugh of St. Cher. Although Hugh of St. Cher's postill on Ecclesiastes is the major ecclesiastical source behind Bonaventure's commentary, it plays a small role in his total creative work, one of whose main features is his use of *quaestiones* that explain difficult points in the text of Ecclesiastes and comprise about one third of his exposition.

TRANSLATION OF BONAVENTURE'S TEXT OF ECCLESIASTES

This translation is based on the Douay version and employs inclusive language. Bonaventure's text was the Latin Vulgate of the original Hebrew, a translation that St. Jerome reputedly accomplished in one day. After providing the translation of Bonaventure's text, we will compare his text to a select number of passages from the NRSV.

Chapter 1

[1] The words of Ecclesiastes, son of David, king of Jerusalem.

[2] Vanity of vanities, said Ecclesiastes, and all is vanity. [3] What profit do people have for all the labor that they engage in under the sun? [4] One generation passes away, and another generation comes, but the earth stands forever. [5] The sun rises and goes down, and returns to its place, and there rising again, [6] makes its round by the south and turns again to the north. The spirit goes forward surveying all places round about and returns to its circuits. [7] All the rivers run into the sea, yet the sea does not overflow. Unto the place whence the rivers come, they return to flow again. [8] All things are hard. Human beings cannot explain them in words. The eye is not filled with seeing. Neither is the ear filled with hearing. [9] What is it

that has been? The same thing that will be. What is it that has been done? The same that will be done. [10] Nothing under the sun is new. Neither is any person able to say: Behold, this is new. For it has already gone before in the ages that were before us. [11] There is no remembrance of former things. Nor indeed of those things which hereafter are to come, will there be any remembrance with those who will be in the latter end.

[12] I, Ecclesiastes, was king in Jerusalem. [13] And I proposed in my mind to seek and search out wisely concerning all things that are done under the sun.

This worst occupation God has given to men and women to be exercised therein. [14] I have seen all things that are done under the sun. And behold, all is vanity and vexation of spirit. [15] The perverse are corrected with difficulty, and the number of fools is infinite.

[16] I have spoken in my heart, saying: Behold, I have become great, and in wisdom I have gone beyond all who were before me in Jerusalem. And my mind contemplated many things wisely, and I have learned. [17] And I have given my heart to know prudence and learning and errors and folly. And I have perceived that in these also there was labor and vexation of spirit. [18] Because in much wisdom there is much indignation. The person who adds knowledge also adds sorrow.

Chapter 2

[1] I said in my heart: I will go and abound with delights and enjoy good things. And I saw that this, too, is vanity. [2] Laughter I counted error. And to joy I said: Why are you vainly deceived? [3] I thought in my heart, to withdraw my flesh from wine, so that I might turn to wisdom and might avoid folly, till I might see what was profitable for men and women, what they ought to do under the sun, all the days of their lives.

⁴ I have made great works for myself. I built houses for myself. I planted vineyards. ⁵ I made gardens and orchards and set them with trees of all kinds. ⁶ I made for myself ponds of water to water therewith the wood of the young trees. ⁷ I acquired menservants and maidservants and had a large family and herds of oxen, and great flocks of sheep beyond all that were before me in Jerusalem. ⁸ I heaped together for myself gold and silver and the wealth of kings and provinces. I made for myself male and female singers and the delights of men and women, cups and vessels to serve and pour out the wine.

⁹ And I surpassed in riches all who were before me in Jerusalem. My wisdom also remained with me. ¹⁰ And all my eyes desired, I refused them not. I withheld not my heart from delighting itself in the things that I had prepared. I esteemed this my portion, to make use of my own labor. ¹¹ And when I turned myself to all the works that my hand had wrought and to the labors wherein I had labored in vain, I saw in all things vanity and vexation of spirit and that nothing was lasting under the sun. ¹² I passed further to behold wisdom and error and folly.

What are human beings, said I, that they can follow the King, their maker? ¹³ And I saw that wisdom excelled folly, as much as light differs from darkness. ¹⁴ The eyes of the wise are in their heads. Fools walk in darkness. And I learned that both alike were to die. ¹⁵ And I said in my heart: If the death of the fool and mine shall be one, what does it avail me that I have applied myself more to the study of wisdom? And I have spoken with my own mind and have perceived that this also is vanity. ¹⁶ For there shall be no more remembrance of the wise than of the fool forever, and the times to come shall cover all things together with oblivion. The learned die in like manner as the unlearned. ¹⁷ Therefore, I was weary of my life, when I saw that all things under the sun are evil, and all vanity and vexation of spirit.

[18] Again I hated all my application wherewith I had earnestly labored under the sun. I would have an heir after me [19] and do not know whether he would be a wise person or a fool. And he will have rule over all the labors with which I have labored and have been solicitous. Is there anything so vain? [20] Wherefore, I left off, and my heart renounced laboring any more under the sun. [21] For when a person labors in wisdom and knowledge and carefulness, he leaves what he has gotten to an idle person. So this also is vanity and a great evil. [22] For what profit will human beings have from all their labor and vexation of spirit, with which they have been tormented under the sun? [23] All their days are full of sorrows and miseries. Even in the night they do not rest in mind. And is this not vanity?

[24] Is it not better to eat and drink and to show their souls good things from their labors? And this is from the hand of God. [25] Who will so feast and abound in delights as I? [26] God has given to a person who is good in his sight wisdom and knowledge and understanding, but to the sinner he has given vexation and superfluous care to heap up and to gather together and to give to the person who has pleased God. But this also is vanity and a fruitless solicitude of the mind.

CHAPTER 3

[1] All things have their season, and in their times all things pass under the sun.

[2] A time to be born and a time to die. A time to plant and a time to pluck up what has been planted.

[3] A time to kill and a time to heal. A time to destroy and a time to build.

[4] A time to weep and a time to laugh. A time to mourn and a time to dance.

[5] A time to scatter stones and a time to gather. A time to embrace and a time to be far from embraces.

[6] A time to get and a time to lose. A time to keep and a time to cast away.

[7] A time to rend and a time to sew. A time to keep silence and a time to speak.

[8] A time of love and a time of hatred. A time of war and a time of peace.

[9] What advantage do human beings have from their labor? [10] I have seen the trouble which God has given human beings to be exercised in it. [11] He has made all things good in their time and has delivered the world to their consideration, so that human beings cannot find out the work which God has made from the beginning to the end. [12] And I have known that there was no better thing than to rejoice and to do well in one's life. [13] For all, who eat and drink, see good in their labors. This is a gift from God.

[14] I have learned that all the works which God has made continue forever. We cannot add anything, nor take away from those things which God has made with the result that God may be feared. [15] That which has been made, the same continues. Things that will be have already been. And God restores what is past.

[16] I saw under the sun in the place of judgment wickedness, and in the place of justice iniquity. [17] And I said in my heart: God will judge both the just and the wicked, and then will be the time of everything. [18] I said in my heart concerning the men and women that God would prove them and show them to be like beasts. [19] Therefore, the death of humans and of beasts is one, and the condition of them both is equal. As a human being dies, so they also die. All things breathe alike. And human beings have nothing more than beasts. All things are subject to vanity. [20] And all things go to one place. Of earth they were made, and into earth they return together. [21] Who knows if the spirit of the children of Adam ascends upward, and if the spirit of the beasts descends downward?

²² And I have found that nothing is better than for people to rejoice in their work, and that this is their portion. For who will bring them to know the things that will be after them?

CHAPTER 4

¹ I turned myself to other things, and I saw the oppressions that are done under the sun, and the tears of the innocent, and they had no comforter. They were not able to resist their violence, being destitute of all help. ² And I praised the dead rather than the living. ³ And I judged that person happier than them both who is not yet born nor has seen the evils that are done under the sun.

⁴ Again I considered all the labors of men and women, and I remarked that their industries are exposed to the envy of their neighbors. So in this also is vanity and fruitless care. ⁵ Fools fold their own hands and eat their own flesh, saying: ⁶ Better is a handful with rest than both hands full with labor and vexation of mind.

⁷ Considering, I found also another vanity under the sun. ⁸ There is but one, and he has not a second, no child, no brother, and yet he ceases not to labor. Neither are his eyes satisfied with riches. Neither does he reflect, saying: For whom do I labor and defraud my soul of good things? In this also is vanity and a grievous vexation.

⁹ It is better, therefore, that two should be together than one, for they have the advantage of mutual companionship. ¹⁰ If one fall, he will be supported by the other. Woe to the person who is alone, for when he falls, he has no one to lift him up. ¹¹ And if two lie together, they shall warm one another. How will one alone be warmed? ¹² And if a person prevail against one, two will withstand that person. A threefold cord is not easily broken.

¹³ Better is a child that is poor and wise than a king who is old and foolish, who knows not to foresee for here-

after. [14] Because out of prison and chains sometimes a person comes forth to a kingdom. And another, who is born king, is consumed with poverty. [15] I saw all the living who walk under the sun with the second young man, who will rise up in his place. [16] The number of all the people who were before him is infinite, and those who will come afterwards will not rejoice in him. But this too is vanity and vexation of spirit.

[17] Guard your foot when you go into the house of God and draw near to hear. For much better is obedience than the victims of fools, who know not what evil they do.

CHAPTER 5

[1] Do not speak anything rashly, and let not your heart be hasty to utter a word before God. For God is in heaven, and you upon the earth. Therefore, let your words be few. [2] Dreams follow many cares, and in many words will be found folly. [3] If you have vowed anything to God, do not defer to pay it. For an unfaithful and foolish promise displeases God. But whatsoever you have vowed, pay it. [4] And it is much better not to vow, than after a vow not to perform the things promised. [5] Give not your mouth to cause your flesh to sin, and do not say before the angel: There is no providence, lest God be angry at your words and destroy all the works of your hands. [6] Where there are many dreams, there are many vanities and words without number. But do you fear God. [7] If you shall see the oppressions of the poor and violent judgments and justice perverted in the province, do not wonder at this matter. For the person who is high has another higher, and there are others still higher than these.

[8] Moreover, there is the king who reigns over all the land subject to him.

[9] A covetous person will not be satisfied with money, and the person who loves riches will reap no fruit from them. So this also is vanity.

[10] Where there are great riches, there are also many to eat them. And what does it profit the owner, but that he sees the riches with his eyes? [11] Sleep is sweet to laborers, whether they eat little or much. But the fullness of the rich will not allow them to sleep. [12] There is also another grievous evil which I have seen under the sun: Riches kept to the harm of the owner.

[13] For they are lost with very great affliction. He has begotten a son who will be in extremity of need. [14] As he came forth naked from his mother's womb, so shall he return and will take nothing away with him of his labor. [15] A most deplorable evil: As he came, so shall he return. What then does it profit him that he has labored for the wind? [16] All the days of his life he eats in darkness, and in many cares, and in misery and in sorrow. [17] This, therefore, seemed good to me that people should eat and drink and enjoy the fruit of their labors, wherewith they have labored under the sun, all the days of the lives which God has given them. And this is their portion. [18] And all to whom God has given riches and substance and has given them power to eat thereof and to enjoy their portion and to rejoice in their labors. This is a gift of God. [19] For they will not remember much of the days of their lives, because God entertains their heart with delight.

CHAPTER 6

[1] There is also another evil that I have seen under the sun, and that frequent among men and women. [2] A man, to whom God has given riches and substance and honor, and his soul wants nothing of all that he desires. Yet God does not give him power to eat thereof, but a stranger will eat them up. And this is vanity and a great misery.

³ If someone begets a hundred children and lives many years and attains to a great age and his soul made no use of the goods of his substance and he will be without burial, of this person I will pronounce that the untimely born is better than he. ⁴ For he came in vain and goes into darkness, and his name will be wholly forgotten. ⁵ He has not seen the sun nor known the distance between good and evil. ⁶ Although he lived two thousand years and has not enjoyed good things, do not all make haste to one place?

⁷ All human labor is for one's mouth, but one's soul will not be filled. ⁸ What more has the wise person than the fool? And what the poor person, but to go there where there is life? ⁹ It is better to see what you may desire than to desire what you do not know. But this also is vanity and presumption of spirit.

¹⁰ The person who will be, his name is already called. And it is known that he is a human being and cannot contend in judgment with him who is stronger than himself. ¹¹ There are many words that have much vanity in disputing.

Chapter 7

¹ Why do people need to seek things that are above them whereas they do not know what is profitable for them in their lives, in all the days of their pilgrimage, and the time that passes like a shadow? Or who can tell them what will be after them under the sun?

² A good name is better than precious ointments, and the day of death than the day of one's birth.

³ It is better to go to the house of mourning than to the house of feasting, for in that we are put in mind of the end of all, and the living think of what is to come.

⁴ Anger is better than laughter, because by the sadness of the countenance the mind of the offender is corrected.

⁵ The heart of the wise is where there is mourning. The heart of fools is where there is mirth.

⁶ It is better to be rebuked by a wise person than to be deceived by the flattery of fools.

⁷ For as the crackling of thorns burning under a pot, so is the laughter of the fool. Now this also is vanity.

⁸ Oppression troubles the wise person and will destroy the strength of his heart.

⁹ Better is the end of a speech than the beginning. Better is the patient person than the presumptuous.

¹⁰ Do not get angry quickly, for anger rests in the bosom of a fool.

¹¹ Do not say what do you think is the cause that the former times were better than they are now. For this manner of question is foolish. ¹² Wisdom with riches is more useful and brings more advantage to those who see the sun.

¹³ For as wisdom is a defense, so money is a defense. But learning and wisdom excel in this, that they give life to the person who possesses them. ¹⁴ Consider the works of God that no one can correct whom he has despised.

¹⁵ In the good day enjoy good things and beware beforehand of the evil day. For God has made both the one and the other, so that human beings may not find any just complaint against God. ¹⁶ These things I also saw on the day of my birth: Just people perish in their justice and the wicked live a long time in their wickedness. ¹⁷ Do not be too just and do not be more wise than is necessary, lest you become senseless. ¹⁸ Do not be too wicked. Do not be foolish, lest you die before your time.

¹⁹ It is good that you should hold up the just. Yes and from him do not withdraw your hand. The person who fears God neglects nothing.

²⁰ Wisdom has strengthened the wise more than ten princes of the city.

²¹ For on the earth there is no just person who does good and sins not. ²² But do not apply your heart to all words that are spoken, lest perhaps you hear your servant reviling you. ²³ For your conscience knows that you also have often spoken evil of others.

²⁴ I have tried all things in wisdom. I have said: I will be wise, and it departed further from me, ²⁵ much more than it was. It is a great depth. Who will find it out? ²⁶ I have surveyed all things with my mind to know and consider and seek out wisdom and reason, and to know the wickedness of the fool and the error of the imprudent.

²⁷ And I have found more bitter than death a woman, who is the hunter's snare, and her heart is a net and her hands are bands. The person who pleases God will escape from her, but the person who is a sinner will be caught by her. ²⁸ Behold, this I have found, said Ecclesiastes, weighing one thing after another, that I might find out the reason ²⁹ which my soul still seeks. And I have not found it. One man among a thousand I have found. A woman among them all I have not found. ³⁰ Only this have I found, that God made human beings right, and they have entangled themselves in an infinity of questions. Who is as the wise person? And who has known the resolution of the word?

Chapter 8

¹ The wisdom of people shine on their countenance, and the most mighty will change their face. ² I observe the mouth of the king, and the commandments of the oath of God. ³ Do not be hasty to depart from his face, and do not continue in an evil work, for he will do all that pleases him. ⁴ And his word is full of power. Neither can any one say to him: Why do you do this? ⁵ The person who keeps the commandment will find no evil. The heart of a wise person understands time and answer.

[6] There is a time and opportunity for every business, and great affliction for men and women,[7] who are ignorant of things past, and things to come they cannot know by any messenger. [8] It is not in a people's dominion to stop the spirit. Neither have they power on the day of death. Neither are they suffered to rest when war is at hand. Neither will wickedness save the wicked.

[9] All these things I have considered, and I applied my heart to all the works that are done under the sun. Sometimes one person rules over another to his own hurt. [10] I saw the wicked buried, who also when they were yet living were in the holy place and were praised in the city as people of just works. But this also is vanity.

[11] For since sentence is not speedily pronounced against the evil, men and women commit evils without any fear. [12] But though a sinner does wrong a hundred times, and by patience be borne with, I know that it will be well with those who fear God, who dread his face. [13] But let it not be well with the wicked. Neither let their days be prolonged, but as a shadow let those pass away who fear not the face of the Lord. [14] There is also another vanity, which is done upon the earth. There are just people to whom evils happen, as though they had done the works of the wicked. And there are wicked people, who are as secure as though they had done the deeds of the just. But this also I judge most vain.

[15] Therefore, I commended mirth, because there was no good for people under the sun, but to eat and drink, and that they should take nothing else with them of their labors in the days of their lives, which God has given them under the sun.

[16] And I applied my heart to know wisdom and to understand the spread of things that are upon the earth. For there are some who day and night take no sleep with their eyes.

[17] And I understand that a human being can find no reason for all those works of God that have been done under the sun. And the more human beings shall labor to seek, so much the less will they find. Yea, though the wise shall say that they know it, they will not be able to find it. All these things I considered in my heart, that I might carefully understand them.

Chapter 9

[1] There are just and wise people, and their works are in the hand of God. And yet men and women do not know whether they be worthy of love or hatred. [2] But all things are kept uncertain for the time to come, because all things equally happen to the just and to the wicked, to the good and to the evil, to the clean and to the unclean, to persons who offer holocausts and victims and to those who despise sacrifices. As the good is, so also the sinner. As the perjurer, so he also who swears truth. [3] This is a very great evil among all things that are done under the sun, that the same things happen to all people, whereby also the hearts of men and women are filled with evil and contempt while they live. And afterwards they will be brought down to hell. [4] There is no one who lives always or who hopes for this thing. A living dog is better than a dead lion. [5] For the living know that they will die, for the dead know nothing more. Neither have they a reward anymore, for the memory of them is forgotten. [6] Their love also, and their hatred, and their envy have all perished. Neither have they a part in this world and in the work that is done under the sun.

[7] Go, then, and eat your bread with joy, and drink your wine with gladness, because your works please God. [8] At all times let your garments be white, and let not oil depart from your head.

[9] Live joyfully with the wife whom you love all the days of your unsteady life, which are given to you under the sun, all the time of your vanity. For this is your portion in life and in your labor wherewith you labor under the sun. [10] Whatsoever your hand is able to do, do it earnestly. For neither work nor reason nor knowledge nor wisdom will be in hell, whither you are hastening.

[11] I turned myself to another thing, and I saw that under the sun the race is not to the swift nor the battle to the strong nor bread to the wise nor riches to the learned nor favor to the skillful. But time and chance in all. [12] No one knows his own end. But as fish are taken with the hook and as birds are caught with a snare, so men and women are taken in the evil time, when it will suddenly come upon them.

[13] This wisdom I have also seen under the sun, and it seemed to me to be very great. [14] A little city, and few men in it. There came against it a great king and built bulwarks round about it, and the siege was perfect. [15] Now there was found in it a man poor and wise, and he delivered the city by his wisdom. And no one afterward remembered that poor person. [16] And I said that wisdom is better than strength. How then is the wisdom of the poor person slighted and his words not heard? [17] The words of the wise are heard in silence, more than the cry of a prince among fools. [18] Better is wisdom than weapons of war, and the person who will sin in one will lose many good things.

CHAPTER 10

[1] Dying flies spoil the sweetness of the ointment. Wisdom is more precious and a little glory for a time than foolishness.

[2] The heart of the wise are in their right hands, and the heart of fools is in their left hands.

³ But, and the fool when he walks in the way, whereas he himself is a fool, esteems all people to be fools.

⁴ If the spirit of the one who has power ascend upon you, leave not your place, because care will make the greatest sins to cease.

⁵ There is an evil that I have seen under the sun, as it were by an error proceeding from the face of the prince.⁶ A fool set in high dignity, and the rich sit beneath. ⁷ I have seen servants upon horses and princes walking as servants.

⁸ The person who digs a hole will fall into it, and the person who breaks a hedge, a serpent will bite him. ⁹ The person who removes stones will be hurt by them, and the person who cuts trees will be wounded by them. ¹⁰ If the iron be blunt, and be not as before, but be made blunt, with much labor it will be sharpened. And after industry wisdom will follow. ¹¹ If a serpent bites in secret, the person who backbites in secret is no better. ¹² The words of the mouth of a wise person are grace. The lips of a fool will throw him down headlong. ¹³ The beginning of his words is folly, and the end of his talk is a mischievous error. ¹⁴ A fool multiplies words.

People cannot tell what has been before them. And what will be after them, who can tell them?

¹⁵ The labor of fools will afflict them who do not know how to go to the city.

¹⁶ Woe to you, O land, when your king is a child and your princes eat in the morning. ¹⁷ Blessed is the land, whose king is noble, and whose princes eat in due season for refreshment and not for riotousness.

¹⁸ By slothfulness a building will be brought down, and through the weakness of hands the house will leak.

¹⁹ For the sake of laughter they make bread and wine that those drinking may feast, and all things obey money.

²⁰ Do not speak detraction against the king in your thought, and in your private chamber speak no evil of the rich person, because even the birds of the air will carry

your voice, and the one who has wings will tell what you have said.

CHAPTER 11

[1] Cast your bread upon the running waters, for after a long time you will find it again. [2] Give a portion to seven, and also to eight, for you do not know what evil will be upon the earth.

[3] If the clouds be full, they will pour rain upon the earth. If the tree fall to the south or to the north, in whatever place it will fall, there will it be. [4] The person who observes the wind will not sow, and the person who considers the clouds will never reap. [5] As you know not what is the way of the spirit nor how the bones are joined together in the womb of her who is with child, so you do not know the works of God who is the maker of all. [6] In thy morning sow your seed, and in the evening let not your hand cease. For you do not know which may rather spring up, this or that. And if both together, it will be the better.

[7] The light is sweet, and it is delightful for the eyes to see the sun. [8] If people live many years and have rejoiced in them all, they must remember the darksome time, the many days, which, when they shall come, the things past will be accused of vanity.

[9] Rejoice, therefore, O youth, in your youth, and let your heart be in that which is good and walk in the ways of your heart and in the sight of your eyes. And know that God will bring you into judgment.

[10] Remove anger from your heart, and put away evil from your flesh. For youth and pleasure are vain.

CHAPTER 12

[1] Remember your Creator in the days of your youth, before the time of affliction comes and the years draw nigh of which you will say: They please me not.

[2] Before the sun and the light and the moon and the stars are darkened, and the clouds return after the rain. [3] When the keepers of the house will tremble and the strong men will stagger, and the grinders will be idle, in small number. And they that look through the holes will be darkened. [4] And they will shut the doors in the street, when the grinder's voice will be low. They will rise up at the voice of the bird, and all the daughters of music will grow deaf. [5] And they will fear high things, and they will be afraid in the way. The almond tree will flourish. The locust will be made fat. The caper tree will be destroyed, because a human being will go into the house of his eternity, and the mourners will go round about in the street.

[6] Before the silver cord is broken and the golden fillet shrink back and the pitcher be crushed at the fountain and the wheel be broken upon the cistern, [7] and the dust return into its earth, from whence it was, and the spirit return to God who gave it.

[8] Vanity of vanities, said Ecclesiastes, all things vanity.

[9] And whereas Ecclesiastes was very wise, he taught the people and declared the things that he had done. And seeking out, he set forth many parables, [10] which are profitable words, and he wrote words most right and full of truth. [11] The words of the wise are as goads and as nails deeply fastened in, which by the counsel of the masters are given by one shepherd.

[12] More than these, my son, require not. Of making many books, there is no end, and much study is an affliction of the flesh.

[13] Let us all hear together the conclusion of the discourse. Fear God and keep his commandments. This is the whole person. [14] And all things that have been done, God will bring into judgment for every error, whether it is good or evil.

VARIATIONS BETWEEN BONAVENTURE'S TEXT AND THE NEW REVISED STANDARD VERSION

There are slight and major variations between Bonaventure's text and that of the NRSV. Among the slight variations are chapter divisions. In Ecclesiastes 1-3 and 10-12 the NRSV and Bonaventure's text begin and end the same. However, in Ecclesiastes 4-9 they do not begin and end the same. For example, the NRSV has 16 verses in Ecclesiastes 4 whereas Bonaventure has 17 verses. Thus, NRSV will commence Ecclesiastes 5:1 with what in Bonaventure's text is Ecclesiastes 4:17. Another slight variation is that the NRSV will call "the author" *the Teacher* (Ecclesiastes 1:1, 2, 12; 12:9-10) where Bonaventure's text will call him *Ecclesiastes*. A final representative minor variation is that the editors of the NRSV have decided to set off as poetry certain passages in Ecclesiastes, e. g., Ecclesiastes 3:1-8; 7:1-13. Bonaventure makes no such determination.

Our consideration of the major variations between Bonaventure's text and the contemporary inclusive language translation of the NRSV begins with the observation that the NRSV is based on a Hebrew text that has a number of difficult and rare words. Four times (2:8; 5:9; 8:10; 12:11) the NRSV has a footnote that reads "meaning of Heb(rew) uncertain." If the meaning of the Hebrew is uncertain to contemporary translators, it stands to reason that it might also have been uncertain to Jerome in the fourth century. Thus, our first four examples feature those verses where the NRSV has the footnote: "meaning of Heb uncertain." The next two examples are representative of the theological problems that arise for Bonaventure because of Jerome's translation. I have put the major variations in bold type.

First example:

The NRSV of 2:8 reads: "I also gathered for myself silver and gold and the treasure of kings and of the provinces; I got singers, both men and women, **and delights of the flesh, and many concubines.**"

Bonaventure's text of 2:8 states: "I heaped together for myself gold and silver and the wealth of kings and provinces. I made for myself male and female singers **and the delights of men and women, cups and vessels to serve and pour out the wine.**"

Second example:

The NRSV of Ecclesiastes 5:9 reads: "But all things considered, this is an advantage for a land: **a king for a plowed field.**"

Bonaventure's text of 5:9 states: "Moreover, there is the **king who reigns over all the land subject to him.**"

Third example:

The NRSV of Ecclesiastes 8:10 reads: "Then I saw the wicked buried; they used to go in and out of the holy place, and were praised in the city **where they had done such things**. This also is vanity."

Bonaventure's text of 8:10 says: "I saw the wicked buried, who also when they were yet living were in the holy place and were praised in the city **as people of just works**. But this also is vanity."

Fourth example:

NRSV of Ecclesiastes 12:11 reads: "The sayings of the wise are like goads, and like nails firmly fixed are **the collected sayings** that are given by one shepherd."

Bonaventure's text of 12:11 states: "The words of the wise are as goads and as nails deeply fastened in, which *by the counsel of the masters* are given by one shepherd."

FIFTH EXAMPLE:

The NRSV of Ecclesiastes 5:6 reads: "Do not let your mouth lead you into sin, and do not say before the messenger *that it was a mistake*; why should God be angry at your words, and destroy the work of your hands?"

Bonaventure's text of same verse in Ecclesiastes 5:5 says: "Give not your mouth to cause your flesh to sin, and do not say before the angel: *There is no providence*, lest God be angry at your words and destroy all the works of your hands."[23]

SIXTH EXAMPLE:

The NRSV of Ecclesiastes of 10:4 states: "If the anger of the ruler rises against you, do not leave your post, for *calmness will undo great offenses*."

Bonaventure's text of 10:4 has: "If the spirit of the one who has power ascend upon you, leave not your place, because *care will make the greatest sins to cease*."[24]

In summary, as readers engage in a detailed comparison of Bonaventure's text with that of NRSV, they will find that both reflect the same original text. Yet there are unmistakable variations that will stop readers in their tracks. It goes without saying that interpretations will vary depending on what text is read. While readers may lament the faulty nature of some of Bonaventure's text, which Jerome produced in one day, they must remember that this is the text that tradition handed on to him. For better or worse, he had to make sense of it.

---

[23]See #15 where Bonaventure addresses the issues arising from this verse.

The contemporary relevance of Bonaventure's Commentary on Ecclesiastes

As far as I can tell, there is only one English language commentator who even knows of the existence of Bonaventure's *Commentary on Ecclesiastes*. That commentator is Roland E. Murphy, who devotes two appreciative pages to it in the section of his commentary on "History of Interpretation."[25] So my task is one that Ecclesiastes would have relished: to explain the unknown to the learned, to interest those who are looking for something new under the sun, and perhaps to tease wise contemporary commentators that there is nothing new under the sun, for Bonaventure grappled quite well with their exegetical issues some seven hundred and fifty years ago.

Those who are proficient in the historical critical method and use this method exclusively in their exegesis may learn little from Bonaventure. That is, one does not go to Bonaventure for insights on the meaning of obscure Hebrew words, for he is commenting on the Latin text of the Vulgate. Bonaventure will give no hints as to the actual *Sitz im Leben* of Ecclesiastes, because he is content to follow the tradition that wise King Solomon was its author. While Bonaventure has fine individual comments about the literary structure of Ecclesiastes, he doesn't specifically ask the question about its literary genre.

---

[24]Bonaventure's theological issue in this verse will be: What really causes the greatest sins to cease?

[25]Roland E. Murphy, *Ecclesiastes*, Word Biblical Commentary 23A (Dallas: Word Books, 1992), li-lii. Murphy's treatment is largely indebted to Dominic V. Monti, "Bonaventure's Interpretation of Scripture in his Exegetical Works" (Chicago: University of Chicago Dissertation, 1979), 83-104. Murphy and Monti were also influenced by the brilliant medievalist, Beryl Smalley, whose work on wisdom literature Murphy edited. See *Medieval Exegesis of Wisdom Literature*, 39-46.

But those whose methods are eclectic may learn much from Bonaventure. I single out four areas for consideration. With regard to the book's *structure* Bonaventure follows Hugh of St. Victor in stating that there is a clear structure in Ecclesiastes consisting of: Heading, a treatise of three parts, and an epilogue. The three parts concern the three vanities: vanity brought about by change, by sin, and by punishment due to sin.[26]

Relative to the question of *canonicity* I note that Bonaventure devotes four of his thirty-four *quaestiones* to analyses of literary and methodological issues. At times these analyses have a distinctive contemporary flavor. For example, Bonaventure does not flee away from the question that agitates commentators and those who encounter the book of Ecclesiastes in liturgy, that is, how did this book of pessimism and impertinent interrogation ever get into the canon? I beg my readers' indulgence for quoting a long section from question three of Bonaventure's *Quaestio* #1. Bonaventure raises an objection: "What the author says in the name of fools is to be rejected. But it is not clear when he is speaking in his own name or in the name of another. Therefore, one does not know what is to be heeded in this book and what is to be rejected. So the teaching of this book leads to error. But since canonical books should purge error, this book should be taken from the canon." Bonaventure's reply is similar to that of commentators who maintain that the epilogue of Ecclesiastes made the preceding twelve and a half chapters orthodox: "It is to be said in reply that one side of an argument is not known until the argument has been resolved, because only in the solution do we find out what is to be accepted and what is to be rejected. Thus, I say that Ecclesiastes con-

---

[26] See the Table of Contents for more detail.

tinues with his argument until the end of the book where he gives his solution when he says in 12:13-14: "Let us all together hear the conclusion of the discourse. Fear God ... and know that God will bring you to judgment for every error." In this conclusion Ecclesiastes condemns every opinion of the foolish, the carnal, and the worldly. So in this last statement he is speaking in his own name, but what he rejects is spoken in the name of others. Hence the book cannot be understood without paying attention to all of it."

With respect to issues of *theodicy* Bonaventure may have some helpful approaches for us twenty-first century folks. I refer specifically to the small question four of his *Quaestio* #8 where he probes the meaning of Ecclesiastes 2:17: "I was weary of my life when I saw that all things under the sun are evil." Bonaventure counters this scriptural quotation with another: Genesis 1:31 states: "God saw all the things God had made, and they were very good." Bonaventure resolves this contradiction between scripture passages by appealing to Romans 7:12: "The law is holy and the commandment good."[27] His point is that wicked or grace-less people can turn what is good into something that is death-dealing. He comments: "But on occasion the commandment can be deadly and death-bearing for any who are without grace. . . .For Wisdom 14:11 reads: 'The creatures of God are . . . a temptation . . . and a snare for the feet of the unwise.' And Sirach 39:32 states: 'All these things . . . will be turned into evil for the ungodly and sinners.'"

I am of the opinion that in Bonaventure's commentary we see Ecclesiastes *redivivus*, for Bonaventure, too, has *to*

---

[27]For an insightful article on biblical contradictions see Nils Astrup Dahl, "Contradictions in Scripture" in his Studies in Paul: Theology for the Early Christian Mission (Minneapolis: Augsburg, 1977), 159-177.

struggle mightily with the tradition he inherited and with which he didn't agree. Simply put, the tradition going back to Origen dictated that the purpose of Ecclesiastes is to instill contempt for the world. In his Introduction and especially in Quaestio #1 Bonaventure contends with this viewpoint, which was contrary to his theological position that creation speaks eloquently of God. We have just seen in the previous point about theodicy that Bonaventure preserves the goodness of creation by assigning blame to the unwise and sinners who abuse creation. Franciscan men and women, who have been nourished on Bonaventure's *Itinerarium Mentis in Deum*,[28] which accentuates creation as God's footprints, may want to walk in Bonaventure's shoes as he struggles with the message of a canonical book that tradition said proposes a different view of creation.[29]

---

[28]See Bonaventure's *Itinerarium Mentis in Deum*, ed. by Philotheus Boehner and Zachary Hayes, Works of St. Bonaventure II/Revised and Expanded (St. Bonaventure, NY: Franciscan Institute Publications, 2002).

[29]For an excellent treatment of sight as temptation and sight as contemplative delight, see Suzannah Biernoff, *Sight and Embodiment in the Middle Ages* (New York: Palgrave Macmillan, 2002).

TABLE OF CONTENTS

ABBREVIATIONS

ACW   Ancient Christian Writers

CCSL   Corpus Christianorum Series Latina

Douay Version

> *The Holy Bible Translated from the Latin Vulgate . . . The Douay Version of The Old Testament; The Confraternity Edition of The New Testament.* New York: P. J. Kenedy & Sons, 1950.

FC   Fathers of the Church.

Hugh of St. Cher

> *Hugonis de Sancto Cher . . . Tomus Tertius in Libros Proverbiorum, Ecclesiastae, Canticorum, Sapientiae, Ecclesiastici.* Venice: Nicolas Pezzana, 1732.

LCL   Loeb Classical Library

NAB   New American Bible

NRSV   New Revised Standard Version

Opera Omnia

> *S. Bonaventurae Opera Omnia.* Studio et Cura PP. Collegii a S. Bonaventura (Ad Claras Aquas). Quaracchi: Collegium S. Bonaventurae, 1882-1902. There are nine volumes of text and one volume of indices. The volume number is first given and then the page number, e. g., 5:24.

PG   Patrologiae Cursus Completus. Series Graeca. Ed. J. P. Migne.

PL   Patrologiae Cursus Completus. Series Latina. Ed. J. P. Migne.

QuarEd   The editors who produced the text and the notes of Bonaventure's Opera Omnia 6, which contains the text of Bonaventure's *Commentary on Ecclesiastes (Commentarius in librum Ecclesiastae).*

SBOp   *Sancti Bernardi Opera I-VIII.* Ed. J. Leclercq and H. M. Rochais with the assistance of C. H.

Talbot for Volumes I-II. Rome: Editiones
Cisterciensis, 1957-1977.

Vulgate   *Biblia Sacra Iuxta Vulgatam Versionem.*
Adiuvantibus B. Fischer, I. Gribomont (†), H. F.
D. Sparks, W. Thiele recensuit et brevi apparatu
critico instruxit Robertus Weber (†) editionem
quartam emendatam cum sociis B. Fischer, H.
I. Frede. H. F. D. Sparks, W. Thiele praeparavit
Roger Gryson. Stuttgart: Deutsche
Bibelgesellschaft, 1969. 4th ed. 1994.

WAE   *The Works of Aristotle.* Volumes 1-12. Translated into English under the Editorship of W.
D. Ross. London: Oxford University Press, 1928.

ACKNOWLEDGMENTS

The Franciscan Institute gratefully acknowledges gener-
ous funding from the Academy of American Franciscan
History; the OFM Province of St. John the Baptist; the
OFM Province of the Sacred Heart in Saint Louis; and the
OFM General Definitorium in Rome, Italy. The two trans-
lators of this volume also owe a debt of gratitude to Sr.
Margaret Carney, O.S.F., director of the Franciscan Insti-
tute; Fr. Zachary Hayes, O.F.M., general editor of the
Bonaventure Texts in Translation Series; to Dr. Jean
François Godet-Calogeras, managing editor of the BTTS;
to Sr. Roberta McKelvie, O.S.F., managing editor of
Franciscan Institute Publications; to Ms. Noel H. Riggs,
executive administrative assistant, and to Sr. Daria
Mitchell, O.S.F. , editorial assistant.

INTRODUCTION TO THE *COMMENTARY* ON *ECCLESIASTES*

GENERAL INTRODUCTION

1. *Blessed is the man,[1] whose trust is in the name of the Lord and has no regard for vanities and lying follies.[2]* For, as Blessed Dionysius says: Good is above all else desirable.[3] Now good is twofold, namely, temporal and eternal, according to what 2 Corinthians 4:18 says: *The things that are seen are temporal, but the things that are not seen are eternal.[4]* Good stirs up in us a twofold love or desire, namely,

---

[1]The Latin reads *vir* ("man"), not *homo* ("human being").

[2]Psalm 39:5.

[3]On p. 3 n. 1 QuarEd state that Dionysius suggests this is his *De divinis nominibus*, chapter 4 n. 4, 10, 31. See PG 3:698-699, 706-707, 751 where Bonaventure's exact wording does not occur.

[4]On p. 3 n. 2 QuarEd refer to Augustine's treatments of this twofold love. See Book XI, chapter 15, n. 19-20 of his *De Genesi ad litteram* and *On Genesis*, Introductions, Translation and Notes by Edmund Hill, The Works of Saint Augustine I/13 (Hyde Park, NY: New City Press, 2002), 439-440. See further question 36 n. 1 in *Eighty-Three Different Questions*, translated by David L. Mosher, FC 70 (Washington, DC: Catholic University of America Press, 1982), 67-69, esp. 68: "However, the poison of charity is the hope of getting and holding onto temporal things. The nourishment of charity is the lessening of covetousness, the perfection of charity, the absence of covetousness." Also see Book XIV chapter 28 in *The City of God* Books VIII-XVI, translated by Gerald G. Walsh and Grace Monahan, FC 14 (New York: Fathers of the Church, Inc., 1952), 410: "What we see, then, is that two societies have issued from two kinds of love. Worldly society has flowered from a selfish love which dared to despise even God, whereas the communion of saints is

of *love* or *inordinate desire* with the result that charity becomes love returning to what is eternal while inordinate desire to what is earthly. And since the concord and disharmony of *actions* follow upon the concord and difference of *desires* and since the *unity of a city* consists in the concord between laws and behavior, a twofold *city* arises from this twofold love, that is, the city of the heavenly Jerusalem and the city of Babylon.[5] The foundation of the first city is ordered charity whereas the foundation of the second is perverse inordinate desire. Therefore, the heavenly city, since it is founded on charity, which raises one up to eternal things, is at peace in eternal things and finds blessedness in them. But the city of Babylon, which is weighed down by inordinate desire to earthly things, finds blessedness in these earthly things. – And so it is clear from the preceding that just as there is a twofold good, a twofold love, and a twofold city, so too is there a twofold blessedness, namely, a true blessedness in what is eternal and a false blessedness in what is temporal and earthly. Psalm 143:15 states: They have called the people blessed, who have these things, etc.[6] – The love of charity and inor-

---

rooted in a love of God that is ready to trample on self." The editors also state that Augustine, who calls *libido* ("inordinate desire") *cupiditas* ("covetousness"), defines *libido* in his book *De mendacio,* chapter 7 n. 10: "A desire of the mind, by which some temporal goods are put before eternal goods." See PL 40:496 and *Saint Augustine: Treaties on Various Subjects*, ed. Roy J. Deferrari, FC 16 (New York: Fathers of the Church, Inc., 1952), 69.

[5]On p. 3 n. 3 QuarEd refer to Book XV, chapters 1-2 of Augustine's *City of God*. See *The City of God* (FC 14), pp. 413-417. They also refer to Augustine's exposition of Psalm 64, n. 1-2. See *Expositions of the Psalms 51-72*. Translation and notes by Maria Boulding The Works of Saint Augustine III/17 (Hyde Park, NY: New City Press, 2001), 264-267, esp. n. 2 on 265: "Babylon signifies 'confusion,' and Jerusalem 'vision of peace.' You need to study the city of confusion now, in order to understand the vision of peace; you must endure the one, and yearn for the other."

[6]Psalm 143:15 continues: ". . . .But blessed are the people whose God is the Lord."

dinate desire are so opposed to one another that they cannot exist together. About these two forms of blessedness Matthew 6:24 says: *No person can serve two masters*. So if people want to be blessed, it is necessary that they love future goods and despise present goods. Therefore, the Holy Spirit through the Psalmist describes the blessed man by means of this twofold action: From the love of heavenly things, which makes him *blessed*, since he says: *Blessed is the man, whose trust is in the name of the Lord* and from the contemning of earthly things, since he states: *And has no regard for vanities and lying follies*. Truly, *blessed is the man, whose trust is in the name of the Lord*.

2. Now the Lord alone makes one blessed. Nor is there any other name under heaven that makes one blessed.[7] For the Lord alone is blessed *in essence*. 1 Timothy 6:14-15 reads: *Keep the commandment without stain, blameless until the coming of our Lord Jesus Christ. This coming he in his own time will make manifest, who is the Blessed and only Sovereign, the King of kings and Lord of lords*. Therefore, blessedness and power belong alone to God by essence, but our blessedness comes *through participation*. What we participate in has its origin in the one who is blessed by essence. Consequently, we are blessed by participating in the source of blessedness, that is, God. For Revelation 19:9 says: *Blessed are they who are called to the marriage supper of the Lamb*. For first God communicates blessedness to the Lamb through a marriage contract, and subsequently to all who are called by the Lamb.

3. Further, only God has *abundance*. For in a special way Proverbs 3:15-16 speaks of Wisdom, who is God: *She is*

---

[7]On p. 3 n. 5 QuarEd rightly indicate that Bonaventure is alluding to Acts 4:12: "For there is no other name under heaven given to men and women by which we must be saved."

more precious than all riches. And all the things that are desired are not to be compared to her. Length of days is in her right hand, and in her left hand riches and glory. But our blessedness consists *in acquiring all good things.* Therefore, God alone has an abundance of all things. This is inferred from what follows right afterwards in Proverbs 3:18: *She is a tree of life to those who lay hold of her, and the person who shall retain her is blessed.* Wisdom 7:11 states: *All good things came to me together with her,* etc.[8]

4. God alone has *the quiet of not changing*, because all other things change, while God does not change. James 1:17 reads: *With whom there is no change nor shadow of alteration.* But our blessedness consists in *the tranquil possession* of accumulated goods because there can be no blessedness without tranquility. But since perfect tranquility exists in God alone, we can find peace and be blessed only in God. For this reason Revelation 14:13 has: *Blessed are the dead, who from now on die in the Lord. Yes, says the Spirit, let them rest from their labors.*

5. Moreover, God alone has *the immortality of eternity*, as it is stated in 1 Timothy 6:16: *Who alone has immortality and dwells in light inaccessible.*[9] But our blessedness consists in *an unending duration* of good possessed, for a state of life that can come to an end is not blessed, but subject

---

[8]Wisdom 7:11 concludes: ". . . and innumerable riches through her hands." On p. 3 n. 7 QuarEd indicate that Bonaventure's discussion of blessedness builds upon that of Boethius. See Book III, second preface of *Boethius, The Theological Tractates and The Consolation of Philosophy,* trans. S. J. Tester, LCL (London: Heineman/Cambridge: Harvard University Press, 1973), 233: Blessedness or happiness "is that state which is perfect since all goods are gathered together in it."

[9]The Vulgate reads *habitans* ("dwelling") while Bonaventure has *habitat* ("dwells").

to misery. Wherefore, since one cannot have interminability except from the source of immortality, one is blessed in God alone. So it is said in Psalm 83:5: *Blessed are those who dwell in your house, O Lord. They will praise you forever and ever*, because they will have everlasting joy. Isaiah 35:10 states: *They will come into Zion with praise, and everlasting joy will be upon their heads.*[10] *They will obtain joy and gladness.* Therefore, *Blessed is the man, whose trust is in the name of the Lord.*

6. But people who put their trust in *the world* are not *blessed*. Rather they are in fact *vain*. For they have regard for *vanities and lying follies*. Their trust vanishes, according to what Jeremiah 2:5 states: *Your fathers have gone far from me and have gone*[11] *after vanity and have become vain*. They have gone after vanity, that is, after the world. – For the world with its own is vain because it does not provide *support for the person who leans on it*. For Isaiah 30:7 reads: *Egypt will provide assistance to no purpose and in vain*, in that it gives no support to the person who leans upon it. For it is a bunch of reeds, and those who lean on it will cut both hands, because the world and all that belongs to the world weaken and make sick all who trust in them and render them unfit for every good work. Thus, it is said that *the hand is cut*. In desperation the Prophet in Psalm 59:13 asks the Lord for help against the things of the world: *Give us help from trouble, since vain is human salvation.*

7. The world is also vain because it does not provide *abundance for the one who possesses it*. For Ecclesiastes 5:9 says:

---

[10]On p. 4 n. 4 QuarEd accurately indicate that the Vulgate reads *caput* ("head") while Bonaventure has *capita* ("heads").

[11]On p. 4 n. 5 QuarEd correctly mention that the Vulgate reads *ambulaverunt* ("have walked") while Bonaventure has *abierunt* ("have gone").

A covetous person will not be satisfied with money. The reason for this is that all earthly things are vain, and what is vain does not satisfy. Thus, it is said in Sirach 34:1-2: *The hopes of a man who is void of understanding are vain and deceitful. . . .The person who gives heed to lying visions is like the person who catches at a shadow and follows after the wind.* So just as the wind does not satisfy the belly, nor shadows fill it, neither do temporal things since they are but shadows of the eternal things for which the soul has been created.

8. The world is also vain because it does not give *rest to the laborer.* So the person who works for earthly goods works in vain. Ecclesiastes 2:22-23 reads: *For what profit do people have from all the labors . . . by which they labor[12] under the sun? All their days are full of labors[13] and miseries. Even at night they do not rest in mind. And is this not vanity?* It is vanity because people labor in vain, because they do not rest. This world cannot give rest, because it does not endure, but is always in motion. Therefore, whoever clings to it must be in motion. Thus, it is said in Psalm 11:9: *The wicked walk about in motion.*

9. It is also vain because it does not give *fruit to the person who loves it.* So Ecclesiastes 5:9 says: *The person who loves riches will reap no fruit from them. And so this also is vanity.* Such a person reaps not fruit, but rather damnation, for by gaining the world that person loses God and loses himself, and this in accord with what Matthew 16:26 states: *For what does it profit people if they gain the whole world and suffer the loss of their own souls?*

---

[12]The Vulgate does not read *laborat* ("labor").

[13]The Vulgate reads *eius doloribus* ("their sorrows") while Bonaventure simply has *laboribus* ("labors").

10. By gaining the world, men and women suffer the loss of their souls. – For the world, by offering *a false exaltation*, lifts one up to *pride* and through this makes a person pass away according to what Job 11:12 has: *A vain man is lifted up into pride and thinks himself born free like a wild ass' colt*. For when a person is lifted up to vain things, that person is lifted up to vain pride, according to what Job 30:22 reads: *You have lifted me up and set me as it were upon the wind, and you have mightily dashed me*. – Also by offering a false *sweetness*, the world stirs up voluptuousness, just as wine by its sweetness draws one to gluttony and thence to voluptuousness. So 3 Esdras 3:18-19 has: *Wine, which overcomes all who drink it, leads astray the mind. Also it makes vain the mind of king and orphan*,[14] and this by inciting the mind to voluptuousness, according to what Ephesians 5:18 states: *Be not drunk with wine wherein is voluptuousness*. The world drew Solomon to this vanity. Ecclesiastes 2:1 says: *I said. . . .I will go and abound in delights and enjoy good things. And I saw that this also was vanity*.

11. The world also offers a false *abundance* by which it stirs up *greed* and thus makes the human heart vain, according to Proverbs 21:6: *The person who gathers treasures by a lying tongue is vain and foolish*. Greed not only makes men and women *vain*, but also takes away their *heart*. For Sirach 10:10 says of the avaricious that *they throw away their innards*,[15] since according to what Truth says in Matthew 6:21: *Where your treasure is, there is your heart*. But since their treasure is outside, so too is their heart outside.

---

[14]Bonaventure has slightly adapted the text to make his point. See Vulgate, 1915.

[15]Sirach 10:10 reads: "There is no more wicked thing than to love money, for such a person puts even his own soul up for sale, because while he lives, he has thrown away his innards."

12. The world also offers a false *wisdom* and so entices one to *curiosity*,[16] and by this makes one *vain*. Thus, the Apostle uses a Psalm to say in 1 Corinthians 3:20: *The Lord knows[17] the thoughts of the wise that they are vain.*[18] For as Jeremiah 10:14 states: *Every human being has become a fool because of their knowledge.* This is human wisdom that does not recognize *what is useful*, but *what is passing*. And so the Lord makes this wisdom stupid, as stated in 1 Corinthians 1:20: *God has made the wisdom of this world stupid.* Stupid wisdom is vain because it is wrong. Sirach 34:5 says: *Deceitful divinations and lying omens and the dreams of evildoers are vanity.*

13. From this fourfold *interior* vanity of the heart, a person is lessened *exteriorly* in a fourfold way. For first, the vanity of *pride* makes a person *barren*, according to Sirach 6:2-3: *Extol not yourself in the thoughts of your soul like a bull, lest your strength be quashed by folly. . . .And you be left as a dry tree in the wilderness.* And so is the vain person left without the fruit of good works. About this person Jeremiah 10:15 reads: *Their works are vain and worthy of*

---

[16]On "curiosity" in Bonaventure, see Charles Carpenter, *Theology as the Road to Holiness in St. Bonaventure,* Theological Inquiries (New York: Paulist Press, 1999), 144-147 (*Curiositas*: enemy of the gifts). See further Etienne Gilson, *The Philosophy of St. Bonaventure* (Paterson: St. Anthony Guild Press, 1965), 408: "Curiosity consists in the desire to know what is hidden simply because we do not know it, to see what is beautiful for its beauty merely, and to seize what we like simply to have it for ourselves. Curiosity thus necessarily implies avarice, and this is what ruined the first man – the passion to know simply for the sake of knowing, to see for the sake of seeing, and to take what he coveted."

[17]The Vulgate reads *novit* ("knows") while Bonaventure has *scit* ("knows"). Psalm 93:11 reads *scit* ("knows").

[18]Paul is referring to Psalm 93:11. The Vulgate, however, reads *cogitationes hominum* ("the thoughts of men and women"). Paul and Bonaventure have *cogitationes sapientium* ("the thoughts of the wise").

ridicule. In the time of their visitation they will perish.[19] –
The vanity of *avarice* keeps a person *full of business* and
addicted to much labor, according to Ecclesiastes 4:7-8: *In
my considerations I found yet another vanity under the
sun. There is but one, and he has not a second . . . and yet
he ceases not to labor. Neither are his eyes satisfied with
riches.* For riches are the strange gods, of which Jeremiah
16:13 speaks: *You shall serve . . . strange gods, who will not
give you rest day and night.*[20] – The vanity of *voluptuousness* makes people *attentive to their appearances* because
the voluptuous are accustomed to use external adorn-
ments. Speaking for them, Wisdom 2:8 says: *Let us crown
ourselves with roses, before they wither away.* And this is
indeed a vanity, for Proverbs 31:30 states: *Favor is deceitful, and beauty is vain.* It is vain because *all the glory* and
the beauty *of flesh is like the flower of the field.*[21] – The
vanity of *earthly wisdom* makes a person *a vain babbler.*
For when the heart is in error, the mouth speaks vanities.
1 Timothy 1:5-8 says: *The end of the commandment is charity, from a pure heart, and a good conscience, and an un-
feigned faith. From which things some, going astray, have
turned aside unto vain babbling . . . understanding neither the things they say nor the things they affirm.* And
because they have been corrupted and deceived by worldly
wisdom, they want to seduce others by vain words. Thus,
Titus 1:10-11 reads: *There are many disobedient, vain talk-
ers, and seducers, especially those who are of the circumci-
sion, who must be reproved.* – Hence, vanity of the heart
flows from vanity of exterior things, and from this arises
vanity of exterior works.

---

[19]On p. 5 n. 3 QuarEd correctly indicate that Bonaventure has
adjusted the first part of Jeremiah 10:15 which reads: "They are vain
things and a work worthy of ridicule. . . ."

[20]The Vulgate has "day and night" modifying "you shall serve."

[21]Bonaventure is referring to Isaiah 40:6. On p. 5 n. 5 QuarEd also
refer to 1 Peter 1:24, which cites Isaiah 40:6.

14. So from all this it follows that there is a triple vanity, namely, of *change, evil, and punishment*.[22] And Hugh of St. Victor says of these: "The first is natural and appropriate. The second is culpable, because perverse. The third is a punishment and wretched."[23] As has been seen, each of these comes from the other. Whoever wants to escape from the vanity of *wretchedness*[24] should run from the vanity of guilt. And whoever wants to escape from this should not think of the vanity of *changing nature*, but hope and cling to the divine and so become blessed. Therefore, *blessed is the man whose trust is in the name of the Lord*.[25]

15. Therefore, since it is the duty of the wise to teach how a person may reach beatitude, this was the main concern and value of the work of wise Solomon. But as it is clear from what has been said, one who wants to reach beatitude must of necessity love what is eternal and despise what is present, and further, know how to live in a becoming manner *in the midst of a depraved generation*.[26] So he wrote three books, namely, *Proverbs* in which he teaches a

---

[22]For more clarity on this threefold division see Bonaventure's commentary on Ecclesiastes 1:13-15 (#30-35), the questions that immediately follow, and the notes thereon. In brief, it was medieval theology that between the first sin of apostasy committed by our first parents and the final punishment of eternal fire, there are sins and punishments for sin.

[23]See Homily 1 of Hugh of St. Victor's *In Salomonis Ecclesiasten Homiliae XIX* in PL 175:119A. Hugh of St. Victor, however, describes the three vanities as: change, curiosity or greed, and mortality. Hugh says that the first "is natural and appropriate or congruous."

[24]*Miseria* has many meanings: wretchedness, misery, unhappiness, distress, unhappy condition. It might also be used in contrast to *beatitudo* ("blessedness").

[25]Psalm 39:5.

[26]On p. 5 n. 8 QuarEd rightly indicate that Bonaventure is alluding to Philippians 2:15: "So as to be blameless and guileless children of God without blemish in the midst of a depraved and perverse generation."

son how to live wisely in this world; *Ecclesiastes*, in which he teaches a contempt for present realities; and *The Song of Songs*, in which he teaches the love of what is heavenly, especially, of the Bridegroom himself.[27]

ON THE FOURFOLD CAUSE OF THIS BOOK

16. Therefore, it is clear what *the aim* of the book of Ecclesiastes is. And since "the aim necessarily affects whatever relates to the aim"[28] and since the aim of the book is the contempt of the present realities, Ecclesiastes discusses these not from the point of view of their attraction, but from the point of view of despising them. They attract by seeming to be good, but are despised in as far as they are vanities. So it follows from this that the *matter* of this book is the vanities of the present realities or, expressed better, such things in so far as they are vanities. For he proves that vanity is like a passion for objects. He first proposes, second proves, and third concludes. He moves from per-

---

[27]On p. 5 n. 8 QuarEd point to Jerome's *Commentarius in Ecclesiasten* and the similar comments he makes about Proverbs, Ecclesiastes, and The Song of Songs in his exposition of Ecclesiastes 1:1. See *Commentarivs in Ecclesiasten*, ed. M. Adriaen in *S. Hieronymi Presbyteri Opera, Pars I: Opera Exegetica*, CCSL lxxii (Turnhout: Brepols, 1959), 250. See further the Sixth Collation n. 24-25 in St. Bonaventure's *Collations on the Six Days*, trans. José de Vinck, The Works of Bonaventure V (Paterson, NJ: St. Anthony Guild Press, 1970), 104: "And such is blessedness. And so, the first of these virtues are political, the second are for cleansing, and the third, for the soul already cleansed. The political virtues consist in action, the cleansing in contemplation, and those for the soul already cleansed, is the vision of light. 25. And, as Origen writes, it is with these that Solomon is concerned; with the political, in Proverbs, with the cleansing, in Ecclesiastes, and with those for the soul already cleansed, in the Song of Songs."

[28]On p. 5 n. 9 QuarEd refer to Book II, chapter 9 of Aristotle's *Physica*. See WAE, vol. 2, 199b as a general reference.

suasion to proof about the triple vanity, which was discussed above, namely, of *nature, guilt*, and *misery*.[29]

From this his *method of proceeding* or form is clear. Compared to other books his method of proceeding is singular, for he proceeds as a preacher, weighing the various opinions of the wise and foolish, so that from the opinions of many the one truth may be clear in the minds of his audience.

From what has been said one can draw the conclusion of what *the efficient cause* is. For in this book pleasures, riches, honors, and curiosities are taught as vanities to be despised. And a person would not be believed about the contempt of such things unless that person has some experience. Thus, a poor person with no possessions would not be believed about despising riches since that person *has no experience* and therefore *knows nothing*.[30] So the author of this book had to be a person with experience of all these things, that is, a person who was powerful, rich, voluptuous, and curious or wise. We have not read or heard of anyone who so excelled in all these as Solomon. So he was more suitable than all others to be the author of this book. – Wherefore, the *material, formal, efficient*, and *final* causes of this book are clear. But particular questions can be raised about each of these four causes.

---

[29]See #12 above where Bonaventure first mentions the vanities of change, evil, and punishment and then in reverse order the vanities of misery, guilt, and changing nature.

[30]On p. 6 n. 2 QuarEd suggest that Bonaventure is alluding to Sirach 34:10: "The person who has no experience knows little."

Questions 1

I. On the purpose of Ecclesiastes

First, about *the purpose*. For it is said that the purpose of the book is *contempt of the world*. Now that this is correct is proven by:

1. James 4:4 where it says: *The friendship of this world is an enemy to God.*[31] Now it is good to despise everything inimical to God.

2. Furthermore, 1 John 2:5 reads: *Love not the world, nor the things that are in the world.*

But against this:

1. To praise a work is to give praise to the worker,[32] and so to despise a work reflects back on the worker. So the person who despises the world, despises God. For either the world was not made by God or it is not to be despised.

2. Likewise, Proverbs 16:4 states: *The Lord made all things for himself.* Therefore, all things are directed towards God. But something directed towards its goal should not be despised, but rather accepted and loved. Therefore, this world, with all that is in it, is to be loved.

I reply: It should be said, as Augustine and Hugh hold,[33] that this world is like a ring given by the bridegroom to

---

[31]On p. 6 n. 3 QuarEd correctly mention that the Vulgate reads *inimica est Dei* ("is an enemy of God") whereas Bonaventure reads *inimica est Deo* ("is an enemy to God").

[32]On p. 6 n. 5 QuarEd allude to Sirach 9:24: "Works will be praised ecause of the hand of their makers."

[33]On p. 6 n. 7 QuarEd draw their readers' attention to Hugh of St. Victor's *Soliloquium de Arrha animae* where he suggests a distinction between chaste and adulterous love. See, e.g., PL 176:961B-962A. See

the soul itself. Now the bride can love the ring given her by her husband in two ways, namely, with *a chaste* or *an adulterous* love. The love is *chaste* when she loves the ring as a memento of her husband and on account of her love for her husband. The love is *adulterous* when the ring is loved more than the husband, and the husband cannot regard such love as good. For just as there is a twofold love, so too there is a twofold hatred or contempt, because "as soon as one of two things that are opposites is mentioned, the other is implied."[34] Contempt for a ring by treating it as a poor and ugly gift reflects on the husband, but contempt of a ring by regarding it as almost nothing compared to the love of a husband, gives glory to the husband. This contempt is referred to in The Song of Songs 8:7: *If a man should give all the substance of his house for love, he*

Soliloquy on the Earnest Money of the Soul, trans. Kevin Herbert, Mediaeval Philosophical Texts in Translation 9 (Milwaukee: Marquette University Press, 1956), 24-25: "What a singular gift was given you, one not granted to all but only to those who are loved and are worthy to be loved by Him. . . .Yet, consider what you have done, my Soul. You have deserted your Lover and have squandered your affections on others. You have lost your probity, defiled your beauty, wasted your substance. . . .You have forgotten your Espoused and have failed to respond rightly to His great generosity. You have become a harlot. . . ." The editors also cite Augustine's Sermon 85 c. 5, n. 6. See *Sermons,* trans. and notes by Edmund Hill, The Works of Saint Augustine III/1 (Hyde Park, NY: New City Press, 1995), 389: "But if you forsake the one who made you and love the things he made, by forsaking the one who made you, you become an adulterer. . . .The soul which forsakes the creator for love of the creature is an adulteress. There is nothing more chaste than love of him, nothing more delightful; once you forsake him, my soul, and embrace the other, you become unclean." Nowhere in this rich note do the editors give the source for Bonaventure's use of the ring.

[34]On p. 6 n. 8 QuarEd cite Book V, chapter 1 of Aristotle's *Ethica nicomachea*: "It often follows that if one of two things that are opposites is mentioned in various ways, the other is also said. So if there is a law against something, there was also some wrong." See WAE, vol. 9, 1129a.

will despise it as nothing. It is of such contempt that we are speaking, and so the matter is clear.

II. THE SUBJECT MATTER OF ECCLESIASTES

The question now is of *the subject matter*, and our position is that it deals with *vanity*. But against this: 1. All knowledge is about what is good and true,[35] but *vanity* drives out goodness and truth. Therefore, there is no knowledge of vanity.

2. Moreover, it seems that there is no vanity in things, because Genesis 1:31 says: *God saw all the things that God had made, and they were very good*.[36] So if all are very good, then nothing is vain.

3. Furthermore, something vain and useless is not directed to a purpose. For example, someone who washes himself to make the sun lose its power acts in vain, because these two things are not directed one to the other. But all creatures tend in their own way to the highest good. For Dionysius[37] and Boethius[38] maintain that all things de-

---

[35] On p. 6 n. 10 QuarEd write: "Cfr. Aristot., I. Poster. C. 2." See Book I, n. 2 of Aristotle's *Analytica posteriora* in WAE, vol. 1, 71b.

[36] This objection is implied by Jerome, *Commentarius in Ecclesiasten*, 1:2. See CCSL lxxii, 252.

[37] On p. 6 n. 12 QuarEd suggest *De divinis nominibus*, chapter 4 n. 4, 10, 31 and PG 3:698-699, 706-707, 751. See, e.g., PG 3:707: "Therefore, the beautiful and the good are desirable and lovable by all things and are loved by all things."

[38] See especially Book III, n. 9 of *The Consolation of Philosophy* in LCL, 285: "That is why it is rightly held that the chief or cardinal cause of all things sought after is goodness. Now the cause for which a thing is sought is seen to be most greatly desired, as for example if a man wanted to ride for the sake of his health, he does not so much desire the motion of riding, but the effect, health. Therefore, since all things are sought after for the sake of good, they are not so much desired by all as the good itself."

sire good. And also the Philosopher[39] says this. Therefore, there is nothing vain to be found in all things.

4. Besides, if vanity is found and knowledge is based on this vanity as on a foundation, the knowledge itself is vain and what is based upon it is also vain. Therefore, this knowledge is vain.

I reply. One way of understanding the preceding points is to say that vanity can be spoken of in two ways. Vanity can be taken *in itself*[40] and as such it has no truth or good. But such a thing does not exist in the world. Or vanity can be used *in comparison with its starting point*, namely, nothing. Used in this way, vanity is not opposed to good, for good and vanity are one and the same thing. In this second way, vanity is good, because it is from good and leads to good. It is vain, because it comes from nothing and, if left to itself, tends toward nothing. Understood in this second way, vanity has goodness and can be the subject of knowledge. And therefore, there can be knowledge and teaching about such vanity. And in this way all the objections can be solved since they proceed as if they were dealing with vanity in itself.

But this solution is not valid since Ecclesiastes is not dealing with things from the viewpoint that they come from nothing. Rather he focuses on things as they are de-

---

[39]See Book I n. 1 of Aristotle's *Ethica nicomachea* in WAE, vol. 9, 1094a: "Every art and every inquiry, and similarly every action and pursuit, is thought to aim at some good; and for this reason the good has rightly been declared to be that at which all things aim." See also Book II, n. 6 of his *Physica* in WAE, vol. 2, 197b: "This implies that what is naturally the means to an end is 'in vain', when it does not effect the end towards which it was the natural means – for it would be absurd for a man to say that he had bathed in vain because the sun was not eclipsed, since the one was not done with a view to the other."

[40]The Latin is *simpliciter*.

sired by human beings. And therefore, he deals with the vanity of *wrongdoing*, which is a privation. So there has to be another solution.

Another way of dealing with the subject is to say that just as *truth* is used with three meanings, so too is its opposite, *vanity*, as explained in the rule above.[41] *Truth* is used in one way as *interchangeable with being*, as when it is said that every being is true. And so *vanity*, its opposite, is called *non-being*, as when we say that a fantasy is a *non-being*.

Truth is used in another way when besides referring to being, it indicates *the relation of a thing to its function and purpose*.[42] So we say *true wine* to indicate a wine that truly functions as a wine should. Also we say *true person* to refer to a person who behaves in a way befitting a human being, and that is the practice of virtue. *Vanity*, then, is the lack of being ordered to a purpose, and thus all sins and abuses are vanities.

Truth is also used to refer to being that has no element of non-being within nor any potential to become non-being. So we say that to have *true being* a thing has *un*-

---

[41]See Question 1, Reply: "As soon as one of two things that are opposites is mentioned, the other is implied."

[42]Bonaventure's multivalent *operatio* is translated here by "function," "behaves," and "practice." On p. 7 n. 2 QuarEd cite Book IV text. 54 (last chapter) of Aristotle's *Meterologia*: "All things are related to their purpose. All things that can achieve their purpose truly exist, as an eye it sees. But an eye that cannot see exists in an equivocal sense, as if it is dead, etc." See WAE, vol. 3, 390a: "What a thing is is always determined by its function: a thing really is itself when it can perform its function; an eye, for instance, when it can see. When a thing cannot do so it is that thing only in name, like a dead eye or one made of stone. . . ."

changeable being. And in this way *vanity* is the opposite of the true in that it is changeable and transmutable. So every *creature is vain, because it was subjected to vanity,*[43] that is, mutability.

So the aforementioned vanity can be spoken of in three ways. One is its lack of *being in itself.* Another is its lack of *a purpose in being.* The third is its lack of *being unchangeable.* Of the first way there is no knowledge or teaching, unless it happens *to exist in something that can cause it* and in this way *be known and taught.* And in this it is not vanity. But in as far as it is *vain*, there is knowledge of it neither *in itself* nor *through something accidental.*[44] In the second way there is no knowledge *in itself*, but *through something accidental.* For just as medical art is the knowledge of the healthy and the sick, that is, in the Philosopher's view, of the healthy *in themselves* and the sick *through something accidental*, so too knowledge of guilt or sin is theoretical and is based on the nature of virtue.[45] In the

---

[43]On p. 7 n. 3 QuarEd helpfully refer to Romans 8:20: "For creation was made sub-ject to vanity...." The editors also refer to Book I, d. 8, p. 1, a. 1, q. of Bonaventure's *Sentence Commentary.*

[44]Bonaventure is using the philosophical distinction between *per se* and *per accidens.* On p. 7 n. 4 QuarEd cite Book I, n. 2 of Aristotle's *Analytica posteriora*: "What does not exist cannot be known, for example, that a diameter is symmetrical." See WAE, vol. 1, 71b: "We suppose ourselves to possess unqualified scientific knowledge of a thing, as opposed to knowing it in the accidental way in which the sophist knows, when we think that we know the cause on which the fact depends, as the cause of that fact and of no other, and further, that the fact could not be other than it is....The premises must be true: for that which is non-existent cannot be known – we cannot know, e.g., that the diagonal of a square is commensurate with its side."

[45]On p. 7 n. 5 QuarEd cite Book VI, n. 5 of Aristotle's *Topica* where he is discussing the definition of medicine, health, and sickness: "For medicine indeed deals with health in itself, but with sickness *through something accidental.* For it is foreign for medicine to produce sickness *in itself.*" See WAE, vol. 1, 143a: "It is only, however, in some cases that what has been said corresponds to the actual state of things: in some it

third way, namely, about the changeableness of creatures, knowledge is *in itself*, as is clear from the movement of the sun, the planets, and other objects.

So in this book the author deals with the vanity of *mutability* or of nature, since it is beautiful and suitable. He also treats the vanity of *guilt* or *sin*.[46] But he does not deal with the other vanity, that is, of *total privation,* because there is no knowledge or teaching about it.

1. So about the first objection that all knowledge is about good and truth. Truth exists *in itself*, but vanity can exist only by reason of the truth. And the person who knows true principles also knows false principles. It is the same with the healthy and the sick person, and this is to be applied to the objection.[47]

2,3,4. The second, third, and fourth objections claim that creatures are not vain, because they are very good and have a purpose. This is answered by pointing out that they

---

does not, e.g., all those terms which are not used essentially in relation to both things: as medicine is said to deal with the production of disease and health; for it is said essentially to do the latter, but the former only by accident: for it is absolutely alien to medicine to produce disease."

[46]*Culpa* in Latin has a wide range of meanings: guilt, fault, blame, wrongdoing, error.

[47]On p. 7 n. 6 QuarEd cite Book I, text. 85 (c. 5) of Aristotle's *De Anima*: "It suffices to know one part of contraries to be able to make a judgment about its opposite. From what is straight we know what is oblique. One rule is the judge of both. But what is oblique does not enable us to distinguish either itself nor judge what is straight." See WAE, vol. 3, 411a: "If we must construct the soul out of the elements, there is no necessity to suppose that *all* the elements enter into its construction; one element in each pair of contraries will suffice to enable it to know both that element itself and its contrary. By means of the straight line we know both itself and the curved – the carpenter's rule enables us to test both – but what is curved does not enable us to distinguish either itself or the straight."

are not called *vanities* because they lack good or a purpose, but because they lack *unchangeable existence*. And so every vain creature is not so vain that it has no truth and goodness.[48] And therefore, there is knowledge and teaching about creatures that is true.

III. The method used by Ecclesiastes[49]

When we ask about his *method* in this book, it is said that he acts and speaks through different people, namely, the foolish and the wise.

But:1: As expressed in Sirach 20:22: *A parable coming out of a fool's mouth will be rejected*. Therefore, an opinion stated by a fool is not to be heeded. So if the opinions in sacred writ are to be heeded, fools should not utter them.

2. Likewise, what he says in the name of fools and carnal people is to be rejected. But it is not clear when he is speaking in his own name or in the name of another. Therefore, one does not know what is to be heeded in this book and what is to be rejected. So the teaching of this book leads to error. But since canonical books should purge error, this book should be taken from the canon.

I reply: 1. There are two ways of saying something in the name of a foolish or carnal person: either to approve or to rebuke and show that the statement is vain. The first way is not fitting for the knowledge of the truth, but the second way is fitting. For example, if a person wants to reject an error, he first explains it and then subsequently disproves it. Ecclesiastes speaks in the second way, not in

---

[48]Jerome in his *Commentarius in Ecclesiasten* 1:2 answers this objection: "So in this way we can also say that the sky, the earth . . . are indeed good in themselves, but compared to God, they are nothing." See CCSL lxxii, 252.

[49]Although Bonaventure does not explicitly say so, he is dealing with the formal cause.

the first. And so the book is not to be rejected, but commended, because it rejects what is to be rejected.

2. This objection states that it is not clear when the author is speaking in his own name. It is to be said in reply that one side of an argument is not known until the argument has been resolved, because only in the solution do we find out what is to be accepted and what is to be rejected. Thus, I say that Ecclesiastes continues with his argument until the end of the book where he gives his solution when he says in 12:13-14: *Let us all together hear the conclusion of the discourse. Fear God . . . and know that God will bring you to judgment for every error. . . .*[50] In this con-clusion Ecclesiastes condemns every opinion of the foolish, the carnal, and the worldly. So in this last statement he is speaking in his own name, but what he rejects is spoken in the name of others. Hence the book cannot be understood without paying attention to all of it.

IV. THE EFFICIENT CAUSE OF THE BOOK

Finally, a question can be asked about *the efficient cause* of the book, and it has been said that the efficient cause was Solomon. But it seems that it would not be appropriate for him to be the author for the following reasons:

1. Solomon was a sinner and carnal. But when a carnal person preaches spirituality, the result is scandal rather than edification. Therefore, this book causes more scandal than edification.

2. Furthermore, Psalm 49:16 states: *But to the sinner God has said: Why do you declare my justices?*[51] Therefore, if

---

[50]Bonaventure's major adaptation of Ecclesiastes 12:14 is to read *te* ("you") which is not in the Vulgate.

[51]Psalm 49:16 concludes: ". . . and take my covenant in your mouth?"

Solomon was a sinner, he sinned by speaking of divine justice.

3. Moreover, a good author inspires trust, and *the authority of such a person*[52] strengthens what is said while a bad author inspires no trust. But the books of Sacred Scripture ought to generate trust. Wherefore, etc.

I reply. 1. It is to be said in reply to this that, according to Jerome, the Jews hold that Solomon wrote this book while doing penance.[53] Since God does not reject, but accepts penitents, Solomon was not in a state to be condemned when he wrote this book. One can give another response. The Holy Spirit speaks what is true and good not only through good people, but also through evil people. For the Lord himself says in the Gospel: *Do what they say, but do not do what they do.*[54] The Spirit most clearly proph-

---

[52]Literally, *locus ab auctoritate*. On p. 8 n. 4 QuarEd cite Book II of Boethius' *De Differentiis Topicis*. See PL 1190C: "The maxim is: one should not contradict what is thought to be right by all or by many or by the wise." The editors also cite Petrus Hispanus (d. 1277). See Tractatus V. 36 *de loco ab auctoritate* in *Peter of Spain, Tractatus*, called afterwards *Summule logicales*, ed. L. M. de Rijk, Philosophical Texts and Studies 22 (Assen: Van Gorcum, 1972), 75-76: "Authority, as understood here, is the judgment of the wise person in that person's area of expertise. Hence this topic is normally referred to as the judgment of fact....The maxim is: All experts are to be trusted in their area of expertise." See the English translation of Tractatus V. 36 by Francis P. Dinneen in *Peter of Spain, Language in Dispute*, Amsterdam Studies in the Theory and History of Linguistic Science 39 (Amsterdam/Philadelphia: John Benjamins Publishing Co., 1990), 36: "Authority, as taken here, is the judgement of an expert in his field. So this Topic is commonly called the Topic from Judgement of Fact....The Maxim: all experts are trustworthy in their own field."

[53]See Jerome's commentary on Ecclesiastes 1:12 in CCSL lxxii, 258: "The Jews say this book was written by Solomon when doing penance because overconfident in his wisdom and riches, he offended God through women."

[54]Bonaventure seems to give a paraphrase of Matthew 23:3: "All things, therefore, whatsoever they shall say to you, observe and do, but do not act according to their works, for they say and do not act."

esied through Balaam,[55] and so the Spirit said many good
things also through carnal Solomon.

2. To the second objection that he was a sinner, it should
be pointed out that the gift of wisdom was given to him
among others in a most special way. And because one
should not hide the talent given by the Lord,[56] he had to
teach the people of the Lord in both the spoken and the
written word, especially since he was appointed to rule
them. So he did not sin by teaching, but by not acting
rightly.

3. To the objection that the book is not to be trusted because its author is not worthy of trust, I answer: Just as
we believe the Prophets, who spoke not from themselves,
but from the Holy Spirit, so we also believe that all the
books of Scripture were written at the prompting of the
Holy Spirit. Wherefore, the goodness of an author does
not inspire greater or less trust. The trust depends on the
Spirit speaking through the author. It is clear to us from 1
Kings 3:5-9 that Solomon was filled with the spirit of wisdom, and so the Church accepts his books without hesita-
tion.

JEROME'S PROLOGUE TO HIS *COMMENTARY ON ECCLESIASTES*[57]

I recall when, almost five years ago, I was in Rome and
read Ecclesiastes to holy Blesilla, so that I might move
her to despise the world and to regard all that is in the
world as nothing. She asked me to write a small commen
tary explaining obscure passages, so that when I was gone
she could understand what she read. She was taken away
by a sudden death while I was making preparations for

---

[55]See Numbers 23-24.
[56]See Matthew 25:14-30.
[57]See CCSL lxxii, 249. Bonaventure's quotation is verbatim.

this work. I did not merit, Paula and Eustochium, to have such a companion and I was struck dumb from such a loss. Now living in Bethlehem, a small town, I offer you what I have written in her memory. I give you a brief warning that I have not followed any authority, but, working from the Hebrew text, I have followed the usage of the translators of the Septuagint only in those things that do not differ greatly from the Jews. Meanwhile I have made of use of Aquila, Symmachus, and Theodotion so as not to deter a reader by excessive novelty. Nor against my conscience have I followed the currents of opinion which have abandoned the fountain of truth.

EXPOSITION OF THIS PROLOGUE

St. Jerome wrote this Prologue, first, to give the reason for his work, and secondly, to determine the method of translation: *I give you a brief warning.*

Concerning his first point he makes three observations. First, he says why he began this work, namely, at the request of saintly Blesilla. Second, he touches on what prevented him from continuing, namely, her death: *a sudden death.* Third, what moved him to finish it, namely, her memory and the request of Paula and Eustochium: *now living in Bethlehem.*

I give you a brief warning. Jerome here speaks of his *method* in translating. First, he states that his method is that of not agreeing nor differing totally from others. Rather, he imitated them when he could do so with profit. Second, he adds the *reason*, namely, *not to deter a reader by excessive novelty.* This is the reason why he followed others in some points so as to avoid excessive novelty. But he did not follow them all the time, so as not to betray the truth.

COMMENTARY ON THE BOOK OF ECCLESIASTES

CHAPTER 1

1. *The words of Ecclesiastes*, etc. This whole work is divided into three parts: *a heading* or prologue and *a treatise* which begins in Ecclesiastes 1:2: *Vanity of vanities*, etc. The third part is *the epilogue* which begins in Ecclesiastes 12:9: *And whereas Ecclesiastes was very wise.* – The heading shows *the efficient cause*, the treatise shows *the matter* and *the form*, and the epilogue shows *the purpose*.

THE HEADING

2. (Verse 1) In *the heading* are stated *the wisdom, goodness*, and *kingly power* of the author. – Referring to *wisdom* verse one says: *The words of Ecclesiastes*, and the reader has to understand that the following words are words of Ecclesiastes, because he is called *a preacher*. And one cannot be a preacher without wisdom because Proverbs 26:9 says: "As if a thorn should grow in the hand of a drunkard, so is a parable in the mouth of a fool." Also Proverbs 17:7 states: "Eloquent words do not become a fool."[1] – Referring to *goodness* the verse continues: *Son of David.*

---

[1] Proverbs 17:7 concludes: ". . . nor lying lips a prince."

For David was holy, and descendents who imitate him are holy. In Scripture his name is kindness and clemency. Matthew 15:22 has: "Have mercy on me . . . Son of David." – Referring to *kingly power* the verse concludes: *King of Jerusalem* since Jerusalem was a most noble city and head of the entire kingdom. Ecclesiastes 1:12 below has: *I, Ecclesiastes, was king over Israel in Jerusalem*, because he lived most of the time there.

Questions 2

I. A question arises here: As Solomon wrote three books, why did he use a heading containing his name for the book of Proverbs and for this book, but put no heading on The Song of Songs?

I reply: In the book of Proverbs Solomon is introduced as a wise person instructing a disciple, and so he refers to the listener as his *son*. Similarly in the present book he is introduced as a person experienced in many things, while in The Song of Songs a bride and bridegroom speak. The Song of Songs should not be read as words of Solomon to his wife – rather they are words of Christ to his Church – and so he does not begin the work with his own name. But because in the present book and in Proverbs he speaks often in his own name, he uses an introductory heading in which he points out and identifies his own name.[2]

---

[2]In his commentary on Ecclesiastes 1:1 Jerome addresses this same question and responds in CCSL lxxii, 251: "Now in The Song of Songs neither son of David nor king of Israel or Jerusalem occur in the first verse, but merely *The Song of Songs of Solomon*. As Proverbs is aimed at teaching the ignorant, it is directed to the twelve tribes and to the whole of Israel. And likewise, contempt for the world (the theme of Ecclesiastes) is only a fitting theme for city dwellers, that is, to the inhabitants of Jerusalem. The Song of Songs is properly directed to those whose sole desire is heavenly things. Paternal dignity and the authority of one's king are rightly claimed for beginners and those who

II. It is also asked why in Proverbs he uses *parables*,[3] but in this book he uses *words*?[4] If *you say* that in Proverbs he is speaking in parables and figuratively, while in Ecclesiastes he is speaking openly, then *I ask*: Why does he use these different ways of speaking?

I reply: There is a way of speaking that is in *one's own words* and open while another way is to speak in parables and this in a twofold manner. One speaks in parables and *open* comparisons or by *hidden* and deep comparisons. Since Solomon in Proverbs is speaking to young and unlearned people, he speaks in *parables* and *openly*. In Ecclesiastes he is speaking to the proficient, and so he speaks *openly* and *in his own words*. But in the Canticle addressed to the perfect who enjoy *solid food*,[5] he speaks in *parables* and in *hidden ways*.

III. Another question is: Why did he use his own name in the heading of Proverbs, but in Ecclesiastes he uses the name Ecclesiastes?

I reply: As Jerome notes, Solomon had three names.[6] This is fitting in accord with the three writings he completed. He is known as *Solomon, Ecclesiastes,* and *Idida*.[7]

---

are proficient. But for the perfect, disciples who are not taught by fear but by love, a proper name suffices and the teacher is equal and no one knows that he is the king, etc."

[3] See Proverbs 1:1: "The parables of Solomon, the son of David, king of Israel."

[4] See Ecclesiastes 1:1: "The words of Ecclesiastes, the son of David, king of Jerusalem."

[5] On p. 10 n. 2 QuarEd rightly cite Hebrews 5:14: "But solid food is for the perfect."

[6] See his commentary on 1:1 in CCSL lxxii, 250.

[7] *Idida* is based on a Hebrew word (*dod*) which means "lover, beloved." See 2 Samuel 12:25 which says about Solomon: "And he sent by the hand of Nathan the prophet and called his name, Beloved to the Lord, because the Lord loved him."

He is *Solomon*, a person of peace, because he ruled over the whole kingdom in peace. And so he taught everyone in parables. He is *Ecclesiastes*, a preacher, because he speaks in the name of diverse persons. *Idida* means beloved of God. Therefore, he calls himself *Ecclesiastes* because in this book he produces the opinions of various people and persuades in various ways. He is called *Idida* from the title found in verse one of Psalm 44, a title applied literally to him.[8]

IV. A further question is: Why does he call himself in Ecclesiastes *son of David* and *king of Jerusalem*, while in Proverbs he says *king of Israel*.

I reply: One reason comes from the author's situation because, as the Jews believe, Solomon wrote this book when he was doing penance and humiliating himself.[9] So in Proverbs he uses a name that indicates his power over the whole kingdom, while in Ecclesiastes he is humiliating himself and so uses a name that indicates only part of his power, not all of it. And therefore, etc.

Another reason is from the nature of *the books*. In Proverbs the author persuades people on what is to be done, while in Ecclesiastes he deals with the contempt of the world. And since many prefer to think more of themselves[10] rather than despise present realities, he calls himself in one book king of *Israel* and in the other king of *Jerusalem*. The reason for this is that those who despise the world

---

[8]The title is "A canticle for the Beloved."

[9]See Jerome's commentary on Ecclesiastes 1:12 in CCSL lxxii, 258: "The Jews say this book was written by Solomon when doing penance."

[10]On p. 10 n. 6 QuarEd helpfully suggest that Bonaventure is alluding to Romans 12:3: " . . . let no one think more of themselves than they ought. . . ."

are citizens of the heavenly Jerusalem and do not have *here a lasting city, but seek one that is to come.*[11]

V. And from all this the solution becomes clear to the question: Why does he not express the purpose of Ecclesiastes as he did in Proverbs? The purpose of Proverbs is *wisdom*,[12] something attractive to listeners. But the purpose of this book is the contempt of the world, and few want to hear about this.

From these considerations it is clear why he said *words, Ecclesiastes, son of David*, and *king of Jerusalem*, and why he did not state the purpose of this book as he did for Proverbs.

ECCLESIASTES 1:2-12:7   THE TREATISE

3. (Verse 2). *Vanity of vanities, said Ecclesiastes, vanity of vanities, and all is vanity.* This is the beginning of the treatise. Because "a purpose imposes a necessity on what leads to the purpose,"[13] and his purpose is both the contempt of all things and fear of God alone, he wants to show the vanity in all things. Since he works as a preacher persuading and proving, he divides the treatise into three parts. The first part states what he wants to prove, namely, that there is vanity in everything. The second proves what is stated in Ecclesiastes 1:3: *What profit do people have from all their labor*, etc.? The third concludes with the point proven, as Ecclesiastes 12:8 has: *Vanity of vanities*, etc.

---

[11]See Hebrews 13:14: "For here we have no lasting city, but we seek for the city that is to come."

[12]See Proverbs 1:2: "To know wisdom and instruction."

[13]On p. 10 n. 8 QuarEd refer to Book II, chapter 9 of Aristotle's *Physica*. See WAE, vol. 2, 199b as a general reference.

The formulation of what has to be proven

4. So he proposes that there is a triple vanity in objects, namely, of *guilt, sin*, and *changeableness*.[14] As regards the vanity of *guilt*, the text states: *Vanity of vanities, said Ecclesiastes*, that is, he proposes this statement. Later in 2:23 he says of it: *All their days are full of sorrows and miseries. Even in the night they do not rest in mind. And is not this vanity?* – With respect to the vanity of *sin* he says again: *Vanity of vanities*. Thus, Jeremiah 10:15 reads: *Their works are vain and worthy of ridicule. In the time of their visitation they will perish*.[15] – With regard to the vanity of *changeability* he says: *All is vanity*, because all things are subject to change. Romans 8:20 states: *The creature was subjected to vanity, not willingly*.[16] And in Ecclesiastes 3:19-20 below we read: *All things are subject to vanity. And all things go to one place.* So he does not use vanity three times as a form of emphasis, but as a wonderful distinction.[17]

5. Note that in this triple vanity there is a succession as one comes from the other. Thus, the vanity of *sin* comes from the vanity of *changeableness*, even though this is not the whole cause. The vanity of *guilt* comes from the vanity of *sin*. He arranges these vanities in what he sees as a reverse order while still examining the relationships. And since the double vanity of sin and guilt comes from the vanity of changeableness, but this third does not come from them, he says *vanity of vanities* twice, but later *vanity* once.

---

[14] *Poenalitas* also bears the translation of "guilt" and "punishment."

[15] On p. 11 n. 1 QuarEd correctly indicate that the Vulgate reads: "They are vain things and a work worthy of ridicule...."

[16] Romans 8:20 concludes: "... but by reason of him who made it subject, in hope."

[17] On Bonaventure's use of *distinctiones* in his *Commentary on Luke's Gospel*, see Robert J. Karris, "St. Bonaventure's Use of *Distinctiones*: His Independence of and Dependence on Hugh of St. Cher," *Franciscan Studies* 60 (2002): 209-250, esp. 209-211, 245.

6. Note also that this threefold vanity is found in human beings, because it is upon them that punishment and sin fall. And therefore, the Psalm 38:6 says: *All things are vanity, every person living.*[18] For in humans there is a vanity of *nature*, a vanity of *sin*, and a vanity of *punishment*. About vanity of *nature* Psalm 143:4 states: *Human beings have become similar to vanity. Their days pass away like a shadow.* Concerning vanity of *sin* Psalm 93:11 says something similar: *The Lord knows the thoughts of men and women, that they are vain.* On vanity of *punishment* we read in Job 14:1: *Human beings, born of a woman, live for a short time and are filled with many miseries.*[19]

7. Note further that Solomon speaks as if it were another person speaking as John did in John 21:24: *This is the disciple who gives testimony of these things.* And like Moses.[20]

8. A triple reason can be given for this: One reason is the role of the *first efficient cause*, namely, the Holy Spirit who is the author of Scripture, not Solomon or any other. When the Spirit is referred to in Sacred Scripture, Scripture must make mention of the Spirit as if it were talking of another person. For example, Balaam said in Numbers 24:4: *The hearer of the words of God has said*, etc.[21] – Another reason comes from the role of *the immediate efficient cause.*

---

[18]Hugh of St. Cher, p. 71v, c also cites Psalm 38:6 and considers the triple condition of human beings: innocence, sin, punishment and then quotes Romans 8:20.

[19]On p. 11 n. 4 QuarEd refer to Homily 1 of Hugh of St. Victor, *In Ecclesiasten.* See PL 175:119A where Hugh of St. Victor treats the three vanities of nature, sin, and punishment, but provides no Scripture citations. Hugh of St. Cher, p. 71v, c says that human beings are subject to the triple vanity in thought, speech, and work.

[20]On p. 11 n. 5 QuarEd refer to Numbers 12:3: "For Moses was a man exceeding meek above all men and women who dwelt upon earth."

[21]Hugh of St. Cher, p. 71v, b comments: "And Solomon speaks in the third person, as if speaking about another for the sake of humility. So

Because Scripture avoids all pride and aspires to humility, teachers in Scripture should not speak of themselves as if the words come from them. Rather they should speak as if another were speaking.[22] – The third reason is that when Scripture refers to great and wonderful things, it must point to them as if from a distance. Thus, Hugh says: "As often as this manner of speaking is used in Scripture, it is because of humility or praise . . . .For we should put away from us great things and point out wonders for praise as if from afar."[23] Examples of this are seen in Paul and John.[24]

DIVISION OF THE WHOLE PROOF

9. (Verse 3). *What profit do people have for all the labor*, etc. This text states what he intends to prove, and now he begins the proof. Just as a triple vanity in things has been posited, so there is a triple proof that has three parts. First, he shows there is a vanity in things because they are *subject to change*. Second, he shows the vanity of *wickedness* where 3:16 reads: *I saw wickedness under the sun in the place of judgment*. Third, he shows the vanity of *guilt* where 7:24 states: *I have tried all things in wisdom*. As Hugh says: "The first is natural and fitting, the second culpable, the third punishable and miserable."[25]

---

too Balaam spoke of himself, as if he were speaking about another in Numbers 24. . . .Likewise, in John 21 he said: This the disciple. . . ."

[22]On p. 11 n. 7 QuarEd indicate that the Vatican manuscript refers to the way Paul speaks of himself in 2 Corinthians 12:2: "I know a man in Christ who fourteen years ago . . . such a one was caught up to the third heaven."

[23]See Homily 1 of Hugh of St. Victor's *In Salomonis Ecclesiasten Homiliae XIX* in PL 175:122D.

[24]See 2 Corinthians 12:2 and John 19:35 and 21:24 (presupposing that "the beloved disciple" is John the Apostle).

[25]See Homily 1 of Hugh of St. Victor's *In Salomonis Ecclesiasten Homiliae XIX* in PL 175:119A.

PART 1. PROOF OF THE VANITY OF BEING SUBJECT TO CHANGE

10. There is a double way of thinking about *changeableness* in things. One is due to the fact of *change*. The others comes from a measurement of a designated *time*. First, he treats the vanity of changeable nature in so far as things *change*. Second, with reference to *time* where 3:1 below states: *All things have their time or season.*

ECCLESIASTES 1:3-2:26   THE VANITY OF CHANGEABLE
NATURE FROM THE POINT OF
VIEW OF CHANGE

11. The first section has two parts. First, he shows that there is *mutability* in things, and so vanity. Second, he blames his curiosity where in verse 12 he says: *I, Ecclesiastes, was king*, etc.

ECCLESIASTES 1:3-11   CHANGEABLENESS IN THE BEING
OF CREATURES

12. First, changeableness is proven in the existence of creatures. Creatures exist in three ways, namely, in *the Word* by reason of exemplarity; in *the world* as being material; in *the human mind* as an abstraction.[26] The first way of existing is unending and unchangeable, and so there is no vanity in it. There is vanity in the others, and so this section has two parts. There is a vanity of subjection to change

---

[26]On p. 11 n. 12 QuarEd refer to Book II, chapter 8, n.16-18, Book IV chapter 23 n. 40-41 and chapter 29 n. 46 of Augustine's *De Genesi ad litteram*. The clearest passage is in Book IV, chapter 29 n. 46. See *On Genesis*, 268-269: "Accordingly, someone may perhaps wish to take me up and argue that the angels of the loftiest heavens do not successively gaze, first upon the ideas of creatures which are there unchanging in the unchangeable truth of the Word of God, and next upon the creatures themselves, and thirdly refer their own knowledge of them to the praise of the creator, but that their minds have the marvelous facility of being able to do all three things at once."

in things according to the *being* they have in the world.
Second, there is a vanity according to the *being* they have
in the human mind. Ecclesiastes 1:8 states: *All things are
hard*, etc.[27]

ECCLESIASTES 1:3-7

**THE VANITY OF CHANGEABILITY
ACCORDING TO THE EXISTENCE
OF THINGS IN THE WORLD**

13. The first part is divided into three sections according
to the three kinds of creatures subject to change. First are
rational creatures. Second are *heavenly* creatures where
verse 5 reads: *the sun rises*. Third are *the elements* where
verse 6 states: *surveying all things*.

14. (Verses 3-4). He shows that rational creatures, that is,
human beings, are subject to change, from which no work
can liberate them. So he says: *What profit do people have
for all the labor that they engage in under the sun?* The
reader should add: Other than vanity and mutability, as if
to say: nothing. Of such work Job 5:7 says: "The bird is
born to fly, and human beings to labor."[28] And Genesis 3:17
reads: "Cursed is the earth in your work. With labor[29] you
shall eat thereof[30] all the days of your life."

15. He shows that humans have nothing other than vanity by adding: *One generation passes away, and another
generation comes*. Therefore, there is change and a succession both of people and of their works. Sirach 14:19 states:
"Thus is the generation of flesh and blood: one comes to

---

[27]Ecclesiastes 1:8 continues: ". . . Human beings cannot explain them
by word. The eye is not filled with seeing. Neither is the ear filled with
hearing."

[28]The Vulgate has the reverse: "Human beings are born to labor, and
the bird to fly."

[29]The Vulgate reads *laboribus* ("labors") while Bonaventure has *labore*
("labor").

[30]The Vulgate has *eam* ("it") while Bonaventure reads *ex ea* ("thereof").

an end, and another is born." This is according to James 4:15: "What is your life? It is a mist that appears for a little while."[31] But when they decay, they do not become nothing, but something in the earth, as it was said to Adam: "Dust you are, and into dust you shall return."[32] He adds: *But the earth stands forever*, as the matter into which we break down. Psalm 103:5 reads: "God has founded the earth upon its own bases. It will not be moved forever and ever." And Proverbs 8:29 says: "When God balanced the foundations of the earth."

16. (Verses 5-6a). *The sun rises and goes down*, etc. Here in a second point he shows that *heavenly* nature is subject to change. For example, the sun never rests, but once it rises it goes towards it setting, and so does not continue to rise. So he says: *the sun rises and goes down*, so that it remains neither in the place of rising nor of setting. Therefore, he adds: *And returns to its place*. Nor does it remain there, for he adds: *And there rising again makes its round by the south*. It does not even remain in this central place. Therefore, the text continues: *And turns again to the north*.

17. This can be applied to *daily* movement or even *annual*. Hugh says of sun's *daily* movement: "*The sun rises daily* when it . . . becomes visible to human eyes. *It goes down* when, descending to lower parts, . . . it withdraws from our eyes. *It returns to its place* because, from the force of its whirling motion below, *it returns* again to its place. But it makes its *round by the south*, because by a slanting path it reaches its midday position. . . .Then *turning again to the north*, it goes down to its setting, again by a slanting passage going to the north."[33] Of its *annual* movement

---

[31]James 4:15 concludes: ". . . and then vanishes." Hugh of St. Cher, 72c also cites James 4:15.

[32]Genesis 3:19.

[33]See Homily 2 of *In Ecclesiasten* in PL 175:135C.

Hugh says: "*The sun rises* when it reaches our pole at its spring equinox. *It goes down*, when it descends to lower parts at its autumn equinox. It makes its *round by south*, when it lingers in winter boundaries. It turns again *to the north* when it comes to summer boundaries nearer to the northern pole."[34] And so the sun does not stand still by its nature, but only by a miracle, as we read in Joshua 10:12: "Stand still, O sun, and move not toward Gibeon, nor you, O moon, toward the valley of Hailon."[35]

18. (Verse 6b). *Surveying all places.* Here in a third place he treats of change in *the elements* of nature. First in *air*, then in *water* where the text reads: *All the rivers run into the sea.* – He treats of *air* when speaking of change in a spirit or wind, that is, either a movement of air according to some philosophers, or, according to Aristotle, a movement of vapor in the air, by which movement the air is also moved.[36] So he says: *The spirit goes forward surveying all places round about*, that is, the wind goes around examining everything. Now Spirit means wind. Exodus 15:10 states: "Your wind blew, O Lord, and the sea covered them."[37] And in Psalm 148:8 we read: "Fire, hail, snow, ice, winds of storms."[38] – The wind *returns to its circuits* be-

---

[34]See Homily 2 of *In Ecclesiasten* in PL 175:135CD.

[35]On p. 12 n. 7 QuarEd rightly indicate that the Vulgate reads *Ahialon* ("Ahialon") while Bonaventure has *Hailon* ("Hailon").

[36]On p. 12 n. 8 QuarEd refer to Book II, n. 4 of Aristotle's *Meterologica*. See WAE, vol. 1, 359b-361b, e.g., 361b: "The facts bear out the view that winds are formed by the gradual union of many evaporations just as rivers derive their sources from the water that oozes from the earth." See WAE, vol. 1, 349a for the opinion of philosophers such as Hippocrates: "Some say that what is called air, when it is in motion and flows, is wind, and that this same air when it condenses again becomes cloud and water, implying that the nature of wind and water are the same. So they define wind as a motion of the air."

[37]Bonaventure has added *Domine* ("O Lord"). Exodus 15:10 concludes: ". . . they sank as lead in the mighty waters."

[38]In the Latin Bible *spiritus* is the word for "wind" as well as for "Spirit."

cause it comes from the four corners of the earth. Zechariah 2:6 reads: "Flee out of the land of the north . . . for I have scattered you into the four winds of the heaven." And Ezekiel 37:9 states: "Come, spirit, from the four winds," etc.[39] For the four winds are principals, and eight accompany them.[40] – *And returns to its circuits*, when the wind drops, when the vapor rests and returns to earth from which it came. And since the cause of this is hidden, Psalm 134:7 says: "He brings forth winds out of his stores," that is, from hidden places.[41] Or according to the Glossa: This verse can be understood of the sun in its *annual* movement, as it surveys all and returns to circle the zodiac.[42] The sun is called *a spirit*, because it is the source and cause of all life, making everything breathe.

19. (Verse 7). *All the rivers*, etc. This verse treats of change in a visible element of nature, namely, water, which does not have a fixed place. For all water moves toward the sea, the great ocean. So he says: *All the rivers run into the sea*. About this Job 38:8 asks: "Who shut up the sea with doors, when it broke forth, as issuing out of the womb?" Its movement does not end, for the sea is not filled. So he

---

[39]Ezekiel 37:9 concludes: ". . . and blow upon these slain and let them live again."

[40]On p. 12 n. 10 QuarEd cite Book XIII, chapter 11, n. 2-3 of Isidore's *Etymologiarum Libri XX*. See PL 82:480BC and *Isidori Hispalensis Episcopi Etymologiarvm sive Originvm,* Volume II, ed. W. M. Lindsay (Oxford: Clarendon Press, 1911): "Four of the winds are principal spirits. The first of these is from the east *Subsolanus*, the south is *Auster*, the west is *Favonius*, the fourth is called by the same name, north. Each of these has twin spirits of wind." Among the passages the editors refer to from Aristotle I cite *De mundo*, chapter 4, WAE, vol. 3, 394b: "The winds which blow continuously from the rising sun are called Euri; those from the north, Boreae, those from the setting sun, Zephyri; those from the south, Noti."

[41]On p. 13 n. 1 QuarEd refer to the *Glossa interlinearis* from Augustine on Psalm 134:7: "From hidden causes."

[42]On p. 13 n. 1 QuarEd state that this is the *Glossa Ordinaria* on Ecclesiastes 1:6 from Jerome. See CCSL lxxii, 255.

adds: *Yet the sea does not overflow.* Because this seems wonderful, he gives a reason for it: *Unto the place from whence the rivers come, they return,* not to rest there, but *to flow again.* Rivers flow out in a hidden way, but return openly, because they come out through underground passages and springs. So all things move in a circle and are subject to vanity. Hugh says: "See how everything . . . is moved in a circle and is subject to vanity. We know that a circle has no end, so whatever moves in a circle, moves indeed, but does not reach an end. What rest can be hoped for when there is no fixed position?. . . So it is said of the wicked: 'The head of them compassing me about'[43] and further: 'The wicked walk round about' and again: 'O my God, make them like a wheel'"[44]

20. Note the *spiritual* interpretation of *the sun, the spirit going forth,* and *the rivers coming and flowing again. The sun* is Christ, about whom Malachi 4:2 says: "But unto you who fear my name, the Sun of justice will arise." This sun *arose* in the nativity to enlighten. Isaiah 60:1 reads: "Arise, be enlightened, O Jerusalem." And John 1:9 has: "He was the true light that enlightens every human being." – This sun *set* in the passion for our redemption. Amos 8:9 says: "The sun shall go down at midday," that is, in a strong love of charity. – This sun *returned to its place* in the ascension. Luke 19:12 states: "A certain nobleman went into a far country," etc.[45] – This sun *makes its round by the south,* that is, in a fervent love of the Saints. The Song of Songs 1:6 reads: "Show me, O you whom my soul loves,

---

[43]A literal translation of the Latin is: "Their head a circle."

[44]Hugh cites in succession: Psalms 139:10; 11:9; 82:14. See PL 175:138D-139A. Bonaventure inverts the citations from Psalms 11:9 and 139:10.

[45]Luke 19:12 concludes: ". . . to obtain for himself a kingdom and then return."

where you feed, where you lie down at midday."[46] And John 14:23 has: "If anyone loves me . . . we will come to him and will make our abode with him."– It *turns again to the north* in a final searching. Jeremiah 1:14 says: "From the north every evil will break," etc.[47]

21. The *spirit surveying* is the Holy Spirit, who is consequently said *to examine*, because the Spirit makes us search everything. 1 Corinthians 2:10 reads: "The Spirit searches all things, even the deep things of God."[48] – The spirit is said *to return in its circuits*, because it makes us go around. Thus Wisdom 7:12 states: "The Spirit of wisdom is active." It goes around to make us aware of the circuit of *misfortune and misery*. Job 1:21 says: "Naked came I out of my mother's womb, and naked shall I return thither." It likewise makes us aware of the circuit of *grace*. About this John 16:28 has: "I came forth from the Father and came into the world. Again I leave the world and go to the Father." Also of *glory*. Ezekiel 1:28-2:1 says: "This was the appearance of the brightness round about . . . the like

---

[46]The Latin *meridies* means both "midday" and "south." Hugh of St. Cher, 72v, b also cites The Song of Songs 1:6, but uses it support a different interpretation: "Makes its rounds by the south, that is, considers the good and their works, who are understood by the word south/midday on account of their splendor and the warmth of their virtues, by which they are hot and splendid. The Song of Songs 1. . . ."

[47]Bonaventure reads *omne malum* ("every evil") whereas the Vulgate has *malum* ("evil"): "From the north an evil will break forth upon all the inhabitants of the earth."

[48]On p. 13 n. 7 QuarEd cite what Augustine, *Enarratio in Psalmum 52* n. 5 says about 1 Corinthians 2:10. See *Exposition of the Psalms 51-72*, p. 36: "He does not mean that the Spirit, who knows everything, needs to search; he means that the Spirit who is given to you causes you to search those depths; and what you do through his gift, he is said to do, because you would not be doing it without him." See further *Sancti Avrelii Avgvstini Enarrationes in Psalmos LI-C*, CCSL xxxix (Turnhout: Brepols, 1956), 641.

ness of the glory of the Lord."[49] The Spirit of God makes us reflect this. 2 Corinthians 3:18 reads: "With faces unveiled, we will be reflecting the glory of the Lord," etc.[50] – This circuit makes us reflect that everything is from God and is directed to God.[51] And Dionysius says that the angels move around the throne in a circular motion.[52]

22. *The rivers* are the rivers of grace. About these John 7:38 says: "The person who believes in me, as the Scripture says, out of his belly rivers ... will flow." *The sea*, from which the waters *come*, is the immensity of divine largess that is neither increased nor lessened. "Great is our Lord, and great is his power. And of his wisdom there is no limit."[53] – The rivers of thanksgiving *return* to this sea and again flow out. John 4:14 states: "The person who drinks of the water which I will give him, in him a fountain of water will spring up for everlasting life." The waters *flow out* from the sea. James 1:17 reads: "Every best gift and every perfect gift is from above." And just as rivers cease to be and dry up when they cease to flow and are at rest, so too the gifts of grace. Psalm 73:15 has: "You

---

[49]Bonaventure has adapted this citation. Ezekiel 1:28-2:1 reads: "As the appearance of the rainbow when it is in a cloud on a rainy day. This was the appearance of the brightness round about. This was the vision of the likeness of the glory of the Lord...."

[50]Bonaventure has adapted 2 Corinthians 3:18: "But we all, with faces unveiled, reflecting as in a mirror the glory of the Lord, are being transformed into his very image from glory to glory, as through the Spirit of the Lord."

[51]See Hugh of St. Cher, 72v, h: "Therefore, the Saints are said to be circles, for they move in a circular motion from God into God. Their center is Christ, from whom lines proceed to the circumference of the Church."

[52]See *De divinis nominibus*, chapter 4, n. 8 and PG 3:703D: "The divine minds are said to move in a circular motion, since lacking beginning and end, they are united in the splendors of the beautiful and the good."

[53]Psalm 146:5.

have opened up the fountains and the torrents" by abundance. "You have dried up the rivers of Ethan" by the severity of judgment.

QUESTIONS 3

I. First, it is asked what is the meaning of: *What gain do people have for all the labor?*[54]

1. This seems to be a heretical opinion that agrees with the statement that all *labor in vain who serve God.*[55]

2. Also it is said in Psalm 9:19: "The patience of the poor will not perish forever." Therefore, patience has some gain.

3. Moreover, Proverbs 12:11 states: "The person who tills his land will be satisfied with bread." Therefore, it is good to work and labor.

I reply: Hugh says *by which they labor under the sun* has "the same meaning as if he were saying 'under time.'"[56] Note here that some things are *with time*, for example, things that did not begin before time such as angelic natures and prime matter. Some things are *in time*, for example, things which began after time started, but do not cease in time as the soul of Peter. Some things are *in time* and *under time*, namely, things that begin after the start of time and finish in time such as things that are changeable. Such changeable things are of two kinds: some are *for time* and *under time* and these cease work and bearing

---

[54]See Ecclesiastes 1:3.
[55]See Malachi 3:14 which lacks *omnis* ("all").
[56]On p. 14 n. 4 QuarEd refer to Homilies 1 and 3 of Hugh of St. Victor and maintain that the *distinctiones* that follow in Bonaventure are suggested by these passages. The opinion of Hugh quoted here is suggested esp. in PL 175:127CD.

fruit. Others are *for eternity* and cease work, but remain planted and bear fruit because good will is to be rewarded in eternity.[57]

When the author says that *people have nothing but vanity*[58] *from all the labor that they engage in under the sun,* he means: in so far as work is done and planned *under time.* In this it has no place among good things.

II. It can also be asked what he means by: *The earth stands forever.*[59]

Contra: 1. Matthew 24:35 reads: *Heaven and earth will pass away.* Therefore, the earth does not stand forever.

2. Also Revelation 21:1 states: *I saw a new heaven and a new earth.* Therefore, the earth grows old and does not stand forever.

I reply: The words *the earth stands* can be taken in two ways: with regard to *substance* or with regard to *appearance* or arrangement. I say that in its *substance* the earth stands forever, but its *appearance* will pass away. 1 Corinthians 7:31 says: *The appearance of this world is passing away.*[60] Human beings are born, and their substance corrupts, so that they are no longer called *human beings,* but are rightly called *the dead.*

Or the word *eternal* is used in many ways. In one way it refers in Scripture to what will not end, for example, the promised land as given to the children of Israel as an

---

[57]Bonaventure is dependent upon Hugh of St. Victor here. See PL 175:128D-129A and 175:151BC.

[58]The Vulgate of Ecclesiastes 1:3 does not read *nisi vanitatem* ("nothing but vanity").

[59]See Ecclesiastes 1:4.

[60]On p. 14 n. 7 QuarEd have this reference: "Cfr. IV. Sent. d. 43. 1. 1. q. ad l. et d. 48. a. 2. q.3."

eternal possession. In another way it refers to what comes to an end, but not in time. In this way *time* is said to be eternal. In the third way it refers to what never ends.[61] In the fourth way it refers to a body of which the substance never ends. In the fifth way it refers to something of which the substance neither began nor ended. This last way applies only to God. The fourth way applies to earth in its substance. The third way applies to what is signified. The first two ways apply to appearances. And this is the reply to the two objections.

III. It can also be asked: Of what is he speaking when he says: *The sun rises and goes down?*[62]

1. Since other heavenly bodies rise, it is asked why he makes more of the sun than of the others?

2. Also, he seems to write in a disordered way, because he says first that the sun goes down and then says that it *makes its way by the south*. It would go by the south before it set.

I reply: 1. When the changeableness of the sun, the most noble and brightest of the heavenly bodies, is affirmed, this is sufficient indication that it happens in the others.

2. To the second objection it has to be said that he does not write according to the way things progress, but according to their extent and the limits of their extent. Hence, since rising and setting are opposites, they are immediately re-

---

[61]On p. 14 n. 8 QuarEd write: "The Vatican MSS offers as an example the priesthood of the Law, which prefigured the priesthood of Christ, about which Psalm 109 says: You are a priest, etc. They give as an example of the fourth way the angels and rational souls as well as the earth. They add Psalm 101:13 ("But you, O Lord, remain forever") as an example." The editors also refer to: "IV. Sent. d. 3 p. II. a. 3. q. 1. ad 1"

[62]Ecclesiastes 1:5.

lated. So also south and north are immediately put together in the form of a cross.

IV. 1. There is a doubt about the words: The sun *returns to his place*, because the sun does not have one place in the firmament rather than another. *If you say*, where it began its course is its place, this is clearly false. The sun always moves by its own movement, either going up or going down. Therefore, it never returns to the same place.

2. Also, what does it mean to say: *turns again to the north?* If the sun is moved in its daily movement by the movement of the firmament, then the firmament is moved in one and the same manner. Therefore, it does not turn more to the Arctic than to Antarctic pole or vice versa. – *If you say*, the text refers to its own movement, we know that its own movement is to ascend and descend in the zodiac. When it ascends, it goes to the north. When it descends, it goes to the south. Therefore, it does not turn more to the north than to the south.

I reply: There is a *daily* and an *annual* movement of the sun. When speaking of the sun's *annual* movement, it is true that the sun returns to the place from which it began to move. But in its *daily* movement, it does not return in fact to the place from which it began to move, but it does in our common way of thinking, because it does not move in a spherical, but in a spiraling movement.

2. To the second objection, if we speak of an *annual* movement, it is true in the four seasons, as stated above.[63] For it rises in spring, sets in autumn, moves around by the south in winter, and turns to the north in summer. But if you speak of the *daily* movement, this is only true in our common way of thinking. We see the firmament moved

---

[63]See the commentary on Ecclesiastes 1:6 (#6) above.

and imagine that the poles are on our right and on our left. This is not so. Indeed one pole is, as it were, above our heads, like the north, the other, as if under our feet. So when the sun turns according to the poles of the firmament, it does not in fact go over our heads and under out feet, bur rather crosses over. Because we do not see everything equally well, it seems to us that by day the sun goes to the south and at night to the north.

V. Also it is asked what he means by saying: *All the rivers run into the sea?*[64]

Contra: The sea is bitter, but rivers are sweet. Contraries do not arise from a common source, nor does one contrary come from another.[65] Therefore, the sea does not come from rivers nor rivers from the sea.

I reply: All water by nature, as the Philosopher says, is sweet or tasteless, but it becomes bitter by accident. This happens either from the vapor of subtle particles, the earthly traces remaining in it, or by a mixture of earthly parts. On the contrary, water made bitter by accident, can be made sweet by being filtered as in the experiment of the earthen vase placed in the sea. Rivers, although they return to the sea in great abundance, leave the sea silently under the ground and are strained. In this way the water is filtered and made sweet.[66]

---

[64]Ecclesiastes 1:7.

[65]On p. 15 n. 3 QuarEd refer to Book II, chapter 10 of Aristotle's *De generatione et corruptione*. See WAE, vol. 2, 336a: "Contrary effects demand contraries as their causes."

[66]On p. 15 n. 4 QuarEd refer to a number of places in Aristotle. See *De sensu et sensibili*, chapter 4 in WAE, vol. 3, 441a: "Now the natural substance water *per se* tends to be tasteless." See also Book II, chapter 3 of *Meterologica* in WAE, vol. 3, 359b: "There is more evidence to prove that saltness is due to the admixture of some substance, besides that which we have adduced. Make a vessel of wax and put it into the sea, fastening its mouth in such a way as to prevent any water getting in.

To the objection that one contrary does not come from another, it has to be said that water is not contrary to water. If some water is contrary to another in a property, this difference does not come from the nature of water, but by accident, as is clear in hot and cold water. Rivers do not come from the sea by reason of *a characteristic property*, because by nature there is sweetness in water, but they come as *an efflux*, like a drink of wine from a jar. The sea holds an abundance of water and so there is a ceaseless outpouring.

Ecclesiastes 1:8-11   **The vanity of the changeability of things according to their existence in the human mind**

23. *All things are hard*, etc. It has been shown above that there is a vanity in things according to their *existence* in the *world*. Here the discussion is concerned with the mode of their *existence* in the *human mind*. It is shown that there is a triple vanity in this: first, because they are not *evident*; second, because they do not *satisfy* where verse 8 says: *The eye is not satisfied with seeing*.[67] Third, they do not *endure* where verse 11 states: *There is no remembrance of former things*. These vanities are not evident and easy to interpret or teach. They do not satisfy by refreshing and calming the person who is learning. They do not endure in the memory. These three vanities correspond to three abilities in us: to interpret, to know, and to remember.

Then the water that percolates through the wax sides of the vessel is sweet, the earthy stuff, the admixture of which makes the water salt, being separated off as it were by a filter."

[67]The Vulgate of Ecclesiastes 1:8 reads *non saturatur* ("is not filled") whereas Bonaventure has *non satiatur* ("is not satisfied").

24. (Verse 8a). It is to be noted first that they are not *evident and easy* to interpret. So he says: *All things are hard*, namely, to discover their reason. Thus, Wisdom 9:16 reads: "With difficulty do we consider the things upon the earth, and with labor do we find the things that are before us." Ecclesiastes 8:17 below states: "I have understood that human beings can find no reason for the works of God."[68] And therefore, since they are difficult, *human beings cannot explain them in words*. Job 38:37 has: "Who will declare the reason and order of the heavens?"[69] Sirach 43:29 says: "We will say much, and yet want for words, but the sum of our words is: He himself is."

25. (Verses 8b-10). *Is not filled*, etc. Here in a second point the author considers how a student seeking refreshment is not *filled*. Because we learn mostly through two senses, namely, sight and hearing, he shows that in neither is there satiety.[70] And therefore, he says: *The eye is not filled with seeing*. Proverbs 27:20 reads: "For the eyes of men and women are insatiable." *Neither is the ear filled with hearing*, because the ear itches to hear novelties and curiosities. 2 Timothy 4:3 states: "According to their own desires, they will heap to themselves teachers, having itching ears." And the reason for this is that the eye does not see nor does the ear hear what provides genuine satiety.

---

[68]The Vulgate reads *omnium operum Dei* ("all the works of God") while Bonaventure has *operum Dei* ("the works of God").

[69]The Vulgate reads *enarravit* ("has declared") while Bonaventure has *enarrabit* ("will declare").

[70]On p. 15 n. 6 QuarEd refer to what Aristotle says about these two educatable senses in *De sensu et sensibili*, chapter 1 in WAE, vol. 3, 437a: "Of the two last mentioned, seeing, regarded as a supply for the primary wants of life, and in its direct effects, is the superior sense; but for developing intelligence, and in its indirect consequences, hearing takes the precedence." See also Book I, chapter 1 of Aristotle's *Metaphysica*, in WAE, vol. 8, 980a.

1 Corinthians 2:9 says: "Eye has not seen, nor ear heard,"
etc.[71] He shows that we cannot be refreshed in these earthly
matters because the eye and ear want to learn new things.
But nothing stays new, and therefore, the ear and eye do
not find satisfaction in anything. The *major premise* is
presupposed and made clear in Acts 17:21: "Now all the
Athenians . . . employed themselves in nothing else but
either in telling or hearing some new thing." The author
proposes here the *minor premise* that there is nothing new
in *being* or *becoming*. – So he says: *What is it that has
been?* He asks this question and gives an answer: *The same
thing that will be*. Therefore, by a simple conversion he
says: What is in the future has been.[72] He continues in the
same way: *What is it that has been done? The same that
will be done*. Therefore, by a simple conversion, what has
to be done is what was done. – From this he concludes:
*Nothing under the sun is new; neither is any person able to
say: Behold this is new*. Therefore, one cannot say nor hear
anything new. He repeats the proof: *For it has already gone
before in the ages that were before us*. 2 Peter 3:4 says:
"Since the time that our fathers slept, all things continue."[73]

26. (Verse 11). *There is no remembrance of former things*.
Here the author treats of the third point, namely, that
things do not *endure* in memory, because all things are
forgotten. So he says: *There is no remembrance of former
things*, namely, among us who come later. Wisdom 2:4
states: "Our name in time will be forgotten, and no one

---

[71]1 Corinthians 2:9 concludes: ". . . neither has it entered into the
human heart what things God has prepared for those who love him."

[72]On p. 16 n. 1 QuarEd explain "simple conversion or change": " Simple
conversion in the proposition is to change the predicate into the subject,
and vice versa, with quality and quantity unchanged. For example, no
man is a stone; no stone is a man."

[73]2 Peter 3:4 concludes: ". . . all things continue as they were from the
beginning of creation."

will have any remembrance of our works." Since it is the same for the past and the present, he says: *Nor indeed of those things which hereafter are to come, will there be any remembrance with those who will be in the latter end.* That is to say that those who come later will have no memory of former times and this happens because of the passage of time that brings on forgetfulness. Ecclesiastes 2:16 below reads: "The times to come will cover all things together with oblivion."

QUESTIONS 4

I. What does he mean by the words: *All things are hard?*[74]

Contra: 1. There are many things known to us and animals. Therefore, it is not difficult for us to know what is known by beasts.

2. Also there are some things in which it is not possible to err, for example, the knowledge of sensible objects because the senses are never deceived when dealing with their own proper object. This is also true of the knowledge of clear principles, for example, of fundamental truths.[75] It is easy to know such things.

3. What does he mean by the words: *Men and women cannot explain them in words?*[76] It is easier for humans to

---

[74]Ecclesiastes 1:8.

[75]On p. 16 n. 4 QuarEd refer to Book IV, chapter 8 of Aristotle's *Metaphysica*. See e.g., WAE, vol. 8, 1012b: "For he who says that everything is true makes even the statement contrary to his own true, and therefore his own not true (for the contrary statement denies that it is true), while he who says everything is false makes himself also false." See also Book II, chapter 6 of Aristotle's *De anima*. See WAE, vol. 3, 418a: "Each sense has one kind of object which it discerns, and never errs in reporting that what is before it is colour or sound (though it may err as to what it is that is coloured or where that is, or what it is that is sounding or where that is)."

[76]Ecclesiastes 1:8.

speak than for some creatures to work with ease. Therefore, if a creature works with ease, humans can easily explain the work.

I reply: There is an *incomplete* knowledge as when something is known through its accidents or through some work. There is a *perfect* knowledge that a person has who knows perfectly the substance, power, work, causes, and reasons for something. All things are hard for us, because power is hidden and substance remote from the senses.

1. To the objection that we know some things in common with animals, I say that there is some truth in this. For example, both know what is bitter, but an animal does not know fully.

2. The answer to the second objection is clear, because a sensible object is evident.

3. The third objection is answered by pointing out that there is a difference between *saying* and *explaining*. *To explain* is to bring into the open reasons that are hidden and obscure. Only a person who understands can do this, something that is difficult and done by few.

II. What does he mean by saying: *The eye is not filled with seeing*, etc.?[77]

1. Why does he not speak of the other senses by which one also comes to knowledge?

2. Why does he say: *Is not filled*? Someone is filled when one does not want more of something. It sometimes happens that a person does not want to see or hear more, but to rest. Therefore, etc.

---

[77]Ecclesiastes 1:8.

3. Also, if the eye is not filled, then the desires of the eyes are never at rest, since desire, something that does not rest, is frustrated in achieving its goal. Such a desire is unprofitable and, therefore, sight is unprofitable.[78]

I reply: He speaks only of these two senses, because he is speaking of the senses as ways of knowing and as they relate to sensual pleasure. There are two words by which we know, namely, by a *divine* and a *human* word. A *divine* word is every creature because each creature speaks of God. This word the eye sees. A *human* word is a spoken word that is heard by the ear.[79] – Or there are two ways of learning. One is by *discovery*; the other by *teaching*. The first of these concerns sight; the second hearing.

1.2. To the objection about being filled, I say that the author is speaking of being filled in so far as they are organs of the heart and will or desire, because a heart is not filled

---

[78]On p. 16 n. 6 QuarEd refer to Book I, chapter 2 of Aristotle's *Ethica Nicomachea*. See WAE, vol. 9, 1094a where Aristotle is arguing about the final purpose of human life and says: "If, then, there is some end of the things we do, which we desire for its own sake (everything else being desired for the sake of this), and if we do not choose everything for the sake of something else (for at that rate the process would go on to infinity, so that our desire would be empty and vain), clearly this must be the good and the chief good."

[79]On p. 16 n. 7 QuarEd cite a long passage from Homily 2 of Hugh of St. Cher's *In Ecclesiasten*. See PL 175:140D-142B: "The other bodily senses serve a necessity or pleasure, but these two senses, that is, sight and hearing, draw their nourishment more from spiritual pleasure. . . .These two, that is, knowledge and affection, direct the whole substance of a rational soul so that by wisdom one may find truth, and by love embrace virtue. While external things might serve to further happiness in a rational soul, these two instruments of the senses are placed in the human body, so that by them ideas of wisdom or virtue might enter in. Should such ideas not be present they can be introduced, or if they are present in a small way, that they be increased. . . .The work of God is like a word of God speaking to us. The eyes are like instruments by

nor are these senses. Thus Hugh comments: "Every beauty, pleasure, sweetness of created things can affect the human heart, but they cannot fill it. It can be filled only by the sweetness for which the heart was made."[80]

3. The objection about being *frustrated* is false since its goal is elsewhere.

2. To the objection that the eye and ear do not want more, that is, because of weariness or dislike, not because they are satisfied.[81]

III. What does he mean by saying: *Nothing under the sun is new?*[82]

Contra: 1. Jeremiah 31:22 says: *The Lord will create a new thing upon the earth.*[83]

2. Furthermore, Revelation 21:1 states: *I saw a new heaven and a new earth.*

3. Moreover, the text seems to confirm an error, namely, that things end up in a circular movement, so that they are the same as they were. This is stated in the rest of the text: *It has already gone before in the ages that were before us.* This confirms the error that after the great year containing fifteen thousand years, all things will be renewed.[84]

---

which we see the words of God in contemplation. Just as the instrument of the ear is for hearing a human word, so the instrument of the eye is for seeing the word of the Creator, etc."

[80]Homily 2 of *In Ecclesiasten*. See PL 175:142D where Hugh has the order: pleasure, sweetness, beauty.

[81]It is not clear how this point fits into the overall schema.

[82]Ecclesiastes 1:10.

[83]The Vulgate reads *creavit* ("created") while Bonaventure has *faciet* ("will create/make").

[84]On p. 17 n. 5 QuarEd give many references. See chapter 13. n. 38 of Augustine's *Unfinished Literal Commentary on Genesis* in *On Genesis*, p. 138: "And perhaps in this way, when all the stars have returned to the same point, a 'great year' is completed, about which many people

I reply: What concerns the working, conservation, repair, and glorification of the world is above nature and so is not *under the sun* or under time. These are above time with the exception of propagation, and so he is speaking only of this.

This also applies to the other objections. Note that he calls *new* what has not been before. There is nothing new in *propagation*, because it always produces similar from similar. The author objects to it being from the same thing as this is impossible to understand. If every form that was corrupted and then born again were to differ in number, this could not be understood of the same number.[85]

---

have said many things." See Plato's *Timaeus* in *Plato VII: Timaeus, Critias, Cleitophon, Menexenus, Epistles*, trans. R. G. Bury LCL (London: Heinemann, 1929), n. 39 on p. 83: "Nevertheless, it is still quite possible to perceive that the complete number of Time fulfills the Complete Year when all the eight circuits, with their relative speeds, finish together and come to a head, when measured by the revolution of the Same and Similarly-moving." On p. 82 n. 2 Bury explains "the Complete Year" in this way: "the Great World-Year, which is completed when all the planets return simultaneously to their original starting-points. Its length was variously computed; Plato seems to have put it at 36,000 years (cf. *Rep.* 546 B ff.)." In Book II, chapter 11 of his *In Somnium Scipionis* Macrobius says: "This, as the Physicists state, is to happen after the completion of fifteen thousand years." In his *Commentarius in Ecclesiasten* Jerome quotes Epicurus, "who claims that after innumerable periods there will be the same, in the same place, and by the same." See CCSL lxxii, 257.

[85]On p. 17 n. 7 QuarEd refer to Bonaventure, II Sent. d. 15. a. 2. q. 3 at the conclusion and at dubium 4. They also refer to Book II, chapter 11 of Aristotle's *De generatione et corruptione*. See WAE, vol. 2, 338b: "In consequence of this distinction, it is evident that those things whose 'substance' – that which is undergoing the process – is imperishable, will be numerically, as well as specifically, the same in their recurrence: for the character of the process is determined by the character of that which undergoes it. Those things, on the other hand, whose 'substance' is perishable (not imperishable) must 'return unto themselves' in the sense that what recurs, though specifically the same, is not the same numerically. That is why, when Water comes-to-be from Air and Air from Water, the Air is the same 'specifically', not 'numerically'."

IV. It can be asked what does he mean by the words: *There is no remembrance of former things?*[86]

Contra: It is said in Psalm 76:12: *I remembered your works, O Lord.*[87]

I reply: Some say that the text refers to what is evil, not to what is good. – But this is still false, because many evil things remain in the memory. – So it has to be said that this is not to be understood to be true universally, but very often. For more is forgotten than remembered. However, we retain the memory of many things that happen.

ECCLESIASTES 1:12-2:26   **FROM REFLECTING ON THE DOUBLE VANITY IN THINGS HE DECLARES AND REPRIMANDS HIS CURIOSITY**

27. *I, Ecclesiastes, was king,* etc. He has shown the vanity in things. Now from a reflection on the changeableness of reality he reprimands his curiosity. There are two parts. First, he *declares* his curiosity. Second, he *reprimands* the curiosity because of vanity where Ecclesiastes 2:11 says: *And when I turned myself to all the works.*

The first part has two sections, because first he deals with curiosity in works of *prudence* or philosophy, and second curiosity about *wealth* or mechanical skill where 2:4 states: *I made great works for myself.* – The first section has two headings, because he deals with curiosity in the study of *natural* phenomena or speculative science and then deals with the study of *morals* or practical science where verse 16 reads: *I have spoken in my heart,* etc.

ECCLESIASTES 1:12-2:3   **CURIOSITY IN PHILOSOPHY**

---

[86]Ecclesiastes 1:11.
[87]The Vulgate does not read *tuorum* ("your").

ECCLESIASTES 1:12-15   **CURIOSITY IN THE STUDY OF**
                            NATURAL PHENOMENA

28. In this section he describes curiosity about works of *nature* or about reflection on divine works. First, he looks at the *suitability* of the one studying. Second, the *curiosity* of this person. Third, the *severity* of divine judgment. Fourth, he concludes with *vanity*.[88]

29. (Verse 12). So first, on the *suitability* of the person studying, he says: *I, Ecclesiastes*. And since he had *wisdom*, he calls himself *Ecclesiastes*, that is, preacher. He also had *power*. So he says: *I was king*.[89] He also had *peace*. So he adds *in Jerusalem*, a word meaning a vision of peace. Sirach 47:15 says: "Solomon ruled in the days of peace." 1 Chronicles 22:9 reads: "The son, who shall be born to you, shall be peaceful."[90] Because he had all these qualities, he did not refrain from study.

30. (Verse 13). *And I proposed in my mind*, etc. Here in a second point he treats of his own *curiosity*, because he wanted to know and subtly investigate everything. So he says: *And I proposed in my mind to seek*, that is, from someone else, *and search out wisely*, by myself. And this is curiosity. Romans 12:3 has: "Do not be more wise than it behooves to be wise, but be wise unto sobriety." Thus, Proverbs 25:16 states: "You have found honey. Eat what is sufficient for you, lest, being glutted with it, you vomit it up." — *Concerning all things that are done under the sun*. This

---

[88]The English translation is able to capture some of Bonaventure's word play of ending four words with –tas: *idoneitas, curiositas, severitas, vanitas*.

[89]The Vulgate reads *fui rex Israhel* ("was king over Israel").

[90]On p. 18 n. 1 QuarEd correctly indicate that the Vulgate reads *vir quietissimus* ("most quiet man") while Bonaventure has *pacificus* ("peaceful").

is excessive curiosity because it is about *everything*. Sirach 3:24-25 reads: "In unnecessary matters be not over curious, and in many of his works you will have been[91] inquisitive. For many things are shown to you above human understanding."

31. *This worst occupation*, etc. He treats here of the third point, namely, the *severity* of divine *judgment*, because this condition comes from the divine judgment on the sin of the first parent. The sentence is that our rational ability may so freely run riot in the knowledge of earthly matters. So he says: *this worst occupation*, because it is not only culpable, but also a punishment. *God has given to men and women*, that is, allowed it to be given or gave it justly as a punishment. *To be exercised therein*, and so become forgetful of their own salvation.

32. Note that an occupation is *bad*, because it comes from *weakness*. Sirach 40:1 states: "Great labor is created for all men and women, and a heavy yoke is upon the children of Adam, from the day of their coming out of their mother's womb until the day of their burial into the mother of all." – An occupation is *worse*, because it comes from *ignorance*. About this Job 3:5 says: "Let darkness and the shadow of death cover it. Let a mist overspread it, and let it be wrapped in bitterness." – A third occupation is from *curiosity*, and this is *worst*. And it is of this that the author is speaking here.[92]

33. Note what Hugh says: "An *occupation* is a distraction of the mind that turns away, distracts, and traps a soul

---

[91]On p. 18 n. 3 QuarEd accurately mention that the Vulgate reads *eris* ("will be") while Bonaventure has *fueris* ("will have been").

[92]Hugh of St. Cher, p. 74h also discusses a threefold occupation: the bad stems from necessity; the worse from curiosity, the worst from cupidity.

from being able to think of what concerns salvation."[93] *Curiosity*, however, is a willful prostitution of a human mind, embracing any truth it chances on and being adulterous with it, because the first truth is the soul's only spouse.[94]

34. (Verses 14-15). *I have seen all things that are done*, etc. Here in a fourth place he treats of the *vanity he has found*, because he makes no further progress except that in his consideration he has found vanity. And so he says: *I have seen all things that are done under the sun*, that is, I have reflected on everything. *And behold, all is vanity*, that is, vanity is clearly evident in them because according to the Apostle in Romans 8:20: "All creation was made subject to vanity, but not willingly." Indeed, not only subject to vanity, but *also vexation of spirit*. – But because all do not see this and because they work uselessly and do not realize their affliction, he replies to an unspoken question and says: *The perverse*, etc. Since more evil people are found than good, more stupid than wise, he says: *The perverse are corrected with difficulty*. Thus, Proverbs 18:2 cautions:

---

[93]On p. 18 n. 6 QuarEd cite Homily 5 of Hugh of St. Victor's *In Ecclesiasten*. See PL 175:157B: "An occupation is a distraction and entanglement of minds that turns away, dissipates, and traps souls, lest they succeed in thinking of what pertains to salvation." The editors also state that in this same place Hugh adopts the definition of curiosity given in chapter 26 of *De similitudinibus*, a work attributed to Anselm. See PL 159:614B: "Curiosity is an eagerness to examine things it is useless to know."

[94]See Hugh of St. Cher, p. 74h: "An occupation is described by Master Hugh of St. Victor in this way: An occupation is a distraction and an entanglement of the mind that turns away and dissipates and entangles it from being able to think of what concerns salvation. Curiosity, however, is nothing other than the willful prostitution of the human mind, embracing any truth it chances upon, and fornicating with it, or to speak more truthfully, being adulterous with it. For the first truth, which is God, is human mind's only spouse." It seems clear that Bonaventure is adapting Hugh of St. Cher's citation of Hugh of St. Victor.

"A fool does not receive words of prudence, unless you say those things that are in his own heart."[95] *And the number of fools is infinite*, namely, on account of their number. It is not only a vanity to reflect, but also an affliction. So it is said in Psalm 118:158: "I behold the transgressors, and I pined away." And again Psalm 118:139 has: "My zeal has made me pine away."

35. A person is perverted by evil *thoughts*. Wisdom 1:3 reads: "For perverse thoughts separate from God, and his power, when it is tried, reproves the unwise." A person is perverted by evil *affections*. Proverbs 17:20 has: "Those who are of a perverse heart will not find good, and those who pervert their tongues will fall into evil." A person is perverted by evil *speech*. Proverbs 10:32 states: "The lips of the just consider what is acceptable, and the mouth of the wicked utters perverse thoughts." And Proverbs 2:12 says: "May you be delivered from . . . the person who speaks perverse things." A person is perverted by iniquitous *deeds*. Proverbs 2:14 has: "They are glad when they have done evil and rejoice in most wicked things." Isaiah 1:16 reads: "Stop acting perversely."

Questions 5

I. First, what does he mean by: *This worst occupation*?[96]

Contra: This is sin, and so it means that God gave sin. – *If you say: God gave*, that is, allowed to be given, then the same thing applies to theft. Therefore, it would be right to say that God steals.

---

[95] On p. 18 n. 8 QuarEd correctly indicate that the Vulgate reads *eius* ("his") while Bonaventure has *suo* ("his own"). Hugh of St. Cher, 74v, o also cites Proverbs 18:2.

[96] See Ecclesiastes 1:13.

I reply: "The sins between the first apostasy and the final punishment are punishment and sin."[97] Some are due more to guilt, some to punishment. Those due more to punishment are attributed to the just judgment of God, and they are occupation and blindness of this matter.

II. What does he mean by: *The perverse are corrected with difficulty?*[98] It is easy for a person to be perverted, but perversion is against nature.[99] Therefore, if it is very easy to be turned back to nature, for vice is against nature, it is very easy to be corrected.

I reply: The answer is taken from the point of view of an *evil work*, because "good is done in one way, but evil is

---

[97]On p. 19 n. 1 QuarEd write: "In these words the Master (Peter Lombard) in Book II, d. XXXVI, c. 1 of his Sentence Commentary includes the opinion of Augustine in his *Enarratio in Psalmum 57*, chapter 9, n. 18." See PL 36:687 and *Exposition on the Psalms 51-72*, pp. 140-141: "The apostle gives a list of many things which are sins, and calls them punishments for sins. He says that the primary punishment is pride, or rather that pride is not a punishment, but the primordial sin. Pride is the first sin, and the last punishment is eternal fire or the fire of hell – last, because it is the punishment of the damned. Between that first sin and this ultimate punishment there are other things which are both sins and punishments." See further *Magistri Petri Lombardi Sententiae in IV Libris Distinctae*, Volume I, third edition, Spicilegium Bonaventurianum 4 (Grottaferrata: College of St. Bonaventure, 1971), 537: "For between the first sin of apostasy and the final punishment of eternal fire, there are sins and punishments of sin in the middle." Obviously, Bonaventure's citation is not verbatim.

[98]Ecclesiastes 1:15.

[99]On p. 19 n. 2 QuarEd cite Book IV, chapter 20 of John Damascene, *De fide orthodoxa*. See *Saint John of Damascus: Writings*, trans. Frederic H. Chase, FC 37 (New York: Fathers of the Church, Inc., 1958), 386-387: "Now, as they were made, all things that God made were very good. So, if they remain as they were created, then they are very good. But, if they freely withdraw from the natural and pass to the unnatural, then they become evil." See PG 94:1195C. The editors also refer to Book II, d. 28. a. 1. q. 1. arg.1 ad oppositum of Bonaventure's Sentence Commentary where the same objection is found.

done in many ways."[100] And from the point of view of the *power of the one working*, whose power is made weak by sin and so is incapable of strenuous work. And from the point of view of the *opposition of good* and evil according to privation, because it is very easy to fall from a perfect state to privation, but difficult or almost impossible to go back.

Ecclesiastes 1:16-2:3   Curiosity in the study of morality

36. *I have spoken*, etc. The author has dealt with the study of natural phenomena. Here he similarly shows his curiosity in the study of morality, and he does this in the following order. First, he notes his *crossing over* from the study of natural phenomena to morality. Second, he notes *the finding* of affliction. Third, his *turning* to the enjoyment of pleasures. Fourth, his *return* to a reflection on what is useful.

37. (Verses 16-17a). First, he suggests his *crossing over* to a reflection on morality after his reflection on natural phenomena. For this he says: *I have spoken in my heart*, that is, by thought, *saying: Behold, I have become great*, in fame. *And in wisdom I have gone beyond all who were before me in Jerusalem.* I Kings 4:30-31 states: "The wisdom of Solomon surpassed the wisdom of all the Orientals and of the Egyptians, and he was wiser than all men and women." Sirach 47:15-16 reads: "You were wise in your youth. You were filled as a river with wisdom."

---

[100]On p. 19 n. 3 QuarEd refer to four places in Aristotle. See, e.g., Book II n. 6 of *Ethica Nicomachia*. See WAE, vol. 9, 1106b: "Again, it is possible to fail in many ways (for evil belongs to the class of the unlimited, as the Pythagoreans conjectured, and good to that of the limited), while to succeed is possible only in one way (for which reason also one is easy and the other difficult – to miss the mark easy, to hit it difficult); for these reasons also, then, excess and defect are

38. Solomon possessed this knowledge partly from *revelation*. Thus he says: *My mind contemplated many things wisely*, namely, I was divinely enlightened. And partly from *his own effort*. So the text continues: *And I have learned*. Proverbs 4:3-4 states: "I was my father's son, tender and as an only son in the sight of my mother. And he taught me." Proverbs 31:1 reads: "The vision, by which his mother instructed him." – So since he reflected that he had wisdom from the study of natural phenomena because "he had discussed things . . . from the cedar of Lebanon to hyssop," as is said in 1 Kings 4:33, he decided to cross over to the study of *morality*. So he says: *And I have given my heart to know prudence*, what should be done; *and learning*, what should be known; *and errors*, that are contrary to prudence; *and folly*, contrary to knowledge. He did this because a thing is not perfectly known, unless its opposite is known. These things are useful to know, provided they are studied in the right way. For Proverbs 8:10 says: "Receive instruction[101] and not money. Choose knowledge rather than gold."

39. (Verses 17b-18). *And I have perceived*, etc. Here the author treats of the second point, namely, *the finding of spiritual misfortune* in this study. The more men and women know of good and evil, the more they are afflicted when doing wrong. So he says: *I perceived that in these also there was labor and vexation of spirit*, that is, in the knowledge of what is useful. And *labor* in acquiring knowledge. Psalm 72:15 reads: "I studied that I might know this. It is a labor in my sight." *Vexation of spirit*, after acquiring knowledge or from denouncing wrongdoing or because this knowledge was an occasion of pride and impatience. For

---

characteristic of vice, and the mean of virtue; 'For men are good in but one way, but bad in many.'"

[101]On p. 19 n. 6 QuarEd accurately indicate that the Vulgate reads *disciplinam mean* ("my instruction").

knowledge puffs up.[102] – Both of these interpretations agree
with what follows in the next verse: *Because in much wisdom there is much indignation* or *contrition* over wrongdoing or *impatience* arising from pride. High ranking clergy
most easily become indignant when they do not have what
they want. In Job 32-37 Elihu was moved to indignation
because he regarded himself as wise.[103] So the author says:
The person who adds knowledge also adds sorrow,[104] for
an impatient person bears many sorrows, as there is no
one who has all desires fulfilled. The other translation of
Jerome agrees with this interpretation: "I have perceived
that in these is a feeding on wind,"[105] and so it is right that
people find labor and vexation of spirit there. For Hugh
comments: "Curiosity impels him to study. Pride impels
him to show off. And so it is fitting that labor should weigh
down on the one puffed up, and being occupied should put
to flight the one who was curious."[106] – The text can also
be understood of the vexation of *contrition*, because where
there is much wisdom, there is great indignation against
sin. Jeremiah 31:19 says: "After you showed me, I struck
my thigh," that is, of penance. Job 42:5-6 reads: "Now my
eye sees you. Therefore, I reprehend myself and do penance in dust and ashes.

---

[102]See 1 Corinthians 8:1. Hugh of St. Cher, p. 74v, k also refers to 1
Corinthians 8:1.

[103]It is understood that the wisdom of others did not agree with that
of Elihu.

[104]The Vulgate reads *laborem* ("labor") while Bonaventure has *dolorem*
("sorrow").

[105]See Jerome's Commentary on Ecclesiastes 1:17 in CCSL lxxii, 261.

[106]See Homily 7 of *In Ecclesiasten* and PL 175:164A.

CHAPTER 2

1. (Verse 1). *I said in my heart*, etc. Here the author touches on his third point. So after the tedium of study there is a *turning to pleasure*. Since there were labor and vexation in study, he thought to leave that behind and turn to pleasure in which is delight. So he says: *I said in my heart*, that is, I made this decision because of the spiritual vexation in study. His word and reflection now is not of wisdom, but of dissatisfaction, because when he does not find rest interiorly, he looks for it outside. So he said: *I will go and abound with delights and enjoy good things. I will go*, by leaving good behind. Psalm 77:39 states: Human beings are made "a wind that goes and returns not." *I will abound with delights*, namely, carnal rather than spiritual.[1] The Song of Songs 7:6 says: "How beautiful . . . are you and how comely, my dearest, in delights." He went back from spiritual to carnal delights. Isaiah 22:12-13 reads: "The Lord . . . called to weeping and mourning. . . . Behold joy and gladness . . . the slaying of rams," etc.[2] *And enjoy good things*, in rest. For men and women enjoy things when their desire has found rest. Wisdom 2:6 states:

---

[1] Hugh of St. Cher, 75c also calls these delights "carnal."

[2] All of Isaiah 22:12-13 reads: "And the Lord, the God of hosts, in that day shall call to weeping and to mourning, to baldness, and to wearing of sackcloth. And behold joy and gladness, killing of calves, slaying of rams, eating flesh and drinking wine: Let us eat and drink, for tomorrow we shall die."

"Come, therefore, and let us enjoy the good things that are present. And let us speedily use creatures as in youth." And Proverbs 7:18 has: "Come, . . . let us enjoy the desired embraces." Because this reflection was blameworthy and reprehensible, he rebuked himself, for present delight is not a true delight, but a deception. So he adds: *And I saw that this, too, is vanity,* since it does not *endure* nor refresh, but fades away and deceives.

2. (Verse 2). So he says: *Laughter I counted error,* in that it seduces people. *And to joy I said: Why are you vainly deceived?*, because by rejoicing you are deceived. *Laughter* is exterior, while *joy* is interior. Laughter deceives, because it offers good that turns out to be evil. Proverbs 14:13 says: "Laughter shall be mingled with sorrow, and mourning takes hold of the end of joy." And James 4:9 states: "Let your laughter be turned into mourning," because Luke 6:25 proclaims: "Woe to you who laugh now, for you shall . . . weep."[3] This is the laughter of the delirious, for it is mistaken and passing. In the same way *joy* deceives interiorly. Job 21:12-13 reads: "They rejoice at the sound of the organ. They spend their days in good things, and in a moment they go down to hell." And Job 20:5 has: "The joy of the hypocrite is but for a moment."

3. (Verse 3). *I thought in my heart,* etc. The author treats here of the fourth point, namely, a *return* to a reflection on what is useful, a return from pleasure to sobriety. So he says: *I thought in my heart, to withdraw my flesh from wine,* because wine in an astonishing way inclines to pleasure. For Ephesians 5:18 reads: "Be not drunk with wine, wherein is voluptuousness." And Proverbs 20:1 states: "Wine is a voluptuous thing, and drunkenness is riotous. Whoever delights in these things will not be wise."[4] He

---

[3]Hugh of St. Cher, 75g also cites Luke 6:25.
[4]Hugh of St. Cher, 75v, a also cites Proverbs 20:1.

thought to withdraw from the beckoning of pleasure, *so that I might turn to wisdom.* That is, to reflect on the wise and to abandon reflecting on the foolish, such as in the preceding reflection. So he says: *And might avoid folly,* as he is encouraged to do by wisdom. Proverbs 1:22 advises: "Children, how long will you love childishness? Fools, how long will they covet things that are harmful?"[5] He does this not only for his own good, but also for the common good. So he continues: *Till I might see what was profitable for men and women.* And this in the present life. Wherefore, he also adds: *What they ought to do,* that is, what it is opportune to do, *under the sun, all the days of their lives.* He saw this and wrote at the end of the book: "Fear God and keep God's commandments. This is all for men and women."[6]

4. These are the things that are *useful. To keep the commandments of God,* because as he says in 8:5 below: "The person who keeps the commandment will find no evil." And in Proverbs 19:16 we read: "Men and women who keep the commandment keep their own souls, but those who neglect their own way shall die." – *Deliverance from iniquity.* 2 Timothy 2:21 reads: "If anyone will cleanse himself from these, he will be a vessel . . . sanctified and useful to the Lord, . . . for every good work" – *Learning of truth.* 2 Timothy 3:16 has: "All teaching,[7] inspired of God, is useful . . . for instruction in justice," that is, to make a person just. – *Exercise of piety.* 1 Timothy 4:7 says: "Exercise yourself unto piety, for bodily exercise is useful for little, but piety is useful for all things."

---

[5]The Vulgate reads *sibi* ("to themselves"). Also the Vulgate reads *cupiunt* ("covet") while Bonaventure has *cupient* ("will covet").

[6]Ecclesiastes 12:13.

[7]The Vulgate reads *scriptura* ("scripture") whereas Bonaventure has *doctrina* ("teaching").

5. These are the things that are *useless*.[8] *Proud transgression of God's law*. 2 Chronicles 24:20 states: "Why are you transgressing the commandment of the Lord, which will not be useful for you?" – *Wisdom without teaching*. Sirach 20:32 reads: "Wisdom that is hidden and treasure that is not seen, what use is there in them both?" – *Teaching that is not put into practice in life*.[9] Luke 14:34 says: "Salt is good. But if salt loses its flavor, wherewith will it be seasoned?" – *Contentious disputations*. 2 Timothy 2:14 has: "Contend not in words, for it is useless."

Questions 6

What does he means by the words: *The person who adds knowledge also adds sorrow?*[10]

Contra: 1. "All people by nature want to know."[11] But when this is fulfilled, they are happy. Therefore, etc.

2. Further, or he is speaking of *true* knowledge, and this is false. Wisdom 8:16 states: *Conversation with her (wisdom) has no bitterness*. If he is referring to *curiosity*, this is false, because the curious get much delight when they can find something out.

I reply: The words can be applied to both true knowledge and to curiosity. It is true of *curiosity* because just as avarice and the desire to possess increase with riches, so too does the desire to learn increase for the curious per-

---

[8]Hugh of St. Cher has no parallel to Bonaventure's listing of four useful and four useless things.

[9]Literally: "teaching without life."

[10]Ecclesiastes 1:18. The Vulgate reads *laborem* ("labor") while Bonaventure has *dolorem* ("sorrow").

[11]On p. 21 n. 2 QuarEd refer to Book I, n. 1 of Aristotle's *Metaphysica*. See WAE, vol. 8, 980a: "All men by nature desire to know."

son. If he is speaking of knowledge of *the truth* from the viewpoint of *taste*, it delights. If he is speaking of knowledge of the truth from the viewpoint of *recognition*, this sometimes causes sadness either because of a person's besmirched conscience or because of the sight of wickedness in someone else.[12]

ECCLESIASTES 2:4-26   CURIOSITY AS IT PERTAINS TO WEALTH AND PLEASURE

6. *I have made great works for myself*, etc. The author has already stated his curiosity in a search for *wisdom*. Now he goes on to state his curiosity in *mechanical works* that pertain to realities of a bodily nature whereas the search for wisdom is a matter of the spirit. The search for wisdom is a liberal art while human works are a work of skill. – This section has two parts. The first deals with works of skill undertaken to acquire *wealth*. The second is concerned with *pleasures* where verse 8 says: *I made singing men and singing women for myself.*

ECCLESIASTES 2:4-8A   CURIOSITY AND THE ACQUISITION OF RICHES

7. In the following order the author describes his curiosity in what pertains to acquiring *riches*. First, acquiring *lasting* possessions. Second, a large number of *servants*. Third, increasing the number of *sheep and animals*. Fourth, a piling up of *minerals*. These four categories cover almost all worldly delights.

8. (Verses 4-6). First, he expresses his curiosity in the *possession of long lasting goods*, namely, homes, vineyards, vegetable gardens, ponds of water for irrigation. So he says:

---

[12]See Question III which follows after Bonaventure's exposition of Ecclesiastes 2:10.

I made my works great, that is, I made myself great. 1
Kings 10:23 says: "King Solomon exceeded all the kings
on the entire earth."[13] He lists his accomplishments indi-
vidually. *I built houses for myself*, because he built many.
And so we read in 1 Kings 9:10: "After Solomon built[14] two
houses that is, the house of the Lord and the house of the
king," he also built a house for the daughter of Pharaoh.[15]
This was a work of curiosity and blameworthy. For Isaiah
4:8 states: "Woe to you that join house to house." *I planted
vineyards* for drinking. Genesis 9:20-21 has: "Noah . . .
planted a vineyard, and drinking of the wine, became
drunk." – *I made gardens and orchards and set them with
trees of all kinds* for eating. The Song of Songs 6:10 says:
"I went down into my garden[16] . . . to see the fruits of the
valleys and to look if the vineyard had flourished and the
pomegranates budded." – Since these had to be irrigated,
he adds: *I made for myself ponds of water*, that is, places to
collect water, so as *to water therewith the wood of the young
trees* by irrigation. For as it is said in Job 12:15: "If he
withholds the waters, all things will be dried up." This
was necessary in the promised land because of the lack of
water. Deuteronomy 11:10-11 reads: "The land, which you
are going to possess . . . is a land of hills and plains, ex-
pecting rain from heaven."

9. (Verse 7a). *I acquired servants*. Here in a second point
he treats of his curiosity with respect to a *large number of
servants* of both sexes and says: *I acquired menservants
and maidservants*; and also of every age. Thus, the text

---

[13]1 Kings 10:23 concludes: " . . . in riches and wisdom." On p. 21 n. 5
QuarEd accurately mention that the Vulgate does not read *universae*
("entire").

[14]The Vulgate reads *aedificaverat* ("had built") while Bonaventure
has *aedificavit* ("built").

[15]See 1 Kings 7:8 which also mentions that Solomon had married the
daughter of Pharaoh.

[16]The Vulgate does not have *meum* ("my").

continues: *I had a large family.* 1 Kings 10:4-5 reads: "When the queen of Sheba saw all the wisdom of Solomon . . . and the food of his table, the apartments of his servants and the order of his ministers . . . she no longer had any spirit in her."[17]

10. (Verse 7b). *And herds.* Here in a third point he treats of his curiosity in regard to *herds of oxen* and large and small *animals,* for he says: *And herds of oxen and great flocks of sheep.* Supply the verb: I possessed. *Beyond all that were before me in Jerusalem.* It is clear that he owned much, because he consumed much. 1 Kings 4:22-23 states: "The provision for Solomon for each day . . . was ten fattened oxen and twenty oxen from the pastures, and one hundred rams, besides venison of harts, roes, etc."

11. (Verse 8a). *I heaped together for myself.* Fourth, he treats of his curiosity in *piling up minerals* when he says: *I heaped together for myself gold and silver,*[18] that is, precious metals, *and the wealth of kings and provinces,* that is, precious stones and gems. 1 Kings 10:25-27 says: "Everyone brought him presents: vessels of silver and gold, garments and armor. . . .And he made silver to be as plentiful in Jerusalem as stones."

12. In the *spiritual meaning,*[19] this Solomon, who *made great works,* is Christ the Lord,[20] who is *the King of peace.*

---

[17]Hugh of St. Cher, 76i also refers to 1 Kings 10:4-5.

[18]Bonaventure has inverted the order of the Vulgate, which has "silver" before "gold."

[19]Hugh of St. Cher, 75v-76 deals with the mystical understanding of Ecclesiastes 2:7, but does not distinguish between the contemplative and active ways of life as Bonaventure does. In what follows I note the few points he has in common with Bonaventure.

[20]See Hugh of St. Cher, 75v, g: "So the true Solomon is speaking, that is, Christ the Lord."

Of his works we read in Psalm 103:24: "How great are your works, O Lord. You have made all things in wisdom," etc.[21] Now Christ makes great works when he makes many great *servants* in the active and contemplative ways of life. – For contemplatives, in so far as they are great in their way of life, have much conferred on them by Christ the Lord. They have *houses*, namely, peaceful consciences. Proverbs 24:15 reads: "Lie not in wait, nor seek after wickedness in the house of the just, nor spoil his rest." In this house one must rest, not in a strange house, since from a contrary perspective Sirach 21:25 states: "The foot of a fool is soon in his neighbor's house." – *Vineyards*, that is, affections of devotion from which wine is drawn. Judges 9:13 has: "Can I forsake my wine?"[22] – *Gardens*, that is, exterior enclosures. The Song of Songs 4:12 says: "My sister, my spouse is a garden enclosed, . . . a fountain sealed up." – *Trees*, that is, various virtues.[23] Numbers 24:5-6 states: "How beautiful are your tabernacles, O Jacob, . . . like valleys filled with woods." – *Orchards*, that is, good and well-regarded works. Job 9:25-26 reads: "My days have passed as ships carrying fruits," that had a good fragrance. 2 Corinthians 2:15 has: "We are the good fragrance of Christ unto God." – *Ponds*, that is, many tears. The Song of Songs 7:4 says: "Your eyes are like the ponds in Heshbon."[24] Jeremiah 9:1 states: "Who will give water to my head and a fountain of tears to my eyes?"

---

[21]Psalm 103:24 concludes: ". . . the earth is filled with your riches."

[22]This passage occurs in Jotham's parable of the trees which want a king to rule over them. Judges 9:12-13 reads: "And the trees said to the vine: Come and reign over us. And it answered them: Can I forsake my wine, that cheers God and human beings and be promoted among the other trees?"

[23]Hugh of St. Cher, 76h writes: "I possessed menservants and maidservants] that is, the virtues."

[24]Hugh of St. Cher, 76g also cites The Song of Songs 7:4.

13. Just as Christ magnifies his works among *contemplatives*, so too he magnifies them among *those in the active way of life*, for they need many things. *Menservants and maidservants* through humility. Luke 17:10 says: "When you will have done all things that have been commanded you, say: We are unprofitable servants."[25] – *Herds of oxen* through strenuous work, because it is not the job of oxen to rest, but to plow. Job 1:14 reads: "The oxen were plowing." Sirach 7:16 states: "Hate not laborious works."[26] – *Sheep*, through simplicity of purpose. Matthew 10:16 has: "Behold, I send you as sheep in the midst of wolves." 1 Peter 2:2 says: "As newborn babes, . . . desire milk."[27] – *Gold* through love. Daniel 2:32 says of this statue: "Its head was of fine gold," because love is the head of the virtues. – *Silver* through eloquence of speech. For Psalm 11:7 reads: "The words of the Lord are pure words, as silver tried by fire." And Sirach 6:5 states: "A gracious word multiplies friends and appeases enemies." – *The wealth of kings* through generous giving. Sirach 13:30 has: "Riches are good to him that has no sin on his conscience."

ECCLESIASTES 2:8B-10   CURIOSITY ABOUT PLEASURES

14. *I made singers for myself*. He has spoken of his curiosity in anything to do with riches, and now he speaks of his curiosity about *pleasures*. He does this as follows. Since pleasures are not found by anyone at all, but by a person who wants them, is capable of them, and knows how to enjoy them, he shows, first, his *care* in preparing delights. Second, his *ability* to complete them. Third, his *wisdom* in planning. Fourth, his *pleasure* in enjoying them.

---

[25]Hugh of St. Cher, 75v, g also cites Luke 17:10.

[26]On p. 22 n. 5 QuarEd rightly indicate that the Vulgate has *non oderis* ("hate not") while Bonaventure reads *ne oderis* ("do not hate").

[27]1 Peter 2:2 reads: "As newborn babes, desire the rational milk without guile."

15. (Verse 8b). First, he shows his great *care* in preparing such pleasures both from the point of view of *hearing* and of *sight*. Of *hearing* he says: *I made for myself male and female singers*, for the sake of pleasure. So he adds: *and the delights of men and women*, and this for pleasure for the ear. For his *eyes* he made beautiful vases, for he says: *cups and vessels to serve and pour out the wine*, made by him for the sake of pleasure. He was then most diligent, and this is blameworthy. Amos 6:1, 5-6 reads: "Woe to you who are wealthy in Zion. . . .You who sing to the sound of the psaltery . . . and drink wine from bowls."

16. (Verse 9a). *And I surpassed in riches*, etc. He treats here of the second point, namely, his *ability* to complete pleasures. For poor people, even though they might begin artificial delights of this kind, do not finish them. But he was able to because he was rich. Therefore he states: *And I surpassed in riches all who were before me in Jerusalem*, for he exceeded all. 1 Kings 3:13 says: "I have given you riches and glory, so that no one has been like you among the kings in all the days heretofore."

17. (Verse 9b). *My wisdom also*, etc. Here he treats of the third point, namely, his *prudence* in planning, for he says: *My wisdom also remained with me*. By this wisdom he ordered all that he made. 1 Kings 10:4-5 has: "When the queen of Sheba saw all the wisdom of Solomon . . . and the order of his ministers, and their apparel and the cupbearers . . . she no longer had any spirit in her." And 1 Kings 4:30-31 reads: "The wisdom of Solomon surpassed the wisdom of all the Orientals and of the Egyptians, and he was wiser than all."

18. (Verse 10). *And all my eyes desired*, etc. He treats now of the fourth point, namely, his *pleasure* in enjoying the delights he had prepared. And since some pleasures come *from outside*, some *from within*, he notes both of them in

himself. Of pleasures coming from outside, he says: *And all my eyes desired*, that is, seeing what was outside me, *I refused them not*. Rather he did wrong by satisfying himself. Lamentations 3:51 comments: "My eye has wasted my soul." And Jeremiah 9:21 observes: "Death has come up through my windows."[28] – Of internal pleasure he says: *I withheld not my heart*, that is, a desire of his heart, *from delighting itself in the things that I had prepared*. Against this we read in Sirach 18:30: "Son,[29] go not after your lusts, but turn away from your own will."[30] And because affection often distorts the judgment of reason, there follows a perversity of mind. Thus the text adds: *And I esteemed this my portion*, that is, I judged it was better for me *to make use of my own labor*, for the present. This is the opinion of the Epicureans who know of no other good or *portion*. On the other hand, the Saints have no *portion* here, but in the future. Thus, Psalm 141:6 says: "O Lord, my portion in the land of the living." And again Psalm 15:5 states: "The Lord is the portion of my inheritance and of my cup."

QUESTIONS 7

I.1. Why was he sinful in delighting in these *songs*, and what kind of sin was it?[31] – *If you say* that it pertains to inordinate pleasure, the question is asked: Since hearing is one of the senses, like taste and touch, it seems that

---

[28]On p. 23 n. 2 QuarEd correctly indicate that the Vulgate reads *fenestras nostras* ("our windows") while Bonaventure has *fenestras meas* ("my windows").

[29]The Vulgate does not have *Fili* ("Son").

[30]On p. 23 n. 2 QuarEd cite Book VI, n. 12 of Aristotle's *Ethica nicomachea*. See WAE, vol. 9, 1144a: "wickedness perverts us and causes us to be deceived about the starting points of action."

[31]See Ecclesiastes 2:8.

hearing should be a capital sin[32] as is the case with touch. And if it is not a capital sin, then why not?

2. Also I ask whether it is a sin to delight in such songs? It would seem *not* to be a sin, because the Saints wrote songs to the glory of God.

Now for the opinion that it is a sin, listen to what Augustine says in his Confessions: "As often as the songs themselves pleased me more than the words, I confess I sinned gravely."[33]

I reply: It has to be said that to take delight in such songs comes from internal *devotion* that looks only for a song and words that are good, or from inner *pleasure* and voluptuousness, or from a certain *curiosity*. The first of these is not a sin, but meritorious. The second is a sin closely related to voluptuousness. The third is the sin of curiosity which is remotely related to voluptuousness.

To the question: Why is a sin of hearing not a capital sin like touch and taste, I reply: Because there is not so much corruption or delight in it.

II. What does he mean by the words: *I surpassed in riches all that were before me in Jerusalem?*[34] What is this? What he says does not claim much, because the only one to reign over Jerusalem before him was his father who rose up, founded the city, and expelled the Jebusites.[35] Some say to

---

[32]See Roy J. Deferrari, *A Latin-English Dictionary of St. Thomas Aquinas* (Boston: St. Paul Editions, 1960), 768: "*capital sin,* by which is understood either that which brings capital punishment with it or that which gives rise to and directs other sins."

[33]On p. 23 n. 4 QuarEd cite Book X, chapter 33 n. 50: "However, when it happened that I was moved more by the song than by the reality behind the song, I confess that my sin was punishable (*poenaliter*).

[34]Ecclesiastes 2:9.

[35]See 2 Samuel 5:6-10. See Jerome's remarks on 2:7 in his *Commentarius in Ecclesiasten* in CCSL lxxii, 265: "There is no great

this that he is speaking not only of the kings of Israel, namely, David and Saul, but also of the judges.[36] – But this was not much. – Therefore, it is said that before Solomon there were kings in Canaan, and these were rich and great. He was speaking of them. – Or the verse can be read to mean that the words, *in Jerusalem*, refer to the riches which he possessed in Jerusalem, not to kings. The meaning would be: *I surpassed in the riches I had in Jerusalem all that were before me*, for no one before him was like him.

III. Further, it is asked what is the meaning of the words: *My wisdom also remained with me?*[37]

Contra: Sirach 6:23 says: *The wisdom of doctrine is according to her name.*[38] Therefore, people are not wise unless they discern things as they should be discerned.[39] But Solomon did not discern correctly, because he despised eternal goods and loved temporal goods. So he was not wise, but stupid.

---

glory to Solomon who was richer than the one father who reigned before him. For Saul had not yet ruled in Jerusalem which was held by the Jebusites who had resided in the city itself."

[36]See Jerome's exposition of 2:9 in *Commentarius in Ecclesiasten* in CCSL lxxii, 267: "When he says *all that were before me in Jerusalem*, he is speaking of those who governed the congregation of the Saints and the Church before his coming."

[37]Ecclesiastes 2:9.

[38]On p. 23 n. 7 QuarEd accurately mention that the Vulgate reads *illius* ("her") while Bonaventure has *eius* ("her").

[39]On p. 23 n. 7 QuarEd cite Sermon 50 n. 6 of Bernard of Clairvaux' *Sermones super Cantica Canticorum*. See SBOp 2.81 and *Bernard of Clairvaux On the Song of Songs III*, trans. Kilian Walsh and Irene M. Edmonds, Cistercian Fathers Series 31 (Kalamazoo: Cistercian Pubications, 1979), 35: "But not so affective love, since it always leads the ordering from the first. It is the wisdom by which all things are experienced as they are; as for example, the higher the nature the more perfect the love it evokes; the lower evokes less, the lowest nothing."

I reply: *Wisdom* in one way brings about knowledge only, and so it is said "wisdom is the knowledge of things sacred and human."[40] In another way it brings about a taste and the savor and order of affection, and so is called *wisdom* by savor. In the first way there is an understanding of good and evil for those who have an enlightened mind to see the many truths about God and creatures. The second way deals only with good things. Wisdom has endured through the first way, because understanding was not lost. Understanding in the second way was lost when people sinned and became stupid.[41]

IV. What does he mean by the words: *And I esteemed this my portion, to make use of my own labor?*[42]

1. So it seems that Solomon followed the opinion of the Epicureans who claim that joy is to be found only in the present, and this is heretical.

2. Also, if he was wise and intelligent and said this, one has to presume it is true.

---

[40]On p. 23 n. 8 QuarEd point to Book V, chapter 3 of Cicero's *Tuscalan Disputations*. See *Cicero, Tusculan Disputations*, trans. J. E. King, LCL (Cambridge: Harvard University Press, 1945). I adjust King's translation on p. 431: "And by wisdom's knowledge of things sacred and human, as well as of the beginnings and causes of every phenomenon, it gained its glorious name with the ancients."

[41]See the discussion of Bonaventure's four meanings of wisdom in *Itinerarium Mentis in Deum*, Ed. Zachary Hayes and Philotheus Boehner, Works of St. Bonaventure II (St. Bonaventure, NY: Franciscan Institute Publications, 2002), 217-221, esp. p. 218: "The fourth is wisdom in a stricter sense (*magis stricte*), and means the cognition of God by experience (*cognitionem Dei experimentalem*). For wisdom is also one of the gifts of the Holy Spirit, the act of which is to taste the sweetness of God. This wisdom truly pertains to the mystical state; it begins in cognition and ends in affection, and has no limits as to its intensity. . . .For all these names mean to him one and the same thing, the real goal of humanity here upon earth, the wisdom of the mystical union with God, which is knowledge by tasting."

[42]Ecclesiastes 2:10.

I reply: We make judgments in two ways, namely, by a *considered and thought-out process* or by a process of *seeing a value* in something. I say that Solomon never held this opinion as a result of a *considered and thought-out process*, but only by *seeing a value* in it, just as all sinners put a value on what they are doing that it is good. Hence, Solomon's error was not one of infidelity, but an error of deviating from good. On the other hand, the Epicureans not only see good in this, but also assert it as something certain. For them there is no other good, and so they are heretics and infidels.

2. To the objection that he was wise and therefore, etc., it has to be said that, even though he was wise, in this he acted stupidly and is not to be imitated. David was good, but did not do good in having Uriah killed.[43] This was not said for us to imitate, but to condemn.

ECCLESIASTES 2:11   HE BLAMES HIS CURIOSITY FOR THE VANITY HE FOUND

19. *And when I turned myself*, etc. He has dealt with his curiosity, and he now *blames* it for the vanity he has found, a vanity that consists in changeableness. This section has two parts. First, he condemns what he did out of curiosity *in general*, and second, *in particular* where verse 12 reads: *I passed further to behold.*

20. (Verse 11). So by careful reflection he found vanity and vexation in what he had done out of curiosity. For this reason he says: *And when I turned myself to all the works that my hand had wrought*, that is, when I had carefully reflected upon them, according to what the Apostle says in Galatians 6:4: "But let everyone prove the worth of his own work." *And to the labors wherein I had labored in*

---

[43]See 2 Samuel 11:6-27.

vain. They were in vain, because they were not done for God, and so he had labored in vain. Wisdom 3:11 states: "Their hope is vain, and their labor[44] without fruit." *I saw in all things vanity and vexation of spirit and that nothing was lasting under the sun.* The works were *vain* and *troublesome*, because they were not lasting. Whatever does not last is *vain* in so far as it slips away, does not last, and causes *vexation*. Sirach 40:13 reads: "The riches of the impious[45] will be dried up like a river and will sound forth[46] like a great thunder in rain." Thus, 1 John 2:17 states: "The world passes away and its concupiscence." "Its[47] favor is deceitful, and its beauty is vain."

ECCLESIASTES 2:12-17   HE BLAMES HIS CURIOSITY IN LEARNING WISDOM

21. *I passed further to behold wisdom.* He now shows *in detail* the vanity in his works. He divides the material to show, first, vanity in the work to learn *wisdom* and, second, in the work to gain *riches* according to the double work of curiosity already explained.[48] This he picks up in verse 18: *Again I hated all my application.* So first he blames his curiosity in the study of wisdom as follows. First, he implies *the diligence* of his study. Second, the *preeminence* he found in a wise person when compared to a foolish person. Third, the finding of another *comparison*. Fourth, from this he concludes to *the vanity* and *blameworthiness* of his own work.

---

[44]On p. 24 n. 2 QuarEd accurately mention that the Vulgate reads *labores* ("labors") while Bonaventure has *labor* ("labor").

[45]On p. 24 n. 3 QuarEd rightly indicate that the Vulgate reads *iniustorum* ("the unjust") while Bonaventure has *impiorum* ("the impious").

[46]The Vulgate reads *manebunt* ("will endure") while Bonaventure has *personabunt* ("will sound forth").

[47]Bonaventure has adapted Proverbs 30:31 to his context by adding *eius* ("its"), which I, in turn, have added to "beauty."

[48]See above on Ecclesiastes 1:12 and 2:4.

22. (Verse 12). So first he implies *the diligence* of his study in examining those things he chose to study. So he says: *I passed further to behold wisdom*, as something *to be chosen, and error and folly*, as things *to be avoided. I passed*, he says, from pleasure. For Sirach 24:26 reads: "Pass over to me, all you that desire me," etc. And while there was diligence in this, it was not *enough*. So he adds: *What is a human being, said I, that he can follow the King, his maker?* As if to say: It is insufficient to reflect upon and see what the Lord sees beforehand. *What is a human being?* As if to say: Small and insufficient. Psalm 8:5 states: "What are human beings that you are mindful of them?" *So that he can follow the King, his maker*, that is, God the creator. Isaiah 64:8 says: "And now, O Lord, you are our father, and we are clay. And you are our maker, and we are all the works of your hands." So no one can follow God. Job 11:7 counsels: "Perhaps, you will comprehend the traces of God and will find out the Almighty perfectly?"

23. (Verses 13-14a). *And I saw that wisdom*, etc. Second, he notes that he found the *preeminence* of wisdom over folly, as if there is no proportion between them. So he says: *And I saw that wisdom excelled folly*, that is, it is more noble, *as much as light differs from darkness*. This is a good comparison, because wisdom enlightens and folly blinds or darkens. Therefore, he adds: *The eyes of the wise are in their heads*, namely, to guide them while *fools walk in darkness*, as if there were no eyes in their head. That wisdom enlightens we know from Wisdom 6:23: "Love the light of wisdom, all you who rule over people." For Christ, the wisdom of God,[49] calls himself light. John 8:12 states: "I am the light of the world." Contrary to this folly is darkness. Isaiah 5:20 reads: "Woe to you who call evil good,

---

[49] See 1 Corinthians 1:24: "... Christ, the power of God and the wisdom of God."

and good evil, who put forward darkness for light and light for darkness." For John 1:5 says: "The light shines in the darkness, and the darkness did not comprehend it." Thus since "they have not known nor understood, they, therefore,[50] walk in darkness."[51] John 3:19 has: "For they loved darkness rather than light."[52]

24. (Verses 14b-16a). *And I learned that both alike were to die.* Here he treats of his third point, namely, the *likeness* of the wise to the stupid both *in* and *after death.* Relative to their likeness in *dying*, the text says: *I learned that both alike were to die*, that is, in a similar way, because no one escapes the sentence of death simply by being wise. For 2 Samuel 14:14 states: "We all die, and like waters that return no more, we fall down into the earth." Just as the foolish take nothing away, neither do the wise. Job 1:21 reads: "Naked I came from my mother's womb, and naked shall I return." – And because of this likeness, he despised wisdom: *And I said in my heart: If the death of the fool and mine shall be one, what does it avail me that I have applied myself more to the study of wisdom?* This is the same as saying: Nothing as far as *death* is concerned.

---

[50]On p. 25 n. 1 QuarEd rightly mention that the Vulgate does not read *ideo* ("therefore").

[51]Psalm 81:5.

[52]Hugh of St. Cher, 77v, d-f also comments in a christological vein: "Because wisdom is light; and foolishness is darkness or blindness. Or wisdom may be taken to be Christ or wisdom as gift. . . .Note that there are three preliminary things required for a human being to possess wisdom. First, that human beings understand the dignity they have in this that in acquiring wisdom they can follow their creator, that is, imitate and be assimilated to God. Romans 13 says: Put on the Lord Jesus Christ. Second, that they may understand the difference between wisdom and foolishness, because wisdom assimilates human beings to the true light which is God, but wisdom to the devil, who is darkness. This is indicated here. . . .Third, that they understand that wisdom, by enlightening the eyes of the mind, gives human beings the eyes of an eagle, so that they can see the true Sun, in whose contemplation is the highest beatitude."

Sirach 40:2-3 says: "The day of their end," that is, death, "from the one sitting," etc.[53] – There is not only a likeness in death, but also *after death*. Wherefore, he adds: *And I had spoken with my own mind*, that is, reflecting in my mind, *I perceived that this also is vanity*, namely, to study wisdom more than a foolish person does, because the wise are not remembered any more than the fools. – So he says: *For there shall be no more remembrance of the wise than of the fool forever*. And he adds the reason: *And the times to come shall cover all things together with oblivion*. In 1:11 above the author stated: "For there is no remembrance of former things, nor indeed of those things which hereafter are to come." Wisdom 2:4 reads: "And our name will be forgotten in time, and no one will have any remembrance of our works." Job 13:12 states: "Your remembrance will be compared to ashes, and your necks will be brought to clay."

25. (Verses 16b-17). From the likeness he has found between wisdom and folly, he concludes that his study has been vain and blameworthy. So he repeats the likeness by saying: *The learned die in like manner as the unlearned*, and thus they are equal. From this he concludes: *Therefore, I was weary of my life*, as if he refused to live because of weariness, as in Job 10:1: "My soul is weary of my life." On account of *occasions of sin*. In Genesis 27:46 Rebekah says: "I am weary of my life because of the daughters of Heth."[54] On account of *labor*. Numbers 21:4-5 states: "The people began to be weary of their journey and labor and spoke against God," etc. On account of *trials*. 2 Corinthians 1:8 reads: "We were pressed beyond measure . . . , so that

---

[53]Sirach 40:2b-3 reads: ". . . and the day of their end: From the person who sits on a glorious throne unto the person who is humbled in earth and ashes."

[54]Genesis 27:46 concludes: ". . . if Jacob (also) takes a wife of the stock of this land, I choose not to live." Genesis 26:34-35 describes Esau as taking foreign wives.

we were weary even of life." On account of a *delay of future glory*. Job 10:1 says: "My soul is weary of my life." On account of *imminent temptation*. Psalm 118:28 implores: "My soul has slumbered through weariness, strengthen," etc.[55] On account of *the horror of imminent death*. Mark 14:33 reads: "Jesus began to fear and to be weary." – *When I saw that all things under the sun are evil, and all vanity and vexation of spirit*. Wisdom 9:15 counsels: "The corruptible body is a load upon the soul, and the earthly habitation presses down the mind that muses upon many things." Wherefore, it is a vexation to meditate frequently on the flesh.

QUESTIONS 8

I. First, what does he mean by: *What are human beings that they can follow God?*[56]

Contra: 1. Sirach 23:38 says: *It is a great glory to follow the Lord.*

2. Moreover, Job 23:11 states: *My foot has followed God's steps.*

I reply: To follow by *being like God* is not given to any creature. Because Satan wanted this, he fell. But one can follow by *subjection* and *obedience*. This is a possibility for human beings, but not for all, but for those to whom it is given by grace from God and whom God draws.[57] And therefore, no one by themselves can follow God without God's help.

---

[55]Psalm 118:28 concludes: ". . . strengthen me by your words."

[56]Ecclesiastes 2:12.

[57]On p. 25 n. 8 QuarEd helpfully cite John 6:44: "No one can come to me unless the Father . . . draws them." They also refer to Augustine's *Enarratio in Psalmum 70*, sermon 2, n. 6 on the double likeness to God. See PL 36:896 and *Exposition of the Psalms 51-72*, 442-444.

II. What does he mean by: *What does it avail me that I have applied myself more to the study of wisdom?* According to this it seems that a person is being advised not to study, while the contrary is often encouraged. Proverbs 27:11 exhorts: *Study wisdom, my son,* etc.

I reply: Wisdom can be studied in two ways, namely, for *an advantage in the present life,* or for *a reward of eternal glory.* As *an advantage in the present life,* wisdom is of benefit before death in that it guides us in our work. But it is of *no advantage* in death itself since *the learned die in like manner as the unlearned,* and it does not prolong a person's life. But if wisdom is studied for *the advantage of eternal life,* then it does not die, but lives.

Wisdom is useful for *doing good.* Sirach 21:24 reads: *Learning to the prudent is an ornament of gold,* etc. – It is useful in *avoiding evil.* Sirach 3:32 admonishes: *A wise and understanding heart will refrain from sin.* – It is useful in *increasing grace.* Sirach 4:9 says: *She will give to your head increases of graces.* – It is useful for *increasing glory.* Proverbs 3:35 has: *The wise will possess glory.* – A person is exhorted, therefore, not to study wisdom for any present advantage or out of curiosity, but for eternal salvation. And so the writer blames himself, because he had labored out of curiosity and worldly vanity.

III. What does he mean by the words: *For the wise will not be remembered any more than the foolish?*[58]

Contra: 1. Proverbs 10:7 states: *The memory of the just is with praises, and the name of the wicked will rot.*

2. Likewise, Sirach 39:13 reads: *His memory will not depart, and his name will be asked after,* etc.[59]

---

[58]See Ecclesiastes 2:16.
[59]Sirach 39:13 concludes: ". . . from generation to generation."

I reply: Some say that here the writer is giving the opinion of the carnal person, so that what he says is simply false. But it is true according to the opinion of carnal people. – But this clearly does not answer the question, because the opinion of carnal people is not to be upheld, but denied. Rather it has to be said that he is speaking of the memory of a *wise person* and of a *foolish person*, both in relation to *God* and in relation to *human beings*. If we speak with reference to *God*, the memory is of a good wise person who studies wisdom for the glory of God. But if we speak with reference to *human beings*, the memory of both good and evil people passes away, as most frequently happens as people remember little.[60] – If the question is about an *evil wise person*, who is vain, there is no memory with *God* nor with *human beings*. Rather their name passes away like the name of a foolish person. Wherefore, it is foolish to work in wisdom to make a famous name for oneself. But Ecclesiastes is speaking of a *vain wise person*, who look to what is of the earth and who speaks of *human* memory, not of *divine*.

IV. What does he mean by saying: *I was weary of my life when I saw that all things under the sun are evil?*[61]

Contra: Genesis 1:31 states: *God saw all the things God had made, and they were very good.* Therefore, they are not evil, and this statement is heretical.

I reply: As the Apostle says in Romans 7:12: *The law is holy and the commandment holy.*[62] But on occasion the

---

[60]See the reply to Question IV on Ecclesiastes 1:11 above: " . . . the text is not to be understood to be true universally, but very often. For more is forgotten than remembered."

[61]Ecclesiastes 2:17.

[62]On p. 26 n. 6 QuarEd helpfully quote Romans 7:11: "For sin, having taken occasion from the commandment, deceived me, and through it killed me."

commandment can be deadly and death-bearing for any who are without grace. Just as creatures are good to the just who love God very much and *work together for good* and are of themselves good, but to wicked sinners and to the foolish all things are turned into an occasion for evil.[63] For Wisdom 14:11 reads: *The creatures of God are . . . a temptation . . . and a snare for the feet of the unwise.* And Sirach 39:32 states: *All these things. . . will be turned into evil for the ungodly and sinners.*"

ECCLESIASTES 2:18-26 REBUKE OF HIS CURIOSITY OVER THE WORKS OF HUMAN INDUSTRY THAT LEAD TO WEALTH

26. *Again I hated all my application*, etc. Above he refuted his curiosity with regard to works of *wisdom*. Now he refutes his curiosity with respect to his work of human skill aimed at *wealth* or skilled work of a mechanical nature. He does this as follows. First, he refutes his curiosity because of *the uncertainty of a good outcome*. Second, because of *the wearisome worry*. Third, for *preferring present comfort* to this. Fourth, he condemns the worry itself because of *the equity of divine judgment*.

27. (Verses 18-21). He argues, first, against his curiosity in acquiring earthly goods because of *the uncertainty of a good result*. For he was not able to hold onto them forever, and he was fearful of having a useless successor. So he says: *I hated all my application*, that is, the curious care, *wherewith I had earnestly labored under the sun*, namely, to increase these goods. Jeremiah 6:13 remarks: "From the least even to the greatest all are given to covetousness." –

---

[63]In the background is Romans 8:28, as QuarEd point out on p. 26 n. 6: "Now we know that for those who love God all things work together unto good, for those who, according to his purpose, are saints through his call."

And the reason for this hatred is inferred from what follows: *I would have an heir after me and do not know whether he would be a wise person or a fool.* In fact the heir of Solomon was Rehoboam, a foolish son, who followed the advice of the young people and divided the kingdom according to 1 Kings 12:6-33.[64] *And he shall have rule over all the labors with which I have labored,* in my body, *and have been solicitous,* in my soul. Of such *sweat* we read in Genesis 3:19: "In the sweat of your face shall you eat your[65] bread." Of such *solicitude* we read in Matthew 6:25: "Be not solicitous for your life, what you shall eat, nor for your body, what you shall put on." And this is exceedingly vain. Therefore, he says: *Is there anything so vain?* One should supply: as to work solicitously for a foolish and lazy person, as if to say, no.

28. Therefore, from this reflection on vanity he stopped being curious and says: *Wherefore I left off, and my heart renounced laboring any more under the sun,* that is, for temporal goods. *I left off,* in work. *And my heart renounced,* in my will. But an avaricious person does not stop for this reason. Ecclesiastes 4:8 below says: "There is but one, and he has no second, . . . and yet he does not cease to work."[66] – And he repeats the reason why he stopped: *For when a person labors in wisdom,* in his heart, *and knowledge,* in his mouth, *and carefulness,* in his work, *he leaves what he has gotten to an idle person.* From this he concludes to vanity: *So this also is vanity and a great evil. Vanity* because riches are left to a useless person, but also a great *evil.* For Hugh comments: "It is a great evil that what one has won by work, should be misused in a lazy and wrong-

---

[64] Hugh of St. Cher, 78i also refers to Rehoboam, who foolishly dissipated what Solomon had wisely garnered.

[65] On p. 26 n. 8 QuarEd accurately indicate that the Vulgate does not have *tuo* ("your").

[66] Ecclesiastes 4:8 reads: "There is but one, and he has not a second, no child, nor brother, and yet he ceases not to labor. . . ."

ful manner by someone else."[67] It is *evil*, because it goes to someone who destroys. Jeremiah 51:18 states: "Their[68] works are vain," etc. Deuteronomy 28:32-33 says: "May there be no strength in your hand. May a people, who you do not know, eat the fruits of your land and all your labors."[69]

29. (Verses 22-23). *For what profit*, etc. Second, he refutes his curiosity to acquire because of *the wearisome worry*. Thus, he says: *For what profit will human beings have from all their labor*, in their bodies, *and vexation of spirit*, in the soul, *with which they have been tormented under the sun?* As if to say, nothing. For Proverb 23:4 says: "Labor not to be rich, but set bounds to your prudence." It does not benefit the person working to possess visible objects. Thus, Bernard observes: "The fruits of riches are with others, but their name and worry remain with the rich."[70] And so it does not benefit. For Ecclesiastes 5:10 below asks: "What does it profit the owner except that he sees his riches with his own eyes?" – Not only is it not a benefit, but it is also an obstacle. So he adds: *All their days are full of sorrows and miseries*, exteriorly; *even in the night they do not rest in mind*, interiorly. For it is said in Job 7:3: "I . . . have numbered for myself empty months and wearisome nights." And Proverbs 15:15 reads: "All the days of the poor are evil, a secure mind is like a continual feast." From this he concludes that such work is vain, because it is useless.

---

[67]On p. 27 n. 2 QuarEd refer to Homily 12 of *In Ecclesiasten*. See PL 175:200B.

[68]The Vulgate does not read *eorum* ("their").

[69]Hugh of St. Cher, 78i also cites this passage from Deuteronomy.

[70]See chapter 8 n. 14 of *De conversione ad clericos* in SBOp 4.88-89: "Finally, *where there are many riches, there are also many to consume them*. And indeed, others use the riches and leave the wealthy only the reputation of being wealthy and the worry over their wealth." Bernard cites Ecclesiastes 5:10. Bonaventure's citation is not verbatim.

And therefore, he says: *And is this not vanity?* As if to say, yes indeed. In Ecclesiastes 5:9 below he remarks: "Those who love riches will reap no fruit from them. So this, also, is vanity," for riches are an obstacle. Thus, Ecclesiastes 5:12 below expresses the matter: "There is another . . . sickness, which I have seen under the sun, riches gathered," etc.[71]

30. (Verses 24-25). *Is it not better*, etc. Third, *he prefers pleasures of the flesh* to the aforementioned solicitude of curiosity. *Is it not better to eat and drink and to show their souls good things from their labors?* Supply: Rather than continuously and always working. As if to say, it is better, that is, less evil, because that evil is an evil of sin and punishment, but this is an evil of sin, but with gladness. Isaiah 22:13 states: "Behold joy and gladness. . . .Slaying rams," etc.[72] And that it is *better* is clear, because it is a gift from God, and so he says: *And this is from the hand of God*. Jeremiah 5:7 states: "I fed them to the full, and they committed adultery," etc. – He puts himself forward as an example to confirm this: *Who shall so feast*, in desire, *and abound in delights*, with abundance, *as I?* As if to say, no one. 1 Kings 4:22-23 reads: "Now the provision of Solomon for each day was thirty measures of fine flour, and sixty measures of meal, ten fattened oxen, and twenty oxen from the pastures," etc.

31. (Verse 26). *God has given*, etc. Fourth, he condemns his solicitude through *the equity of divine judgment*, because such solicitude is not given to good people, but to evil, and this is by divine judgment. Wherefore, he says:

---

[71]Ecclesiastes 5:12 concludes: ". . . to the hurt of the owner." Bonaventure reads *congregatae* ("gathered") while the Vulgate has *conservatae* ("kept").

[72]Isaiah 22:13 reads: "And behold joy and gladness: Killing calves and slaying rams, eating flesh and drinking wine. Let us eat and drink, for tomorrow we will die."

To a person who is good in his sight, namely, who pleases God, not men and women like a hypocrite. Psalm 67:4 states: "Let the just feast," etc.[73] *God has given wisdom,* concerning what is eternal, *and knowledge,* concerning the use of temporal goods, *and understanding,*[74] concerning what needs to be understood or pondered.[75]   Job 38:36 reads: "Who has put wisdom into the human heart or who gave the cock understanding?" God does this from an abundance of mercy. But he adds from the equity of justice: *But to the sinner he has given vexation and superfluous care,* that is, God has allowed this to be given by just judgment, *to heap up and to gather together and to give to the person who has pleased God.* Proverbs 13:22 says: "The substance of the sinner is kept for the just." Proverbs 28:8 observes: "The person who gathers[76] riches by usury and loan gathers them for the person who is generous to the poor." And from this he concludes to vanity: *But this also is vanity and a fruitless solicitude of the mind,* for, as Proverbs 11:7 notes, "the expectation of the solicitous will perish."

32. Note what an effort and study[77] it is *to acquire wisdom.* Proverbs 27:11 states: "Study wisdom, my son, . . . so that you can give an answer to the person who reproaches

---

[73]Psalm 67:4 concludes: ". . . and rejoice before God. And be delighted with gladness."

[74]The Vulgate reads *laetitiam* ("joy") whereas Bonaventure has *intelligentiam* ("understanding").

[75]Hugh of St. Cher, 78e comments: "Wisdom, by which God is contemplated and loved. And knowledge, by which one conducts one's life well in the world. And understanding, by which the mysteries of the Scriptures are penetrated. Or wisdom, by which they savor things according to their proper taste. And knowledge, by which things are considered according to their own value. And understanding, by which things are understood according to their total *esse.* And this reading is better."

[76]The Vulgate reads *coacervat* ("heaps up") while Bonaventure has *congregat* ("gathers").

you." *To act justly*. Jeremiah 7:3 has: "Now make your ways and your deeds good." *To satisfy concupiscence*. Proverbs 23:29-30 reads: "Who has woe? Whose father has woe? Is it not those who pass their time in wine and studiously drink off their cups?" – *To obey avarice*. Jeremiah 6:13 observes: "From the least to the greatest all studiously engage in avarice." – The first two efforts and studies are good while the last two are evil. And in these we discern what is good for humans. Thus, Proverbs 20:11 states: "From his studies and efforts a young child will understand whether his deeds are clean and right." Therefore, Ecclesiastes condemned his study, because he had not yet studied the first two, but had studied and engaged in avarice and gluttony.

---

[77]In this paragraph Bonaventure plays on two of the meanings of *studium*: "study" and "effort." The translation tries to capture Bonaventure's word play.

CHAPTER 3

ECCLESIASTES 3:1-15   **THE VANITY OF CHANGEABLE
NATURE FROM THE VIEWPOINT
OF TIME**

1. *All things have their season*, etc. Ecclesiastes has already dealt with the vanity of things by showing there is in them a changeableness because of *movement*. Now in a second part he wants to show their vanity in relation to their boundary and variety *in time*.[1] He shows the changeableness of things and their variety, not in contempt of them, for they are works of God, but in so far as we love them. So in this part he shows, first, *the variety of times*, and, second, he blames *our curiosity* where verse 9 reads: *What advantage does a human being have from his labor?* Third, he shows *the permanence of the divine works* where verse 14 says: *I have learned that the works of God*, etc.

ECCLESIASTES 3:1-8   **THE VARIETY OF TIMES**

2. The first section has two headings because he deals, first, with the variety and changeableness of things in time *in general*, and, second, *in particular*, by persuasion and proof, where verse 2 says: *A time to be born*.

---

[1]Part One dealt with Ecclesiastes 1:3-2:26.

ECCLESIASTES 3:1   **CHANGEABLENESS OF THINGS IN**
                              TIME IN GENERAL

3. (Verse 1). He makes a *general* proposal by saying: *All things have their season*, that is, a variety of times, because Romans 8:20 states: "The creature was made subject to vanity, not willingly." *And in their times all things pass under the sun*,[2] to the boundary of a fixed time. Wisdom 11:21 reads: "You have ordered all things in number, weight, and measure."[3] 1 Corinthians 7:31 states: "The figure of this world is passing away," especially in the space of time fixed for it. Job 14:5 says: "You have appointed his bounds that cannot be passed."[4]

QUESTIONS 9

I. A question is asked about the meaning of the words: *All things have their season*.[5]

1. An objection is that, according to Jerome, "spiritual substances are contained in neither place nor time."[6]

---

[2]The Vulgate reads *sub caelo* ("under the heaven") whereas Bonaventure has *sub sole* ("under the sun").

[3]I translate the Vulgate: "measure, and number, and weight."

[4]Job 14:5 reads: "The days of a human being are short, and the number of his months is with you. You have appointed his bounds that cannot be passed."

[5]Ecclesiastes 3:1.

[6]See his *Commentarius in Ecclesiasten* on 3:1 in CCSL lxxii, 273: "For all spiritual substances are contained in neither heaven nor time." It may well be that Bonaventure is quoting Jerome through Hugh of St. Cher, for their wording of "Jerome" is the same. See Hugh of St. Cher, 78v, a: "For spiritual substances are contained in neither place nor time." On p. 28 n. 3 QuarEd cite Jerome's *Commentarius in Epistolam ad Titum* on 1:3. See PL 26:594B: "How great must one think the eternities . . . were, in which the Angels . . . served God and at God's command existed without changes or measures of time." The editors also refer to Book II, d. II. c. 3 of Peter Lombard's Sentence Commentary.

2. Also, everything that is in time and has time is corporal.[7] But spiritual substances are not corporal, and therefore, they are not in time nor do they have a place. That they are in time seems to be the case, for first, Augustine said to Dardanus: "Uncreated spiritual substance does not move in time nor place. Created spiritual substance moves in time, but not in place. A corporal created substance moves in time and place."[8] Second, what is in place is also in time, but "only God is uncircumscribed," as Damascene says.[9] Therefore, only God is outside time, and all other things have their season.

I reply: This verse has *a limited application*,[10] as when a person says that the sky covers all things, he is referring to what is under the sky. And so it does not apply to a *spiritual* substance. – But if we extend the application, we

---

[7]On p. 28 n. 4 QuarEd refer to Book IV, n. 12 of Aristotle's *Physica*. See WAE, vol. 2, 221b: "For time is by its nature the cause of decay since it is the number of change, and change removes what is."

[8]On p. 28 n. 5 QuarEd state that this is the reference and citation given in the manuscripts, but Augustine's Letter 187 deals with the omnipresence of God. They quote from what they believe is a better reference among the works of Augustine, that is, Question 40 of *Dialogus Quaestionum LXV sub titulo Orosii percontantis et Augustini respondentis* in PL 40:746: "God moves without time or place. A created spirit moves in time without a place. A corporal creature moves in time and place. Substance that moves only in time takes precedence over a substance that moves in time and place. Therefore, a substance that does not move in time or place takes precedence over a substance that moves only in time."

[9]See Book I, chapter 13 of *De fide orthodoxa* in PG 94:854B. See *Saint John of Damascus, Writings*, 198-199: "Now, to be circumscribed means to be determined by place, time, or comprehension, while to be contained by none of these is to be uncircumscribed. So the Divinity alone is uncircumscribed, who is without beginning and without end, who embraces all things and is grasped by no comprehension at all."

[10]Technically Bonaventure is referring to an "accommodated distribution." See Tractatus XII n. 26 of Peter of Spain, *Tractatus*, 225-226: "It is customary to posit an accommodated distribution, as 'the heaven covers everything,' that is, all other things apart from itself and 'God created all things,' that is, all other things than God."

will say that *time* is used in three ways: *commonly* and *properly* and *more properly*. *Commonly*, as in saying that the transition from non-being to being is a measure. And in this manner time is in all, because all things had a beginning. And the text seems to imply this, because it says that *all things have their season*, but not that all things *make a transition* except *under the sun*. – In another way time is used *properly*, as when it implies a variation either in substance or in affection. And so a spiritual substance has time in changing affections. – In the third way, *more properly*, as when it is a surpassing measure and thus of what is corruptible, but not of all things.

So what has been asked, namely, whether spiritual substances have time, is solved in the first sense with regard to *substance*. In the second with regard to some *affections*. But in the third they do not have time. – And in this way the contraries of both parts are reconciled.[11]

II. Concerning the second part of the proposition, *And in their times all things pass under the sun*,[12] one asks whether the elements pass away. It seems that this is so.

1. Revelation 21:1 states: *I saw a new heaven and a new earth*. Therefore, the old had passed away.

2. Furthermore, 1 John 2:17 says: *The world passes away and the concupiscence thereof*. And Matthew 24:35 reads: *Heaven and earth will pass away*.

Contra: Elements are of the constitution of the earth, and so if the universe endures, it is clear that the elements also endure.

---

[11]On p. 29 n. 1 QuarEd refer to Book II d. 2 p. 1 n. 1 and 2 of Bonaventure's *Sentence Commentary*.

[12]Ecclesiastes 3:1.

I reply: To say that something *passes away* in its space has a threefold meaning: in relation to the corruption of *the whole substance* as when brute animals corrupt; or in relation to a *partial* corruption of something as when elements are generated and corrupted along the end by which they touch one another; or *to pass*, that is, to be moved across from the state of corruptibility to another state, and in this way this sensible world is renewed. – So what is said here, namely, that *all things pass away*, is to be understood in the second of these three ways.[13]

Relative to the second objection – *The world and the concupiscence thereof is passing away* – it is solved by the clarification that this applies to the world as an occasion of pleasure.

Relative to the first objection – *I saw a new heaven* – a Gloss has: "that is, renewed."[14]

A Gloss explains what is said in Matthew – *Heaven and earth will pass away* – by stating that they will pass from a changeable form to an unchangeable one.[15]

---

[13]On p. 29 n. 5 QuarEd refer to Book III, n. 6ff. of Aristotle's *De caelo*. See WAE, vol. 2, 302b-307b and to Book II, n. 2 of his *De generatione et corruptione*. See WAE, vol. 2, 329b.

[14]On p. 29 n. 5 QuarEd quote the *Glossa Interlineris apud Lyranus*: "That is, a renewed air." They also refer to Book III, chapter XXI of Bede's *Explanatio Apocalypsis, Epistola ad Eusebium* in PL 93:194C: "Then the figure of this world will pass away through the conflagration of heavenly fire, so that, heaven and earth having been changed for the better, the appropriate quality of their change may correspond to the incorruption and immortality of the bodies of the saints."

[15]See the *Glossa Ordinaria* on Matthew 24:35 in PL 114:162B: "*Heaven and earth* will be renewed, having put aside the previous form, but permanent in substance. For it is said: *The earth will stand forever*." The *Glossa Ordinaria* cites Ecclesiastes 1:4 and reads *stabit* ("will stand") instead of *stat* ("stands"). The editors also refer to Book IV of Jerome's *In Matthaei Evangelium Expositio* on Matthew 24:35. See PL 92:104CD: "For heaven and earth through the change of renovation

Ecclesiastes 3:2-8   Changeableness of things in time in particular

4. *A time to be born*. Ecclesiastes has put forward a general proposition, and he now proves it in detail by showing the different kinds of times in things. First, he treats of the kinds of times in *beginning* and *ending*. Second, he treats of the different *states* where verse 4 states: *A time to weep and a time to laugh*. Third, he treats of *use* where verse 5b reads: *A time to embrace and a time to be far from embraces*. And fourth, he considers *the manner* of correct speech in verse 7b says: *A time to keep silence*.

Ecclesiastes 3:2-3   Times with beginnings and endings

5. So first he introduces the kind of time regarding *the beginning* and *ending* of things. He sees four differences here. First, for *the living*. Second, for *vegetable matter*. Third, for *sensible creatures*. Finally, for *the work of artisans*.

6. (Verse 2). Concerning the beginning and ending of *living creatures* he sees a difference when he says: *A time to be born and a time to die*, and this is true for all the living, because they move from birth to death. Job 14:1 states: "A human being, born of woman, living for a short time, is filled with many miseries." Sirach 40:1 reads: "Great labor is created for all human beings, and a heavy yoke is upon the children of Adam from the day of their coming

---

will pass away, but the word of the Lord will in no way pass away without its successful completion." They also refer to Bede. For Bede's commentary on Mark 13:31 see CCSL cxx, 602: "But if *heaven and earth will pass away*, the question can be raised how Ecclesiastes says: *One generation passes away, and another generation comes, but the earth stands forever*. But the reason is that heaven and earth pass from the image that they now have, but they exist without end according to their essence. *For the figure of this world is passing away* (1 Cor 7:31)."

out of their mother's womb until the day of their burial into the mother of all." And so Wisdom 5:13 says: "Having been born, we continually cease to be."[16] Sirach 14:19 has: "Some grow, and some fall off. Thus is the generation of flesh and blood. One comes to an end, and another is born."

7. Concerning the beginning of *vegetation* he says: *A time to plant*. And for the ending: *A time to pluck up what has been planted*. Genesis 2:8 reads: "The Lord God had planted a paradise of pleasure from the beginning." But there is *a time to pluck up* what has been unfruitful. For Luke 13:7 states: "Behold, for three years I came seeking fruit on this fig tree[17] and have found none. Therefore, cut it down."

8. (Verse 3). Concerning the beginning and ending of *sensible creatures* he adds: *A time to kill*. He puts first: *A time to kill* and then adds: *A time to heal*, because of the state of corrupt nature that becomes so engrained that sound health has no place.[18] Of this kind of time we read in Deuteronomy 32:39: "I will kill, and I will make to live."[19] And further, 2 Samuel 8:2 says: "He measured the two lines: one to put to death and one to save alive."[20]

9. Fourth, concerning the beginning and ending of *the work of artisans* he adds: *A time to destroy*, that is, their end. And *a time to build*, that is, the restoration of what was destroyed. What must be destroyed are things falling into

---

[16]On p. 29 n. 7 QuarEd accurately mention that the Vulgate reads *desivimus* ("ceased") while Bonaventure has *desinimus* ("cease").

[17]On p. 29 n. 8 QuarEd correctly indicate that the Vulgate reads *ficulnea* ("fig tree") whereas Bonaventure has *ficu* ("fig tree").

[18]On p. 29 n. 9 QuarEd cite Book II, n. 3 of Aristotle's *Ethica nicomachea*. See WAE, vol. 9, 1105a: "Again it (pleasure) has grown up with us all from our infancy; this is why it is difficult to rub off this passion, engrained as it is in our life."

[19]Hugh of St. Cher, 79d also cites Deuteronomy 32:39.

[20]This is what David does to defeated Moab.

ruins. Luke 19:44 reads: "One stone upon a stone will not be left in you."[21] *A time to build*, when an abundance of goods is available. Luke 12:18 states: "I will pull down my barns and build greater." Haggai 1:8 has: "Bring timber. Build the house. And it will be acceptable to me." And so there was no permanence in the ending of things.

ECCLESIASTES 3:4-5A   VARIETY OF TIMES IN THE STATE OF THINGS

10. *A time to weep, and a time to laugh*. After considering the variety of times in the way things begin and end, he now treats of the variety of times in *the state* of things, for example, in prosperity and misfortune. He notes a triple difference in this, namely, *prosperity, joyfulness*, and *security* and their opposites.

11. (Verse 4). Thus, concerning a time for *prosperity*, that is, a time for laughing, and for *adversity*, that is, for weeping, he says: *A time to weep*, in *adversity*. 1 Maccabees 1:28 reads: "Every bridegroom took up lamen-tation, and the brides that sat on the marriage bed mourned." And Lamentations 1:2 states: "Weeping, she has wept in the night, and her tears are on her cheeks." *And a time to laugh*, in *prosperity*. Esther 8:16 has: "To the Jews a new light seemed[22] to rise and joy . . . and dancing." He puts weeping before laughing either because it comes first in fallen nature, as Wisdom 7:3 comments: "The first voice that I uttered was crying, as all others do." Or because we should weep first, for Luke 6:21 states: "Blessed are you who weep now, for you shall laugh." On the contrary, we read of evil-

---

[21]The Vulgate reads *non relinquent in te lapidem super lapidem* ("they shall not leave in you a stone upon a stone") while Bonaventure has *non relinquetur in te lapis super lapidem*.

[22]The Vulgate reads *visa est* ("was seen") while Bonaventure has *videbatur* ("seemed/was seen").

doers in Proverbs 14:13: "Laughter will be mingled with sorrow."

12. Concerning the state of *rejoicing* and its opposite he says: *A time to mourn and a time to dance.* There is a difference between *mourning* and *weeping, laughter* and *dancing,* because weeping is in tears while *mourning* is in the voice, and *laughter* is in a sign[23] while *dancing* is in the elevation of the body. About *mourning* we read in Genesis 50:11: "This is a great mourning to the Egyptians," for the occasion was a burial.[24] But *dancing* is for wonderful solemnities, as when it is said in Mark 6:21 that on the birthday of Herod the daughter of Herodias entered to dance.

13. (Verse 5a). Concerning a time for *security* and its opposite, the text says: *A time to scatter stones,* namely, when there is security. Micah 4:3 reads: "Man shall not take up a sword against man."[25] *A time to gather,* so as to build fortifications, namely, when there is fear of an enemy. 2 Chronicles 32:5 says: "He built up . . . all the wall that had been broken down and built tower. . . ."

ECCLESIASTES 3:5b-7a   KINDS OF TIME WITH RESPECT TO USE

14. *A time to embrace,* etc. Ecclesiastes has already dealt with the variety of times in the beginning and ending of things and their state. He makes a third point here with

---

[23]Bonaventure gives a masked indication here of his theory of laughter.

[24]Joseph is burying his father Jacob. Genesis 50:10 reads: ". . . where celebrating the exequies with a great and vehement lamentation, they spent seven full days."

[25]On p. 30 n. 3 QuarEd rightly mention that the Vulgate reads *non sumet gens adversus gentem gladium* ("nation shall not take up sword against nation") while Bonaventure has *non sumet vir contra virum gladium* ("man shall not take up a sword against man").

regard to *use*. And there is a fourfold difference, namely, in the use of *wives, possessions, treasures,* and *clothes*.

15. (Verse 5b). So the use of *wives* consists in carnal union for the generation of children. Of this he says: *A time to embrace and a time to be far from embraces*. 1 Corinthians 7:29 says: "It remains that they also who have wives, be as if they had none." And again: "Defraud not one another, except, perhaps by consent, for a time, that you may give yourselves to prayer, and return together again."[26]

16. (Verse 6). With regard to the use of *possessions* he says: *A time to get and a time to lose*. We get by industry, but lose by laziness. Proverbs 14:1 reads: "A wise woman builds[27] her house, but the foolish will also pull down with her hands what is built."[28] – Or we acquire in life and lose in death. Job 20:15 says: "The riches which he had swallowed, he will vomit up," etc.[29] – Or we get when we are joined to God, but lose when separated from God. Psalm 106:38-39 has: "He blessed them, and they were multiplied exceedingly. . . .And they became few."

17. Concerning the use of *treasures* the text continues: *A time to keep*, when there is abundance. And *a time to cast away*, when there is need among the poor. See the example of Joseph in Genesis 41:47-57, who gathered in the fertile years and distributed in the barren years. For riches are to be kept for this purpose, namely, to be distributed, for Psalm 111:9 reads: "He has distributed. He has given to the poor."

---

[26] 1 Corinthians 7:5 in the context of spouses' rendering to one another their conjugal rights.

[27] The Vulgate reads *aedificavit* ("has built") while Bonaventure has *aedificat* ("builds").

[28] The Vulgate reads *instructam* (built "through instruction") while Bonaventure has *exstructam* ("what is built").

[29] Job 20:15 concludes: ". . . and God will draw them out of his belly."

18. (Verse 7a). With respect to the use of *clothing* he adds: *A time to rend*, when worn out. And *a time to sew*, because our clothes wear out by day and are not renewed other than by a divine miracle, as in Deuteronomy 8:4: "Your raiment, with which you were clothed, has never worn out because of age."[30] But our clothes wear out quickly, and this should not cause us to worry. 1 Timothy 6:8 advises: "Having food and wherewith to be clothed, we are content with these."

ECCLESIASTES 3:7B-8   KINDS OF TIME WITH REGARD TO SPEECH

19. *A time to keep silence*, etc. This is the fourth kind of time and deals with the correct *manner of speaking*. In this there is a triple succession of acts, namely, an act of *reasonable* virtue, which is to speak; an act of *desire*, which is love; an act of *anger*, which is to make war, and their opposites.[31]

20. (Verse 7b). With regard to the alternative acts of *speaking*, he says: *A time to keep silence, and a time to speak*, because one should not speak at all times or be silent all the time. Sirach 20:7 admonishes: "Wise persons will hold their peace till they see an opportunity, but a babbler and a fool will keep no time." For a wise person will remain silent and speak at the right time. Thus, Proverbs 21:11 states: "To speak a word in due time is like apples of gold on beds of silver." And he prefers silence to speech, because one must weigh what one says. Proverbs 13:3 counsels: "The person who keeps his mouth, keeps his soul, but the person who has no guard on his speech will meet with evils."

---

[30]The addressees are the people of Israel who journeyed in the desert for forty years.

[31]On p. 31 n. 1 QuarEd refer readers to Opera Omnia 3:579.

21. (Verse 8). Concerning the succession of acts of *desire* he says: *A time of love*, when the object is good. And *a time of hatred*, when it changes to evil. Psalm 118:163 reads: "I have hated and abhorred iniquity." Romans 12:9-10 says: "Hating that which is evil, cleaving to what is good, loving one another with the charity of brotherhood."

22. Relative to succession of acts of *anger* the text continues: *A time of war*, against an attacking enemy. 2 Samuel 11:1 reads: "And it came to pass at the return of the year, at the time when kings go forth to war, that David sent Joab," etc. And *a time of peace*, when fighting stops. 1 Maccabees 14:4 states: "All the land of Judah was at rest during the days of Simon," etc. And Micah 4:3 has: "Nation shall not take the sword against nation.[32] Neither shall they learn war any more."

23. In the *spiritual sense* this fourfold difference refers to the four states of people living in the Church. First, *the reborn*. Second, *the penitents*. Third, *the just*. Fourth, *the prelates*. – First, among the baptized there is *a time to be born and a time to die*, for they are born unto God. John 3:5 states: "Unless a person be born again of water and the Holy Spirit," etc. As they die to the world, see Romans 6:4: "We have been buried together with him by baptism into his death." – Second, there is *a time to plant and a time to pluck up what is planted*, because the virtues are planted in them. Psalm 127:3 says: "Your children are as olive plants." But vices are pulled up. Wisdom 4:3 reads: "Bastard slips[33] will not take deep root," for Matthew 15:13

---

[32]In his commentary on Ecclesiastes 3:5a (#5) above Bonaventure quoted a different version of Micah 4:3.

[33]The Vulgate reads *spuria vitulamina* ("spurious shoots") while Bonaventure has *adulterinae plantations* ("bastard slips"). On p. 31 n. 6 QuarEd quote Book II, chapter 12 n. 18 of Augustine's *De Doctrina Christiana* on the proper derivation of *vitulamina* ("shoots") which does not come from *vitulus* ("calf").

says: "Every plant that my heavenly Father has not planted will be rooted up." – Third, in the baptized there is *a time to kill* the movement of concupiscence. Colossians 3:5 states: "Put to death your members which are upon the earth." And there is *a time for healing the force of nature.* Jeremiah 30:17 has: "I will close up your scar and will heal you from your wounds." – Fourth, there is *a time to destroy and to build* in the baptized, because the dwelling of the devil is destroyed, and it is made a dwelling for Christ.[34] 1 Peter 2:4-5 says: "Coming to him as a living stone, . . . may you also be built up . . . into spiritual houses."[35] Jeremiah 1:10 states: "I have set you this day over the nations and over kingdoms to root up and to destroy and to lay waste . . . and to build and to plant."

24. The second kind of time refers to *penitents* from three points of view, namely, *contrition, confession,* and *satisfaction. A time to weep and a time to laugh,* in *contrition,* in which there is joy and sorrow. Proverbs 14:10 notes: "The heart knows its own bitterness of soul. The stranger will not mix in with his joy." – *A time to mourn and a time to dance,* in *confession* during which one must confess with mourning. Job 10:20 states: "Suffer me that I may lament my sorrow a little." One should confess in a naked manner and openly. 2 Samuel 6:14 reads: "David danced . . . girded . . . before the ark."[36] – There is *a time to scatter*

---

[34]Hugh of St. Cher, 79ef comments: "In the moral sense a time to destroy Babylon and Jericho, that is, confession and instability of mind that the devil builds in us, is now, f. and a time to build the temple of God, that is, purity and stability of conscience, which the devil destroys wherever he can."

[35]The Vulgate reads *domus spiritalis* ("a spiritual house") while Bonaventure has *in domus spiritales* ("into spiritual houses").

[36]2 Samuel 6:14 reads: "And David danced with all his might before the Lord, and David was girded with a linen ephod." The comments of Michal, Saul's daughter, to David in 2 Samuel 6:20 indicate Bonaventure's point: "How glorious was the king of Israel today,

stones and a time to gather, in *satisfaction.* Stones on which
a person stumbles are occasions of sin. Sirach 21:11 reads:
"The way of sinners is leveled with stones, and in their
end is hell and darkness and pains." These stones are collected through reflection and scattered by cautious avoid-
ance and mortification of the flesh. Few are freed from
these occasions unless they are preserved by the Lord.
Psalm 90:12 says: "In their hands they will bear up you,
lest you dash your foot against a stone."

25. The third kind concerns *the just* in their twofold state,
namely, *active* and *contemplative.* Concerning *contem-*
platives he says: *A time to embrace and a time to be far*
from embraces, because at one time they need to act, and
at another they should be taken up with contemplation.
Of such an embrace we read in Proverbs 4:8: "You will be
glorified by her, when you will have embraced her." They
should be far from embraces of the flesh, of which Proverbs 7:18 cautions: "Come, let us be inebriated with . . . the
desired embraces." – Concerning *active* just people who
should be busy in works of mercy, he adds: *A time to get*
and a time to lose, that is, to distribute as alms what has
been gotten. Sirach 29:13 counsels: "Lose your money for
your brother and friend and do not hide it under a stone. .
. ." – This verse refers to perfect justice, but to give away
all is a work of supererogation. The words, *a time to keep*
and a time to cast away, refer to such a giving away of
everything. Matthew 19:21 says: "If you will be perfect,
go, sell what you have, and give to the poor." – He says
further to active people: *A time to rend and a time to sew,*
and this applies to clothing. Job 31:19-20 states: "If I have

---

uncovering himself before the handmaids of his servants, and was
naked, as if one of the buffoons should be naked."

abandoned[37] . . . the poor person who has no clothing and if his sides have not blessed me," etc.[38]

26. The fourth kind refers to *prelates*. First, in their teaching when the text says: *A time to keep silence and a time to teach*,[39] for a person must first learn and later teach. Sirach 18:19 reads: "Learn before you speak." Sirach 32:9 advises: "Hear in silence." – *A time of love and a time of hatred*, in repelling evil by hating sin and loving nature. 2 Thessalonians 3:15 reads: "Do not consider him[40] as an enemy, but admonish him as a brother." And Psalm 138:22 says: "I have hated them with a perfect hatred." – *A time of war and a time of peace. Of war*, against the incorrigible who are to be struck with the sword of excommunication. Sirach 7:6 states: "Do not seek to be made a judge, unless you have strength enough to extirpate iniquities." *Of peace*, for those returning. Luke 10:6 has: "If a child of peace be present in that house,[41] your peace will rest upon him. But if not, it will return to you."

QUESTIONS 10

A question is asked about the number of these times. It seems that he has listed an insufficient number in the varieties of time, because they are many that cannot be listed under the ones mentioned, such as a time to eat and a time to fast and so on. *If you answer* that they are just examples, then they are superfluous, because far fewer would have been sufficient.

---

[37]The Vulgate reads *despexi* ("have despised") while Bonaventure has *dimisi* ("have abandoned").

[38]Job 31:20 concludes: ". . . when they were warmed by the fleece of my sheep."

[39]Ecclesiastes 3:7 actually deals with "speaking."

[40]On p. 32 n. 2 QuarEd correctly intimate that the Vulgate does not read *illum* ("him").

[41]On p. 32 n. 2 QuarEd rightly intimate that the Vulgate reads *ibi* ("there") while Bonaventure has *in domo illa* ("in that house").

I reply: It has to be said with Augustine that any change in the universe, when considered in itself, is an imperfection, but in the context of the whole universe the result is a perfect song.[42] Solomon, therefore, wanted to state variety in such a way that he might show the imperfection in single things, but the perfection of the whole. So he used numbers that include everything and its perfection. He lists twenty-eight times and fourteen differences, because *twenty-eight* is a perfect number and includes *a seven*, that is, the whole of time. Although a passage of *six* is perfect, it does not include *a seven*.[43] Therefore, Ecclesiastes could use many numbers, not fewer, to embrace universality, but

---

[42]On p. 32 n. 4 QuarEd point to three passages in Augustine. See, for example, Book VI, chapter 11, n. 29-30 of his *De Musica*. See "On Music," trans. Robert C. Taliaferro in *Saint Augustine, The Immortality of the Soul, The Magnitude of the Soul, On Music, The Advantage of Believing, On Faith in Things Unseen*, FC 4 (New York: CIMA Publishing Co., 1947), 355: "So terrestrial things are subject to celestial, and their time circuits join together in harmonious succession for a poem of the universe. And so many of these things seem to us disturbed and perturbed, because we have been sewn into their order according to our merits, not knowing what beautiful thing Divine Providence purposes for us."

[43]On p. 32 n. 5 QuarEd refer to two passages from Augustine. See Book IV, chap. 2, n. 2-5 of his *De Genesi ad Litteram* and *On Genesis*, 242-244: "So then we find the number six to be the first perfect number for the reason that it is completed by its parts . . . .So more numbers are to be found of any of these sorts, than of those which are called perfect in that they are completed by their parts of this kind being added up together. I mean, after six the next one we find is twenty-eight, which likewise consists of the total of its parts. Of these, you see, it has five; a twenty-eighth, a fourteenth, a seventh, a quarter, a half; that is, one and two and four and seven and fourteen, which added up together complete twenty-eight." See also Augustine's Sermon 31 n. 4 of his *Enarratio in Psalmum 118* in *Avrelii Avgvstini Enarrationes in Psalmos CI-CL*, CCSL xl (Turnhout: Brepols, 1956), 1771: "To say *seven times a day* means always. The number seven is customarily used as an indication of all. For this reason, to the six days on which God worked there is added a seventh day of rest. And by seven days coming and being repeated, all times are included."

not too many, for universality also is to be found in perfection.[44]

ECCLESIASTES 3:9-13   OUR CURIOSITY IS BLAMED

27. *What advantage do human beings have from their labor*? He has shown the variety of things in their diverse times and now he condemns human curiosity over this. He does this as follows. First, he suggests *the futility of curiosity*, and second, he commends *present pleasure* while despising curiosity.

28. (Verses 9-11). He condemns our *curiosity* for its futility, saying: *What advantage do human beings have from their labor*? Supply: other than being subject to change and variation and therefore, to vexation. – And he makes it clear that he has this vexation: *I have seen the trouble which God has given human beings to be exercised in it. God has given*, that is, allowed to be given, according to what Romans 1:8 states: "God delivered them up to a reprobate sense." *Human beings*, that is, sinners. Ecclesiastes 2:26 above says: "God has given to the sinner vexation and superfluous care." *To be exercised*, namely, with various worries. Sirach 11:10 reads: "My son, meddle not in many matters." And he explains that this vexation is one of reflection, and that is why he continues: *He has made all things good in their time.* For Sirach 39:39-40 says: "All the works of the Lord are good, and he will furnish every work in due time. It is not to be said: This is worse than that, for all will be well approved in their time." And although God made all things good, God did not give us knowledge of everything, but God did give us the ability to study. Wherefore, he adds: *And God has delivered the*

---

[44]A basic and helpful book on the meaning of numbers in the Middle Ages is Vincent Foster Hopper, *Medieval Number Symbolism: Its Sources, Meaning, and Influence on Thought and Expression* (Mineola, NY: Dover, 2000 [1938]).

world to their consideration, that is, to their inquiry. We read in Sirach 17:5: "God gave them counsel, and a tongue, and ears, and a heart for careful consideration," but not *to finish the inquiry*. Thus he continues: *So that human beings cannot find out the work which God has made*, that is, so that he may not come to perfect knowledge because of doubts. *From the beginning to the end*, namely, of his life. Job 36:24 reads: "Remember that you do not know his work, about which men have sung." And Ecclesiastes 8:17 below states: "I understood that I could find no reason for the works of God."[45]

29. (Verses 12-13). *And I have known*, etc. In his second point he commends *present pleasure*, and he does this to censure curiosity. For he says: *And I have known that there was no better thing*. Supply: in these transitory things. *Than to rejoice and to do well in one's life*, namely, *to rejoice* in one's heart, and *to do well* in work. – Or *to rejoice* by enjoying things. Wisdom 2:9 reads: "Let us everywhere leave tokens of our joy."[46] *To do well* in preparing delights. Luke 12:19 states: "My soul, you have many goods laid up for many years. Take your ease, eat, drink, be merry." – He adds the reason for this by saying: *For all, who eat and drink, see good in their labors*, have a large abundance in this. The meaning then is that the person who eats and drinks and sees good in his labor has received an immediate reward. So he says: *This is a gift from God*. In Ecclesiastes 5:18 below he says: "To every person, to whom God has given riches . . . and has bestowed on him the power to eat thereof . . . is a gift from God."

---

[45]On p. 33 n. 1 QuarEd rightly indicate that the Vulgate reads *possit homo* ("a human being could") while Bonaventure has *possem* ("I could"). Further, the Vulgate reads *omnium operum* ("all the works") while Bonaventure has *operum* ("works").

[46]Bonaventure has added *nostrae* ("our") to the text.

30. A Gloss explains this in *a spiritual sense.*[47] *And I have known that there was no better thing*, that is, more useful, *than to rejoice*, namely, with joy of the mind. Sirach 30:23 reads: "Joyfulness of the heart is the life of men and women and a never failing treasure of holiness." *And to do well in his life*, namely, through meritorious actions. Galatians 6:10 states: "Therefore, while we have time, let us perform good for all." – *For every person, who eats and drinks.* Supply: from the Scriptures. That person eats what is difficult and drinks what is easy. Wisdom says in Proverbs 9:5: "Come and eat of my bread, and drink from the wine which I have mixed for you." *This is the gift of God*, because to understand the Scriptures is a gift from God. 2 Corinthians 3:5 says: "Not that we are sufficient of ourselves to think anything [we do], as from ourselves, but our sufficiency is from God."

ECCLESIASTES 3:14-15   THE UNCHANGEABILITY OF DIVINE WORKS

31. *I have learned that all the works of God*, etc. He has shown earlier the changeableness of works, and from that he censured human curiosity. Here in a third point he shows *the unchangeability of divine works* while above he was showing changeablness.

---

[47]On p. 33 n. 3 QuarEd refer their readers to the *Glossa Ordinaria* (from Jerome) and the *Glossa Interlinearis apud Lyranum.* They go on to cite Rupert of Deutz' interpretation which is especially close to that of the *Glossa Interlinearis.* See Rupert's commentary on Ecclesiastes 3:12-13 in his *In Librum Ecclesiastes Commentarius* in PL 168:1230D-1231A: "He teaches that there is nothing better than to rejoice during one's life and be busy in doing good. . . .Moreover, because the flesh of the Lord is true food. . . .According to the anagogical interpretation, then the only good we have in this world is to eat his flesh and drink his blood, not only in the mystery, but also in reading Scripture. For the true food and drink, taken from the Word of God, is knowledge of the Scriptures."

32. (Verses 14-15). So he says: *I have learned that all the works which God has made continue forever*. This perpetuity is the reason why our reflection can change nothing. Thus he continues: *We cannot add anything, nor take away from those things which God has made with the result that God may be feared*. And so they are not in our power. Proverbs 30:6 reads: "Do not add anything to his words, lest you be reproved and found a liar." – And he shows this, because God himself neither diminishes nor increases. Thus he says: *That which has been made, the same continues*. No need to add these. He makes the inference: *Things that will be have already been*, because similar things have gone before. Wherefore, he also states: *And God restores what is past*, because "the corruption of one thing is the generation of another."[48] Ecclesiastes 1:10 said earlier: "There is nothing new under the sun. Nor is any person able to say . . . this is new." Genesis 2:2 reads: "God rested on the seventh day."

Questions 11

The question arises here: While he aims to show *the vanity of what is changeable*, how does he decide on *what is continually permanent*?

1. This seems to be outside his stated aim.

2. Also, the question is asked about perpetuity itself, because he says: *The works which God made continue forever*.[49] But corporal things do not endure forever. Therefore, God made no corporal things. This is to return to the

---

[48]On p. 33 n. 5 QuarEd refer to Book I, n. 3 of Aristotle's *De generatione et corruptione*. See WAE, vol. 2, 319a: ". . . in substances, the coming-to-be of one thing is always a passing-away of another, and the passing-away of one thing is always another's coming-to-be."

[49]Ecclesiastes 3:14.

heresy of the Manichees who claimed that what is corruptible was not made by a good God.

3. Moreover, it seems that he contradicts himself, because he adds immediately: *God restores what is past*. Therefore, some of the works of God corrupt and are restored. So it is wrong to say that *all the works which God has made continue forever*.

But it seems that all the works of God are incorruptible, as he says in the text:

1. Since there is a proportion between cause and effect,[50] the effect of an incorruptible cause should itself by incorruptible. But God remains for all eternity and is incorruptible. Therefore, the works of God are incorruptible.

2. Furthermore, since all the works of God are *very good*, as stated in Genesis 1:31 and since what is incorruptible is better than what is corruptible, it seems that what is corruptible cannot be created by a good God.

I reply to the first question about why Ecclesiastes deals with perpetuity here by stating that he does this not to examine perpetuity in itself, but because he is talking about changeability. He does so for a triple reason. First, *to remove error*, because already in 1:2-11 above he has spoken of the changeability of creatures. And lest it be believed that the works of God are completely faulty, he adds that in some way they are perpetual. A further reason is *to limit curiosity*. He does this because we are not able to examine the changeableness, cause, and origin of things. He also wishes to restrain curiosity, because

---

[50]On p. 34 n. 1 QuarEd refer to Book II, n. 3 of Aristotle's *Physica*. See WAE, vol. 2, 194b-195b where Aristotle treats the four causes and their effects.

we are not able to change or increase the substance of things.[51] A third reason is *to curb pride*, because it seems that although the works of the Lord are weighed down by being changeable, he again returns to imply continual permanence in them, lest anyone condemn God as their author.

I reply to what is asked about continual permanence, that there is a triple *existence* of things, namely, in *their own kind*, in *a living being*, and in *divine foreknowledge*. He has shown above in 1:3-11 that what is changeable exists in *its own kind* and in so far as it is *a living being*. Here he treats of its continual permanence in *divine foreknowledge*.

This can be answered in another way, that is, by speaking of things according to their own proper *existence* in two ways: either according to their *common existence* or their *individual existence*. According to their *individual existence* many things are corruptible but according to their *common existence* they are continually permanent. For God by generation continually preserves their existence. "For although they are distant from the principal source in a lasting way, God completed their *existence* by effecting continual generation in them."[52]

1. To the objection that things are incorruptible in proportion to their cause, I reply that this applies when there is

---

[51]See his comments on Ecclesiastes 3:14-15 (#18) above.

[52]On p. 34 n. 6 QuarEd refer to Book II n. 10 of Aristotle's *De generatione et corruptione*. See WAE, vol. 2, 336b: "Now 'being' . . . is better than 'not-being': but not all things can possess 'being', since they are too far removed from the 'originative source'. God therefore adopted the remaining alternative, and fulfilled the perfection of the universe by making coming-to-be uninterrupted: for the greatest possible coherence would thus be secured to existence, because that 'coming-to-be should itself come-to-be perpetually' is the closest approximation to eternal being."

a *univocal* generation, that is, when a cause produces something similar to itself. This, however, is not the case between the Creator and creatures, because in fact God with infinite power made great and small, corruptible and incorruptible.

2. To the objection about goodness, I reply that all things are good *in themselves*, but very good *in an order*. Where there is an order, there is more and less good. And so some things are corruptible, some are incorruptible. Moreover, goodness is in things not only as more or less good, but also by opposition and likeness. Therefore, the world is compared to a most beautiful song.[53] Hence it is fitting that some things be corruptible and some not.

PART II

ECCLESIASTES 3:16-7:23   **PROOF OF THE VANITY OF SIN AND THE REMEDY AGAINST IT**

33. *I saw under the sun*, etc. He has dealt with *the vanity of nature*, and now treats of *the vanity of sin*. And since this is dangerous, it needs a remedy. So first, he states the vanity. Second, he provides the remedy against it where 4:17 below says: *Keep your foot.*

---

[53] See n. 40 above. On p. 34 n. 7 QuarEd cite chapter 10 n. 3 (sic) of Augustine's *Enchiridion de fide, spe, et caritate*. See chapter 3 n. 10-11 of *Faith, Hope and Charity*, trans. Bernard M. Peebles in *Saint Augustine, Christian Instruction, Admonition and Grace, The Christian Combat, Faith, Hope and Charity*, FC 2 (New York: CIMA Publishing Co., 1947), 376: "By this Trinity supremely, equally, and unchangeably good, all things were created; yet these are not supremely, equally, and unchangeably good, but good they are, even taken separately, while together they are very good, because it is of all things that the wonderful beauty of the whole consists. In this whole even that which is called evil, well-regulated and confined to its own place, serves to give higher commendation to the good, making it, in comparison with the evil, more pleasing and worthy of praise."

ECCLESIASTES 3:16-4:16   THE VANITY OF SIN

34. Now there is a triple kind of vanity. First is a vanity of *malice*. Second is a vanity of *avarice* where 4:7 reads: *Considering, I found.* Third is a vanity of *imprudence* where 4:13 states: *Better is a child.* Now vanity is found in both rulers and subjects. He treats first of the vanity of malice in *rulers* and judges. A second consideration focuses on subjects where 4:1 says: *I turned myself.*

ECCLESIASTES 3:16-22   VANITY OF MALICE IN RULERS

35. So first the vanity of *malice* in *rulers* is described in this order. First, he introduces a reflection on this vanity. Second, this leads to a meditation on future judgment. Third, it leads to a reflection on the present state. Fourth, there is a consideration of how he fell into an erroneous opinion.

36. (Verse 16). So first he states that he has considered *the malice of judges: I saw under the sun in the place of judgment wickedness,* in examining cases, *and in the place of justice iniquity,* in pronouncing sentence. Isaiah 1:21-23 states: "How has the faithful city, that was full of judgment, become a harlot? Formerly,[54] justice dwelt in it, but now murderers . . . . Your princes are faithless, companions of thieves. They all love bribes. They run after rewards. They judge not for the fatherless, and the widow's cause does not come forward to them." For Psalm 25:10 says: "In whose hands are iniquities. Their right hand is filled with gifts."

37. (Verse 17-18a). *And I said in my heart: God will judge both the just and the wicked.* He shows here in a second

---

[54]On p. 34 n. 11 QuarEd accurately indicate that the Vulgate does not read *olim* ("formerly").

point how he came *to meditate on future judgment*. So he adds: *And I said in my heart: God will judge the just*, for a reward, but *the wicked* for punishment. Job 34:10-12 reads: "Far from God be wickedness and iniquity from the Almighty. For he will render a person his work, and he will reward them according to the ways of each one. For truly God will not condemn without cause. Neither will the Almighty pervert judgment." And therefore, God will judge them according to their works which will then be made manifest. For the text adds: *And then will be the time of every thing*,[55] that is, a time of judgment of every person, when every thing is seen. 2 Corinthians 5:10 states: "For we must all be manifested before the judgment seat of Christ, that everyone may receive the proper things of the body . . . whether it be good or evil." – Another meaning is this: *the time of every thing*, that is, of making all things manifest. 1 Corinthians 4:5 says: "Do not judge before the time, until the Lord comes, who will bring to light the hidden things of darkness and will make manifest the counsels of hearts." – Yet another meaning is: *the time of every thing*, that is, for the retribution of every thing. Romans 8:22 has: "Every creature groans," etc.[56] – From the viewpoint of the present wickedness Ecclesiastes was waiting for this time to be in the future. Isaiah 59:14-17 reads: "Judgment is turned away backward, and justice has stood far off, because truth has fallen down in the street and equity could not come in. . . .And the Lord saw, and it appeared evil in his eyes . . . because it is not manifest,[57] and

---

[55]The Vulgate reads *tempus omni rei* ("a time for every thing") while Bonaventure has *tempus omnis rei* ("a time of every thing").

[56]Romans 8:22 reads: ". . . and travails in pain, even until now." On p. 35 n. 2 QuarEd cite Homily 29 n. 2 of GGHG. See PL 76:1214B: "In the word 'human being' every creature is indicated. . . ."

[57]The Vulgate does not read *quia non est manifestum* ("because it is not manifest"). Rather it has *quia non est iudicium* ("because there is no judgment").

the just one was clothed with the breastplate and the helmet of salvation."[58]

38. *I said in my heart concerning the children of men and women*, etc. Third, he treats here of how this came from a *reflection on the present condition*. That is, why did the Lord want humans to be miserable in this present life? The Lord did this *to test* them, and so made the life of humans like the life of beasts.

39. (Verses 18-21). For this reason he says: *I said in my heart*, that is, I knew. *Concerning men and women*, in their nature.[59] *That God would prove them and show them to be like beasts*, that is, by making them like beasts God would test who were truly good or evil. Evil people, seeing their likeness to beasts in their lives, want to be like them in customs and to live in a bestial way. But the good want to live spiritually. So Psalm 48:13 says: "Human beings, when they were held in honor, did not understand. They are compared to senseless beasts and have become like them."[60] He shows how humans and beasts are alike in *death* and *life* and in *matter*. There are no such clear differences in spiritual substances. – With respect to *death* he says: *Therefore, the death of humans and of beasts is one, and the condition of them both is equal*, namely, to test humans because just as a beast does not live forever but dies at some time, so too with humans. Ecclesiastes 9:4 below reads: "There is no person who lives forever nor hopes for this." So he shows that there is a likeness in death: *As a human being dies, so they also die*.

---

[58]The Vulgate reads *indutus est iustitia ut lorica et galea salutis in capite eius* ("he put on justice as a breastplate and a helmet of salvation upon his head").

[59]On p. 35 n. 3 QuarEd state: "According to the Hebrew and Syriac (Peschitto) text, the sense is: I thought as human beings do."

[60]Hugh of St. Cher, 81v, a also cites Psalm 48:13.

40. Nor is the likeness only at the end of life, but also in *the act of living*. So he adds: *All things breathe alike*, namely, by drawing breath. *And human beings have nothing more than beasts*, that is, in the act of living. Wisdom 7:6 states: "Human beings[61] have one entrance into life, and a similar exit." Thus, a likeness in life is clear. – He adds the likeness in *matter* and says: *All things are subject to vanity*, namely, because they were made from nothing and so are vain. Romans 8:20 reads: "Creation was made subject to vanity."[62] He does not say that matter is nothing, but he wants to say that creatures do not have uncreated matter or essence. Rather they have created matter, which is understood from the word *earth*. – Wherefore, he continues: *And all things go to one place*, namely, to the matter from which they were made. *Of earth they were made, and into earth they return together*, equally, like one another. In this way he notes a likeness in matter. Sirach 40:11 says: "All things that are made[63] of the earth will return to the earth again. Similarly[64] all waters will return to the sea."[65]

41. There is *a clear likeness* only in these three things, while there does not seem to be a *difference in the soul*. *Who knows if the spirit of the children of Adam ascends upward*, to heaven for a reward, or downward in corrup-

---

[61]On p. 35 n. 6 QuarEd rightly indicate that the Vulgate reads *omnibus* ("for all") while Bonaventure has *hominum* ("human beings").

[62]Hugh of St. Cher, 81v, k cites Romans 8:20 in its entirety: "Creation was made subject to vanity – not by its own will but by reason of him who made in subject – in hope."

[63]On p. 35 n. 7 QuarEd correctly mention that the Vulgate does not read *facta* ("made").

[64]On p. 35 n. 7 QuarEd accurately point out that the Vulgate does not read *similiter* ("similarly").

[65]Hugh of St. Cher, 81v, n also cites Sirach 40:11 in a version that agrees with the Vulgate. The text of Hugh of St. Cher erroneously refers to this text as Sirach 20.

tion. Likewise on the other hand, *who knows if the spirit of the beasts descends downward*, by corruption, or upward like humans for the pronouncement of judgment. Few have known this. Many have erred and stated that the spirits of humans and beasts are uniform. But the faithful have known this. In their name Ecclesiastes states in 12:7: "The body[66] returns to its earth from which it was. And the spirit returns to God who gave it." Carnal people do not know this. In their name he says in 9:5: "The dead know nothing more. Neither do they have a reward anymore."

42. (Verse 22). *And I have found*, etc. In a fourth place he adds that because of this likeness he fell into an *erroneous recommendation of pleasure*, as if there is nothing better. For this reason he continues: *And I have found that nothing is better than for people to rejoice in their work*, that is, to rejoice in the present moment as carnal people do. About these Isaiah 56:12 says: "Come, let us take wine, and be filled with drunkenness. And it will be as today, so also for tomorrow and much more." And this advice is wrong, because it sees no other reward and no other life. So he adds: *And that this is their portion*, as if there is nothing else for which one may hope. Speaking in the name of such people, Isaiah says: "Let us eat and drink, for tomorrow we will die." And Wisdom 2:9 reads: "Let us everywhere leave tokens of joy, for this is our portion, and this is our lot." And this wrong opinion comes from an uncertainty in judgment. Therefore, he says: *For who will bring them to know the things that will be after them*, that is, who will show them that some good things are in the future, things for which we have to wait? This is like saying:

---

[66]On p. 36 n. 1 QuarEd rightly mentions that the Vulgate reads *pulvis* ("dust") while Bonaventure has *corpus* ("body").

No one. Certainly people will not be convinced unless they are raised up to contemplate spiritual matters. 2 Corinthians 4:18 states: "While we look not at things that are seen, but at the things that are not seen. For the things that are seen are temporal, but the things that are not seen are eternal." Since carnal persons see only what is temporal, they do not wait for what is eternal. 1 Corinthians 2:14 reads: "The sensual person does not perceive the things that are of God."[67] So whoever wants to know future goods must put aside what is carnal.

QUESTIONS 12

I. What does he mean by saying: *Human beings have nothing more than beasts* since *the condition of both is equal?*[68] That this is false is seen from:

1. Genesis 2:20 states: *For Adam no helper was found like himself.* Therefore, no beast is like a human being, and so a human being is more than a beast.

2. Likewise, it is certain that human beings plan for the future, discern the past, and express ideas. But a beast does not do these things.[69] Therefore, etc.

3. Moreover, human beings tame beasts, but no beast tames a human. Therefore, humans have something more than beasts.

But it seems that this is not a valid point, because a human being is born, lives, dies, and goes to the earth just like a beast.

---

[67] On p. 36 n. 3 QuarEd accurately indicate that the Vulgate reads *sunt Spiritus Dei* ("are of the Spirit of God") while Bonaventure has *Dei sunt* ("are of God").

[68] See Ecclesiastes 3:19.

[69] On p. 36 n. 5 QuarEd refer to three texts from Aristotle, e.g., Book II n. 3 of his *De anima*. See WAE, vol. 3, 415a: "Lastly, certain living

I reply: Some say that he is speaking here as a carnal person would speak, that is, a person who believes humans have no more than beasts. – Or it can be said that he is speaking in his own name and speaks truthfully according to his understanding. He wants to show the uncertainty of a reward for the soul based on the likeness to beasts. He states and understands this likeness in relation to what is *visible*, to what can be observed by the senses. From this he does not conclude to a likeness in what is *spiritual*, but he comes to doubt. Thus, he says: *Who knows if the spirit of the children of Adam ascend upward*, etc. – So it must be concluded that it is true that humans have the power to reason more than beasts, but are similar in being corruptible, in life, and in breathing. But because the power to reason is not something tangible, but understandable, he is speaking of what is tangible. And so there is no objection to this at all.[70]

II. There is a doubt about his words: *Who knows*[71] *if the spirit of the children of Adam ascends upward?*[72] That this is true is seen from:

1. First, from the disposition of the body, which is arranged and organized with a view to its suitability towards what is above. If, then, "he gave to humans an uplifted face to

---

beings – a small minority – possess calculation and thought, for (among mortal beings) those which possess calculation have all the other powers above mentioned, while the converse does not hold . . . ."

[70] On p. 36 n. 6 QuarEd call their readers' attention to d. 19. a. 1. q. 1 of Bonaventure's Second Book of the Sentences. See Opera Omnia 2:461 where Bonaventure cites Ecclesiastes 3:19 and argues that men and women do not die as beasts because of their souls. Opera Omnia 2:461-462 will also provide background for what follows.

[71] The Vulgate reads *novit* ("knows") while Bonaventure has *scit* ("knows).

[72] Ecclesiastes 3:21.

turn their eyes to heaven,"[73] they also look for what is above.[74] Therefore, the spirit goes upward.

2. Furthermore, by nature all long for happiness, but it is certain that no one can be happy while in misfortunes, especially the person to whom death comes unwanted. Therefore, if one cannot have happiness in this life, one is born to have it after this life when the spirit is separated. Wherefore, etc.

3. Moreover, our mind is unmixed and so understands everything,[75] and thus does not depend on the body to be able to act and consequently, much less is it dependent upon it for its *existence*. Therefore, while the body goes downwards, it is possible that the spirit goes upward.

4. Also, from the argument of Ecclesiastes himself: For some have good things and others bad things, and we see

---

[73]On p. 36 n. 7 QuarEd refer to Book I, verses 85-86 of Ovid's *Metamorphoses*. See *Ovid, Metamorphoses I*, trans. Frank J. Miller, LCL (Cambridge: Harvard University Press, 1966), 8-9: *pronaque cum spectent animalia cetera terram, os homini sublime dedit caelumque videre iussit et erectos ad sidera tollere vultus* ("And, though all other animals are prone, and fix their gaze upon the earth, he gave to man an uplifted face and bade him stand erect and turn his eyes to heaven"). Hugh of St. Cher, 81v, a also quotes Ovid: *Os homini sublime dedit coelumque videre jussit* ("He gave to humans an uplifted face and commanded them to look to heaven.") Bonaventure's Latin text is: *Os homini sublime dedit caelumque tueri.*

[74]On p. 36 n. 7 QuarEd also allude to Part II, chapter X of Bonaventure's *Breviloquium*. See Omnia Opera 5:228: "In order that the human body might be conformed to a soul tending upward toward heaven, it possessed rectitude of stature and a head lifted high. In this way bodily rectitude might give witness to mental rectitude."

[75] On p. 36 n. 8 QuarEd quote Book III n. 4 of Aristotle's *De anima*. See WAE, vol. 3, 429a: "Therefore, since everything is a possible object of thought, mind in order, as Anaxagoras says, to dominate, that is, to know, must be pure from all admixture; for the co-presence of what is alien to its nature is a hindrance and a block. . . ."

that in the present life bad things happen to good people and good things to bad people. Therefore, if it is necessary to have one judge, there must also be another time for giving a reward, during which *God will judge both the just and the wicked*. Since our faith holds this, Ecclesiastes seems to have been a heretic who doubted this.

But that soul goes *downwards* is seen:

1. From Scripture, because it is said in Wisdom 9:15: *The corruptible body is a load upon the soul*. Therefore, if the soul is corrupted bodily, it is completely corrupted.

2. Also, when a person suffers, the suffering dies with the person. But the soul suffers with the body. Therefore, etc.

3. Furthermore, no substance is idle,[76] and so everything that takes away from it the ability to work, takes from it its very *existence* and continuance. But every soul loses the ability to work when a body is injured. This is clear in the instance of a mind which is able to do less such as in people who are out of their mind. Wherefore, as the body corrupts, its substance is lost.

I reply: 1. Our faith says and presumes that good souls go upward to be rewarded and that the souls of beasts go downward into corruption. Reason and philosophy agree with this. However, reason and philosophy are both ob-

---

[76]On p. 37 n. 2 QuarEd cite Book II, chapter 23 of John Damascene's *De fide orthodoxa*. See *Saint John of Damascus: Writings*, 252: "One should note that all the faculties heretofore discussed are called *acts*, whether they be the cognitive, the vital, the natural, or the technical. Act is the natural force and movement of any substance. Again, *natural act* is the innate movement of every substance. Whence it is clear that those things that have the same substance have also the same act, whereas those that have different natures have different acts. For it is inconceivable that a substance should be devoid of natural act."

scure and provide many grounds for doubt. Hence, almost no one or but a few were able to be sure of the immortality and happiness of the soul unless helped by faith. So Plato, who held the immortality of the soul, erred in its happiness as he argued that the bodies of beasts shelter souls.[77] – Ecclesiastes does not deny or doubt this, but says it is difficult to prove. And this is indeed true for an unbeliever.

2-3. To what is objected on the basis of work and suffering, it has to be said that something can be *united with something else* in two ways. It can be simply *a moving force*, and it then can be separated without any change to it. Or it can be *a moving force that perfects*, and this is in two ways. Either it does not have its own operation as in a soul of a beast, or it has its own operation as in the soul of a human being. Since the soul of a person is joined as a moving power that perfects, it suffers with the body that suffers and is hindered as the body is hindered. But since it is joined as something separate, it is not necessary for it to corrupt. As the union is dissolved, the soul goes away.

---

[77]On p. 37 n. 3 QuarEd refer to three passages in Plato. Plato takes up the immortality of the soul extensively in his *Phaedo*. See, for example, *Phaedo* 80E-81A in *Plato I*, trans. Harold North Fowler, LCL (Cambridge: Harvard University Press, 1982), 281: "But the soul, the invisible, which departs into another place which is, like itself, noble and pure and invisible, to the realm of the god of the other world in truth, to the good and wise god, whither, if God will, my soul is soon to go, – is this soul, which has such qualities and such a nature, straightway scattered and destroyed when it departs from the body, as most men say? Far from it, dear Cebes and Simmias, but the truth is much rather this: – if it departs pure, dragging with it nothing of the body, because it never willingly associated with the body in life, but avoided it and gathered itself into itself alone, since this has always been its constant study – but this means nothing else than that it pursued philosophy rightly and really practiced being in a state of death: or is not this the practice of death?"

Chapter 4

1. *I turned myself to other things*, etc. He has dealt with the vanity of malice in prelates. Now he treats of it in *subjects*. Vanity of malice is considered here under three headings. First, the heading of *oppression* in harming maliciously. Second, the heading of *envy* in being saddened maliciously where verse 4 reads: *Again I considered*. Third, the heading of *sloth* by abandoning a good work where verse 5 has: *The fool folds his hands.*

2. (Verses 1-3). He describes the vanity of *oppression*, and in his *reflection on oppression* he states: *I turned myself to other things*. Supply: for reflection. *And I saw the oppressions that are done under the sun*, that is, in this world. Ezekiel 22:29 reads: "The people of the land have used oppression and committed robbery. They afflicted the needy and poor, and they oppressed the stranger by calumny without judgment." A violent seizing of goods is called *oppression*, when done not in justice, but in malice.

3. And he goes on to state *the increase of misfortune*, because of the oppressions that are done and because people are oppressed *unjustly with no consolation and without remedy.* — *Unjustly*, because he says: *And the tears of the innocent*, namely, on account of such oppression. Job 35:9

states: "By reason of the multitude of oppressors they will cry out and will wail on account of the violence from the arm of tyrants." – *With no consolation*, because *they had no comforter*, a situation that increases cruelty. Lamentations 1:2 says: "There is no one to comfort her among all those who were dear to her." Sirach 7:38 talks about the contrary: "Be not wanting in comforting those who weep. And walk with those who mourn." – Not only do they lack a comforter, but they are also *without remedy*. So he adds: *They were not able to resist their violence, being destitute of all help.* Supply: I saw. Of such malice we read in Proverbs 22:22: "Do no violence to a poor person, because he is poor. Do not oppress the needy in the gate." Thus, 2 Chronicles 20:12 reads: "As for us we have not strength enough to be able to resist this multitude that comes violently upon us."

4. Concerning a *detestation of sin* the text continues: *And I praised the dead rather than the living*, namely, in that they do not see this evil and cruelty which no good person can see without sorrow. In 1 Kings 19:4 Elijah said: "It is enough for me, Lord. Take away my soul, for I am no better than my fathers." – *And I judged that person happier than them both*, namely, any dead or living person *who is not yet born nor has seen the evils that are done under the sun*. He speaks as if to see or to have seen such evils is a great misfortune. 1 Maccabees 2:7 reads: "Mattathias said: Woe is me. Wherefore was I born to see the ruin of my people and the ruin of the holy city and to dwell there?" So he has given *a reflection on oppression and an increase of misery*, because the oppressed are desolate and without assistance. And so he comes to *a detestation of the sin*.

5. (Verse 4). *Again I considered*, etc. Second, he treats of the vanity of *envy*, when a person out of malice is sad to see a neighbor's good fortune and prosperity. So he adds:

Again I considered.[1] This consideration or contemplation is a free and penetrating and fixed gaze.[2] *I considered and contemplated,* he says, *all the labors of men and women,* with regard to the body; *and their industries,* with respect to the soul. – Or: *labors and industries,* that is, efforts. For the other translation reads: *every effort at work.*[3] Note what he had said earlier in 2:18: "Again I hated all my application wherewith I had earnestly labored under the sun." *And I remarked,* that is, saw in my soul. *That their industries are exposed,* that is, laid open to *the envy of their neighbors,* because when they see them, they are immediately sad. Sirach 14:8 says: "The eye of the envious is wicked, and he turns away his face and despises his own soul." *So in this also is vanity,* namely, the vanity of malice. Proverbs 28:22 reads: "A man that makes haste to be rich and envies others," etc.[4] *And fruitless care,* namely, of sin, because while envious people should be thinking of their own goods, they are always thinking of the goods of others. So we read in Proverbs 23:6-7: "Eat not with an envious person and desire not his food, because like a soothsayer . . . he is delving into something about which he knows nothing."

---

[1]The Vulgate is *contemplatus sum* or literally: "I contemplated."

[2]On p. 38 n. 1 QuarEd quote Homily 1 of Hugh of St. Victor's *In Salomonis Ecclesiasten Homiliae XIX.* See PL 175:116D-117A: "There are three visions of a rational soul: thought, meditation, and contemplation. Thought exists when the mind dwells in a passing way on an idea of something, when the thing itself is suddenly put before a soul by its image or through the senses or arising from memory. Meditation is a careful and wise reflection of thought trying to explain something complicated or searching to delve into what is hidden. Contemplation is a penetrating and free gaze of the soul onto things to be perceived, but that are scattered everywhere." Obviously, Bonaventure's definition of consideration/contemplation is almost identical to that of Hugh of St. Victor.

[3]On p. 38 n. 2 QuarEd state that this reading is found in the Septuagint and in Jerome. The LXX reads: *syn pasan andreian.*

[4]Proverbs 28:22 concludes: ". . . is ignorant that poverty will come upon him."

6. (Verses 5-6). *Fools fold their hands*, etc. Third, he treats of the vanity of *sloth*, by which a person becomes weary and lazy in everything that is good and so becomes stupid. Therefore, Ecclesiastes says: *Fools fold their hands*. And so is stupid because of *laziness*. Proverbs 12:11 states: "The person who pursues idleness is very foolish." Proverbs 6:6 reads: "Go to the ant, O sluggard, and consider its ways and learn wisdom." These *stupid people fold their hands*, because they refuse to work. Proverbs 26:15 says: "The slothful person hides his[5] hands under his armpit, and it grieves him to turn them to his mouth."[6] Since the slothful refuse to work, they become poor and skinny from a lack of food. Wherefore, the text continues: *And they eat their own flesh, saying*. This is said in hyperbole, for he has become emaciated and has no food. Proverbs 21:25 states: "Desires kill the slothful, for his hands have refused to work at all." – But from this laziness of sloth a person can gain a lesson in wisdom, for he says: *Better is a handful with rest than both hands full with labor and vexation of mind*. This is how a slothful person thinks as an excuse. And so we read in Proverbs 26:10: "The sluggard is wiser in his own conceit than seven men who voice their opinions." In this way Ecclesiastes describes *the inactivity of the slothful*, because he folds his hands; *the diet of poverty*, for *he eats his own flesh*; *the excuse of ignorance*, because he praises rest.

QUESTIONS 13

I. What does he mean by: *I praised the dead rather than the living*?[7]

---

[5]The Vulgate does not read *suas* ("his").

[6]The NAB of Proverbs 26:15 has: "The sluggard loses his hand in the dish; he is too weary to lift it to his mouth."

[7]Ecclesiastes 4:2.

Contra: 1. Ecclesiastes 9:4 below says: *A living dog is better than a dead lion.*

2. Moreover, *reason* proves this, because it is better to have than not to have. Therefore, to have life is better than to be dead. So *from things that come in pairs,*[8] better are the living than the dead.

I reply: To praise or prefer one thing more than another can happen in two ways, namely, *simply* or *according to some condition.* Speaking *simply*, a person prefers what is living to what is dead, unless you add the condition of beatitude. But speaking *according to some condition*, what is dead can be preferred to what is living. First, because the dead do not have so many occasions of sin. For the Apostle used to say in Romans 7:24: *Unhappy human being that I am, who will deliver me from the body of this death?* Second, when there are not so many occasions for sadness, because one no longer sees so many evils. Jonah 4:5 reads: "It is better for me to die than to live." In this condition death is preferred to life as an exaggeration of the present evils and miseries.

II. What does he mean by: *I judged that person happier than them both, who is not yet born?*[9]

Contra: 1. Such a person enjoys no good, and therefore is not happier.

2. Moreover, everything that provides in any way a reason for happiness is to be desired, but no one is able to desire

---

[8]On p. 38 n. 6 QuarEd cite Book II n. 9 of Aristotle's *Topica*: "All pairs are named from their inter connection, as justice, a just person, just, and justly; it is clear that each of these is named because of an inter connection, as good or praiseworthy, when one is named all the others are included, as when justice is praised, so too justly, a just person and to be just are praised." See also WAE, vol. 1, 114a.

[9]Ecclesiastes 4:3.

non-existence, as Augustine maintains.[10] Therefore, whoever is not yet born is in no way happy.

III. It is also asked whether, if one's desire is ordered, anyone can wish non-existence rather than suffer punishment. That this is so we read in Matthew 26:24: *Therefore, it were better for him if he had not been born.* So if what is better is to be desired and preferred, then one can choose this.

That this is *not so* is proved, because death takes away all good. And so nothing is worse than death.

I reply: Happiness exists in someone in two ways: *in fact* or *putatively*. There is only one way of being happy *in fact*, but one can be *reputed* to be happy from many points of view and conditions found in diverse circumstances. Because the good is most delightful, Epicurus found happiness in pleasures and other things. For a *happy* person is not troubled by any malice or misfortune. And since someone not born is in this condition, Ecclesiastes, thinking of this condition, says: *I judged that person happier*, etc. I also add that because of the nature of this condition, it is desired by many troubled people.

When it is asked whether this should be desired or preferred, it has to be said that there is a double punishment: *temporal* and *eternal*. Neither punishment takes away *the whole*, but eternal punishment *always* takes it away. Corruption takes *the whole* away into *non-existence*, but *only once*. So if such corruption into *non-existence* is compared to *temporal* punishment, it is simply worse. If it

---

[10]On p. 38 n. 8 QuarEd refer to Book III, chapters 6-9 n. 18-24 of Augustine's *De libero arbitrio*. See *The Teacher, The Free Choice of the Will, Grace and Free Will*, trans. Robert P. Russell, FC 59 (Washington: Catholic University of America Press, 1968), 181-192.

be compared to *eternal*, we are dealing with an excess, because temporal punishment exceeds in taking away while eternal punishment exceeds in duration. Eternal punishment is infinite in duration while temporal punishment is but momentary. And so eternal punishment exceeds in this and can reasonably be fled and rejected.[11]

IV. What does he mean by saying: *I remarked that their industries are exposed to the envy of their neighbors?*[12] I ask if a person should abandon a good work because of someone's envy? – That it should be abandoned seems clear, for a neighbor is to be loved more than any present benefit. Therefore, if a neighbor were to perish from envy, the work should be abandoned.

Contra: A good work gives a good example and inspires others to good. Therefore, if a good work is exposed to praise, it should not be hidden because of the envy of a neighbor.

I reply: A work is done either out of *necessity* or out of *usefulness*. If a work is performed out of *necessity*, it should never be stopped. If it is done out of *usefulness*, one can either be as well off if it is done or not done. If one is as well off without the work being done, it should be abandoned to take away any occasion of envy, when it is probable that there would be such an occasion. If one cannot be well off without the work being done, he should do it, and this does not give an occasion for envy, although someone might take such an occasion from it.

---

[11]On p. 39 n. 2 QuarEd refer the interested reader to Book IV of Bonaventure's *Sentence Commentary*: "IV. Sent. d. 50. p. 1. a. 1. q. 2."
[12]Ecclesiastes 4:4.

ECCLESIASTES 4:7-12   VANITY OF AVARICE

7. *Considering, I found*, etc. Having treated of the vanity of malice, he now deals with the vanity of *avarice*. He does this, first, with *a reflection on avarice*. Second, since the avaricious person does not want a companion, Ecclesiastes judges him by praising *the company of a companion* where verse 9 reads: *It is better, therefore, that two should be together.*

8. (Verses 7-8). So he says about the vanity of avarice: *Considering, I found also another vanity under the sun*, that is, *another*, because he has already spoken of the vanity of malice. – So he adds: *There is but one, and he has not a second, no child, no brother*, and so he should be content with little as he is alone, because he does not even want a companion. Sirach 11:19 says: "I have found me rest, and now I will eat of my goods alone." However, all vanishes in avarice: in *effect* and *affection* and *understanding*. In *effect*, for the text continues: *And yet he ceases not to labor.* Sirach 31:3 states: "The rich person has labored in gathering riches together. . . ."[13] In *affection*, as the text adds: *Neither are his eyes satisfied with riches.* Sirach 14:9 reads: "The eye of the covetous person is insatiable in his portion[14] of iniquity; he will not be satisfied. . . ."[15] In *understanding*, for he adds: *Neither does he reflect, saying: For whom do I labor and defraud my soul of good things?* We read in Psalm 38:7: "He stores up and knows not for whom he will gather these things."[16] So from all this he draws a

---

[13]Sirach 31:3 continues: ". . . and when he rests, he will be filled with his goods."

[14]On p. 39 n. 4 QuarEd rightly indicate that the Vulgate reads *in parte* ("in portion") while Bonaventure has *in partem* ("in portion").

[15]Sirach 14:9 continues: ". . . till he consumes his own soul, drying it up."

[16]Hugh of St. Cher, 83a also cites Psalm 38:7.

conclusion about vanity: *In this also is vanity and a grievous vexation*. Ecclesiastes 5:12-13 below states: "Riches
kept to the hurt of the owner, for they are lost with grievous vexation."[17]

9. (Verses 9-12). *It is better, therefore, that two should be
together*. He treats here, secondly, of *praise for the company of another*. And he does this in the context of his condemnation of the solitude of an avaricious person. So he
says: *It is better, therefore, that two should be together*, although the avaricious person may prefer to be alone. He
adds the reason: *For they have the advantage of mutual
companionship*.[18] For Luke 10:1 states: The Lord "sent the
disciples[19] two and two before his face."

10. He shows a triple benefit in this, namely, in *relieving,
protecting*, and *defending*. About *relieving* he states: *If one
fall, he will be supported by the other*. Deuteronomy 22:4
says: "If you see that your brother's ass or his ox has fallen
along the way, you shall not slight it, but shall lift it up
with him." A solitary individual lacks this help, and so he
adds: *Woe to the person who is alone, for when he falls, he
has no one to lift him up*. This applies to the miserly person, for Psalm 24:16 says: "Look upon me and have mercy
on me, for I am alone and poor."

11. Relative to the benefit of *protecting*, he adds: *And if
two lie together, they shall warm one another*, that is, they
are protected from the cold. Ephesians 5:29 has: "For no

---

[17]The Duoay masks the fact that both Ecclesiastes 4:8 and 5:13 contain
the same words, that is, *afflictio pessima* ("grievous affliction") by
translating those words in 5:13 by "very great affliction."
[18]The Vulgate reads *societatis suae* ("their companionship") while
Bonaventure has *societatis mutuae* ("mutual companionship").
[19]The Vulgate reads *illos* ("them") while Bonaventure has *discipulos*
("disciples").

man ever hated his own flesh, but nourishes and cherishes it." A solitary person lacks this help, and so he continues: *How will one alone*, when he sleeps, *be warmed?* There is an example of this in 1 Kings 1:1-4, where it is told how David, old and unable to keep warm, was given Abishag the Shunamite, who slept in the king's bosom and warmed him. He could not warm himself since he was alone.

12. With regard to the benefit of *defense* he adds: *And if a person prevail against one, two will withstand that person*, and so is valuable for defense. 2 Samuel 10:11 reads: "If the Syrians are too strong for me, then you will help me. But if the children of Ammon are too strong for you, then I will help you." He makes this clear with an example: *A threefold cord is not easily broken*. Just as one cord joined to another is stronger, so it is with people. Proverbs 18:19 says: "A brother, who is helped by his brother, is like a strong city."[20]

13. In the *spiritual interpretation* one notes here the triple effect of charity, namely, mutual *relief*, mutual *consolation*, and mutual *defense*. Concerning *relief* he says: *If one fall*. We read in Galatians 6:1: "If a person is overtaken in any fault, you, who are spiritual, instruct such a one in the spirit of meekness." For it is said in Sirach 37:17: "Establish within yourself a heart of good counsel. – About the benefit of *consolation* he says: *They will warm one another*. 1 Thessalonians 5:14 states: "Console the pusillanimous." And also in 1 Thessalonians it is said: "We became little ones in your[21] midst, as if a nurse were comforting her children."[22] – For the benefit of *defense* he says:

---

[20]Hugh of St. Cher, 83s also cites Proverbs 18:19.

[21]On p. 40 n. 2 QuarEd accurately mentions that the Vulgate reads *vestrum* ("your") while Bonaventure has *vestry* ("your").

[22]1 Thessalonians 2:7.

Two will withstand. Isaiah 50:8 reads: "Let us stand together. Who is my enemy?" – Because of this triple effect of charity it is called a threefold cord.[23] Hosea 11:4 has: "I will draw you[24] with the cords of Adam, with the bands of charity."

QUESTIONS 14

I. It can be asked here whether a solitary life should be preferred to communal living.[25] That this is so is seen from what follows:

1. Since it is said about a good youth in Lamentations 3:28 that *he will sit solitary and hold his peace*, it is good to be alone.

2. Moreover, Bernard says: "As often as I was with people, I returned less a person."[26] Therefore, it is not good to be among people.

---

[23]Hugh of St. Cher, 83v, a gives these explanations of the triple cord: "faith in the Trinity . . . faith, hope, and charity. . . .Power of the Father, wisdom of the Son, goodness of the Holy Spirit. . . .Threefold manner of loving God, with one's entire heart, mind, and strength. . . .Or total thought, affection, and operation. . . .Or contrition, confession, and satisfaction or thought, speech, and deed; or love, fear, shame or . . . the height of love . . . the width of love . . . the strength of love."

[24]On p. 40 n. 2 QuarEd correctly indicate that the Vulgate reads *eos* ("them") while Bonaventure has *te* ("you").

[25]See Ecclesiastes 4:8-12.

[26]On p. 40 n. 4 QuarEd indicate that this opinion is also cited in Book 1, chapter 20 n. 2 of Thomas à Kempis, *On the Imitation of Christ.* See his *De Imitatione Christi Libri Quatuor,* Ex nova recensione Jacobi Merlo Horstii (Cologne: Balth. Ab Egmond, 1675), 45: *Dixit quidam: Quoties inter homines fui, minor homo redii* ("Someone has said: As often as I was with people, I returned a lesser person"). Both Bonaventure and Thomas à Kempis seem to be indebted to Seneca's *Epistulae morales* 7.2-3. See *Seneca ad Lucilium Epistulae Morales I,* trans. Richard M. Gummere, LCL (Cambridge: Harvard University Press, 1934), 31: "But nothing is so damaging to good character as the habit of lounging at the games; for then it is that vice steals subtly upon one through the avenue of pleasure. What do you think I mean?

3. Furthermore, when in society it is necessary for one to think how one has to conform to social norms. But the Apostle says in 1 Corinthians 7:32-34 that it is good not to marry so as to avoid the worry of pleasing a wife. Therefore, it is good to flee from all company.

Contra: 1. Genesis 2:18 states: *It is not good for a person to be alone.* Therefore, solitude is blameworthy, and on the other hand company is praiseworthy.

2. Likewise, Matthew 18:20 reads: *Where there are two or three gathered in my name, there am I in the midst of them.* He does not say: Where there is *one*, but where there are *two* or *three*. Therefore, it is better to live in a group than alone.

3. Furthermore, it is proved also by Ecclesiastes himself in 4:9-12, because a group *lifts up, warms,* and *defends.* And those who live alone lack these three good things.

I reply: There are three kinds of *solitude.* One comes from *a lack of love,* as in an avaricious person who does not want a companion to share his riches, in an envious person who does not want to share good things, in a proud person who does not want to share great things. Such solitude is completely wrong. – Another kind of solitude comes from *a lack of consolation,* as it is said in Psalm 24:16: *I am alone and poor,* and this solitude is miserable. – Another kind of solitude comes from *the quiet of contemplation,* and this is praiseworthy and honorable.

I mean that I come home more greedy, more ambitious, more voluptuous, and even more cruel and inhuman, – because I have been among human beings." The editors also follow MSS Vat. and point to Sermon 40 n. 4-5 of Bernard's *Sermons on the Canticle of Canticles,* but stress that Bernard only exhorts people to love solitude and on the correct way to converse with people. See the next note.

Similarly, there are three kinds of *company or society*. One kind is *disturbing and holds one back*, such as the company of evildoers. Another kind is a company of *those needing support and solace*, as in the company of wives and of the sick. Yet another kind is a group *helping and causing one to advance*, as in the company of the perfect. One must *flee* from the first, *tolerate* the second, and *desire* the third. This third is found in religious orders. When, therefore, Scripture commends company or society, it is to be understood of this last kind. And this is not inconsistent with the solitude of contemplation, because Bernard says: "When among others a person can be entirely alone, provided he flees curiosity."[27] – And in this way the objections are resolved.

ECCLESIASTES 4:13-16   THE VANITY OF IMPRUDENCE

14. *Better is a child*, etc. He has dealt with the vanity of malice and avarice. Here he treats the vanity of *imprudence*. Since the vanity of imprudence is culpable and detestable, he speaks against it in two ways. First, because of *the present* evil. Second, because of evil that *follows it* or *is caused by it* where verse 15 says: *I saw all those living*.

15. (Verse 13). Evil that is *present* and accompanies imprudence is what puts the rich, old king under the poor child who was prudent. This is indeed a great vanity. So he says: *Better is a child that is poor and wise than a king that is old and foolish*, even though the king has more

---

[27]On p. 40 n. 10 QuarEd cite Sermon 40 n. 5 of Bernard's *Sermons on the Canticle of Canticles*. Bonaventure's citation is not exact. See SBOp 2.27 and *On the Song of Songs II*, trans. Kilian Walsh, Cistercian Fathers Series 7 (Kalamazoo: Cistercian Publications, 1976), 203: "Do you not see that you can be alone when in company and in company when alone? However great the crowds that surround you, you can enjoy the benefits of solitude if you refrain from curiosity about other people's conduct and shun rash judgment."

power than the child and more wealth and age. Ecclesiastes 10:1 below states: "Wisdom and a little glory[28] are more precious than short-lived folly." And Proverbs 12:9 reads: "Better is a poor man who provides for himself than the person who is glorious and wants for bread." He explains what he means by *foolish*, in that he is slack in providing for the future, which is one element of prudence.[29] Thus, he says: *Who knows not to foresee for hereafter*, namely, future events. Deuteronomy 32:29 states: "O that they would be wise and would understand and would provide for their last end."

16. (Verse 14). *Because out of prison and chains sometimes a person comes forth to a kingdom.* We read in Wisdom 10:13-14: "She did not abandon the just when he was sold bound in chains, but delivered him from sinners, . . . till she brought him the scepter of the kingdom."[30] *And another, who is born king, is consumed with poverty*, because of his pride. Sirach 10:17 reads: "The Lord[31] has overturned the thrones of proud princes and has set up the meek in their stead."

17. (Verse 15). *I saw all the living.* Here he treats of the evil that *follows* from imprudence, because one person is put down and another raised up. Thus, he says: *I saw all*

---

[28]On p. 41 n. 1 QuarEd intimate that the Vulgate reads *et gloria parva* ("and a little glory") while Bonaventure reads *parvaque gloria* ("and a little glory").

[29]On p. 41 n. 1 QuarEd refer readers to Book III, d. 33, dubium 2 of Bonaventure's *Commentary on the Sentences* for the elements of prudence. See Omnia Opera 3:728: "There are three elements of prudence, as Cicero says, namely, 'memory, understanding, and providence,' and only providence looks to the future." The reference is to Book II chapter 54 of Cicero's *Rhetorica*.

[30]The "she" is Wisdom. The Vulgate reads *in vinculis* ("bound in chains") in verse 14, not in verse 13: "13. She did not abandon the just when he was sold, but delivered him from sinners. . . .14. And she did not abandon him bound in chains, till she brought him the scepter of the kingdom."

the living who walk under the sun, that is, many or a limitless number in the sense of hyperbole. *With the second young man*, that is, who follows him in the kingdom. So he continues: *Who will rise up in his place*. And others follow this youth who took over and despised the older man. There is an example of this in David who rose up in the kingdom of Saul, and the people of Israel followed him and abandoned the house of Saul. So it is said in 2 Samuel 5:1 that all came to David.[32]

18. (Verse 16). The reason why they follow the younger man and abandon the older man is that the foolish old man did no good for them. This is implied in the verse that follows: *The number of all the people who were before him is infinite*, that is, those who were under the foolish king before the coming of the young man whom they joined. *And those who will come afterwards*. Supply: who are still loyal to the old king. *Will not rejoice in him*, that is, in the foolish old king, since he does no good for them and will do no good for them, for he does not know how to do good. Sirach 20:17-19 states: "A fool will have no friend, and there will be no thanks for his good deeds,[33] . . . for he does not distribute with right understanding that which was to be had." From this he draws the conclusion of vanity: *But this too is vanity and vexation of spirit*. This is another vanity from the ones mentioned earlier in Ecclesiastes 1:14: "I have seen all things that are done under the sun, and behold, all is vanity."[34] In Ecclesiastes 1:15 he adds the

---

[31]The Vulgate reads *Deus* ("God") whereas Bonaventure has *Dominus* ("the Lord").

[32]2 Samuel 5:1 reads: "Then all the tribes of Israel came to David in Hebron, saying: Behold, we are your bone and your flesh."

[33]On p. 41 n. 4 QuarEd accurately indicate that the Vulgate reads *et non erit gratia bonis illius* ("and there will be no thanks for his good deeds") while Bonaventure has *et nec erit gratia in bonis illius* ("and there will be thanks for his good deeds").

[34]Ecclesiastes 1:14 continues: ". . . and vexation of spirit."

reason: "The perverse are hard to be corrected, and the number of fools is infinite." – This concludes the section of the vanity of sin.[35]

19. In a *spiritual sense* this can be applied to Christ. *The poor and wise child* is Christ, who is *a child* by reason of innocence. For Isaiah 42:1 says in another translation: "Behold, my child, my elect, in whom my soul has been pleased."[36] Since he was made needy for us, he is *poor*. 2 Corinthians 8:9 states: "You know, brothers and sisters,[37] the grace of our Lord Jesus Christ that, although he was rich, he became poor for your sakes." He is *wise*, indeed Wisdom itself. 1 Corinthians 1:24 reads: "We speak of[38] Christ, the power of God and the wisdom of God." And Ecclesiastes 9:15 below says: "There was found in it a man poor and wise."

20. *The old and foolish king* is the devil.[39] He is *old*. Job 40:14 reads: "He was the beginning of the ways of God." Thus "he has grown old in evil days."[40] He is *king*, because

---

[35]That is, Ecclesiastes 3:16-4:16.

[36]The English of the Vulgate of Isaiah 42:1 is: "Behold, my servant, I will uphold him, my elect, in whom my soul has delighted." The English of the Septuagint is: "Jacob, my child, I will take him up; Israel, my elect, my soul has taken him." Matthew 12:18 reads: "Behold, my servant, whom I have chosen, my beloved, in whom my soul was well pleased."

[37]The Vulgate does not read *fratres* ("brothers and sisters").

[38]The Vulgate does not read *dicimus* ("we speak of").

[39]On p. 41 n. 5 QuarEd quote Jerome's commentary on Ecclesiastes 4:13. See CCSL lxii, 290: "Origen and Victorinus do not differ much among themselves. For after that general opinion which is obvious to everyone that a poor and wise youth is better than an old and foolish king. . . .They interpreted this passage to be about Christ and devil. They take Christ to be the poor and wise child. . . .Now he was poor, because although he was rich, he became poor. . . .He was born during the reign of the old man. . . ."

[40]On p. 41 n. 6 QuarEd rightly point to Daniel 13:52 and the Vulgate's reading of *inveterate* ("O you who have grown old") while Bonaventure

he reigns among the evil. For Job 41:25 states: "He is king over all the children of pride." He is *foolish*, since he attempted what he could not do. Thus, Isaiah 14:13 has: "I will ascend into heaven. I will exalt my throne above the stars of God."[41] Although he is most cunning in deceiving, *he does not know how to foresee* that *sometimes a person comes out of prison to a kingdom*, as Christ came out of the prison of flesh and the chains of the passion to the kingdom of heavenly glory. Hebrews 1:3 reads: "He sits at the right hand of majesty on high." Also the devil, *who is born king*, that is, to take over the kingdom, *is consumed with poverty*, as is stated in Colossians 2:15: "Despoiling the principalities and the powers, he has confidently exposed them."

21. What follows now is an explanation of what comes before Christ's reign. *And I saw all the living who walk under the sun with the second young man*, that is, Christ. John 12:19 says: "Behold, the whole world is gone after him." This one *will rise up* to throw the devil out of the kingdom. John 12:31 reads: "Now is the judgment of the world. Now will the prince of this world be cast out." *The number of the men who were before him is infinite*,[42] that is, before the coming of Christ. And the faithful, *who will come afterwards will not rejoice in him*, that is, in the stupid king, that is, in the devil, because they now rejoice only in Christ. For the Apostle states in Philippians 4:4:

---

has *inveteratus* ("he has grown old"). Daniel is addressing one of the old men who are falsely accusing Susanna of sin."

[41]On p. 41 n. 6 QuarEd correctly mention that the Vulgate reads *In caelum conscendam* ("Into heaven I will mount") while Bonaventure has *Ascendam in caelum* ("I will ascend into heaven").

[42]Bonaventure's citation is not exact: it omits *omnibus* ("all") and has *virorum* ("men") rather than the Vulgate's *populi* ("people").

"Rejoice in the Lord always." A person should rejoice in the Lord, not in the devil.[43]

ECCLESIASTES 4:17-7:23   TRIPLE REMEDY AGAINST TRIPLE VANITY

22. *Guard your foot.* Ecclesiastes has dealt with *the vanity* of sin above. Since this vanity is mortal and destructive, he deals here with *the remedy* against it. Because he has shown that there is a triple vanity, namely, of malice, avarice, and imprudence, he now gives three remedies. First, he gives a remedy against *malice*. Second, against *avarice* where Ecclesiastes 5:9 reads: *A covetous man will not be satisfied*. Third, against *imprudence* where Ecclesiastes 6:8 asks: *What more has the wise person than the fool?* But since the sickness of malice is incurable in itself and can additionally corrupt others, he deals here with a remedy not against *malice*, but against *the corruption of malice* or the evil coming from it in others who see malice in another.

ECCLESIASTES 4:17-5:8   THE REMEDY AGAINST THE VANITY OF MALICE

23. A triple disorder comes from this malice, namely, in *work* because of the *disobedience* of deviation; in the *mouth* through *foolish speech*; in the *heart* through *wrong thinking*. Anyone, who without caution gazes on the malice of another, falls into all these evils. For when someone thinks that evil is not punished, *believing* there is no providence,

---

[43]See Hugh of St. Cher, 84d for a different interpretation: "With the second young man] that is, with the Antichrist, who is said to be the second youth with respect to the poor and wise child about whom the text spoke earlier, that is, with regard to Christ, who is the first youth."

this is *erroneous thinking*. And from this a person freely *says what is foolish*, because he does not believe that there is anyone to reprimand him. And finally, a person *transgresses the commandments*, because he does not believe that there is anyone to punish him. So first, he gives a remedy against *disobedience*. Second, against *foolish speech* where Ecclesiastes 5:1 says: *Do not speak anything rashly*, etc. Third, against *wrong thinking* where Ecclesiastes 5:7 reads: *If you see the oppressions of the poor*, etc.

ECCLESIASTES 4:17   REMEDY AGAINST DISOBEDIENCE

24. (Verse 17). As a remedy against *disobedience* he introduces *exhortation* and adds *the reason for exhortation*. Now he exhorts people to keep careful custody over their feet, lest the divine commandments be transgressed. Therefore, he says: *Guard your feet*, lest you stray from the right path. We read in Hebrews 12:13: "Make straight steps for your feet, so that no one who is lame may go out of the way." *When you go into the house of God*, that is, into a church or into the service of God, into which a person should enter with fear. For Psalm 5:8 reads: "I will come into your house. I will worship towards your holy temple in fear of you." So you are to keep your feet from disobedience and ready to obey. For this reason he continues: *And draw near to hear*, that is, to obey. He says *draw near*, because Deuteronomy 33:3 states: "Those who draw near to his feet will receive from his teaching." *To hear*, that is, by obeying. Jeremiah 17:20-21 reads: "Hear the word of the Lord, all who enter in by these gates. Thus says the Lord: Guard your souls."

25. And he adds *the reason for the exhortation*: *For much better is obedience than the victims of fools, who know not what evil they do*, for they do not acknowledge their transgressions nor take care to obey. Gregory states: "Obedience is better than victims, because in obedience one's own

will is offered up. In a victim the flesh of another is offered."[44] The comparison is *faulty*, because obedience is good and so is pleasing.[45] Lamentations 3:27 says: "It is good for a man when he has borne the yoke from his youth." On the other hand the victims offered by fools are displeasing. Proverbs 15:8 has: "The victims of the wicked are abominable to the Lord." For Saul was condemned, because he transgressed a divine commandment out of love for an offering.[46] 1 Samuel 15:22 reads: "Does the Lord desire holocausts and victims and not rather that the people obey him?[47] For obedience is better than sacrifices and to listen attentively is greater than to offer the fat of rams."[48]

---

[44]On p. 42 n. 5 QuarEd indicate that in Book XXXV, chapter 14 n. 28 of his *Moralia in Iob*, Gregory is interpreting 1 Samuel 15:22: "*Obedience is better than victims*. . . .Indeed, obedience is rightfully preferred to victims, for through victims the flesh of another is sacrificed, but through obedience one's own will is offered up." See *S. Gregorii Magni Moralia in Iob, Libri XXIII-XXXV*, ed. M. Adriaen, CCSL cxliiib (Turnhout: Brepols, 1985), 1792. Hugh of St. Cher, 84p also cites Blessed Gregory on 1 Samuel 15: "Because by obedience one's own will is offered up, but another's flesh by a victim."

[45]On p. 42 n. 6 QuarEd refer to Book VII n. 4 of Aristotle's *Physica* for the conditions required for a strict comparison. See WAE, Vol. 2, 249a: "Must we then say that, if two things are to be commensurable in respect to any attribute, not only must the attribute in question be applicable to both without equivocation, but there must also be no specific differences either in the attribute itself or in that which contains the attribute – that these, I mean, must not be divisible in the way in which colour is divided into kinds? Thus in this respect one thing will not be commensurable with another, i.e. we cannot say that one is more coloured than the other where only colour in general and not any particular colour is meant; but they are commensurable in respect of whiteness."

[46]See 1 Samuel 15:15: Saul tells Samuel of his disobedient action: "the people spared the best of the sheep and of the herds that they might be sacrificed to the Lord your God, but the rest we have slain."

[47]On p. 42 n. 6 QuarEd correctly maintain that the Vulgate reads *voci Domini* ("voice of the Lord") while Bonaventure has *ei* ("him").

[48]Hugh of St. Cher, 84p devotes seven lines to the example of Saul and the citation of 1 Samuel 15:22.

CHAPTER 5

REMEDY AGAINST FOOLISH
SPEECH

1. *Do not speak anything rashly.* He now gives a remedy
against *foolish* or disordered *speech*. Now speech is disordered by being *thoughtless*, either because it is *false*. And
he forbids this here: *If you have vowed anything,* etc. Or
because it is *wrong.* And he forbids this here: *Give not your
mouth to cause your flesh to sin,* etc. – Relative to *thoughtless* speech *he forbids being hasty with rash speech* and
gives the reason for this and *provides an example to confirm the reason.*

2. (Verse 1). So he forbids *being hasty: Do not speak anything rashly,* that is, without thinking. Sirach 9:25 states:
"The person who is rash in his word will be hateful." And
again Sirach 28:29 reads: "Make a balance for your words
and a just bridle for your mouth." And since a person cannot think all that fast, he adds: *And let not your heart be
hasty to utter a word.*[1] A person should deliberate for a
long time. Proverbs 29:20 counsels: "Have you seen a person hasty to speak? Folly is rather to be looked for than

---

[1] For some reason Bonaventure does not finish this verse with *coram
Deo* ("before God"), which is the reading of the Vulgate.

his amendment." For there must be a distance between the mouth and the heart. Sirach 21:29 has: "The heart of fools is in their mouth." Thus, it is said in James 1:19: "Let every person be in haste to hear and[2] slow to speak." And Seneca says: "I want you to be slow of speech."[3]

3. He adds as *the reason* divine judgment which sees all: *For God is in heaven.* Supply: seeing everything. Thus, we read in Psalm 101:20: "From heaven the Lord has looked upon the earth." *And you upon the earth,* standing in the open before God, so that you are not out of God's sight. Sirach 23:28 reads: "The eyes of the Lord are far brighter than the sun, looking roundabout into[4] all the ways of men and women." *Therefore, let your words be few,* because when you speak before God, God will demand an account of all. Matthew 12:36 states: "For[5] every idle word that men and women will speak, they will render an account for them on the day of judgment."

4. And it can hardly be that the person who says much to God does not displease God. He makes this clear by an example from something similar: *Dreams follow many cares,* and so it is stupid to pay attention to them. Sirach 34:7 says: "Dreams have deceived many." *And in many*

---

[2] On p. 43 n. 2 QuarEd rightly suggest that the Vulgate reads *autem* ("but") while Bonaventure has *et* ("and").

[3] On p. 43 n. 2 QuarEd cite Seneca, *Epistulae Morales* 40. See Letter 40:14 in *Epistulae Morales I*, 270: *Tardilocum esse te iubeo* ("I bid you be slow of speech"). Bonaventure's quotation is: *Tardiloquum te esse volo* ("I want you to be slow of speech"). Hugh of St. Cher, 84v, Introduction: *Et Senec. Tardiloquum te esse volo....* ("And Seneca says: I want you to be slow of speech").

[4] On p. 43 n. 3 QuarEd correctly mention that the Vulgate does not read *in* ("into").

[5] On p. 43 n. 3 QuarEd accurately intimate that the Vulgate does not read *de* ("For").

[6] Hugh of St. Cher, 84v, g also cites Proverbs 10:19.

words will be found folly. Sirach 20:8 reads: "The person who uses many words will hurt his own soul." And Proverbs 10:19 states: "In the multitude of words sin will not be absent."[6] But on the other hand, Ecclesiastes 10:14 has: "A fool multiplies words."

5.(Verses 3–4). *If you have vowed anything*, etc. Second, he treats of *false* speech by which one promises something that is not fulfilled. – So he exhorts people to fulfill what they promise: *If you have vowed anything to God*, that is, you have promised by means of a vow. *Do not defer to pay it*. Thus, we read in Psalm 75:12: "Vow and pay to the Lord your God. All you who are round about him bring[7] presents." And a Glossa comments: "To vow is voluntary, but to pay is necessary," because otherwise a person makes a false promise.[8] So he adds: *For an unfaithful and foolish promise displeases God. Unfaithful*, because truth is not in it. *Foolish*, because there is no discernment in it, and a foolish promise should not be made. For Isidore says: "In evil promises you annul the faith; in a base vow you change a decree."[9] So he adds that truth consists in keeping a

---

[7]The Vulgate reads *omnes . . . afferent* ("all will bring") while Bonaventure has *omnes . . . affertis* ("all you bring").

[8]Bonaventure seems indebted here to Hugh of St. Cher. See Hugh of St. Cher, 84vi: "This is what is said in the Gloss about what Psalm 75[12] has: Vow and pay, that is, if you have vowed, pay. For to vow is voluntary, but to pay is necessary." On p. 43 n. 5 QuarEd track this Gloss back to Peter Lombard's commentary on Psalm 75:12. See PL 191:709A: "To vow is a well-considered decision. After the promise of the vow it of necessity demands to be carried out. So he does not say simply: Vow and be unwilling to vow, but *vow and pay*. That is, if you vow, pay. Otherwise, you are held by the vow in the matter and have damnation, because they have made void their first faith, as the Apostle says (1 Timothy 5:12)."

[9]On p. 43 n. 6 QuarEd point to Book II n. 58 of Isidore's *Synonyma de lamentatione animae peccatricis*. See PL 83:858C where Isidore has quoted Ecclesiastes 5:4 in the previous sentence. The translation has turned imperatives into indicatives for easier comprehension in this

promise: *But whatsoever you have vowed, pay it* and do
not change it. Leviticus 27:9–10 states: "A clean animal
that can be sacrificed to the Lord, if anyone should vow,
shall be holy and cannot be changed, neither for a better
animal or for a worse one."[10]

6. Otherwise, it would be better not to vow, as he says:
And it is much better not to vow, that is, it is a lesser evil
because it is without sin, *than after a vow not to perform
the things promised*. We read in 2 Peter 2:21: "It had been
better for them not to have known the way of justice than
after they had known it, to turn back. . . ."[11] For Luke 9:62
states: "No one putting his hand to the plow and looking
back is fit for the kingdom of God."[12]

7. (Verses 5–6). *Give not your mouth*, etc. In a third point
he forbids *wrong speech*, speaks against *error in speaking*,
and adds *the reason* for this. Afterwards *he shows the source
of the error.* – He speaks against *error in speech* by saying:
Give not your mouth to cause your flesh to sin, that is, do
not utter a wrong word by which you may be led into sin.
He specifies what he means by adding: *And do not say
before the angel: There is no providence*, that is, say it not
in secret or in a hidden place, because the angels hear you

---

context of Isidore's exhortatory style. The editors also point to Book III
distinction 39, chapter 9 of Peter Lombard's *Sentence Commentary*. See
Sententiae in IV Libris Distinctae II, 225 where Peter Lombard cites
the same opinion from Isidore's *Synonyma*.

[10]On p. 43 n. 6 QuarEd correctly indicate that is more a summary of
the Vulgate than an exact quotation. Duoay translates: "But a beast
that may be sacrificed to the Lord, if anyone shall vow, shall be holy
and cannot be changed, that is to say, neither a better for a worse nor a
worse for a better."

[11]2 Peter 2:21 concludes: ". . . .from that holy commandment which
was delivered to them."

[12]Hugh of St. Cher, 85d quotes Luke 9:62 and 2 Peter 2:21, that is, in
reverse order from that found in Bonaventure.

even when you are in a hidden place and are commissioned to guard you. He says later in 10:20: "Speak no detraction against the king in your thought, and speak no evil against the rich person on your private couch[13] because even the birds of the air will carry your voice."[14] He adds *the reason* for the exhortation: *Lest God be angry at your words and destroy all the works of your hands*, that is, render them useless. *Be angry*, not from a disturbance in the mind, but from a strict punishment for sin. God was angry in this way at the words of Rabsaces,[15] and at night an angel destroyed all the works of the kings of Assyria.[16] Isaiah 37:4 reads: "It may be the Lord your God will hear the words of Rabsaces, whom the king of the Assyrians . . . , has sent to blaspheme the living God." Proverbs 20:26 says: "A wise king scatters the wicked," etc.[17]

8. And he goes on to state *the source* of such speech. It does not come from right thinking, but from an illusion of dreams. For this reason he says: *Where there are many dreams, there are many vanities*, because a dream is a vanity. Isaiah 29:8 states: " . . . the person who is hungry dreams and eats, and afterwards when he is aroused,[18] his soul is empty." *And words without number* follow dreams, because

---

[13]On p. 43 n. 8 QuarEd accurately mention that the Vulgate reads *in secreto cubiculi tui* ("in your private chamber") while Bonaventure has *in secreto cubili tuo* ("on your private couch").

[14]The Vulgate reads *avis caeli portabit* ("a bird of the air will carry") while Bonaventure has *aves caeli portabunt* ("birds of the air will carry").

[15]This name is not given in the Hebrew.

[16]See Isaiah 37:36: "And the angel of the Lord went out and slew in the camp of the Assyrians a hundred and eighty-five thousand. . . ."

[17]Proverbs 20:26 concludes: ". . . and brings the wheel over them."

[18]On p. 44 n. 2 QuarEd rightly point to variation(s). The Vulgate reads *cum autem fuerit expertus* ("but when he is awake") while Bonaventure has *et postea, cum expergefactus fuerit* ("and afterwards, when he is aroused").

nothing certain can be known from dreams. For Sirach 34:5 reads: "Deceitful divinations and lying omens and the dreams of evildoers are vanity."[19] No attention should be paid to such dreams, but to God. So he continues: *But do you fear God*, who is the only one able to destroy and to save. Do not fear dreams or auguries. Luke 12:5 has: "I will show you whom you should fear. Fear the person who after he has killed has power to cast into hell."

Ecclesiastes 5:7-8   Remedy against wrong thinking

9. (Verses 7–8). *If you shall see the oppressions*, etc. Third, he holds one back from *wrong thinking*, namely, that when human malice is seen, one does not think that providence is not present. So he says: *If you shall see the oppressions of the poor*. He has already said in 4:1: "I saw the oppressions that are done under the sun and the tears of the innocent." *And violent judgments*, which he had seen as he stated earlier in 3:16: "I saw in the place of justice wickedness." *And justice perverted in the province*. This is similar to what he had seen and expressed earlier in 3:16: "I saw in the place of judgment iniquity." Faced with this it is no wonder, I say, that one would think that no one is ruling or correcting. And so he says: *Do not wonder at this matter*, as if there were no ruler, for there is one who orders all things. Wherefore, he adds: *For the person who is high has another higher, and there are others still higher than these*. Thus, the centurion said in Matthew 8:9: "I also am a person subject to authority, having soldiers under me, and I say to this one: Go, and he goes."

10. *Moreover, there is the king who reigns over all the land subject to him*. Therefore, although they may not serve

---

[19]Hugh of St. Cher, 85n also cites Sirach 34:5.

[20]On p. 44 n. 4 QuarEd correctly indicate that the Vulgate reads *habet* ("has") while Bonaventure has *habebat* ("had").

another nor keep order among themselves, they are kept in order by God who knows how to use evil for good. Genesis 41:44 says: "I am Pharaoh. Without your commandment no one will move hand or foot in all the land of Egypt." Thus, Revelation 19:16 states: "He had[20] on his garment and on his thigh is written: King of Kings and Lord of Lords." And in no way does he himself pervert justice. Deuteronomy 10:17-18 reads: "The Lord our[21] God is the God of gods and the Lord of lords, a great Lord,[22] mighty, terrifying, who accepts no person nor takes bribes. He does justice for the fatherless and the widow." And so if he rules,justice is not perverted.

QUESTIONS 15

I. It is asked what he means by the words: If you have vowed anything to the Lord, defer not to pay it?[23] Is a person bound by a vow made indiscreetly, presuming that the person intended the vow to be binding? If this is *not* true, then:

1. Then the person derives a benefit from his indiscretion.[24]

---

[21]On p. 44 n. 4 QuarEd accurately mention that the Vulgate reads *vester* ("your") whereas Bonaventure has *noster* ("our").

[22]On p. 44 n. 4 QuarEd rightly advise that the Vulgate has *Deus* ("God") while Bonaventure reads *Dominus* ("Lord").

[23]Ecclesiastes 5:3.

[24]On p. 44 n. 5 QuarEd offer this reference: "Cap. *Intelleximus* (7.) X. (Decret. Gregor. Lib. II. tit. 1.) says this about judgments: Lest a benefit seem to derive from one's own malice." See Book II, Titulus I, De judiciis, capitulum VII in *Decretales D. Gregorii Papae IX, suae integritati una cum glossis restitutae Ad exemplar Romanum diligenter recognitae,* Editio ultima (Tavrini: Apud Nicolaum Beuilaquam, 1621), 527: *Ne videatur de sua malitia commodum reportare.* The opening word to the case cited in chapter 7 is: *Intelleximus.*

2. Likewise, a person must do the truth.[25] But a person who does not keep a promise does not do the truth. Rather the person is lying. Therefore, the person is bound to do what was vowed.

3. Also, Jephthah, who made an imprudent vow and kept it, is commended by the Apostle in Hebrews 11.[26] Therefore, we should keep and fulfill indiscreet vows.

Contra: 1. If it is indiscreet to say something, it is also imprudent to do it. If, then, a person vows imprudently, by reason of what is said the person is indiscreet. If the vow is fulfilled, the person is even more imprudent and sins the more. Therefore, by not fulfilling the vow, the person acts well.

2. Also, one evil does not excuse another. Therefore, if a person makes and carries out a foolish vow, he or she is no less blameworthy than if the same thing were done without a vow. Nor is the vow less blameworthy if it is not carried out. Therefore, etc.

3. Likewise, Isidore says: "In evil promises you annul the faith; in a base vow you change a decree."[27]

I reply: Such a vow is not binding. Indeed, if the person keeps the vow, sin is added to sin. Jephthah, by keeping his vow, sinned more than if he had not kept it, be-

---

[25]On p. 44 n. 6 QuarEd refer to John 3:20-21. See also Ephesians 4:15: "Rather we are to do the truth in love, and so grow up in all things in him who is the head, Christ."

[26]The scriptural references are: Judges 11:29-39: Jephthah ends up keeping his vow and sacrificing his daughter, his only child; Hebrews 11:32.

[27]See Book II n. 58 of Isidore's *Synonyma* in PL 83:858C. Bonaventure quoted this passage earlier in his commentary on Ecclesiastes 5:3-4 (#4) above.

cause he was stupid in making the vow and was wicked in keeping it, as Augustine says.[28]

3. To the objection that Jephthah is commended, it has to be said that he is commended neither for *the vow* nor for *keeping it*. In the text the Apostle is commending *faith*,[29] and he commends the faith of Jephthah who believed that he would conquer his enemies with the help of the Lord.

1. When it is objected that this brings a benefit, I say that this is wrong, because the person immediately sins in the vow itself and is worthy of punishment.

2. To the objection about doing the truth, it has to be said that *truth* underlies *judgment*. Because the vow was made without proper *judgment*, it cannot be fulfilled in *truth*. And for this reason truth cannot be present in such a vow, and there is no obligation.

II. It is asked whether a person may change a vow. – That the answer is *no* is clear from what Leviticus 27:10 states: *It cannot be changed . . . neither for a worse animal nor for a better animal.*[30]

That the answer is *yes* is clear, because it is lawful to choose the better part of the Lord. Therefore, although it is not lawful to choose what is worse, it is lawful to choose what is better.

---

[28]Of two passages from Pseudo-Augustine referred to by QuarEd on p. 44 n. 9 the closer parallel is found in Question 43 of *Quaestiones Veteris et Novi Testamenti* in PL 35: 2242: "And Jephthah was still so insensitive that even after he had realized that his vow was stupid, he did not correct the error which his actions had initiated." See also PL 34:812.

[29]See Hebrews 11:33: "who by faith conquered kingdoms, wrought justice, obtained promises, stopped the mouths of lions."

[30]On p. 45 n. 1 QuarEd correctly mention that the Vulgate has a different text. See Ecclesiastes 5:3-4 (#4) and note 9 above.

I reply: It must be said that a vow can be changed into something *completely wrong* or into something *better* that *includes* the lesser good, as in the example of someone, who has made vows in a less perfect religious institute, entering a more perfect religious institute that includes both goods. To change is to take on something *better not included in the present state* as, for example, to change one's land journey to Rome into a journey there by sea.

The first option, to vow what is completely wrong, is forbidden. The second option, to vow something good, is lawful *in itself*. The third option, to vow something more perfect, is lawful, but it is only lawful with *permission of a higher authority*. For since I am committed to God, I cannot change without God's permission. And since God does not speak to me other than through a minister who represents God, I cannot change without the permission of the superior, unless the Lord himself were to inspire me interiorly in a most certain way. This is the answer to the objection.[31]

III. What does he mean by saying: *Do not say before the angel: There is no providence?*[32]

Contra: It would seem that there is no providence:

1. First, because providence gives a proper order to things. But such an order does not exist in the world. Ecclesiastes 10:7 below reads: *I have seen servants upon horses and princes walking on the ground as servants.*

2. Second, because providence provides a due reward. But this does not happen in the world. Ecclesiastes 9:3 below states: *The same things happen to all people.*

---

[31]On p. 45 n. 4 QuarEd refer to Book IV, d. 38. a. 2 q. 2 of Bonaventure's *Sentence Commentary*. See Opera Omnia 4:816.

[32]Ecclesiastes 5:5.

3. Third, because providence provides a fitting length of time. But this is simply not found in the world. Ecclesiastes 7:16 below says: *The wicked live a long time in their wickedness.*[33]

But the following necessary points should be considered:

1. Since it is characteristic of a wise person to provide for his household, this is even more so the case with the One who is most wise.

2. Moreover, it is characteristic of the wise worker not only to fashion an object, but also to preserve it.[34] Therefore, God preserves and governs in like manner. But God is wise, and a wise person governs everything that he governs by providence. Therefore, etc.

3. Furthermore, since God is most wise, God cannot act without seeing our evils. Therefore, since God is most just, he cannot but avenge evil and reward good. Therefore, there is reward for all. Therefore, there is providence too.

IV. It is also asked who sins more: One who denies providence or one who blames divine providence?

It would seem to be that the greater sinner is the one who denies providence, for the person who believes in providence acts well in very fact of believing and has some ele-

---

[33]On p. 45 n. 7 QuarEd correctly indicate that the Vulgate reads *malitia* ("malice") while Bonaventure has *impietate* ("wickedness").

[34]On p. 45 n. 8 QuarEd quote from Book IX n. 7 of Aristotle's *Ethica nicomachia*. See WAE, vol. 9, 1167b: "This is what happens with craftsmen too; every man loves his own handiwork better than he would be loved by it if it came alive." The editors also cite n. 2 of Philo's *De opificio mundi*. See *Philo I*, trans. F. H. Colson and G. H. Whitaker, LCL (London: Heinemann, 1929), 11: "For it stands to reason that what has been brought into existence should be cared for by its Father and Maker."

ment of good. But the person who outright denies providence has no good, and so is more blameworthy.

Contra: Jerome maintains that a person sins more who accepts providence and accuses God than the person who simply denies providence.[35]

I reply to the first that there is providence.

1. To the objection about proper order, I reply that there is a twofold order, namely, *particular* and *universal*. Something can be lacking in a *particular* order, but not in the *universal* order, as Boethius says.[36] *Universal* order covers everything, as when someone falls from the order of *nature* and enters the order of *punishment*. Augustine gives the example of a cloud that becomes a whirlwind. It is turned around in itself in a disordered way, but in fact it is ordered for the benefit of the fruit of the earth.[37]

---

[35]On p. 45 n. 10 QuarEd point to Pars I, inquisitio 1, tractatus 5, sectio 1, quaestio 3, titulus 1, capitulum 8 of Alexander of Hales, *Summa Theologica I* (Quaracchi: College of St. Bonaventure, 1924), 304: "Contra: a. Isaiah 18:1: *Woe to the land, the winged cymbal!* The Glossa of Jerome: 'Epicurus says that there is no providence and pleasure is the greatest good. But they are worse who acknowledge providence, yet accuse its author, as if the Lord by mistake made things that are useless.'" Jerome's opinion is not found in PL 113:1259, namely, the *Glossa Ordinaria* on Isaiah 18:1. See Jerome's commentary on Isaiah 18:1 in PL 24:254D: "Epicurus says that there is no providence and that pleasure is the greatest good. By comparison with this one Marcion and all the heretics, who cut parts out of the Old Testament, are more wicked. For although they acknowledge providence, they accuse the Creator and assert that he has erred in many works and has not done what he should have done."

[36]On p. 45 n. 11 QuarEd quote from Book IV, Prosa 6 of Boethius, *De consolatione philosophiae*. See PL 63:820A and *Boethius, The Consolation of Philosophy*, trans. H. F. Stewart, LCL (London: Heinemann, 1926), 351: "For a certain order embraces all things, so that even that which departs from the order appointed to it, though it falls into another, yet that is order also, lest confused rashness should bear any sway in the kingdom of Providence."

2. Likewise, it has to be said about reward that in the present life good things come to sinners in a just way in that they are rewarded here and will be tortured for all eternity in the future. Also bad things come to good people, so that they might be purified here and rewarded for all eternity.

3. I reply to the objection that sinners live for a long time for the aforementioned reason, but the good die. For it is said of Enoch that *he was taken away, lest wickedness should alter his understanding.*[38] Divine judgments in the present are hidden to test us. And since simple and un-educated people do not notice what is hidden, everything seems to them to be in disorder. So Ecclesiastes teaches us to look to the One under whom all things are in order.

---

[37]On p. 45 n. 12 QuarEd cite Book III, chapter 10 n. 14 of Augustine's De Genesi ad litteram. See On Genesis, 224 where Augustine distinguishes between two areas in the atmosphere. In the lower area "it is still air but now intertwined with a fine humidity. This causes winds when stirred up, and lightning and thunder when more vehemently roused; clouds when contracted and rain when thickened even more; snow when the clouds freeze, hail when the denser clouds freeze more turbulently; fair weather when it is stretched out; and all this at the hidden orders and working of God controlling from its heights to its depths the universe he created. So that psalm, after mentioning *fire, hail, snow, ice, spirits of the tempest,* lest such things should be thought to come about and run their course apart from divine providence, adds straightaway, *that carry out his word* (Ps 148:8)." The editors also cite Augustine's commentary on Psalm 148 in *Sancti Avrelii Avgvstini Enarrationes in Psalmos CI-CL,* CCSL xl (Turnhout: Brepols, 1956), 2173: "*Fire, hail* . . . all of which to certain fools seem to be disturbances . . . he adds *which fulfill his word.* You should not think that these are moved by chance since they serve the word of God in all they do. To where God wants fire, clouds, rain, snow, and hail, there they go."

[38]See Wisdom 4:11. Cf. Sirach 44:16: "Enoch pleased God and was translated into paradise. . . ."

When it is asked who sins more, I reply that providence can be denied in two ways. One way is to believe that God is *ignorant*, while the other way is to believe that God *does not care* about mortal affairs. Similarly, we can accuse in two ways: either by saying that God *does not care* or by saying that God *destroys*. Each of these ways of accusing providence is worse, since each is not only wrong, but also blames God and blasphemes. In this way the sin is greater, and knowledge is no excuse here. Indeed, it increases guilt.

Ecclesiastes 5:9-6:7   Remedy against avarice

11. *A covetous person will not be satisfied with money.* Ecclesiastes has given a remedy against the vanity of malice, and he now goes on to a remedy against the vanity of *avarice*. Now the remedy against avarice is to despise earthly goods. So here he encourages us to despise riches. He does this in three ways. First, he shows that riches are not to be desired, because they *do not enrich* their owners. Second, because often *they are not handed on* to the heirs where verse 12 reads: *There is also another grievous evil.* Third, because frequently *they fall into the hands of strangers* where 6:1 states: *There is another evil that I have seen under the sun*, etc.

Ecclesiastes 5:9-11   Despise riches, for they do not enrich their owners

12. So first, riches are to be despised, because the riches that are desired do not help and *do not enrich* their owners. The reason is that they are *insufficient*. Second, because riches *bring no benefit*. Third, because *they afflict*.

13. (Verse 9a). Riches are to be despised, because they *are not sufficient* for an avaricious person. And the first thing desired by the avaricious is sufficiency. So he says: *A covetous man will not be satisfied with money*. Sirach 14:9

states: "The eye of the avaricious person is insatiable." Thus, Jerome observes: "The avaricious lack both what they have and what they do not have."[39] And Seneca comments: "If you want to make yourself rich, it is not necessary to accumulate money, but to curb greed."[40]

14. (Verses 9b-10). *And the person who loves riches*, etc. Second, he speaks against the love of riches, because *they bring no benefit*. So he says: *And the person who loves riches will reap no fruit from them*, and so bring no benefit. Sirach 10:10 states: "There is no more wicked thing than to love money, for such a person puts his own soul up for sale." Wherefore, riches are of no benefit to the covetous, because they exchange their soul for money. Thus, Matthew 16:26 reads: "For what does it profit a person, if he gain the whole world and suffer the loss of his own soul?" As if to say, nothing. From this he draws the conclusion that it is vanity to love riches: *So this also is vanity*, both of sin and punishment. That it is a vanity of sin is stated in Psalm 4:3: "O you children of men and women, how long will you be dull of heart," etc.[41] That it will be punished is stated in Psalm 77:33: "Their days were consumed in vanity." And Psalm 51:9 has: "Behold the person, who made not God his helper, but trusted in the abundance of his riches and prevailed in his vanity."

---

[39]On p. 46 n. 3 QuarEd refer to *Epistula* 100 n. 15. This is Jerome's translation of the Letter of Theophilus, Bishop of Alexandria to all the bishops of Egypt. See PL 22:826: "A covetous person is always in need, knows no measure; a person for whom as much is lacking as is already possessed."

[40]Hugh of St. Cher, 85z comments: *Et Sen. Si te vis divitem facere, non divitiis addendum est, sed cupiditati subtrahendum* ("And Seneca says: If you want to make yourself rich, it is not necessary to accumulate riches, but to curb greed"). Bonaventure's text is: *Et Seneca: 'Si vis te divitem facere, non pecuniae est addendum, sed cupiditati subtrahendum* ("If you want to make yourself rich, it is not necessary to accumulate money, but to curb greed"). It seems clear that Bonaventure

15. He shows that riches bring no benefit to their owner, because they are used up and the owner no longer has anything to serve him: *Where there are great riches, there are also many to eat them*, so that they are used up. For Seneca observes: "Wolves corpses, flies honey, this crowd follows booty, not the person."[42] Job 39:30 says: "Her young ones will suck up blood and where[43] the carcass will be, she is immediately there." For according to what is said in Proverbs 19:6: "Many honor the person who is mighty and are friends of the person who gives gifts." *And what does it profit the owner, but that he sees the riches with his eyes?* As if to say: nothing more than it profits others, because others eat as much as he eats and so he has no more fruit than others. Rather he has damnation, since he sins more. For Sirach 11:10 reads: "If you are rich, you will not be free from sin. If you pursue riches, you will not overtake them."

---

adapted his quotation of Seneca from Hugh of St. Cher. On p. 46 n. 3 QuarEd provide a lengthy quotation from Seneca's Epistula moralis 119 as a possible source for Bonaventure's citation. See, for example, *Seneca ad Lucilium Epistulae Morales III*, trans. Richard M. Gummere, LCL (London: Heinemann, 1925), 375: "Money never made a man rich; on the contrary, it always smites men with a greater craving for itself."

[41]Psalm 4:3 concludes: " . . . and why do you love vanity and seek after lying?"

[42]On p. 46 n. 6 QuarEd cite "Excerpt. II. (e libris Senecae) de Remediis fortuitorum." See Seneca, *De remediis fortuitorum liber*, Opera Omnia 2 (Leipzig: Teubner, 1892), 451: *Mel muscae sequuntur, cadavera lupi, frumenta formicae, praedam sequitur ista turba, non hominem* ("Flies follow honey, wolves corpses, ants grain, this crowd follows booty, not the person"). Hugh of St. Cher, 85v, d observes: "Where there are great riches, there are also many to eat them: just as where they are many corpses, there is a multitude of vultures and crows and dogs. And where there are plentiful harvests, there are birds aplenty. . . .For this reason Seneca says about the families of the rich: This crowd follows the booty, not the person." It seems that in this instance Bonaventure and Hugh of St. Cher adopt Seneca's dictum independently.

[43]On p. 47 n. 6 QuarEd accurately indicate that the Vulgate reads *ubicumque* ("wherever") while Bonaventure has *ubi* ("where").

16. (Verse 11). *Sweet is sleep*. Third, he shows that riches are to be despised, because *they afflict* and allow a person no quiet. So he continues: *Sleep is sweet to laborers, whether they eat little or much*. And so working and laboring, they at last take their rest. Sirach 31:24 states: "Sound and wholesome sleep with a moderate person: he will sleep till morning, and his soul will be delighted with him."[44] It is different for the rich person who does not rest, and so he adds: *But the fullness of the rich will not allow them to sleep*. Or whoever has great wealth has many worries that drive sleep away. We read in Job 15:21: "The sound of dread is always in [his] ears. And although there is peace, he . . . suspects treason."[45] Thus, Ecclesiastes 2:23 above says: "All his days are full of labors[46] and miseries. Even in the night he does not rest his mind." Or, because he eats and drinks much, but does not labor, he does not rest. Thus, Sirach 31:23 states: "Sleepless nights and stomach ache and twisting and turning are the intemperate man's lot,"[47] and so he does not rest because of satiety.

QUESTIONS 16

But it is asked what he means by saying that *riches do not profit their owner*.[48]

---

[44]On p. 47 n. 1 QuarEd correctly mention that the Vulgate has *cum ipso* ("with him") while Bonaventure reads *cum illo* ("with him"). Hugh of St. Cher, 85v, f also cites Sirach 31:24 and reads *cum ipso* ("with him").

[45]On p. 47 n. 2 QuarEd rightly point out that Bonaventure's citation from Job 15:21 is not verbatim, for example, he does not read *semper* ("always") in the second sentence. Hugh of St. Cher, 86a also quotes Job 15:21 and quotes the entire verse.

[46]The Vulgate of Ecclesiastes 2:23 reads *doloribus* ("sorrows") while Bonaventure has *laboribus* ("labors").

[47]Hugh of St. Cher, 85v, f also quotes Sirach 31:23, although he erroneously refers to it as Sirach 41.

[48]See Ecclesiastes 5:10.

1. For Ecclesiastes 7:12 below states: *Wisdom with riches is more useful and brings more advantage to those who see the sun.*

2. Also, Proverbs 13:8 reads: *The ransom of a man's life are his riches.*[49] Therefore, riches are able to redeem a life.

Contra: 1. Everything that it is simply better to throw away than to keep is simply useless, because if the absence of something is useful, its presence is harmful. Therefore, to throw riches away is good; to keep them is useless.

2. Also, something is profitable because of its relation to the final end. Therefore, what prevents a person from reaching the end is not useful, but useless. But riches are this kind of obstacle, because it is impossible for their owner to enter heaven,[50] and it is difficult to have riches and not love them. Therefore, the possession of riches is an obstacle, and they do not benefit, but obstruct.

I reply to this by saying with Bernard: "Temporal things of themselves are neither good nor evil. Their use is good, their abuse evil. To worry over them is worse. To seek them is more shameful."[51] If it is asked are riches useful or useless, I say that to a person who uses them well they are useful. But to one who hoards them, they are useless. And to those who use them in a wrong way, they are harm-

---

[49]On p. 47 n. 4 QuarEd correctly indicate that the Vulgate reads *divitiae suae* ("his riches") while Bonaventure has *divitiae eius* ("his riches").

[50]See Matthew 19:23: "Amen I say to you: with difficulty will a rich man enter the kingdom of heaven." Mark 10:23 and Luke 18:24 also have "with difficulty."

[51]On p. 47 n. 6 QuarEd quote Book II, chapter 6 n. 10 of Bernard's *De Consideratione*. See SBOp 3.417-418: "Now the things themselves, in as far as they relate to the good of the soul, are neither good nor evil. But their use is good, their abuse evil. To worry over them is worse. To seek them is more shameful."

ful. For he says in Ecclesiastes 5:12 below: *Riches kept to the harm of the owner*. But they are good for a person who uses them well, for example, when distributed in works of mercy. – For riches are able *to redeem sin*. Daniel 4:24 reads: *Redeem your sins with alms*. They are able *to augment grace*. 1 Timothy 4:7–8 states: *Train yourself unto godliness*, etc.[52] They are valid for *receiving a glorious reward*. Luke 16:9 says: *Make for yourselves friends of the mammon of iniquity that when they fail, they may receive you into everlasting dwellings*.

1. To the objection that they are useless, because it is good to throw them away, I say that *to throw* them *away* is to give them to God, and this is a good use of riches. Hence, they are useful for throwing away, for giving to the poor, and for buying the kingdom.

2. To the objection that it is difficult to have riches and not love them, I reply that it does not follow from this that riches are an obstacle, since "every virtue is about what is difficult."[53] Virtue does not impede, but helps. However, a more useful and safer use is to give them all away at one time than to give them bit by bit. To give all away avoids the dangers that occur.

---

[52] On p. 47 n. 7 QuarEd accurately mention that the Vulgate reads *Exerce autem te ipsum* ("But train yourself in godliness") whereas Bonaventure has *Exerce temetipsum* ("Train yourself"). 1 Timothy 4:8 reads: "For bodily training is of little profit, while godliness is profitable in all respects, since it has the promise of the present life as well as that which is to come."

[53] On p. 47 n. 8 QuarEd cite Book II n. 3 of Aristotle's *Ethica Nicomachea*: "But art and virtue are always concerned with what is more difficult." See WAE, vol. 9, 1105a: "But both art and virtue are always concerned with what is harder; for even the good is better when it is harder."

ECCLESIASTES 5:12-19   RICHES ARE TO BE DESPISED, BECAUSE OFTEN THEY ARE NOT HANDED ON TO HEIRS

17. *There is another grievous evil*, etc. He has shown that riches do not enrich their owners, and he now moves to his second point, namely, that riches are to be despised, because often *they are not passed on to their heirs*. He proceeds in the following manner. First, he notes *the thought of a future need in an heir*. Second, from this *he detests the worry and work* in getting the money. Third, through this detestation *he commends the enjoyment of present joy*, adding, that this is a gift of divine generosity.

18. (Verses 12–15a). So first, *he considers a future need for riches in an heir*, because, although these riches were guarded for a long time by the father, they do not last for the son. So he says: *There is also another grievous evil which I have seen under the sun*, that is, an evil different from the preceding one that I said dealt with the possession of riches. Thus he says: *Riches kept to the harm of the owner*, because they cannot be accumulated without the evil of both *punishment* and *sin*. Sirach 31:8–9 reads: "Blessed is the man[54] who is found without blemish and who has not gone after gold nor put his trust in the treasures of money.[55] Who is he? And we will praise him. He has done wonderful things in his life." Or: *to the harm*, for they make a person come to the evil of *punishment*. James 5:1 states: "Come now, you rich, weep and howl in the miseries, which will come upon you."[56] *Of their owner*. In fact,

---

[54]On p. 48 n. 1 QuarEd correctly mention that the Vulgate has *Beatus dives* ("Blessed is the rich person") while Bonaventure reads *Beatus vir* ("Blessed is the man").

[55]On p. 48 n. 1 QuarEd rightly indicate that the Vulgate reads *in pecunia et thesauris* ("in money and treasures") while Bonaventure has *in pecuniae thesauris* ("in the treasures of money").

[56]Hugh of St. Cher, 86a also cites James 5:1.

of the servant of the money, since avarice turns a covetous person into a slave. For Ephesians 5:5 has: "Avarice,[57] which is the serving of idols."

19. Such riches, I say, *are lost with very great affliction*, because it is necessary that the rich person give us his wealth with sorrow. Job 27:19 says: "The rich person, when he falls asleep, will take away nothing with him."[58] Not only does the owner lose them, but the son also loses them. So he adds: *He has begotten a son who will be in extremity of need*. There is an extreme want, namely, the loss of all good things. Of this we read in Proverbs 6:11: ". . . Want will come . . . like a traveler," etc.[59] – So riches hoarded are not[60] handed on to the heir nor can the owner take them away. So he continues: *As he came forth naked from his mother's womb, so shall he return*, not into the womb, but into the earth. *And will take nothing away with him of his labor*, as we read in Job 1:21: "Naked I came out of my mother's womb, and naked shall I return thither." – And this is to be deeply lamented. Thus, he adds: *A most deplorable evil: As he came, so shall he return*. For 1 Timothy 6:7 reads: "We brought nothing into this world, and certainly we can carry nothing out."[61]

---

[57]On p. 48 n. 2 QuarEd accurately notice that the Vulgate has *avarus* ("the avaricious person") while Bonaventure reads *avaritia* ("avarice"). Hugh of St. Cher, 86o writes: "For avarice is idolatry, as the Apostle says in Ephesians 5."

[58]Hugh of St. Hugh, 86vi, cites Job 27:19 in its entirety.

[59]Proverbs 6:11a reads: "And want will come upon you, like a traveler, and poverty like a man armed."

[60]On p. 48 n. 3 QuarEd state that they have supplied this negative ("not") from MSS E and give this sense: "Riches hoarded by a father, then given in a will to a son, are lost by the father and not [yet] handed on to the heir."

[61]Hugh of St. Cher, 86v, f also quotes Job 1:21 and 1 Timothy 6:7 in sequence.

20. (Verses 15b–16). *What then does it profit?* Second, *he condemns anxiety* to increase money by means of a reflection upon future want. He comes to this conclusion from the preceding, namely, that it is vain to afflict oneself with such labor in acquiring goods. So he says: *What then does it profit him*, that is, the rich, covetous person, *that he has labored for the wind*, that is, in vain, if it be true that *as he came forth naked form his mother's womb, so shall he return*, not only he himself, but also his son? This is equivalent to saying: It profits nothing. We read in Psalm 4:3: "O children of men and women, how long will you be dull of heart? Why do you love vanity and seek after lying?" Riches are compared to wind on account of vanity. Sirach 34:2 states: "The person who gives heed to lying visions is like a person that catches at a shadow and follows after the wind." Therefore, *the person who had labored for the wind* is the one who has labored to acquire wealth.

21. He adds the extent of the work: *All the days of his life he eats in darkness*, because of solitude. *And in many cares*, because of the worry. *And in misery*, because of the tenuous nature of his income. *And in sorrow*, because of cost for necessities. For he is sad because he must have something to eat. Sirach 14:10 says: "A person with an evil . . . and envious eye[62] will not have his fill of bread, but will be needy[63] and sorrowful at his own table." As people become rich, they are worried and in misery, for Matthew 13:22 states: "The care of this world[64] and the deceitfulness of riches choke the word."

---

[62]The Vulgate reads *oculus malus ad mala* ("A person with an evil eye toward evil things") while Bonaventure has *Oculus nequam et invidus* ("A person with an evil and envious eye").

[63]The Vulgate does not have *indigens* ("needy").

[64]On p. 48 n. 6 QuarEd accurately indicate that the Vulgate reads *saeculi istius* ("of this world") while Bonaventure has *huius saeculi* ("of this world").

22. (Verses 17–19). *This, therefore, seemed good to me.* Third, *he commends the enjoyment of delight* while despising the torment of avarice. For since the covetous torment themselves and get no profit from it, it seems good to eat. And so he says: *This, therefore, seemed good to me that people should eat and drink* with regard to external pleasure. *And enjoy the fruit of the labors, wherewith they have labored under the sun.* This enjoyment refers to internal pleasure. People have to do this while it is possible, that is, *all the days of the lives which God has given them*, that is, not waiting for another time. *And this is their portion.* About all these things Isaiah 22:13 reads: "Behold, joy and gladness . . . slaying rams, eating flesh, and drinking wine. Let us eat and drink, for tomorrow we will die," as if that were the portion.

23. And he approves this statement, as it pleases God. So he adds: *And all to whom God has given riches and substance*, for these are from God. Sirach 11:14 says: "Good things and evil, life and death, poverty and riches, are from God." *And has given them power to eat thereof*, delighting exteriorly. *And to enjoy their portion*, being at rest in them. *And to rejoice in their labors*, joyfully showing openly what he has acquired. *This is the gift of God*, for this power is from God, because John 15:15 states: "Without me you can do nothing." He shows that this is a great gift, because the torments of cares and worries, which are significant punishments, are tempered by pleasures. And so he adds: I say well that *this is a gift of God*, in so far as it frees one from the torments of avarice.

24. *For they will not remember much of the days of their lives*, that is, not being afflicted greatly by worries about life, *because God entertains their hearts with delight*. The reference here is not to spiritual delights, concerning which The Song of Songs 7:6 sings: "How beautiful are you and

how comely, my dearest, in delights!" Rather it refers to carnal pleasures. About these we read in Ecclesiastes 2:8 above: "I made for myself singing men and singing women and the delights of the children of men and women."

QUESTIONS 17

I. The first question concerns what he means by: *This seemed good to me that people should eat*.[65]

Contra: 1. He says later in Ecclesiastes 10:16: *Woe to you, O land, when your king is a child and when your princes eat in the morning*. Therefore, he contradicts himself.
II. Moreover, he says: *And should rejoice*.

Contra: 1. He says in Ecclesiastes 7:3 below: *It is better to go to the house of mourning than to the house of feasting* and again in 7:5 he states: *The heart of the wise is where there is mourning*.

2. Also, Truth himself says in Luke 6:25: *Woe to you who now laugh, for you shall . . . weep*. Therefore, it is wrong to rejoice, and all of Scripture condemns carnal pleasure. What is it then that he is commending here?

I reply to this by pointing out that the singular method used in this book is distinct from all the other books of Scripture. For he speaks as a preacher, who weaves his argument in such a way that different persons present diverse opinions. Thus, one person speaks as a carnal person while another as a wise person, as in Ecclesiastes 7:3 below: *It is better to go*, etc.[66] But later he speaks in his

---

[65]See Ecclesiastes 5:17.
[66]Ecclesiastes 7:3 reads: "It is better to go to the house of mourning than to the house of feasting."

own person and says in Ecclesiastes 12:13: *Let us all hear together the conclusion of the discourse*, where he passes sentence on those whose arguments he had earlier presented: *Fear God*, and God will judge everything.[67] So anything read in the book that is contrary to that sentence is made void by that sentence. Such are all the things said to recommend present pleasure. And in this way the objections are answered by one solution.

Another reply can be offered, namely, that Ecclesiastes speaks in his own name in whatever is said. However, to understand what he says, attention must be paid to two things, namely, *the reason* for speaking and *the style* of speaking. Further, he uses two styles of speaking, for he says some things *plainly*, others *ironically*. A plain statement is found in Ecclesiastes 11:1 below: *Cast your bread upon the running waters*. An ironic statement occurs in Ecclesiastes 11:9 below: *Rejoice therefore, O young man, in your youth*. That this statement is ironic is clear from what shortly follows in 11:9: *And know that for all these God will bring you into judgment*.

There is another variation in the style of speaking, because Ecclesiastes says some things *to approve them*: *Do not speak anything rashly*, etc.[68] He says some things *to report* what *he has done*, as, for example, in Ecclesiastes 2:10 above: *I withheld not my heart from enjoying every pleasure*, etc. He does not approve this, but reports that he acted in such a way, just as the Apostle says of himself that he was a blasphemer.[69] Likewise, he says some things

---

[67]See Ecclesiastes 12:13.

[68]Ecclesiastes 5:1.

[69]On p. 49 n. 6 QuarEd helpfully point to 1 Timothy 1:13: "For I formerly was a blasphemer, a persecutor and a bitter adversary."

to report what *he has thought*, as when he said above in
Ecclesiastes 2:24: *Is it not better to eat and drink?* He often uses this style in the book as if to report his temptations. Hence this book is a kind of meditation by Solomon.
Just as a person moves from one meditation to another
depending on diverse circumstances, as when someone
thinks that this is good, and afterwards begins another
line of thought. This is how Solomon speaks in this book.

With regard to his *reason for speaking*, it must be noted
that he says some things simply *to approve them*. Other
things he does not approve, but speaks about them *to condemn them by comparing* them to other things. An example
of this occurs when a person wants to condemn avarice by
praising generosity. Thus in this book the author praised
the dead in comparison with the living,[70] pleasure in comparison with avarice,[71] for in avarice there are punishment
and sin. Now he does this to call us back from avarice, not
to draw us to avarice.

A further point is to be noted about his *reason for speaking*. That is, he addresses some words to *everyone*, some to
a single group, whose members take something for granted.
He argues against this latter group on the basis of their
supposition. An example is found in what he said above in
Ecclesiastes 2:16 that there is *no remembrance of the wise
and of the foolish*. He said this to those wise men and
women who place all their reward in human praise.

Therefore, there is a general rule to be observed in his
words. The rule is this: when he speaks *plainly* and *gives
approval*, he is giving his own personal approval, is speak-

---

[70]See Ecclesiastes 4:2.
[71]See Ecclesiastes 5:17.

ing to everyone. The things that he says plainly and assertively, universally and absolutely are to be taken as authoritative. But when he speaks *ironically* or *is reporting*, he is speaking to condemn others or to condemn some presupposition or to contradict others. Such statements are not *assertions*, but *reports*. For example, when he tells of his own temptation, his intention is to report. – Or something is said not *absolutely*, but to condemn avarice.

III. What does he mean by saying that it is *a gift of God to enjoy* riches.[72] But this is a sin. Therefore, etc.

IV. He also says that *God entertains the heart with delight* during life. But this also is a sin.

I reply to III: Goods of *fortune, nature*, and *grace* are gifts of God. Goods of *fortune* are the least gifts, gifts of *nature* the middle gifts, but gifts of *grace* are the best gifts. Among the gifts of *nature* are counted health and courage. Among the gifts of *fortune* are prosperity and quiet. God gives riches to some who do not enjoy health or quiet, and such do not enjoy their goods. To some God adds quiet and health, and such people have the ability to enjoy their gifts. And since they are gifts of God, so too is the ability to enjoy them. But to abuse the ability to enjoy is evil and is not from God.

I reply to IV: When he says that God *entertains the heart with delight*, the answer should be that God does some things in mercy, other things by abandoning people

---

[72]Ecclesiastes 5:18.

to a just judgment as it is said *to deliver up the wise of the world to a reprobate sense.*[73] In this way God is said *to entertain the heart with delights*[74] by allowing it to be entertained by a just judgment and to forget eternal realities.

---

[73]On p. 49 n. 10 QuarEd accurately intimate that Bonaventure has adapted Romans 1:28: "God has delivered them up to a reprobate sense." A major change is to read *sapientes mundi* ("the wise of the world") for the Vulgate's *illos* ("them").

[74]Ecclesiastes 5:19.

CHAPTER 6

AVARICE IS TO BE DESPISED
BECAUSE RICHES OFTEN GO TO
STRANGERS

1. *There is also another evil*, etc. He has shown above that riches are to be despised both because they do not benefit their owner and are often not handed on to the heirs. Here in a third point he shows they are to be contemned, because *they often fall into the hands of strangers*. He proceeds in the following order. First, he intimates *the loss of riches hoarded*. Second, *a detestation of niggardliness* where verse 3 reads: *If a man beget*, etc. Third, he adds *the reason for this detestation* where verse 4 states: *For he came in vain*, etc.

2. (Verses 1-2). First, Ecclesiastes has considered *the vanity* arising from riches and now *states, develops*, and *concludes* this consideration. *He states* it saying: *There is also another evil that I have seen under the sun*. This evil is increased from a circumstance *frequent among men and women*, that is, among the weak lovers of the world and the rich. About these Psalm 4:3 says: "O you children of men and women, how long will you be dull of heart? Why do you love vanity and seek after lying?"

3. He *develops* his point about the vanity that consists in holding on to riches while another devours them. So he continues: *A man, to whom God has given riches*, in movable goods; *and substance*, in immovable goods; *and honor*, in sublime goods. For everything is from God. *Riches* are from God, as Proverbs 3:16 reads: "Length of days is in her right hand, and in her left hand riches and glory." And *substance* is from God, especially that of which Sirach 13:30 says: "Substantial riches are good to the person who has no sin on his conscience." Similarly, *honor* is from God, as seen in the words Daniel spoke to Belshazzar in Daniel 5:18: "O king, the most high God gave to . . . your father a kingdom and greatness . . . and honor." And to complete the perfect abundance of the goods of fortune, he adds: *And his soul wants nothing of all that he desires*, because he has sufficient. In this text the word *soul* means carnal life, about which we read in John 12:25: "The person who loves his life will lose it." So the person has an abundance of possessions, but by hoarding them out of avarice he loses the ability to enjoy them. So he adds: *Yet God does not give him power to eat thereof*, because he continually holds on to them in vain. Thus, Sirach 14:3 reads: "Substantial riches make no sense in the hands of a covetous and niggardly man, and what will an envious person do with gold?" Neither he nor his children get to use them, but strangers get them. So he adds: *But a stranger will eat them up.* Thus, Sirach 14:4 states: "The person who gathers together by wronging his own soul, gathers for others. And another will live luxuriously off his goods." And Proverbs 13:22 says: "The substance of a sinner is kept for the just." – And from this he *infers* vanity: *And this is vanity and a great misery. Vanity*, because he does not enjoy it. *Misery*, because he is sad, as others take away his wealth. Isaiah 1:7 reads: "Strangers devour your country before you."

4. (Verse 3). *If someone beget*, etc. Here he states his *despising of niggardliness* because of the loss just mentioned. And he blames this niggardliness which is aimed at being secure in the future. So he adds: *If a man beget a hundred children*, speaking in hyperbole, that is, many children, for evil people often have evil children who do not provide joy even if they be many. Sirach 16:1 states: "Rejoice not in ungodly children, if they be multiplied. Neither be delighted in them."[1] To have an abundance of children is a temporary prosperity that is followed by another temporary prosperity: *And live many years*, that is, through many years. *And attain to a great age*, namely, more than others. And this prosperity is also a passing one. Often the wicked have this prosperity. Ecclesiastes 7:16 below reads: "A wicked person lives a long time in his wickedness,"[2] if he had an abundance of such prosperity. *And his soul made no use of the goods of his substance*, that is, he was parsimonious and greedy in life. *And he will be without burial* in death, as was said of Jehoiakim in Jeremiah 22:19: "He will be buried with the burial of an ass, rotten and cast forth outside the gates of Jerusalem."[3]

5. After stating the conditions of prosperity and niggardliness, he adds how he despises them: *Of this person I pronounce*, like a judge in the land, *that the untimely born is better than he*, on account of the misery and great vanity which are lacking in an aborted infant. Wherefore, it is said in Job 3:11-12: "Why did I not die in the womb?[4]

---

[1]On p. 50 n. 5 QuarEd accurately indicate that the Vulgate reads *super ipsos* ("in them") whereas Bonaventure has *super illos* ("in them").

[2]On p. 50 n. 6 QuarEd correctly mention that the Vulgate has *in malitia sua* ("in his evilness") while Bonaventure reads *in impietate sua* ("in his wickedness").

[3]Hugh of St. Cher, 87q also cites Jeremiah 22:19.

[4]Hugh of St. Cher, 87t also cites Job 3:11.

Why did I not perish immediately when I came from[5] the womb? Why was I received upon the knees? Why was I suckled at the breast?"[6] And also Job 10:18: "Why did you bring me forth out of the womb?"

6. (Verses 4-7). *For he came in vain*, etc. Third, he adds *the reason for despising*, namely, that an aborted child is better than this niggardliness, because just as an aborted child comes in vain and goes into darkness as it dies immediately, so too do the niggardly. There the text continues: *For he*, namely, the niggardly person, *came in vain and goes into darkness*. Job 3:23 asks: "To a man whose way is hidden, has God surrounded him with darkness?" He shows that such an avaricious and niggardly person came into this world *in vain* because of *the deletion of his name* in death, and because of his *non-experience of good* in life, and because of his *non-fulfillment of desire* in both states. Concerning *the deletion of his name* the text reads: *And his name will be wholly forgotten*, that is, he will not remain in reality or in name, as the Lord threatened Babylon in Isaiah 14:22: "I will destroy the name and the remains and the bud and the offspring of Babylon, says the Lord." And Wisdom 2:4 speaks in the person of the wicked: "Our name in time will be forgotten, and no one will remember[7] our works."

7. He continues about *the non-experience of good*: *He has not seen the sun*, in which is the delight and experience of good, according to what he says later in Ecclesiastes 11:7:

---

[5]On p. 50 n. 7 QuarEd rightly notice that the Vulgate reads *ex* ("out of") while Bonaventure has *de* ("from").

[6]Hugh of St. Cher, 87q also cites Job 3:12.

[7]On p. 51 n. 1 QuarEd correctly indicate that the Vulgate has *memoriam* ("have remembrance of") whereas Bonaventure reads *memor* ("remember").

"The light is sweet, and it is delightful for the eyes to see the sun." The covetous man does not see this, because he is in error. Wisdom 5:6 reads: "We have erred from the way of truth, and the light of justice has not shone on us. And the sun of understanding has not risen upon us." And so *he has not seen the sun*, that is, he has no knowledge of the light *nor known the distance between good and evil*, because he has not experienced it.

8. So he says: *Although he lived two thousand years,*[8] because our knowledge does not come from length of time, but from experience. Sirach 34:10 says: "The person who has no experience knows little." According to what the Philosopher says: "Experience makes art; inexperience makes chance."[9] Because of *the frustration of desire* he adds: *Do not all make haste to one place?* As if to say, their bodies fall into the ground. Sirach 41:13 reads: "All things that have been made[10] from the earth will return into the earth." And Ecclesiastes 3:19-20 above states: "All things are subject to vanity, and all things go to one place." So *the body* turns to ashes, while in *the soul* is an unfulfilled desire.

9. For this reason he continues: *All human labor is for one's mouth. The mouth* stands for the opening of desire, for whoever desires is like a person with an open mouth. So *the labor is for the mouth*, that is, to work to realize the desire. Thus, Proverbs 16:26 states: "The soul of the per-

---

[8]Bonaventure does not comment on the next clause *et non fuerit perfruitus bonis* ("and has not enjoyed good things").

[9]On p. 51 n. 3 QuarEd cite Book I, n. 1 of Aristotle's *Metaphysica*: "For experience, as Polus says correctly, makes art; inexperience makes luck." See WAE, vol. 8, 981a: "For 'experience made art', as Polus says, 'but inexperience luck'."

[10]On p. 51 n. 4 QuarEd accurately indicate that the Vulgate has *sunt* ("are") while Bonaventure reads *facta sunt* ("have been made").

son who labors, labors for himself, because his mouth has obliged him to it." Although the work is done to satisfy the desire, it is not satisfied. Therefore, he says: *But one's soul,* namely, of the rich and niggardly person, *will not be filled with good things,* as it had been said above in Ecclesiastes 5:9: "A covetous person will not be satisfied with money." Thus, Habakkuk 2:5 reads: "He has enlarged his soul like hell, and is himself like death, and will not be satisfied."[11] So what is true of covetous people with regard to money is also true with respect to knowledge. 2 Timothy 3:7 has: "Always learning and never attaining to the knowledge of the truth."[12]

QUESTIONS 18

I. It is asked what he means by the words: *God did not give him power to eat thereof.*[13]

Contra: This is free will, but God gave free will and therefore also gave the power.

I reply: The reference is to the power to enjoy, namely, by which one *is able* to enjoy. But by a just judgment of God the person is impeded by some punishment, because the person incurs excessive care, fear, and sorrow. And since *power* means unhindered power, this power is limited by a just judgment.[14] Therefore, etc.

---

[11]The Vulgate reads *adimpletur* ("is satisfied") while Bonaventure has *adimplebitur* ("will be satisfied").

[12]Hugh of St. Cher, 87g also cites 2 Timothy 3:7.

[13]Ecclesiastes 6:2.

[14]On p. 51 n. 6 QuarEd cite Book V, tractatus 2, c. 12 of Albert the Great's *Metaphysica*. See *Alberti Magni Metaphysica,* ed. Bernhardus Geyer, Opera Omnia XVI Pars I (Aschendorff: Monasterium Westfalorum, 1960), 250: "It should be known that power differs from potency in this: power is a potency, brought into existence, by an action or habit, and therefore, is an active power. Potency, however, is still undetermined and incomplete and so properly speaking material potency is called potency."

II. It is asked what he means by the words: *His soul wants nothing of all that he desires.*[15]

Contra: He said earlier in Ecclesiastes 5:9: *A covetous person will not be satisfied with money.* And Jerome says: "The avaricious lack both what they have and what they do not have."[16] Therefore, he is wrong when he says: *His soul lacks nothing.*

I reply: *To lack something* can happen in two ways: either concerning sufficiency according to *the thing* and nature or according to *an opinion.* I say, therefore, that covetous people are well able to be so rich that they lack nothing according to *things* and nature. However, they will never be so rich as not to be lacking something according to *their own way of thinking.* For there is always the desire to have more, and so there is a lack.

III. It also is asked why an aborted child is preferred. This would seem to be wrong:

1. Because an aborted child has no knowledge of anything while a covetous person does. Further, the covetous, when they sin mortally, enjoy what ought to be used.[17]

2. Moreover, how can he say that *he does not know the distance between good and evil,*[18] unless the person has

---

[15]Ecclesiastes 6:2.

[16]On p. 51 n. 7 QuarEd refer to Bonaventure's earlier reference to *Epistula* 100 n. 15 in his commentary on Ecclesiastes 5:9a (#11). See PL 22:826: "A covetous person is always in need, knows no measure; a person for whom as much is lacking as is already possessed."

[17]On p. 51 n. 8 QuarEd cite Augustine. See Question 30 in Augustine's *Eighty–Three Different Questions,* trans. David L. Mosher, FC 70 (Washington: Catholic University of America Press, 1982), 56: "Consequently every human perversion (also called vice) consists in the desire to use what ought to be enjoyed and to enjoy what ought to be used. In turn, good order (also called virtue) consists in the desire to enjoy what ought to be enjoyed and to use what ought to be used."

[18]Ecclesiastes 6:5.

greatly enjoyed possessions? Therefore, it seems that an aborted child is better than all who have not delighted in present possessions and who are not carnal. But this is heretical.

I reply: If Ecclesiastes is speaking here in the name of *a carnal person*, a response is easy. But if it is said that he is speaking *the truth*, I say that he puts an aborted child before such a niggardly rich person for the following reason. Although the aborted child has not experienced possessions, it has not experienced evil. But the niggardly rich person has experienced evil and has not tasted good things. Therefore, the aborted child is preferable, and this is how Ecclesiastes understands the statement.[19]

1. To the objection about the reason why he has not enjoyed possessions, I say that *to enjoy* means in one sense *a love* of something *with contentment* in its possession. In another sense it means *contentment* and *love*. Therefore, I say that the person who loves God possesses God, as Augustine says in his Book of Eighty-Three Questions.[20] And

---

[19]On the literary styles of speech in Ecclesiastes see the response to question two of *Quaestio* #15, which occurs after Bonaventure's commentary on Ecclesiastes 5:17-19 above.

[20]On p. 52 n. 2 QuarEd provide a lengthy citation from Question 35. Bonaventure does not quote Augustine verbatim, for Augustine nowhere says exactly: *Qui diligit Deum habet* ("The person who loves God possesses God"). For the best parallel see Question 35 of *Sancti Avrelii Avgvstini De diversis qvaestionibus octoginta tribvs; De octo dvlcitii qvaestionibvs*, ed. Almut Mutzenbecher, CCSL xliva (Turnhout: Brepols, 1975), 51: *Quamquam bonum quod non amatur nemo potest perfecte habere uel nosse. Quis enim potest nosse, quantum si bonum quo non fruitur? Non autem fruitur, si non amat; nec habet igitur quod amandum est qui non amat, etiamsi amare possit qui non habet.* See FC 70 whose translation on p. 65 has been adjusted: "However, as far as a good which is not loved, no one can possess it or know it perfectly. For who can know to what extent something is good when he does not enjoy it? But he does not enjoy it if he does not love it, nor therefore does he who does not love it possess what is to be loved, even if he who does not possess it could love it."

so whoever loves God delights in God. But money and earthly possessions bring sadness when they are loved, but not owned. There can be enjoyment of such things, that is, the greatest *love*, and a slight *delight* with great *sadness*. So it does not follow that, although such a covetous person might sin, he rests in any delight, but he does rest in love, because he loves for his own purposes.

2. To the objection that he does not know the distance, it has to be said that the person who always does good knows with a *simple* knowledge what is good and evil. It is similar with the person who always does evil. However, this is not an *experiential* knowledge, unless the person does both good and evil. And since the covetous person always does evil, never good, therefore, etc. – To the objection about a spiritual man, I say, that he is not without spiritual delight, and so *sees the sun and knows the distance*. But the niggardly, covetous person, since he is a sinner, does not have spiritual delight. Since he is *niggardly*, he does not have carnal delight. And so does not know the distance between good and evil.

ECCLESIASTES 6:8-7:23   THE REMEDY AGAINST THE VANITY OF IMPRUDENCE

10. *What has the wise person*, etc. Ecclesiastes has discussed the remedy against the vanity of malice and against the vanity of avarice. Here in a third point he provides the remedy against the vanity of *imprudence*. Now the best remedy against this vanity is to grow in wisdom. But since no one is able to obtain wisdom except through the correct way of learning, this section has two parts. In the first he gives *the method*, and in the second he explains *the sources of wisdom* where 7:2 reads: *A good name is better*, etc.

ECCLESIASTES 6:8-7:1   THE METHOD FOR ACQUIRING WISDOM

11. Now *the method* for engaging in thinking and learning for the person who wants to be wise is handed down in this wise. First, *that he learn useful matters.* Second, *that he leave aside what is hidden.* Third, *that he not search out the sublime.*

ECCLESIASTES 6:8-11   LEARNING USEFUL MATTERS AND LEAVING ASIDE WHAT IS HIDDEN

12. (Verse 8). First, he teaches *to seek what is useful* and to ponder it, that is, how a person can reach the life of glory. So he asks: *What more has the wise person than the fool, and what the poor person?* He does well to join these two, namely, *the poor* and *the wise.* For *the poor person* represents contempt for present goods. Thus, Matthew 5:3 reads: "Blessed are the poor in spirit, for theirs is the kingdom of the heavens."[21] *The wise person,* through taste[22] of what is eternal and right judgment. About these Proverbs 3:35 says: "The wise will possess glory; the exaltation of the fools is disgrace." Indeed, an earthly person is called *a fool,* because the fool despises what is eternal and longs for what is earthly. Job 5:3 states: "I have seen a fool with a strong root, and I cursed his beauty immediately."[23] *What more has a wise and poor person than a fool* in this life? Supply: little. *But to go there where there is life,* namely, to eternal life, for which a person should aspire and not aspiring to earthly things that cannot be retained. For this

---

[21]Hugh of St. Cher, p. 87v, a also cites Matthew 5:3.

[22]Bonaventure plays with the fact that both *sapientia* ("wisdom") and *sapor* ("taste") have the same root, that is, *sap-*.

[2] See the NAB of Job 5:3: "I have seen a fool spreading his roots, but his household suddenly decayed."

reason we have little in this mortal life, because as Ecclesiastes 2:16 above says: "The learned die in equal manner[24] as the unlearned." But in eternal life a person has much more, because its *existence* is delightful, abundant, secure. A person will obtain all in open vision and in enjoyment of the highest good. About this life we read in John 17:3: "Now this is eternal life, that they may know you, the only true God," etc. The wise journey to this life, since they fix their eyes on it, as was said earlier in Ecclesiastes 2:14: "The eyes of a wise person are in his head." And so the wise follow Christ, the light, who as it is said in John 14:6 is "the way, the truth, and the life." But the foolish do not journey forth. Thus, Ecclesiastes 10:15 below reads: "The labor of fools will afflict those who do not know how to journey to the city."

13. (Verse 9). It is not possible to reach this life correctly without knowledge. Therefore, he continues: *It is better to see what you may desire*, that is, to know the life you desire, *than to desire what you do not know*, that is, to want to reach there in ignorance. So it is necessary to fix one's attention on this. Proverbs 4:25 states: "Let your eyes look straight ahead, and let your eyelids go before your steps." It is indeed good to know this, but to desire what a person does not know is foolishness. Wherefore, he adds: *But this also is vanity and presumption of spirit*, namely, to desire what is not known, as when James and John desired and begged to sit at the right hand and asked for this presumptuously. Therefore, he said to them in Matthew 20:22: "You do not know what you are asking for."[25]

---

[24]On p. 52 n. 8 QuarEd accurately intimate that the Vulgate has *similiter* ("in like manner") while Bonaventure reads *pariter* ("in equal manner").

[25]As Matthew 20:20-21 indicate, it is the mother of James and John who does the initial asking about her sons sitting on Jesus' right and left hand.

14. The verse can also be interpreted as an approval of knowing what is useful. The meaning then is that it is better to know what is desirable and useful than to desire *to know things hidden*, namely, things forbidden for us to know, because this is a presumption of spirit, that is, to want to know what God in God's providence has decided.

15. (Verses 10-11). It is forbidden for us to examine what is hidden, and so he says: *The person who will be*, etc. Here he calls us back from *searching out what is hidden* such as divine decisions. For this reason he states: *The person who will be, his name is already called*, from the point of view of eternal election. Romans 4:17 reads: "Who calls those things that are not as those that are." *And it is known that he is a human being* from the point of view of a brief duration of time. Genesis 3:19 says: "Dust you are, and into dust you will return." *And he cannot contend in judgment with him who is stronger than himself*, in matters of justice. For no human being is so just that they can justify themselves at God's judgment. Job 9:2-3 states: "Indeed I know it is so, and that a human being cannot be justified compared with[26] God. If he will contend with God, he cannot answer God one for a thousand." So Job said: "What am I then that I should answer him."[27] And so Job adds, because God is *stronger* and says: "If strength be demanded, God is most strong. If equity of judgment, no

---

[26]On p. 53 n. 3 QuarEd accurately mention that the Vulgate reads *compositus* ("arranged against") while Bonaventure has *comparatus* ("compared with"). Hugh of St. Cher, 87v, o also cites Job 9-2 and reads *comparatus* ("compared with").

[27]Job 9:14.

human being dare bear witness for me."[28] We are told not to examine this hidden providence, because in our words little truth is found, especially when we want to expound things hidden from us.

16. So he adds: *There are many words*, that is, few things are known. Ecclesiastes 10:14 below states: "A fool multiplies words." *There are many words that have much vanity in disputing*, but little truth. Ecclesiastes 3:11 above reads: "He has made all things good in their time and has delivered the world to their disputation, so that a human being may not discover the work which God has made from the beginning to the end." Consequently, those who want to examine these things fade away, according to what the Apostle says in 1 Corinthians 3:20: "God[29] knows the thoughts of the wise that they are vain."

---

[28]Job 9:19. On p. 53 n. 3 QuarEd quote Book IX, chapter 2 n. 2 of Gregory the Great's *Moralia in Iob*. See *S. Gregorii Magni Moralia in Iob, Libri I-X*, ed. M. Adriaen, CCSL cxliii (Turnhout: Brepols, 1979), 456: "A person subordinate to God receives justice, but the person arranged against God loses it, for the person who compares himself to the author of good things, deprives himself of the good he had received. For the person who arrogates to herself the goods she has received is contending against God with God's very gifts."

[29]On p. 53 n. 4 QuarEd rightly notice that the Vulgate reads *Dominus* ("The Lord") while Bonaventure has *Deus* ("God").

CHAPTER 7

DO NOT SEARCH OUT THE
SUBLIME

1. (Verse 1). *Why do people need?* Third, he calls his readers away from inquiring and *searching out the sublime* when they have enough to do to know their own or common evils. So he says: *Why do people need to seek things that are above them?* As if to say, there is no need. We read in Sirach 3:22: "Seek not the things that are too high for you."[1] And Romans 11:20 states: "Be not high-minded, but fear." He adds the reason why a person should not seek what is higher: *Whereas they do not know what is profitable for them in their lives*, that is, what is useful. Wisdom 9:16 says: "Hardly do we guess aright at things that are upon the earth, and with labor do we find the things that are before us. But who will search out the things that are in heaven?" We are ignorant of what may be useful for us in this brief life. Wherefore, he adds: *in all the days of their pilgrimage*. Genesis 47:9 has: "The days of the pilgrimage of my life . . . are few and evil." 2 Corinthians 5:6 reads: "While we are in this body,[2] we are pilgrims away

---

[1]Hugh of St. Cher, 88a cites all of Sirach 3:22.

[2]The Vulgate reads *dum* ("while") while Bonaventure has *quamdiu* ("while"). Also the Vulgate does not read *in hoc corpore* ("in this body"), but simply *in corpore* ("in the body"). Hugh of St. Cher, 88d also quotes 2 Corinthians 5:6 and reads *dum* ("while") and *in hoc corpore* ("in this body").

from the Lord." – *And the time that passes like a shadow*. 1
Chronicles 29:15 states: "We are on pilgrimage before you
and strangers, as were all our fathers. Our days upon earth
are like a shadow, and there is no remaining." And so he is
not able to search out or learn from another. Therefore, he
adds: *Or who can tell them what will be after them under
the sun?* For human beings do not know the future, unless
the Lord reveals it by grace. Therefore, human beings
should not investigate the future. Isaiah 48:7-8 reads: ". . .
before the day when you heard them not, lest you should
say: Behold, I knew them. You have neither heard nor
known. Nor was your ear opened of old."[3] Ecclesiastes 8:7
below says: "Since he is ignorant of things past, and things
to come he cannot know by any messenger." For only god
knows and reveals the future.

QUESTIONS 19

I. What does he mean by the words: *It is better to see what
you may desire than to desire what you do not know.*[4] So he
does not allow that a person can desire what he doesn't
know.

Contra: 1. Augustine says that "we are able to love what is
not seen, but in no way can we love what is not known."[5]
Therefore, against this objection: For something to be loved
and desired, it must be known.

---

[3]Isaiah 48:7 commences in this way: "They are created now, and not
of old. . . ."

[4]Ecclesiastes 6:9.

[5]On p. 54 n. 1 QuarEd refer to Book VIII, chapter 4 n. 6ff. and Book X,
chapter 1 n. 1ff. of Augustine's *De Trinitate* and say that this opinion is
treated extensively in these passages. It seems to me that nowhere
does Augustine actually say what Bonaventure attributes to him. See,
for example, Book X, chapter 1 n. 1 in *Sancti Avrelii Avgvstini De
Trinitate Libri XV Libri I-XII*, ed. W. J. Mountain and Fr. Glorie, CCSL
l (Turnhout: Brepols, 1968): *Ac primum quia rem prorsus ignotam amare
omnino nullus potest* ("And first since no one can love a thing at all
that is entirely unknown").

2. Moreover, affection follows knowledge. Therefore, when knowledge does not come first, there can be no affection. But knowledge does not reach what is not known, and therefore, neither does affection.

I reply: There are two types of knowledge, namely, *sure* knowledge and knowledge of *opinion*. There is also a double ignorance. One kind is the lack of any *certitude* while the other is a lack of any *opinion*. I say, therefore, that for something to be desired, a sure knowledge is not necessary, for desire can come from an opinion. But some knowledge must be the basis for the opinion. Ecclesiastes is speaking here of ignorance from a lack of certainty.[6]

II. What does he mean by the words: *Why do people need to seek things that are above them?*[7] From this it would seem that a person is not to examine or strive to know what is above. – This is proved by Sirach 3:22: *See not the things that are too high for you.* Romans 11:20 says the very same thing: *Be not high-minded, but fear.*

Contra: 1. Human beings stand between visible creatures and God. But Augustine says that a human mind is darkened when the eye concentrates on what is of the earth and lowly, but it is enlightened when it turns to eternal goods.[8] Therefore, one should always seek what is eternal. But eternal goods are higher. Therefore, etc.

---

[6] See Book VIII chapter 4 n.6 of Augustine's *De Trinitate* in CCSL 1, 274-275 and *Saint Augustine The Trinity*, trans. Stephen McKenna, FC 45 (Washington: Catholic University of America Press, 1963), 250-251: "But who loves that which he does not know? For something can be known and not loved; but what I am asking is, whether something can be loved that is not known? If that is impossible, then no one loves God, before he knows Him. And what does it mean to love God, except to see Him and to perceive him steadfastly with our mind?"

[7] Ecclesiastes 7:1.

[8] On p. 54 n. 5 QuarEd cite Sermon 1 n. 18 of Augustine's *Enarratio in Psalmum 58*. See CCSL xxxix, 742. See *Exposition of the Psalms 51-72*, trans. Maria Boulding, Works of St. Augustine III/17, (Hyde Park,

2. Moreover, the soul never attains a total perfection other than in things higher than itself.[9] But whatever can grow in perfection should tend towards and seek the thing in which it is perfected. Therefore, it should seek what is above itself. – *If you say* that the soul does not know, that it ought not to seek nor study things substantially higher than itself, that it should not reflect on what exceeds the limits of its understanding, then one can object. For all matters of faith are beyond our understanding. And so according to this our mind should not concern itself with believing matters of faith.

3. Also, most blameworthy are those who want to discuss articles of faith. Therefore, all who want to discuss the faith are blameworthy.

I reply: What he means by *things that are above them* and by *to seek* needs attention. He calls *things that are above them* those things that exceed our understanding from the point of view that they exceed. *To seek* means for him to search and discuss, as if he were to say that it is stupid to study things that our study cannot reach and for which our ability is inadequate. For there are some things that manifest God to us, and these are not above us. So he is not discouraging us from thinking about God.

NY: New City Press, 2001), 163-164: "Consider how it is with the human soul, brothers and sisters. It has no light of its own, no power of its own. The only beauty the soul has consists of power and wisdom, but it is not wise of itself, not strong of itself, nor is it the source of its own light, or its own power. There is another source and wellspring of strength, there is a root of wisdom; there is a country of immutable truth, if I may so express it. When the soul departs from that country it is darkened, but it is illuminated as it approaches. *Draw near to him and receive his light* Ps 33:6 (34:5), for by moving away you are darkened."

[9]On p. 54 n. 6 QuarEd cite Book I, chapter 3 n. 5 of Augustine's *De Moribus Ecclesiae catholicae*. See PL 32:1312: *Quisquis enim quod se ipso est deterius sequitur, fit et ipse deterior* ("For whoever follows what is lower than himself, also becomes lower himself").

2-3. Regarding the objection about faith, it has to be said that it does not dissuade us from *believing*, but from *seeking*. Moreover, although matters of faith are beyond our mind *by itself*, they are not above a mind *enlightened* by grace. Hence, to seek out and to study to that point to which the light of faith reaches is not to reach out to things above us. Every prudent discussion of the articles of faith is done in this way. But if the discussion goes beyond this, it is a blameworthy excess unless it be from God.[10]

III. What does he mean by: *Who can tell them what will be after them under the sun?*[11]

Contra: In our soul there is an ability *to become everything* and *to do everything*.[12] But the mind, seen from its capacity to receive, allows the soul to think of all that is present, all that is past, and all that is future. Therefore, if the mind, seen from its capacity to act, can realize its potential, persons are able, through their own power, to know the future.

I reply: If the intellect as active can form or abstract in the intellect as possible, it can only do so if certitude about the thing comes from outside the mind and internally from the senses. For "without an object, knowledge stops."[13] And

---

[10]On p. 54 n. 7QuarEd refer to Book I, Prooemii q. 2. See Opera Omnia 1:9-11.

[11]Ecclesiastes 7:1.

[12]On p. 54 n. 8 QuarEd cite Book III, n. 5 of Aristotle's *De anima*. See WAE, vol. 3, 430a: "And in fact mind, as we have described it, is what it is by becoming all things, while there is another which is what it is by virtue of making all things: this is a sort of positive state like light; for in a sense light makes potential colours into actual colours."

[13]On p. 54 n. 9 QuarEd cite chapter 7 of Aristotle's *Categoriae*. See WAE, vol. 1, 7b: "Again, while the object of knowledge, if it ceases to exist, cancels at the same time the knowledge which was its correlative, the converse of this is not true. It is true that if the object of knowledge does not exist there can be no knowledge: for there will no longer be anything to know."

"without the senses, one source of knowledge that is dependent on that sense will stop."[14] Therefore, since future things that may happen do not form a likeness of themselves in the senses, neither *by themselves* nor by an *antecedent determined cause* and since they do not have in themselves the permanence needed for knowledge, our intellect, dependent as it is on objects, cannot of itself come to know them, unless through him whose knowledge does not depend on objects.[15]

ECCLESIASTES 7:2-23   SOURCES OF WISDOM THAT PROVIDE A REMEDY AGAINST THE VANITY OF FOOLISHNESS

2. *A good name is better.* In his earlier treatment Ecclesiastes has given the method of learning. Now in a second place he gives *teachings about wisdom*, in which is found a remedy against the vanity of foolishness. Since, as it is said in Wisdom 8:7, "wisdom teaches temperance, prudence, justice, and strength"[16] or fortitude, he divides this section into four parts. In the first he states instructions on *temperance*. In the second on *steadfastness* where verse 8 reads: *Oppression*, etc. In the third on *prudence* where verse 11 states: *Do not say: What do you think is the cause*, etc. In the fourth on *justice* where verse 17 says: *Do not be overly just*, etc.

---

[14]On p. 54 n. 9 QuarEd cite Book I n. 18 of Aristotle's *Analytica posteriora*. See WAE, vol. 1, 81a: "It is also clear that the loss of any one of the senses entails the loss of a corresponding portion of knowledge, and that, since we learn either by induction or by demonstration, this knowledge cannot be acquired."

[15]On p. 55 n. 1 QuarEd refer to Book I, d. 19. p. 1. dub. 8 and Book II, d. 7. p. II. a. 1. q. 3 of Bonaventure's *Commentary on the Sentences*. See Opera Omnia 1:352 and 2:194 respectively.

[16]On p. 55 n. 2 QuarEd correctly mention that the Vulgate reads *sobrietatem enim et sapientiam docet et iustitiam et virtutem* ("For she teaches sobriety and wisdom and justice and strength").

ECCLESIASTES 7:2-7   **FIVE INSTRUCTIONS ON**
                                  TEMPERANCE

3. He gives five instructions about *temperance*. First, he teaches to prefer what is *good* to what is pleasant. Second, to prefer *the future life* to the present. Third, *trouble* to pleasure. Fourth, *sadness* to enjoyment. Fifth, *severity* to softness or adulation.

4. (Verse 2). So he sets forth the instruction in which he teaches to prefer what is *good*, for example, a good name, to what is *soothing* such as an ointment. So he says: *A good name is better*, that is, a good reputation based on good actions. About this Sirach 41:15 says: "Take care of a good name, for this will continue with you more than a thousand precious and great treasures."[17] *Than precious ointments* which have a strong fragrance, according to what is said in John 12:3: "Mary took a pound of ointment of right spikenard, of great price . . . and the house was filled with the fragrance of the ointment." And although ointments have a fragrance, a good name has a stronger one and therefore better. 2 Corinthians 2:14-15 reads: "We are the good fragrance of Christ unto God in every place,"[18] namely, with regard to our good reputation.

5. *And the day of death.* The second teaching is to prefer *the future life to the present one*, and so to prefer entrance into the other life to entrance into this life. So he contin-

---

[17]Hugh of St. Cher, 88g also cites Sirach 41:15.

[18]On p. 55 n. 3 QuarEd rightly indicate that Bonaventure has adapted this quotation. 2 Corinthians 2:14-15 reads: "But thanks be to God who always leads us in triumph in Christ Jesus, manifesting through us the fragrance of his knowledge in every place. For we are the fragrance of Christ for God. . . ." Thus, Bonaventure has taken "in every place" from the end of verse 14 and placed it at the end of verse 15a. Hugh of St. Cher, 88g cites 2 Corinthians 2:14b-15a and does not adapt the citation as Bonaventure does.

ues: *And the day of death.* Supply: is better than *the day of one's birth,* because *we die so as to rest.* Revelation 14:13 states: "Blessed are the dead who die in the Lord, the Spirit says now . . . that they may rest from their labors." But here a person *is born to labor.* Job 5:7 says: "Human beings are born to labor, and birds to fly." Hence, to die is better. So Sirach 30:17: "Better is death than a bitter life, and everlasting rest than continual distress."

6. (Verse 3). *It is better to go to the house of mourning,* etc. The third instruction concerns the preference of *affliction to pleasure,* for example, to mourn rather than to feast. For this reason he says: *It is better to go to the house of mourning,* where sins are mourned. For Matthew 5:5 reads: "Blessed are they who mourn, for they shall be comforted." *Than to the house of feasting,* where one finds pleasures. Proverbs 23:20 says: "Be not in the feast of great drinkers," etc. The reason is that in feasting one is forgetful of oneself, while in a house of mourning one is mindful of one's judgment. And so he adds: *For in that,* that is, in a house of mourning, *we are put in mind of the end of all.* We read in Sirach 38:23: "Remember my judgment, for this also will be so. Today is for me, and tomorrow will be for you."[19] *And the living thinks of what is to come.* And this is most useful, for Sirach 8:40 counsels: "Remember your last end, and you will never sin" for, as Jerome says, "people, who are always pondering that they will die, easily despise all goods."[20]

---

[19]On p. 55 n. 6 QuarEd rightly notice that the Vulgate reads *mihi heri et tibi hodie* ("yesterday for me and today for you") whereas Bonaventure has *mihi est hodie, tibi erit cras* ("today is for me; tomorrow will be for you"). Hugh of St. Cher, 88v, g also cites Sirach 38:23. His text agrees with the Vulgate's.

[20]On p. 55 n. 6 QuarEd cite Jerome's *Epistula* 140 to Cyprianum n. 16. See PL 22:1177: "For whoever is mindful every day that she will die, despises present things and hastens to the future."

7. (Verses 4-5). He now deals with his fourth instruction: to prefer *sorrow to joy*, because sorrow corrects while joy deceives. And so he says: *Anger is better than laughter.* *Anger*, namely, by which a person gets angry over the sins of others. Hebrews 12:6 states: "He scourges every son whom he receives." And Revelation 3:19 reads: "I rebuke and chastise those whom I love." This anger is better than false laughter. Sirach 30:9 has: "Play with your son, and he will make you sorrowful," etc.[21] And therefore, *anger is better*. He adds the reason: *Because by the sadness of the countenance the mind of the offender is corrected.* Proverbs 25:23 reads: "The north wind drives away rain as a sad countenance drives away a backbiting tongue."

8. And he confirms this instruction with the judgment of the wise. So he says: *The heart of the wise is where there is mourning.* Contrariwise, *the*[22] *heart of fools is where there is mirth.* The wise look for sadness in the present life; the fools look for joy. John 16:20 states: "You will lament and weep, but the world will rejoice." That one group acts wisely and the others foolishly is clear from the consequences. For it is said to the sad in Luke 6:21: "Blessed are you who weep now, because you will laugh." But the contrasting woe is addressed to those who are rejoicing in Luke 6:25: "Woe to you who are laughing now, because you will weep."

9. (Verses 6-7). *It is better to be rebuked by a wise person.* He speaks now of the fifth teaching: prefer *severity to softness*, for example, sharp correction to flattery. So he says: *It is better to be rebuked by a wise person than to be deceived by the flattery of fools.* We read in Proverbs 27:5:

---

[21]NAB of Sirach 30:9 reads: "Pamper your child, and he will be a terror for you. Indulge him, and he will bring you grief." Hugh of St. Cher, 88v, h cites Sirach 30:9 in its entirety.

[22]The Vulgate reads *et cor* ("and the heart").

"Open rebuke is better than hidden love," because correction guides, but flattery deceives. Proverbs 16:29 states: "An unjust man allures his friend and leads him into a way that is not good." And Isaiah 3:12 says: "O my people, those who call you blessed are the same ones who deceive you," etc.

10. He illustrates the reason by a parallel. Flattery does not last long for the fool and makes a lot of noise, like thorns burning under a pot. So he says: *For as the crackling of thorns burning under a pot*, making much noise, *so is the laughter of the fool*. The literal meaning is that the fool is laughing loudly. Sirach 21:23 reads: "A fool lifts up his voice in laughter, but a wise man will scarce laugh low to himself." Or: loud laughter, when the flattery is a clamoring. Proverbs 27:14 states: "The person who blesses his neighbor with a loud voice at early morning will be like the person who curses." *Now this also is vanity*, namely, such flattery. We read in Psalm 61:10: "Vain are the children of men and women, the sons of men and women are liars."

Questions 20

I. What does he mean by: *The day of death is better than the day of birth?*[23]

Contra: 1. Death is a privation while life is a habit. But a habit always has more existence and goodness than a privation.[24] Therefore, life is better than death. Therefore, the day of birth is better than death.

---

[23]See Ecclesiastes 7:2.

[24]On p. 56 n. 3 QuarEd cite Book I, n. 8 of Aristotle's *Physica*: privation "is by its very nature non-being." See WAE, vol. 2, 192b: "Privation in its own nature is not-being." The editors also refer to Book IV, n. 22 of Aristotle's *Metaphysica*. See WAE, vol. 8, 1022b: "(2) 'Having' or 'habit' means a disposition according to which that which is disposed is either

2. Moreover, there is a rule that "if the corruption of some-thing is good, then its generation is bad."[25] But death is a corruption of life. The person whose death is good has a bad life. But only the life of a sinner is bad. Wherefore, only the death of a sinner is better than life. But this is false, because a sinner on dying goes to hell.

I reply: Something is preferred at one time *by reason of itself*, and at another *by reason of something consequent to it*. When something has more good in itself, it is to be preferred *by reason of itself*, for example, a human being is better than a horse. On the other hand, a thing is to be preferred by *reason of something consequent to it*, for ex-ample, death is preferred to life, for its dissolution, namely, death has as its consequence rest *and existence with Christ.*[26] Ecclesiastes is speaking of such a death, because during life a person is in danger, work, and distress. After death a just person is in joy, security, and tranquility.

The answer to the first objection is that death is not preferred by *reason of itself*.

The second objection can be resolved in the same way. Death is called bad from two points of view: either be-cause it takes away a great good, that is, a good life, a life

---

well or ill disposed, and either in itself or with reference to something else; e.g. health is a 'habit'; for it is such a disposition. – (3) We speak of 'habit' if there is a portion of such a disposition; and so even the excellence of the parts is a 'habit' of the whole thing." In footnote 1 the translator writes: "The word *hexis* does duty for 'having', 'habit', and 'permanent state'."

[25]On p. 56 n. 4 QuarEd quote Book II, n. 9 of Aristotle's *Topica*. See WAE, vol. 1, 114b: "For those things whose modes of generation rank among good things, are themselves also good; and if they themselves be good, so also are their modes of generation. If on the other hand their modes of generation be evil, then they themselves are evil."

[26]On p. 56 n. 5 QuarEd rightly allude to Philippians 1:23: "Indeed, I am hard pressed from both sides – desiring to depart and to be with Christ, a lot by far the better."

that is good, true, and useful or because it leads to a bad end. In the first way, the death of the just is bad, that is, destructive. But in the second way it is very good. And from this point of view it is to be preferred.

II. It is also asked what does he mean by: *Anger is better than laughter*.[27]

Contra: 1. Matthew 5:22 reads: *Whoever is angry with his brother will be in danger of the judgment.* But whoever laughs is not liable to any punishment. Therefore, it is worse to be angry than to laugh.

2. Furthermore, to laugh can be without sin. But to be angry, when a disturbance of the mind is involved, is hardly without venial sin. And it is never without some punishment.[28] Hence it is much worse to be angry than to laugh.

I reply: There are *anger over sin* and *anger of nature*. The first comes from virtue and is good. The second comes from sin and is bad.[29] The case is similar with *laughing at good* and *laughing at sin*. The first is good while the second is bad. So Ecclesiastes is speaking of anger and laughter that is bad.

Similarly, another rule can be given about good: laughter is better than anger. – And it has to be said that in the present life there is more bad than good. So there are more things that occasion sadness than occasion rejoicing, and so he prefers anger to laughter.

---

[27]Ecclesiastes 7:4.

[28]On p. 56 n. 7 QuarEd helpfully point to James 1:20: "For wrath of human beings does not work the justice of God."

[29]On p. 56 n. 8 QuarEd cite Book I, chapter 18 n. 4 of Augustine's *Retractiones*. See *Saint Augustine, The Retractations*. Translated by Mary Inez Bogan. (FC 60; Washington: Catholic University of America Press, 1968) 81: ". . . one who is angry at the sin of his brother is not angry with his brother. He, then, who is angry with his brother, but not because of his sin, is angry without cause."

ECCLESIASTES 7:8-10   INSTRUCTIONS ON CONSTANCY

11. *Oppression troubles the wise person.* He has given above his instructions about temperance. In this second part he presents lessons about *acquiring constancy.* And since constancy is lost through oppression and anger and preserved by patience and perseverance, he divides the material into four parts. In the first part he shows that *oppression is to be avoided.* In the second that *perseverance is to be loved.* In the third that *patience is to be kept.* In the fourth that *anger is to be shunned.*

12. (Verse 8). In the first part he shows that *oppression is to be avoided,* because when a person is disturbed, that person becomes inconstant. So he says: *Oppression troubles the wise person.* Calumny, a special form of oppression, is a litigious criminal accusation, and therefore is to be avoided.[30] Isaiah 54:14 reads: "Depart far from oppression, for you will have no fear." *And it will destroy the strength of his heart,* that is, the fortitude of love. Matthew 24:12 states: "Since iniquity has abounded, the charity of many will grow cold."

13. (Verse 9). *Better is the end,* etc. Here he treats of the second instruction, in which *perseverance is preferred* to justice merely begun. So he says: *Better is the end of a speech than the beginning.* It is better to persevere in good than only begin. Matthew 10:22 reads: "The person who perseveres to the end is the one who will be saved." Thus, Bernard comments: "Perseverance is the culmination of

---

[30]On p. 57 n. 1 QuarEd quote q. 68 of Augustine's *Quaestiones in Leviticum.* See PL 34:707: "Calumny is nothing other than when a neighbor is hurt by the accusation of a false crime." The editors also quote Justinian. See Book XLVIII, section 16, n. 1 of *The Digest of Justinian,* Vol. 2, ed. Alan Watson, (Philadelphia: University of Pennsylvania Press, 1998): "Calumny is the bringing of false charges."

all the virtues."[31] *Better is the patient*, etc. Here he gives the third lesson in which *patience is commended*, because without it there can be no constancy. So he continues: *Better is the patient person than the presumptuous*. The comparison is misapplied, for patience is good while presumption is wrong. Proverbs 16:32 states: "The patient man is better than the valiant," etc.

14. (Verse 10). *Do not get angry quickly*. He gives now the fourth instruction, in which he teaches that *anger is to be shunned*. So he says: *Do not get angry quickly*. We read in James 1:19: "But let every person be swift to hear, but slow to speak, and slow to anger."[32] He supplies the reason: *For anger rests in the bosom of a fool*. Job 5:2 observes: "Anger indeed kills the foolish man, and envy slays the little one." Well does the text say *rests*, because anger lingers, and the wise person ought not to stay angry day by day. Ephesians 4:26 reads: "Let not the sun go down upon your anger." Do not be like the fool, of whom it is said in Proverbs 27:3: "The sand is heavy" *in the bosom of a fool*.

QUESTIONS 21

I. There is doubt about the words: *Oppression troubles the wise person*.[33]

Contra: Proverbs 12:21 states: *Whatever shall befall the just person, it will not make him sad*. Therefore, if the wise are just, they will not be saddened by oppression or calumny.

---

[31]On p. 57 n. 2 QuarEd cite Bernard's *Epistola* 129 n. 2. See SBOp 7.323: "Strength of strengths, it (perseverance) is the culmination of the virtues. . . . Finally, it is not the person who begins, but the one *who perseveres to the end who will be saved*."

[32]Hugh of St. Cher, 89v, a also cites James 1:19.

[33]Ecclesiastes 7:8.

This is answered in one way, that is, the sadness of *impatience* does not sadden a just person, but the sadness of *compassion* does sadden a just person. Thus, the Apostle says in 2 Corinthians 12:29: *Who is scandalized, and I am not on fire?*[34] As if to say: no one. – But the second half of the verse cancels this exposition by adding: *And will destroy the strength of his heart.* So the solution is that the text in Ecclesiastes refers, as stated in the Glossa, to a wise person who is just and *perfect*.[35] To him the text of Proverbs 12:21 applies. And to an *imperfect* person, about whom the present text is speaking.

II. Also, what does he mean by: *Do not get angry quickly?*[36]

Contra: Psalm 4:5 reads: *Be angry and do not sin.*

I reply: It has to be said that anger has many forms.[37]

ECCLESIASTES 7:11-16   INSTRUCTIONS ON PRUDENCE

15. *Do not say what do you think is the cause*, etc. After giving instructions about temperance and steadfastness, he now provides lessons on *prudence*. Since it is prudence's

---

[34]On p. 57 n. 6 QuarEd refer to Book I, d. 48, a. 2, q. 2 and dubium 4 of Bonaventure's *Sentence Commentary*. See Opera Omnia 1:857 and 861 respectively.

[35]On p. 57 n. 7 QuarEd cite the *Glossa Ordinaria* on Ecclesiastes 7:6, which is taken from Jerome's observations on 7:8. See PL 113:1123: "A wise, perfect person has no need of proof, is not troubled by oppression. Therefore, it is to be understood of such a wise and perfect person that he will sometimes be troubled by the iniquity of a judgment, when God does not immediately punish."

[36]Ecclesiastes 7:10.

[37]On p. 57 n. 9 QuarEd offer five references, of which two are selected here. MSS Vat. observes: "Note that there is an anger that is *permitted*, and this is a venial fault. *Be angry and sin not* (Psalm 4:5). And the condition just stated is essential. There is anger that is *forbidden*, and this is a mortal fault: *Anger has no mercy, nor fury when it break forth* (Proverbs 27:4). There is a anger that is *commanded*, and this is an anger of justice and zeal. Of this anger Ecclesiastes has said earlier:

task to discern where error occurs,[38] he gives four instructions about discretion. The first is discernment of what is *useful*. The second is discernment of *divine works*. The third is the discernment of *the times*. The fourth is discernment of *the merits* of men and women.

16. (Verses 11-13). So his first instruction deals with *the discernment of what is useful*. For at different times what is useful varies from diverse causes. So he says: *Do not say what do you think is the cause that former times*, that is, of the ancients, *were better?* That is, because there was scarcity of things during them. *Than they are now*, that is, when there is now an abundance of things. Since this question stems from a lack of thought, he continues: *For this manner of question is foolish*. And the reason is that the person does not consider the usefulness of wealth. Therefore, he instructs the person to discern when he states: *Wisdom with riches is more useful*. Proverbs 13:8 reads: "The ransom of man's life are his riches."[39] *And brings more*

Anger is better than laughter (Ecclesiastes 7:4), provided that the anger is controlled and does not go to excess." See Book IV, n. 5 of Aristotle's *Ethica nicomachea* and WAE, vol. 9, 1125b: "The man who is angry at the right things and with the right people, and, further, as he ought, when he ought, and as long as he ought, is praised. This will be the good-tempered man, then, since good temper is praised. For the good-tempered man tends to be unperturbed and not to be led by passion, but to be angry in the manner, at the things, and for the length of time, that the rule dictates; but he is thought to err rather in the direction of deficiency; for the good-tempered man is not revengeful, but rather tends to make allowances."

[38]On p. 57 n. 10 QuarEd refer to Book VI, n. 5 and 8ff. of Aristotle's *Ethica nicomachia*. See WAE, vol. 9, 1140b: "Practical wisdom, then, must be a reasoned and true state of capacity to act with regard to human goods. But further, while there is such a thing as excellence in art, there is no such thing as excellence in practical wisdom; and in art he who errs willingly is preferable, but in practical wisdom, as in the virtues, he is the reserve. Plainly, then, practical wisdom is a virtue and not an art."

[39]Hugh of St. Cher, 90a also quotes Proverbs 13:8.

advantage to those who see the sun, that is, to those who have a right intention. For we read in Sirach 13:30: "riches are good to the person who has no sin on his conscience, and poverty is very wicked in the mouth of the ungodly."

17. He shows that money is useful from its effect: *For as wisdom is a defense*, namely, from sin. Proverbs 2:10-11 states: "If wisdom shall enter into your heart and knowledge please your soul, counsel shall keep you and prudence shall preserve you." *So money is a defense*, provided it is spent well. Sirach 29:16 says: "The alms of a man are like a purse with him and will preserve the grace of a human being as the apple of his eye."[40] And although both are useful, wisdom is more useful. So he adds: *But learning and wisdom excel in this, that they give life to the person who possesses them*. Thus, Proverbs 4:10 reads: "Hear, O my son, and receive my words that years of life may be multiplied to you." And Proverbs 3:18 has: "Wisdom is a tree of life to those who lay hold of her." But money without wisdom brings death. James 5:1 states: "Come now, you rich, weep and howl over your miseries." And so wisdom is to be preferred to money. Proverbs 8:10 says: "Receive wisdom[41] and not money, choose knowledge rather than gold."

18. (Verse 14). *Consider the works of God*, etc. This is the second instruction, in which he teaches a *discerning consideration of divine works* or judgments, because no one brings back the person whom God despises by a judgment of rejection. So he says: *Consider the works of God*, that is,

---

[40]On p. 58 n. 1 QuarEd accurately indicate that Sirach 28:16 does not exist in the Vulgate. The exact same words that Bonaventure cites as Sirach 28:16 occur in Sirach 17:18. Hugh of St. Cher, 90b also quotes Sirach 28:16, but as Sirach 29:16.

[41]On p. 58 n. 2 QuarEd rightly indicate that the Vulgate reads *disciplinam meam* ("my instruction") whereas Bonaventure has *sapientiam* ("wisdom").

divine judgments, *that no one can correct whom he has despised*, that is, whom God himself by his judgment has decided to visit. So we read of the sons of Eli in 1 Samuel 2:25: "And they hearkened not to the voice of their father, because the Lord had determined to kill them." Such works and judgments are for our reflection to increase fear. Habakkuk 3:2 reads: "I considered your works and was afraid."[42]

19. (Verse 15). *In the good day*, etc. This is the third instruction, in which he teaches the need *to discern the times*, because God did not make all times uniformly, but different one from another. And a person has to watch the different times. So he says: *In the good day enjoy good things*, that is, do the good joyfully. Sirach 14:14 states: "Defraud not yourself of the good day, and let not part of a good gift pass you by,"[43] because that day is the place and time for working. Thus, John 9:4 reads: "I must work . . . while it is day." Similarly the Apostle warns us in Galatians 6:10: "While we have time, let us do good to all." *And beware beforehand of the evil day*, namely, that of which Zephaniah 1:15 speaks: "That day is a day of wrath, a day of tribulation and distress, a day of calamity and misery."[44] Whoever want to beware of that day must keep in mind what Sirach 11:27 states: "In the day of good things be not unmindful of evils." The Lord made the days and ordered them justly. Therefore, Ecclesiastes says: *For God has made both the one and the other*, that is, the good and the evil days. And God did this justly: *So that human beings may*

---

[42]On p. 58 n. 3 QuarEd accurately mention that the text of the Vulgate does not match Bonaventure's text. Habakkuk 3:2 says: "O Lord, I have heard your hearing and was afraid. O Lord, your work, in the midst of the years bring it to life." The editors note that the Septuagint reads: "I considered your works and was speechless."

[43]Hugh of St. Cher, 90m also cites Sirach 14:14.

[44]Hugh of St. Cher, 90o also quotes Zephaniah 1:15.

not find any just complaint against God. Wherefore, God makes good things for the good, and evil against evil people. For Psalm 144:17 reads: "The Lord is just in all his ways."

20. (Verse 16). *These things I also saw on the day of my birth.*[45] Here he states the fourth instruction, in which he teaches *the careful discernment to be made of merits,* because they hide much. So he says: *These things also I saw on the day of my birth,* that is, after I was born *I saw* what would happen. What happens is this: *Just people perish in their justice,* because they are judged to be wicked. We read in Isaiah 57:1: "The just perish, and no one lays it to heart." *And the wicked live a long time in their wickedness,* as if they were righteous. About this Jeremiah was indignant in Jeremiah 12:1: "Why does the way of the wicked prosper? Why is it well with all those who transgress and do wickedly?" And Ecclesiastes 8:14 below says: "There are just people, to whom evils happen, as though they had done the works of the wicked. And there are wicked people, who are as secure as though they had done the deeds of the just."

QUESTIONS 22

I. What is the meaning of: *Wisdom with riches is more useful?*[46]

1. Therefore, it is better to be a rich wise person than a poor wise person. Therefore, it is not a more perfect state to be poor.

2. Moreover, "art and virtue are concerned about what is difficult."[47] But it is more difficult for a rich person to be

---

[45]The Vulgate reads *vanitatis* ("vanity") while Bonaventure has *nativitatis* ("birth").

[46]Ecclesiastes 7:12.

[47]On p. 58 n. 7 QuarEd refer to Book II, n. 3 of Aristotle's *Ethica nicomachea.* See WAE, vol. 9, 1104a: "But both art and virtue are always

saved than for a poor person. Therefore, the poor person has the greater virtue. Therefore, poverty is the more praiseworthy state.

Contra: The Lord preferred the state of poverty both in deed and in word, as in Matthew 19:21.[48]

I reply: 1. There is a triple poverty: one in which a person is *happy* to be poor. Another in which poverty is *tolerated*. A third is poverty with *impatience*. The first is good and perfect. The second is imperfect. The third is to be avoided. Sirach 13:30 states: "Poverty is very wicked in the mouth of the ungodly." When it is said that wisdom is better with wealth than without wealth, it is to be understood of poverty that is *tolerated* or that causes *impatience*.[49]

2. Relative to the objection about the difficulty, it has to be said that there is a difficulty by reason of *the kind of work*, and this leads to greater virtue. There is also a difficulty by reason of *a disordered will*, as when a covetous person finds it more difficult to give a gift than does a generous person. And this does nothing for greater virtue. In this sense it is more difficult for a rich person to be saved. – Another solution is to apply the words to abundance and excessive need.

---

concerned with what is harder; for even the good is better when it is harder." Bonaventure also cited this passage from Aristotle in his second response after his commentary on Ecclesiastes 5:11 (#14) above.

[48]Matthew 19:21 reads: "Jesus said to him: If you want to be perfect, go, sell what you have, and give to the poor, and you will have treasure in heaven. And come, follow me."

[49]On p. 59 n. 2 QuarEd refer to Bonaventure's *Quaestiones disputatae de perfectione evangelica*, q. 2, a. 1, ad 1 where a solution to the following objection is suggested. See Omnia Opera 5:128 where Bonaventure cites Ecclesiastes 7:12.

II. It is asked what he means by: *That no one can correct whom God has despised.*[50]

1. But God despises all sinners, because Sirach 12:3 says: *The highest hates sinners.* Wisdom 14:9 states: *To God the wicked and their wickedness are hateful alike.*

2. Also, whoever cannot be corrected cannot be saved. Therefore, this text should not be applied to such a person.

I reply: There is a double love, namely, an *eternal* love and one *according to present justice.*[51] In the same way there is a double *despising of people.* The text is speaking not of any person whatever, but of a reprobate person. Nor is it speaking of any despising whatever, but of a despising based on eternal rejection, a sign of which is hardness of heart in this present life. So the reference is not to every sinner, but only to the reprobate.

To the objection that the text should not be applied to oneself, it has to be said that God despises no one without reason. Hence, although a person could not rise unless God extends a hand, this is no excuse, because it is one's own fault that a hand is not extended. In his book on Correction and Grace Augustine says that no one is corrected unless they want to be corrected.[52]

---

[50]See Ecclesiastes 7:14. The Vulgate reads *possit* ("could") while Bonaventure has *potest* ("can"). The Vulgate does not have *Deus* ("God").

[51]On p. 59 n. 1 QuarEd refer to Book I, d. 40, 1. 2, q. 2, ad 1 and 2 of Bonaventure's *Sentence Commentary.* See Omnia Opera 1:711.

[52]On p. 59 n. 6 QuarEd refer to chapter 5, n. 7 and chapter 14, n. 43-44 of Augustine's *De correptione et gratia.* On chapter 14, n. 43 see *St. Augustine, Admonition and Grace,* trans. John Courtney Murray, FC 2 (New York: CIMA Publishing Co., 1947), 298: "Actually, when men come, or come back, to the way of justice as the result of an admonition, who is it that effects salvation in their hearts, but God?. . . .To say 'yes' or 'no' is indeed in the power of the man who says it, but in such a way that he may not thwart the will of God nor overcome His power."

III. It is also asked what he means by: *Just people perish in their justice, and the wicked live a long time in their wickedness.*[53]

Contra: 1. Psalm 54:24 states: *Bloody and deceitful men will not live out half their days.*

2. Furthermore, about good people Exodus 20:12 says: *Honor your father and your mother, that you may be long lived upon the land* and live for a long time. Therefore, to observe the commandments is to prolong life.

I reply: What we read about the just in Wisdom 4:13 has to be said: *Being made perfect in a short space, he fulfilled a long time,*[54] showing that few is to be construed as many. But it is different with evil people, and also with the number to be saved and to be damned. The days of good people are longer, because they are better and not because they live longer.

Note, however, that the years of people are sometimes *shortened,* lest they become evil. Wisdom 4:11 reads: *He was taken away, lest wickedness should alter his understanding,* etc. This happens sometimes, lest people become worse. Psalm 54:24 says: *Bloody and deceitful men will not live out half their days.* – The days of good people are *lengthened* for the sake of *purgation.* Sirach 2:5 has: *For gold and silver are tried in the fire.* Romans 2:4 states: *Do you not know that the goodness of God is meant to lead you to repentance?*

---

[53]Ecclesiastes 7:16.
[54]On p. 59 n. 9 QuarEd rightly indicate that the Vulgate reads *explevit* ("fulfilled") while Bonaventure has *complevit* ("fulfilled").

ECCLESIASTES 7:17-23   INSTRUCTIONS ABOUT JUSTICE

21. *Do not be too just.* He has already dealt with instructions about temperance, steadfastness, and prudence. Here in a fourth point he deals with instruction about acquiring *justice*. Since justice is not genuine when it is excessive in rigor or cruelty, unless it be tempered by compassion, he provides four lessons here. In the first *he forbids a rigorous severity* or an excess of justice. Second, he forbids *a lapse into mercilessness*. Third, he *commends a display of mercy*. Fourth, he commends *a hiding of one's own injury*.

22. (Verse 17a). In the first instruction *he warns against being excessively just when imposing punishment* by saying: *Do not be too just*, that is, do not be excessive in *the rigor of justice*, because it is wrong to pursue every wrong. Thus, James 2:13 states: "Judgment without mercy will be to him[55] who has not acted mercifully."[56] Nor should you be relentless in *searching out faults*. Therefore, he says: *And do not be more wise than is necessary*, because we read in Proverbs 30:33: "The person who squeezes forcefully brings out blood." Therefore, Romans 12:3 states: "Do not be more wise than it is necessary to be wise, but be wise with moderation."

23. (Verses 17b-18). *Lest you become senseless*, etc. Here he deals with his second instruction which *forbids a lapse into mercilessness*. For mercilessness renders a person *senseless in affection* and rigorous. So he says: *Lest you become senseless*. Jeremiah 31:30 reads: "Every person who shall eat the sour grape, his teeth will become senseless."[57]

---

[55]On p. 59 n. 11 QuarEd correctly state that the Vulgate has *illi* ("to him") whereas Bonaventure reads *fiet ei* ("will be to him").

[56]Hugh of St. Cher, 90v, f also cites James 2:13 and reads *fiet ei* ("will be to him").

[57]Hugh of St. Cher, 91a also quotes Jeremiah 31:30.

Mercilessness makes a person *cruel*. So he says: *Do not be too wicked*, that is, do not act with cruelty. Psalm 74:5 states: "I said to the wicked: Do not act wickedly." And Sirach 7:3 has: "Do not sow evils in the furrows of injustice, and you will not reap them sevenfold." Mercilessness also *blinds the mind*, and so he says: *Do not*[58] *be foolish*. We read in Proverbs 24:8: "The person who devises to do evils will be called a fool. The thought of a fool will be called sin."

24. Since sin and foolishness hasten death, he adds the reason: *Do not be foolish, lest you die before your time*, that is, lest you hasten the time of your death, for Psalm 54:24 reads: "Bloody and deceitful men will not live out half their days."[59] And again Luke 12:20 says: "You fool, this night do they require your soul of you." An example of this is seen in Dathan and Abiram who "went down alive into hell."[60]

25. (Verses 19-21). *It is good that you should hold up the just*. He states now his third instruction, in which *he warns us to show mercy*. He begins with *an exhortation* and supplies *a reason*. – *He exhorts* by saying: *It is good that you should hold up the just*, namely, in justice. Proverbs 24:15

---

[58]The Vulgate reads *et noli esse* ("and do not be").

[59]Hugh of St. Cher, 91d will cite the example of Dathan and Abiram from Numbers 16 (he erroneously has Numbers 26) and will quote Psalm 54:24; he does not refer to Luke 12:20.

[60]See Numbers 16:33. On p. 60 n. 1 QuarEd rightly indicate that the Vulgate of Numbers 16:33 reads *descenderuntque vivi in infernum* ("and they went down alive into hell") while Bonaventure has *descenderunt viventes in infernum* ("went down alive into hell"). Bonaventure's point is actually articulated in Numbers 16:29-30: Moses said: "If these men die an ordinary death, merely suffering the fate common to all humanity, then it was not the Lord who sent me. But if the Lord does something completely new, and the ground opens wide its mouth and swallows them alive into hell, with all their belongings, then you shall know that these men have defied the Lord."

reads: "Do not lie in wait, nor seek after wickedness in the house of the just nor spoil his rest." For it is said in Proverbs 17:26: "It is not a good thing to do harm to the just nor to strike the prince who judges rightly." Not only is a just person to be held up in a just cause, but the hand should be extended to him in almsgiving. And so he adds: *Yes and from him do not withdraw your hand.* Sirach 12:2 states: "Do good to the just, and you will find great recompense, and if not from him, then assuredly from God."[61] After this exhortation he adds *a threefold reason.* And the first is *the divine will.* About it he says: *The person who*[62] *fears God neglects nothing,* namely, of those things that God wants to be done. Sirach 7:31-34 says: "With all your soul fear the Lord . . . and for your negligence purify yourself with a few."[63]

26. The second reason is *the dignity of the just person.* About this dignity he says: *Wisdom has strengthened the wise more than ten princes of the city.* Wisdom 6:1 states: "Wisdom is better than strength, and a wise man is better than a strong man."

27. The third reason is *human weakness.* About this weakness he says: *For on the earth there is no just person who does good and sins not,* and therefore, a sinner is to be shown mercy. Proverbs 24:16 reads: "A just person falls seven times a day[64] and will rise again." Indeed, even the

---

[61]On p. 60 n. 3 QuarEd accurately mention that the Vulgate has *et si non ab ipso, certe a Domino* ("and if not from him, then assuredly from the Lord") while Bonaventure reads *et si non ab illo, certe a Deo* ("and if not from him, then assuredly from God").

[62]The Vulgate reads *quia qui* ("for the person who").

[63]The context would seem to indicate that "a few" include sacrificial gifts to the priestly ministers.

[64]On p. 60 n. 5 QuarEd rightly indicate that the Vulgate reads *Septies enim cadet iustus* ("For a just person will fall seven times") while Bonaventure has *Septies in die cadit iustus* ("A just person falls seven times a day").

most perfect person sins sometimes. 1 John 1:8 proclaims: "If we say that we have no sin, we deceive ourselves, and the truth is not in us."[65]

28. (Verses 22-23). *But do not apply your heart to all words*, etc. He deals here with the fourth lesson, in which *he exhorts us to hide our own injury*. One should not search into nor believe every word, and so he says: *But do not apply your heart to all words that are spoken*, that is, do not trust every word, because little trust is to be put into words. For many say many things. For this reason Sirach 19:4 states: "The person who is swift to trust is light of heart."[66] And since it is difficult to hear and not believe, Sirach 28:28 reads: "Hedge in your ears with thorns. Do not hear a wicked tongue." So people should not be anxious to hear what is said about them. He gives the reason: *Lest perhaps you hear your servant reviling you*, as happened when David heard Shemei curse him as 2 Samuel 16:9 says. As a result Abishai said to David: "Why should this most wretched[67] dog curse my lord the king? I will go and cut off his head."

29. And this often happens, as human beings know from their own experience: *For your conscience knows that you also have often spoken evil of others*. And so you must not pay careful *attention nor punish*. Sirach 31:18 states: "Judge the matters of your neighbor as you do your own." For as it is said in Matthew 18:33: "Should not you, then, have had compassion also on your fellow servant, even as I had compassion on you?"

---

[65]Hugh of St. Cher, 91o also cites 1 John 1:8.

[66]Sirach 19:4 reads: "The person who is swift to trust is light of heart and will be lessened; and the person who sins against his own soul will be despised."

[67]The Vulgate reads *moriturus* ("about to die") while Bonaventure has *pessimus* ("most wretched").

QUESTIONS 23

I. First, what does he mean by: *Do not be too just?*[68]

Contra: 1.In itself this is true, because the just person is good. Therefore, the more just a person is, the more good. Therefore, the completely just person is the completely good person. Therefore, in the area of justice there is not too much.

2. Also, whatever is said of God, is said in the highest way. But God is said to be *just*. Therefore, God is supremely just. And it is assured that this is not evil. Therefore, if the height of justice is not evil, then there is no superfluity there.

II. It is also asked what he means by: *Do not be more wise than it will be necessary.*[69]

1. For whoever has more love is wiser, but no one can love too much. Therefore, no one is too wise when speaking of love directed to God.

2. Moreover, no one is exceedingly wise nor can one be. Therefore, no one can be wiser than it is necessary.

Contra: Virtue consists of the middle way and is damaged by too much and by too little.[70] Therefore, just as there can be sin in excessive forgiving, so also in excessive punishing.

---

[68]Ecclesiastes 7:17.

[69]The Vulgate reads *necesse est* ("it is necessary") whereas Bonaventure has *necesse erit* ("it will be necessary").

[70]On p. 60 n. 8 QuarEd refer to Book II, n. 6 of Aristotle's *Ethica nicomachea*. See WAE, vol. 9, 1106b: ". . . virtue must have the quality of aiming at the intermediate. I mean moral virtue. . . .Now virtue is concerned with passions and actions, in which excess is a form of failure, and so is defect, while the intermediate is praised and is a form of success; and being praised and being successful are both characteristics

I reply: 1. The word *just person* is understood in one way as the person having *such a virtue*. In this sense an excess of justice means to move to the middle way, and so there can be no superfluity there. For no one can be exceedingly virtuous nor have come too close to the middle way.[71] Another way of speaking of the just person is in reference to an action of that virtue, namely, *to punish*. Excess in this sense does not refer to the middle way, but to superfluity. Thus the person is said to be *too just* who punishes too much. And to punish in an extreme way is not good.[72] The text is to be understood in this sense.

---

of virtue. Therefore virtue is a kind of mean, since, as we have seen, it aims at what is intermediate." The Latin dictum is: *virtus stat in medio*.

[71]See the previous note on "virtue occupies the middle ground." In this understanding of virtue, striving excessively to be virtuous means to strive to always be in the middle ground.

[72]On p. 61 n. 1 QuarEd cite Book I, chapter 10 of Cicero's *De officiis*. See *Cicero, De officiis*, trans. Walter Miller, LCL (London: Heinemann, 1947), 35: "Injustice often arises also through chicanery, that is, through an over-subtle and even fraudulent construction of the law. This it is that gave rise to the now familiar saw, 'More law, less justice.' Through such interpretation also a great deal of wrong is committed in transactions between state and state; thus, when a truce had been made with an enemy for thirty days, a famous general went to ravaging their fields by night, because, he said, the truce stipulated 'days,' not nights." The Latin for "more law, less justice" is *summum ius summa iniuria*. The editors also call attention to Bernard of Clairvaux' interpretation of Ecclesiastes 7:17 in Book I, chapter 8 n. 10 of his *De consideratione*. See SBOp 3.405: "*Do not be excessively just*, says the Wise Man, showing by this that that justice is least to be approved which is not braked by the controls of temperance." The editors also quote Augustine. See Tractate 95 n. 2 of *St. Augustine, Tractates on the Gospel of John –111*, trans. J.W. Rettig, FC 90 (Washington: Catholic University of America, 1988), 188: "Because as it has been written, *There is not a just man upon earth who will do good and will not sin* [Eccl 7:21]. And therefore, even when a just man is convicted, he is convicted of sin, not of justice. Because even in that divinely expressed remark that we read *Be not over just* [Eccl 7:17], it is not the justice of the wise man that has been identified, but the pride of the presumptuous. Therefore, he who becomes *over just* by his very excess becomes unjust. For he makes himself just to excess who says that he does not have sin, etc."

2. The second objection states that whatever is said of God is said in the highest way possible. That is true for what is said of God *absolutely* and when it refers to something *constant in God*. But it is not true of God's *actions* that they are done in the highest way possible. Thus, God does not punish nor pardon in the highest way possible, but according to what is fitting.[73]

To the question about wisdom, it has to be said that *the habit* of wisdom can never be in excess. But note that *in acting wisely* there are three elements, namely, *to taste, to know*, and *to discern*. In *tasting* and *knowing*, no one can do so excessively, but *in discerning* well there can be excess. And the reason for this is that excessive discerning leads to a bad taste, but love, when directed to God, cannot be excessive, because God is to be loved in the highest way.[74]

III. It is also asked what he means by: *Do not be foolish, lest you die before your time.*[75]

Contra: Job 14:5 states: *You have appointed his bounds which cannot be passed.*[76] So it seems that they cannot be increased on account of goodness. Therefore, neither can they be diminished because of malice.

If this is true, how is it that in Scripture God promises long years?[77] – Also, how is it that God increased the life of

---

[73]On p. 61 n. 2 QuarEd refer to Book IV, d. 46, a. 2, q. 1, ad 4 of Bonaventure's *Sentence Commentary*. See Omnia Opera 4:963.

[74]On p. 61 n. 3 QuarEd refer to Book III, d. 27, a. 2, q. 5 of Bonaventure's *Sentence Commentary*. See Omnia Opera 3: 611.

[75]Ecclesiastes 7:18.

[76]Job 14:5 reads: "The days of man are short, and the number of his months is with you. You have appointed his bound which cannot be passed."

[77]On p. 61 n. 5 QuarEd quote Exodus 20:12: "Honor your father and your mother, that you may live long upon the land which the Lord your God will give you."

Hezekiah by fifteen years according to 2 Kings 20:6?[78] –
Likewise, God also shortens lives. Psalm 54:24 says: *Bloody
and deceitful men will not live out half their days.*

I reply: *To die at one's time* has a threefold meaning. In
one sense it means to die at the time of *one's salvation*,
something to which everyone is destined. In this sense all
the good die in their time, but no evil people do, because
evil people never reach this. I am speaking of people who
are evil to the end. – In the second sense to die in one's
time is to die *a natural death*, which occurs through using
up the basic fluids of life.[79] The elderly and decrepit die in
this way. – In the third sense to die in one's time is to die
at the time which *God has determined for a person.* This is
a time set in the divine foreknowledge that is never mistaken. No one anticipates or extends this time. In the first
sense, *evil people* die in a time which is not their own. In
the second sense *both good and evil people* die when they
suffer an accidental death. *No one* dies in the third sense.

Therefore, Ecclesiastes and Scripture are speaking of
death in the first sense. But Job speaks of death in the
third sense. Similarly it is said of Hezekiah that God
changed his mind.[80]

IV. It is also asked what he means by: *The person who
fears God neglects nothing.*[81]

---

[78]2 Kings 20:6 reads: "And I will add to your days fifteen years."

[79]On p. 61 n. 7 QuarEd refer to Opera Omnia 1:316 note 12 and 2:736
note 3.

[80]See 2 Kings 20:1-6 and Isaiah 38:1-5 for the story of how Hezekiah
through his prayers is freed from the sentence of death pronounced on
him by Isaiah. 2 Kings 20:5-6: "I have heard your prayer and seen your
tears. I will heal you. . . .I will add fifteen years to your life."

[81]Ecclesiastes 7:19.

But whoever sins neglects something. Therefore, no one who sins fears God. But *there is no just person who does not sin.*[82] Therefore, there is no just person who might fear God.

V. It is asked further whether any just person could be sinless. – It is clear that the answer to this is no because of what is said here and in 1 John 1:8: *If we say that we have no sin, we deceive ourselves, and the truth is not in us.*

But that it is possible seems to be true:

1. It is proved by Job 17:2: *I have not sinned, and my eye abides in bitterness.*[83]

2. Also, if it is not possible, how can we say that no one sins in what he cannot avoid?[84] Therefore, etc.

I reply: In one sense *negligence* implies *contempt*, and so is a mortal sin. And this is the sense used in the text here. In another sense negligence implies *an omission of some circumstance*, and this is a venial sin. And from this no one is free. – It is also used of *mortal sin*, from which many are free, and of *venial sin* from which no one, who has free will, is free other than Christ. We also believe this of the most blessed Virgin.

1. To the objection based on Job, I reply that Job does not say that he has not sinned, but that he has not sinned in a way that deserves such punishment. Also our heart blames

---

[82]Ecclesiastes 7:21 reads: "For on the earth there is no just person who does good and sins not."

[83]The NAB translates the last clause: "My eyes grow dim."

[84]On p. 61 n. 12 QuarEd quote Book III, chapter 18 n. 50 of Augustine's *De Libero Arbitrio*. See FC 59, 210: "Who sins in what cannot be prevented?"

us when we take pleasure in sin. But when we do what we do not want to do, even if it is sinful, our heart does not accuse us.[85]

2. From what has been said about the impossibility of avoiding sin, it has to be said that a person has been thrust into this state from sin. And therefore, that person is not absolved from sinning in some way. Moreover, although sin cannot be completely avoided, particular sins can be avoided. Therefore, etc.[86]

Part III
Ecclesiastes 7:24-12:7   The vanity of being subject to punishment

30. *I have tried all things*, etc. He has treated above the vanity of being subject to change and of iniquity. In this part he intends to deal with the vanity of *being subject to punishment*. There is a double punishment, namely, *the occasion of sin* such as concupiscence, and another which is *a simple affliction* such as death and bodily infirmity. So he first treats of the first subjection to punishment, namely, *an occasion of sin*, and then, about those things which are *simple afflictions* where Ecclesiastes 12:1 reads: *Remember your Creator*, etc.

Ecclesiastes 7:24-12:1   Occasions of sin

31. The punishment in an occasion of sin is twofold, namely, one from a lack of love, and this is a *propensity*. The other is from a lack of fear, and this is *unconcern*. The first makes

---

[85]On p. 61 n. 13 QuarEd helpfully point to 1 John 3:20-21 as a source for this thought: "Because if our heart blames us, God is greater than our heart and knows all things. Beloved, if our heart does not condemn us, we have confidence towards God." The editors also refer to Book XIII, chapter 30 n. 34 of Gregory's *Moralia in Iob*.

[86]On p. 61 n. 14 QuarEd refer to Book II, d. 41, a. 2, q. 1 of Bonaventure's *Sentence Commentary*. See Opera Omnia 2:947.

a person prone to evil while the second makes the person unconcerned, since he has no fear and does not think of being punished. So this section has two parts. The first deals with the vanity of *propensity*. The second treats the vanity of *feeling secure* and commences in Ecclesiastes 8:9 below: *All these things I have considered and applied my heart*, etc.

ECCLESIASTES 7:24-8:8   THE VANITY OF PROPENSITY

32. And since the vanity of *the propensity* to concupiscence is dangerous and since no one is free from it without the help of divine wisdom, he treats first of *the discovery of concupiscence*. Second, he gives *the remedy of wisdom* where verse 30 states: *Who is as the wise person*, etc.

ECCLESIASTES 7:24-29   THE FINDING OF CONCUPISCENCE

33. As in the situation when something hidden is found after a careful search, so he describes in the first place the careful *search* for it, and, in the second place, the finding of concupiscence where verse 27 says: *And I have found a woman more bitter than death*, etc.

ECCLESIASTES 7:24-26   THE SEARCH FOR CONCUPISCENCE

34. So his diligent *search* for it, which in fact was so diligent that it degenerated into curiosity, is described by speaking first of *the presumption* in his curiosity, the extent of his *search*, and the intensity of his *thinking*.

35. (Verses 24-26). So with regard to *the presumption of curiosity* he says: *I have tried all things in wisdom*, that is, in my search, which is a search of curiosity. Sirach 3:22 states: "In many of his works do not be curious." *I have said: I will be wise*, and this is the height of presumption.

We read in Isaiah 5:21: "Woe to you who are wise in your own eyes," etc. And 1 Corinthians 3:18 says: "If any among you seems to be wise in this world, let him become a fool that he may be wise."

36. Concerning *the extent of the search* he continues: *And it departed further from me, much more than it was.* For the more he searched, the more he realized that this is a more difficult question because of the *severity of divine judgment.* Romans 1:22 reads: "Professing themselves to be wise, they became fools." It was also more difficult because of *the depth of the question*, and so he says: *It is a great depth. Who will find it out?* The depth of the search for wisdom is profound. Sirach 24:7 states: "I dwelt in the highest places, and my throne is in a pillar of a cloud."[87] Hence, who can find it? Few do so adequately, but none perfectly. Sirach 43:34 has: "Be not weary, for you can never go far enough." And Romans 11:33 says: "O the depths of the riches of the wisdom and of the knowledge of God," etc.

37. Relative to *the intensity of his thinking* he adds: *I have surveyed all things with my mind*, that is, I have looked at and reflected on the question from every side. Sirach 6:19 says: "Come to her as one that plows and sows and wait for her good fruits." And he touches on the reason motivating him when he says: *to know*, and retain as a habit; *and consider*, in actual study; and *seek out wisdom*, in the desires, and *seek out reason*, in works. Viewed from the opposite perspective, the reason is *to know the wickedness of the fool*, in what is to be done, *and the error of the imprudent* in what is to be believed. Ecclesiastes 1:17 above says: "I have given my heart to know prudence, and learning and errors and folly.

---

[87]Wisdom is the "I" speaking.

ECCLESIASTES 7:27-30A   THE FINDING OF CONCUPISCENCE

38. *And I have found*, etc. Having described the diligent search, he now describes *the finding of carnal concupiscence*, and this in a threefold condition. First, *the propensity of concupiscence itself is noted*. Second, its *universality*. Third, its *causality*.

39. (Verse 27). First, he treats of the powerful *attraction* of concupiscence, because it leads to extreme bitterness under the guise of sweetness. So he says: *And I have found more bitter than death a woman*, and this after the perpetration of a wicked deed, to which concupiscence drew him. Thus, we read in Proverbs 5:3: "For the lips of a harlot are like a dripping honeycomb, and her throat is smoother than oil." It is concupiscence that drew him to this, concupiscence that began with a woman and finds its fuel in a woman, who by her beauty *snares* through love. So he says: *Who is the hunter's snare*, that is, of the demons, who hunt for the souls of men and women. She snares by *words* and *looks*. Proverbs 7:21 reads: "She entangled him with many words and drew him away with the flattery of her lips." She snares by the *beauty* of her face. Sirach 9:9 states: "Many have perished because of the beauty of a woman." She snares also by *words*. Sirach 9:11 has: "Her conversation burns like fire." Not only does she *snare in love*, but she also *swallows up* in wicked *deeds*. Therefore, he says: *Her heart is a net*, when at her wish one consents to an evil deed. This is the net of the devil. Habakkuk 1:15 states: "He lifted up all with his hook and gathered them into his net." But afterwards she *binds* by affection, and so he says: *And her hands are bands*. We read in Proverbs 7:22: "He follows her, not knowing that he is drawn like a fool to chains." This *attraction* is so strong that a person escapes from it only with the Lord's help. Wherefore, he says: *The person who pleases God will escape from her*, according to what 1 Corinthians 6:18 has: "Flee from fornication." Wis-

dom 8:21 states: "I knew that I could not otherwise be continent, unless God gave it." *But the person who is a sinner will be caught by her.* Proverbs 5:22 cautions: "His own iniquities catch the wicked, and he is fast bound with the ropes of his own sins."

40. (Verses 28-29). *Behold, this I have found*, etc. Second, he treats *the universality* of concupiscence, the reason for which it was difficult to see. So he says: *Behold, this I have found, said Ecclesiastes, weighing one thing*, namely, *the propensity* to concupiscence itself, *after another*, that is, its *universality*. – Supply: I labored, *that I might find out the reason which my soul still seeks*. This is *the reason* for the universality of concupiscence and why it is in everyone. *And I have not found it*, namely, by his own ability, because the philosophers had not come to find it. But *by faith* the reason is known and *by experience* its *effect* is known, namely, its universality. So he continues: *One man among a thousand I have found. A woman among them all I have not found.* This is hyperbole and means that he found very few men in whom concupiscence did not hold sway. But he found no women. This is not surprising, for Sirach 25:26 says: "All[88] malice is short lived in comparison to the malice of a woman." – We might be able to interpret this text of Christ,[89] who alone escaped from the corruption of original concupiscence and who alone was "free among the dead."[90]

---

[88]The Vulgate does not have *omnis* ("all").

[89]See Hugh of St. Cher, 92n: "Mystically, this text is interpreted of Christ, who alone is outside this universality."

[90]On p. 63 n. 5 QuarEd indicate that this is a citation from Psalm 87:6 and go on to quote Alcuin's commentary on Ecclesiastes 7:28-29. See Alcuin's *Commentaria super Ecclesiasten* in PL 100: 698C: "I have carefully considered all things in my search, so that I might find the reason for the one or the other, that is, for every thing or might distinguish between peoples and their customs and might ascertain who is perfectly good. But of all men only one did I find to be perfectly

41. (Verse 30a). *Only this have I found.* Third, he deals with *the causality* of concupiscence, which truly is not from God, but from the first sin. So he says: *Only this have I found, that God made human beings right.* Sirach 17:1 says: "God created the human being out of earth and made him after his own image." And the sign of this is the uprightness of human stature which still remains in the body.[91] *And they have entangled themselves,* that is, by their own freedom, *in an infinity of questions,* because by abandoning the one human beings have become prone to many and indeed to an infinite number of things. For in these their concupiscence is not finished or satisfied. Proverbs 30:15-16 reads: "There are three things that never are satisfied, and the fourth never says: It is enough: Hell and the mouth of the womb and the earth," etc.[92]

QUESTIONS 24

I. When he says, *I have tried all things in wisdom,*[93] it can be doubted whether he is blameworthy in this. It would seem to be so:

---

good, that is, Christ, as the Prophet says [Psalm 13:1.3]: *There is none that does good, no not one.* Only Christ was found to be good, without any stain of sin. The number thousand stands for the saints as distinct from the sinners, who are represented by the word woman in this text. For man comes from virtue or strength while woman comes from softness." The last derivation of meaning might be seen in the Latin: *vir = VIRtute; mulier = MoLlis.*

[91]See Part II, chapter X of Bonaventure's *Breviloquium* in his Omnia Opera 5:228: "In order that the human body might be conformed to a soul tending upward toward heaven, it possessed rectitude of stature and a head lifted high. In this way bodily rectitude might give witness to mental rectitude." See also what Bonaventure has to say in Question II. 1 after his commentary on Ecclesiastes 3:22 above.

[92]Proverbs 30:16 reads: "Hell, and the mouth of the womb, and the earth which is not satisfied with water, and the fire never says: It is enough."

[93]Ecclesiastes 7:24.

1. From the text itself: *I have said: I will be wise, and it departed further from me.*

2. Also from what is said in Sirach 3:22: *Do not be curious in many of his works.*

Contra: 1. *The spiritual person judges all things, and he himself is judged by no one.*[94] Therefore, if Solomon had the spirit of wisdom, he was able to judge all things.

2. Moreover, the Apostle says in 1 Thessalonians 5:21: *Test all things. Hold fast to that which is good.* So it is good to test all things.

I reply: There are two ways *to test something.* One way is to know by *experience,* for example, when someone knows and tests the taste of a wine. Another way is through *examination* and *approbation* and *rejection.* In the first way only things that are useful are tested. To go beyond this is curiosity. In the second way *to test* and *to examine* mean the same thing, and this is the sense in which Paul takes *to test.* And so all things are to be examined, not only the good and useful, but also the useless. In this sense it is said that *the spiritual person judges all things.*[95] The Apostle also says: *Test all things,* that is, examine all those things in *our* works about which we can have doubts whether they are good or bad. But it is curiosity to test and examine *the works of God,* which we must presume were done well. Therefore, since Solomon examined more things than are relevant for salvation, he was engaged in curiosity. And this has to be conceded. – These two authorities are to be understood of things pertaining to sal-

---

[94] 1 Corinthians 2:15.

[95] On p. 63 n. 11 QuarEd cite the *Glossa Ordinaria apud Strabum* on this verse. See PL 114:522D: "*All things,* not indeed everything contained in divine knowledge, but all things sufficient for justice and life. That is the meaning of all things are to be judged."

vation and so concerned Paul himself, but Solomon went beyond this.

II. There is also doubt about what he means by: *One man among a thousand I have found.*[96] According to this statement it would appear to confirm that heresy which stated that no woman is saved. And heretics try to prove this:

1. Because, if only what Christ assumed is to be saved and Christ assumed only the sex of a man, therefore only men are to be saved.

2. They try to prove this from what is said in Mark 16:16: *He who believes and is baptized will be saved.* The text does not say: *She who believes and is baptized.*[97] The same thing is stated in John 3:3.[98]

Contra: 1. The text of Matthew 21:31 reads: *The harlots will go into the kingdom of God ahead of you.*[99]

2. It is also clear that the Lord received both sexes, healed the bodies of both, and called both through the Apostles. Solomon himself praised both sexes and said of the valiant woman in Proverbs 31:25: *She will laugh on the last day.* How then does he say: *A woman among them all I have not found?*

---

[96]Ecclesiastes 7:29.

[97]The key word here is *baptizatus* ("is baptized") which has a masculine ending, not the feminine ending *baptizata* ("is baptized").

[98]John 3:3 reads: *Nisi quis natus fuerit denuo, non potest videre regnum Dei* ("Unless a man be born again, he cannot see the kingdom of God"). Again the word *natus* ("born") has a masculine ending. On p. 64 n. 1 QuarEd cite Book I, Heresy XXV or XLV, Contra Severianos of Epiphanius' *Adversus Haereses.* See PG 41:834BC: "Moreover, they say that woman is the work of Satan. . . .And therefore, those who have intercourse with them in marriage perform the work of Satan. Further, they affirm that one part of humankind is from God, the other from the devil."

[99]The Vulgate reads *praecedunt* ("are going ahead") while Bonaventure has *praecedent* ("will go ahead").

I reply: He is speaking of the universality of concupiscence, and he speaks of this in two ways. One way is by referring to it *being handed on through carnal propagation*. The other way is to refer to *its continuance in actual sin*. If he is using the first way of speaking, his word is true and proper, because only Christ was conceived without sin and did not have original sin. If he is using the second way of speaking, he is using hyperbole. The hyperbole is clear, because not only is there just one good man to be saved, but indeed many. And he spoke in this way because in Solomon's time there were but a few who were free from acts of concupiscence.

1. To the objection of the heretics that Christ assumed the male sex, I reply that even if Christ assumed the male sex, it has to be noted that he assumed it *from a woman*. Christ would not have done this unless it had a bearing on salvation. Moreover, man and woman are of one nature and are one body.[100]

2. Concerning the two Gospel texts, which use the *masculine* form, it has to be said that the masculine stands for both sexes since it refers to nature in those texts, not to gender. And frequently in Scripture the masculine gender in a word includes the feminine.[101]

---

[100]On p. 64 n. 4 QuarEd helpfully point to Ephesians 5:28-33. In the same note the editors also refer to Book III, d. 12, a. 3, q. 1 and 2 of Bonaventure's *Sentence Commentary*. See Opera Omnia 3:263-265.

[101]On p. 64 n. 5 QuarEd offer four additional points of evidence. The blessed of Matthew 25:34 and the accursed of Matthew 25:41 include both men and women. They also cite Book III, Titulus 42 De baptismo et eius effectu, chapter 3 (Maiores ecclesiae). See *Decretales D. Gregorii Papae IX, suae integritati una cum glossis restitutae Ad exemplar Romanum diligenter recognitae*, Editio ultima (Tavrini: Apud Nicolaum Beuilaquam, 1621), 1383: "Now the Gospel text makes no distinction: *Unless a man be born again of water and the Holy Spirit, he cannot enter into the kingdom of God*. From this general statement no sex or

age is excluded." Moreover, the editors cite a Glossa on John 3:5: "In fact, it is inclusive since the feminine is included in the masculine form when it says: *Unless a man*, etc." Finally, see Book IV, chapter 16 n. 1 of *The Digest of Justinian*, Vol. 2, ed. Alan Watson, (Philadelphia: University of Pennsylvania Press, 1998): "1. Ulpian, *Edict, book 1*: This expression 'if anyone' covers both men and women."

CHAPTER 8

ECCLESIASTES 7:30B-8:7[1] THE REMEDY OF WISDOM
AGAINST CONCUPISCENCE

1. *Who is as the wise person?* He has just described the
vanity of concupiscence. Now he wants to give *the remedy
of wisdom* against this vanity, for people are not freed from
concupiscence unless they walk with wisdom. So the reader
is exhorted in this section to cling to wisdom for four reasons. First, from a consideration of its *nobility*. Second, of
its *power*. Third, of its *usefulness*. Fourth, of its *suitable
time*.

2. Thus, the reader is exhorted to cling to wisdom from a
consideration of its *nobility* which is seen in how it makes
a person noble and glorious both in *appearance* and in
speech. He does this first by *asking a question* and then by
giving the answer.

3. (7:30b) *Who is as the wise person*, that is, who is so noticeable? We read in Sirach 8:10: "For her sake I will have
glory among the multitude and honor with the ancients,

---

[1]On p. 64 n. 6 QuarEd accurately indicate that the words with which
Bonaventure commences his commentary on Ecclesiastes 8 actually
stem from Ecclesiastes 7:30b. The editors also point out that Jerome
commences Ecclesiastes 8 with the text from Ecclesiastes 7:30b. See
CCSL lxii, 313.

though I be young." The author is speaking of wisdom here. Who is so noticeable *in word*? And so he adds: *And who has known the resolution of the word*? Supply: except the wise person. Wisdom 8:8 states: "She knows the subtleties of speeches," etc. And therefore, in doubtful matters the wise person is to be heard with reverence. Thus, Wisdom 8:11-12 states further: "I will be admired in the sight of the mighty, and they will look upon me when I speak. And if I talk much, they will lay their hands on their mouths."

4. (8:1). Now that he has asked the question, now he gives *the answer*. So he says: *The wisdom of people shine in their countenances*. Proverbs 17:24 reads: "Wisdom shines on the countenance of the wise,"[2] that is, wisdom is seen in a person's deeds. Sirach 19:26 states: "A man is known by his appearance, and a wise man, when you meet him, is known by his countenance." For as a good person is known by his appearance, so too is a wise person known through his deeds. Nor is it surprising that goodness should be visible in *the face*, because God made this. So he says: *And the most mighty will change their faces*. This most mighty individual is God. Job 36:5 reads: "God does not cast away the mighty, whereas he himself[3] is mighty." And later in Job 36:22 we read: "Behold, God is high in his strength, and none is like him among the lawgivers." God *will change* the external *face* by first changing the interior one, that is, by turning it to himself. For the face of the soul is the higher region of the mind, by which it is destined to see God.[4] Only God changes this face. Proverbs 21:1 says: "As

---

[2]Hugh of St. Cher, 92v, a also cites Proverbs 17:24.

[3]On p. 65 n. 2 QuarEd correctly mention that the Vulgate reads *et ipse* ("he himself also") while Bonaventure has *ipse* ("he himself").

[4]On p. 65 n. 3 QuarEd refer to Peter Lombard and Gregory the Great. See Book II, d. 24 n. 5 of *Magistri Petri Lombardi Sententiae in IV Libris Distinctae*, Tom. I, Pars II, Liber I et II, Spicilegium Bonaventurianum IV (Grottaferrata: Collegium S. Bonaventurae, 1971), 454: "And 'that intent of the mind by which we contemplate things

the divisions of the waters, so the heart of the king is in the hand of the Lord, whithersoever he will turn it."

5. (Verse 2). Not only is a wise person visible in *appearance*, but also in *a word* spoken in wisdom. In the person of such a wise person he says: *I observe the mouth of the king.* This *king* is God, of whom 1 Timothy 6:15 says: "The Blessed and only Sovereign, the King of kings and Lord of lords." *The mouth* of this King is the Son of God, through whom God speaks to us. Hebrews 1:2 reads: "Last of all in these last days God has spoken to us by his Son." So *to observe the mouth of the king* is to listen carefully to the word of the Son of God. Luke 11:28 states: "Blessed are they who hear the word of God and keep it."[5] Wherefore, Wisdom says: *I observe*, and my observing leads to deeds in accordance with what Deuteronomy 6:3 has: "Observe, so that you may do what the Lord has commanded you, and it will be well with you." He explains what he observes, namely, the commandments of God. So he says: *And the commandments of the oath of God*, because they are firm and must not be profaned. Matthew 24:35 states: "Heaven and earth will pass away, but my words will not pass away." Or: they are *the commandments of the oath*, because they were given with a covenant and an oath. Exodus 223:8 reads: "Moses took the blood and sprinkled it upon the

---

eternal is called wisdom, but that by which we utilize in a good way temporal things is called knowledge or skill.'" Peter Lombard is quoting Augustine. See Book X, chapter 15, n. 27 of Gregory's *Moralia in Iob Libri I-X*, ed. Marcus Adriaen, CCSL cxliii (Turnhout: Brepols, 1979), 556-557: "The inner face of a person is the mind, in which we are undoubtedly recognized so that we are loved by our Creator."

[5]Hugh of St. Cher, p. 92v, f comments: "The king can be understood to be God the Father, and his mouth Christ the Lord. . . .Or the king is understood as Christ the Lord ...who through his own mouth preached the Gospel. Matthew 5[2-3]: Jesus, opening his mouth, taught them saying: Blessed are the poor in spirit, etc."

people saying:[6] This is the blood of the covenant of the Lord . . . concerning all these words."

6. (Verses 3-4). *Do not be hasty*, etc. Second, he exhorts his readers to adhere to wisdom from a consideration of God's *power*, when he says: *Do not be hasty to depart from his face*, that is, do not move away from God's will, for it is a sin of the heart, as if one were hiding from God. Of such a moving away we read in Deuteronomy 32:15: "He forsook God who made him and departed from God his savior." So do not depart from his face by wanting to hide in evil. Sirach 16:16 says: "Do not say: I will be hidden from God and who will remember me from on high." Like Cain, who said to the Lord: "Behold, you cast me out this day from the face of the earth, and I will be hidden from your face."[7]

7. And if a person were to move away so as not to remain in evil, he adds: *And do not continue in an evil work*. Sirach 5:8 reads: "Do not delay in being converted to the Lord, and defer it not day to day."[8] And the reason for this is a reflection on divine power, because God works *omnipotently*: *For he will do all that pleases him*. Psalm 113:11 says: "He has done all things whatsoever he willed."[9] And Isaiah 46:10 states: "My counsel will stand, and all my will shall be done." – God also acts *without difficulty*, and so he says: *And his word is full of power*. Psalm 28:4-5 confesses: "The voice of the Lord is in power. . . .The voice of the Lord breaks cedars." And Jeremiah 32:17-18 reads: "No word will be difficult for you. You show mercy unto thousands." God also acts in a *blameless way*: *Neither can*

---

[6]On p. 65 n. 5 QuarEd rightly indicate that the Vulgate reads *et ait* ("and said") while Bonaventure reads *dicens* ("saying"). Further, the Vulgate reads *ille* ("he") whereas Bonaventure has *Moyses* ("Moses").

[7]Genesis 4:14.

[8]Hugh of St. Cher, 93b also cites Sirach 5:8.

[9]In the Duoay this is Psalm 113:3. In the NAB it is Psalm 15:3.

any one say to him: Why do you do this? Romans 9:20 says: "Who are you that replies against God?"[10]

8. (Verse 5a). *The person who keeps the commandment,* etc. Here in a third point he exhorts us to cling to wisdom from a reflection of *our own benefit.* For there is great benefit from clinging to wisdom and keeping its commandments. So he says: *The person who keeps the commandment will find no evil.* Rather such a person will receive many good things. Matthew 19:17 states: "If you want to enter into life, keep the commandments." And John 8:31-32 reads: "If you continue[11] in my word, you will truly be my disciples, and you will know the truth, and the truth will make you free."

9. (Verses 5b-8). *The heart of a wise person,* etc. Fourth, he exhorts us to keep the commandments of divine wisdom from a reflection on *the opportune time* that wise persons ponder in their works. For this reason he says: *The heart of a wise person understands time and answer.* The wise understand *the time* when one should work. Ephesians 5:15-16 states: "See, brothers, how you walk circumspectly, not as unwise, but as wise, redeeming the time, because the days are evil." One should not only consider *the time,* but also *an answer in time.* Colossians 4:5-6 says: "Walk with wisdom towards those who are outside, redeeming the time. Let your speech be always in grace, seasoned with salt, that you may know how you ought answer every one."

10. And the wise person, who weighs the opportune time, does well, as the author proves when he says: *There is a*

---

[10]Hugh of St. Cher, 93e also cites Romans 9:20 in its entirety.

[11]On p. 65 n. 8 QuarEd accurately mention that the Vulgate reads *Si vos manseritis* ("If you continue") whereas Bonaventure has *Si manseritis* ("If you continue").

time and opportunity for every business, and great affliction for men and women. Supply: in reflecting diligently on these things. Ecclesiastes 3:1 above says: "All things have their season, and in their times all things pass under heaven." For there is a suitable time for *study*. Sirach 38:25 reads: "Write down wisdom during the time of leisure."[12] There is also a suitable time for *prayer*. Psalm 118:62 says: "I rose at midnight to give praise to you."[13] There is also a suitable time for *doing good*. Galatians 6:10 has: "While we have time, let us do good to all."

11. And this opportunity occurs in the present time. The author shows that opportunity comes in the present time by showing the danger of future time which cannot *be foreseen.* And so he says: *Who are ignorant of things past, and things to come they cannot know by any messenger,*[14] since much less known is the future than the past. Ecclesiastes 7:1 above says: "Who can tell him what will be after him?"

12. A person cannot *stop* time. So he says: *It is not in people's dominion*, that is, power, *to stop the spirit*, namely, from going out, because no one can prevent the coming of the time of death. He explains this by saying: *Neither have they power on the day of death.* We read in Job 14:5: "You have appointed his bound which cannot be passed." Nor can time *be avoided*, and so he says: *Neither are they suffered to rest when war is at hand*, namely, on judgment day. Wisdom 5:21 says: "The world will fight on his behalf[15] against the unwise." The wicked could not avoid this

---

[12]Hugh of St. Cher, 93v, a also quotes Sirach 38:25 and along with Bonaventure reads *sapientiam scribe* ("write down wisdom").

[13]Hugh of St. Cher, 93v, a also cites Psalm 118:62.

[1] On p. 66 n. 2 QuarEd correctly indicate that the Vulgate reads *Quia* ("Because") at the beginning of Ecclesiastes 8:7 whereas Bonaventure has *Qui* ("Who").

[15]On p. 66 n. 3 QuarEd accurately mention that the Vulgate reads *cum illo* ("with him") while Bonaventure has *pro eo* ("on his behalf").

war. Thus, in Revelation 6:16 they say to the mountains: "Fall on us," etc., because then "flight will perish."[16] Further, time cannot be *disguised*, and so he continues: *Neither will wickedness save the wicked*, as if a wicked person could pretend to be good. Job 36:6 has: "He does not save the wicked, and he gives judgment to the poor." And Proverbs 11:4 reads: "Riches will not profit on the day of revenge. Justice will deliver from death." Wherefore, Job 10:15 states: "If I be wicked, woe unto me."

QUESTIONS 25

I. What does he mean by: *I observe the commandments of the oath of God?*[17] Therefore, God swears.

Contra: 1. Matthew 5:37 has: *Let your speech be yes, yes, no, no*. Therefore, *that which is longer comes from the evil one*.[18] Wherefore, if it is not fitting for the perfect to swear, and nothing is fitting for God other than what is most perfect, then it is not fitting for God to swear.

2. Moreover, it is excessive, because God cannot lie.[19] Therefore, the simple word of God is equally true as an oath.

3. Also, God *is not able* to swear, because *to swear an oath* is to bring someone as a witness and support, but there is no one who can confirm God's word. And so God cannot swear.

I reply: *An oath for confirmation is the end of all controversy*,[20] and so an oath is a straightforward and firm

---

[16]Amos 2:14.

[17]See Ecclesiastes 8:2.

[18]On p. 66 n. 4 QuarEd rightly indicate that the Vulgate reads *his abundantius* ("over and above these") while Bonaventure has *amplius* ("longer/more").

[19]On p. 66 n. 5 QuarEd helpfully cite Hebrews 6:18: "It is impossible for God to lie."

[20]On p. 66 n. 6 QuarEd cite Hebrews 6:16-17: "For men and women swear by one greater than themselves, and an oath given as a guarantee

assertion. There can be nothing more firm, and it establishes a certain trust. So when we want a listener to have certain trust, we swear an oath. So God, condescending to our weakness, indeed swears an oath to make our faith firm.

1. To the objection that this is from evil, I explain that it comes from the evil of *punishment*, not from the evil of the one swearing. Rather it is from the evil of the person to whom the oath is sworn, that is, due to a doubt in that person.[21] – There is still another way of stating the matter: The Lord does not forbid an oath as something evil. But since people are prone to speak untruths, the Lord forbids swearing oaths too easily, lest one sometimes falls both into a lie and into an oath in contempt of God. And because God cannot lie, this reason does not exist in God.

2. To the objection that God cannot lie, I reply, that even though an oath in God adds nothing in fact to a simple statement, it does add something in our understanding, because our faith is made firmer and because it shows a wondrous condescension towards us.

3. To the objection that God cannot call on a witness, I reply that God himself is a witness to himself, because

---

is the final settlement of all their controversy. Hence God, meaning to show more abundantly to the heirs of the promise the unchangeableness of his will, interposed an oath."

[21]On p. 66 n. 7 QuarEd explain Bonaventure's complex thought by citing Augustine. See Book I, chapter 17 n. 51 in *Saint Augustine, Commentary on the Lord's Sermon on the Mount with Seventeen Related Sermons*, trans. Denis J. Kavanagh, FC 11 (New York: Fathers of the Church, Inc., 1951), 75: "If you are forced to take an oath, remember that the necessity for it arises from the infirmity of those whom you are trying to persuade with regard to something. . . .For you do no evil when you make good use of an oath which, although it is not a good thing, is nevertheless necessary for the purpose of persuading someone to believe what you are trying to induce him to believe for a good purpose.

God is truth. So God himself swears by himself and is the best witness, for the light makes himself and other things clear.[22]

II. There is also doubt about his words: *The person who keeps the commandment will find no evil.*[23]

Contra: Ecclesiastes 8:14 below states: *There are just people, to whom evils happen, as though they had done the works of the wicked.*

I reply: A person experiences an evil that *endures* and an evil that *passes away.* Here the author of the experience speaks of an evil that always *endures,* not of one that is *transitory.*[24]

III. There is a further doubt about the words: *The person who keeps the commandment will find no evil.*[25]

But He said that it is 'from evil,' that is, from the evil of the man whose infirmity forces you [to] take an oath." The editors also refer to Book III, d. 39. c. 4 of Peter Lombard's *Sentence Commentary.*

[22]On p. 66 n. 9 QuarEd cite Hebrews 6:13: "For when God made his promise to Abraham, since he had no one greater to swear by, he swore by himself." The editors also refer to Alexander of Hales, *Summa Theologica,* P. 2, inq. 3, tract. 2, sect. 1, q. 2, n.5.

[23]Ecclesiastes 8:5.

[24]On p. 67 n. 1 QuarEd cite *In Ecclesiasten Expositio Mystica* of Salonius, bishop of Vienna who flourished ca. 450. See PL 53:1006C for his interpretation of this verse: "It is true, because whoever keeps the precepts of God . . . will not experience any evil in the future, that is, will suffer no evil nor be burdened with evil on the day of judgment. For even though a person suffers some evils in this life, they are but slight and transitory, while anyone who reaches the glory of eternal happiness will suffer no evil in the future life." The editors also cite Rupert of Deutz, *In Librum Ecclesiastes Commentarius* on this verse. See PL 168:1272C: "Ecclesiastes did not say he will not suffer, but he will find no evil. Whoever, in observing the commandment, have suffered evils, when they have merited to receive the crown of eternal life, have to their benefit and satisfaction found out that they have not suffered evils."

[25]Ecclesiastes 8:5.

1. Since there are many commandments to be kept, why does he speak of a commandment in the singular?

2. Moreover, it is possible for a person to keep the divine precepts out of fear, as did the Jews, and yet such people are not saved.

I reply: Although there are many precepts because of the diversity of deeds, there is a unity among them in relation to the one *commanding*, to the one *observing*, and to *the reason* for keeping them. – With respect to the one *commanding* there is only one who commands. And therefore, the person who transgresses one commandment cannot be obedient to the one commanding, for there is only the one individual commanding. – With regard to the one *observing* there is a unity, because a person observes all things from the one principle governing all things, namely, charity that overcomes all things. Thus, just as charity loves everybody or nobody, so a person observes all the commandments or none of them. – In relation to *the reason* or goal there is a unity, because one reward is offered and the commandments are to be observed for the one reward. Therefore, since this triple unity is found in a proper observance of the commandments, he says correctly: *The person who keeps the commandment will find no evil.*[26]

ECCLESIASTES 8:9-12:1 THE SECOND OCCASION OF SIN: THE VANITY OF FEELING SECURE

13. *All these things I have considered.* He has treated the vanity of *attraction* and now goes on to the vanity of *security*. Since this vanity is dangerous because it pushes one to sin or holds on to one who has been so pushed, he treats

---

[26]On p. 67 n. 2 QuarEd helpfully refer to *Quaestio* #31 that concerns Ecclesiastes 9:18 and occurs after Ecclesiastes 10:3 (#4) below. The editors also refer to Book III, d. 36. q. 4 ad 1 and 2 of Bonaventure's *Sentence Commentary* and the footnotes there. See Opera Omnia 3:800.

first of *the vanity* and second of *the remedy for the vanity* where Ecclesiastes 10:8 reads: *The person who digs a pit will fall into it.*

ECCLESIASTES 8:9-10:7   THE VANITY OF SECURITY

14. *Security* arises in two ways. First, from what is seen as a lack of *just retribution*. Second, from what is seen as a lack of *the rule of providence*. This second point is considered where Ecclesiastes 9:11 below says: *I turned myself to another thing, and I saw,* etc.

ECCLESIASTES 8:9-9:10   SECURITY ARISES FROM WHAT IS SEEN AS A LACK OF JUST RETRIBUTION

15. Now there seems to be *a lack of the retribution of justice* because of *the exaltation of the wicked,* because of *the lack of goods,* because of *the confusion of both.* So there are three sections. First, he shows how the vanity of security comes from *the advancement of the wicked.* Second, from *the lack of goods* where verse 14 reads: *There is also another vanity which is done upon the earth,* etc. Third, how it arises from a *confusion between the just and the wicked* were verse 16 states: *And I applied my heart to know wisdom,* etc.

ECCLESIASTES 8:9-13   THE EXALTATION OF THE WICKED

16. The rise of security from *the exaltation of the wicked* is described in the following way. First, he suggests *the high position of the wicked.* Second, how *the vanity of security* arises from this in the wicked. Third, how *the good derive a benefit* from this.

17. (Verses 9-10). First, he suggests *the high position of the wicked,* a subject that Ecclesiastes reflected on care-

fully. So he says: *All these things I have considered.* Supply: Something I had said earlier. *And I applied my heart to all the works that are done under the sun* that I might consider them all. Ecclesiastes 1:17 above says: "I have given my heart to know prudence and learning and errors and folly." And in this reflection he saw the high position of the wicked both *in power* and *in fame.* With regard to their exaltation *in power* he says: *Sometimes one person rules over another to his own hurt,* namely, when an evil person is ruling, for a good person, when he rules well, exercises his rule for his own good. Thus, 1 Timothy 3:1 says: "If anyone desires the office of a bishop, he desires a good work." But evil people rule to their own hurt. For Sirach 7:8 states: "Do not bind sin to sin, for even in one you will not be unpunished." An evil prelate binds double sins to himself.

18. With regard to exaltation *in fame,* he says: *I saw the wicked buried,* that is, *in the depth of despair.* Proverbs 18:3 reads: "The wicked person, when he has come into the depth of sins, contemns." Or: *buried,* with *a mound of praise.*[27] Matthew 8:22 states: "Let the dead bury their dead."[28] Gregory observes: "The dead bury the dead when they pile a mound of praise on them."[29] Or: *buried,* by *continual transgressions* even until death, as if to say: Those

---

[27]Hugh of St. Cher, 83v, r has this interpretation: "Buried] with a mound of praise." The same Latin words, *aggere adulationis,* are found in the subsequent quotation attributed to Gregory the Great.

[28]On p. 67 n. 8 QuarEd rightly suggest that Bonaventure's quotation is not so much from Matthew 8:22 as from Luke 9:60.

[29]On p. 67 n. 8 QuarEd quote Book IV, chapter 27 n. 52 of Gregory's *Moralia in Iob.* See CCSL cxliii, 196-197: "About this it is well said: *Let the dead that they may bury their dead.* For the dead bury their dead when sinners cover a sinner with favors. For what does it mean to sin other than to fall down? But persons who pursue a sinner with praises is hiding the dead person under the mound of his words."

who were buried in malice also died in malice. 1 Kings 16:18-19 says: "He died in the sins . . . of Jeroboam who made Israel sin."[30] And according to what the Lord said to the Jews in John 8:21: "You will die in your sins." He saw such wicked people exalted in fame, and so he says: *Who also when they were yet living*, Supply: in their malice, *were in the holy place*, that is, in dignity as if they were holy, like the Antichrist of whom Matthew 24:15 says: "When you shall see the abomination of desolation . . . standing in the holy place."[31] *And were praised in the city as people of just works*. In this way they were famous. Psalm 9:24 states: "For the sinner is praised in the desires of his soul."[32] And Proverbs 28:4 reads: "Those who forsake the law praised the wicked person, but those who keep," etc.[33]

19. (Verses 10-11). *But this also is vanity*. Here he treats the second point, namely, how *the vanity of security* arises because others feel secure when the wicked are not punished. So he says: *But this also is vanity*, that is, a cause of vanity. – And he shows this: *For since sentence is not speedily pronounced against the evil*, the wicked wait serenely, as we read in 2 Peter 3:9: "The Lord delays not his promise,[34] as some imagine, but deals patiently for your sake,

---

[30]Bonaventure's quotation is more a summary than an actual quotation of 1 Kings 16:18-19: "And Zimri . . . died in his sins, which he had sinned, doing evil before the Lord, and walking in the way of Jeroboam, and in his sin, wherewith he made Israel to sin."

[31]Hugh of St. Cher, 93v, t quotes Matthew 24:15 in its entirety.

[32]Hugh of St. Cher, 93v, y also quotes Psalm 9:24.

[33]On p. 68 n. 2 QuarEd accurately indicate that the Vulgate reads *laudant* ("praise") whereas Bonaventure has *laudabant* ("praised"). They also note that the Vulgate does not have *autem* ("but"). Proverbs 28:4 says: "Those who forsake the law praise the wicked person; those who keep it are incensed against him."

[34]The Vulgate reads *Non tardat Dominus promissi* ("The Lord of what has been promised delays not") while Bonaventure has *Non tardat Dominus promissionem* ("The Lord delays not his promise").

not willing that any[35] should perish, but that all should return to penance." And *men and women commit evils without any fear*, and so they are secure because they neither think about nor fear the future. Proverbs 28:5 has: "Evil men do not think about judgment," because now they are not being punished. Isaiah 26:10 states: "Let us have pity on the wicked, but he will not learn justice," etc.

20. (Verses 12-13). *But though a sinner*, etc. Third, he treats of how *the good derive a benefit* from this. For from this good people experience divine mercy and are tested in justice. So he says: *But though a sinner. But though from this that a sinner does wrong a hundred times*, should be taken to mean very often according to what Jeremiah 2:36 says: "How exceedingly base have you become, going the same ways over again." *And by patience be borne with*, namely, by God's patience, according to what Romans 2:4 has: "Do you not know that the benignity of God leads you to penance?"[36] Thus, Lamentations 3:22 reads: "The mercies of the Lord that we are not consumed." *I know that it will be well with those who fear God*, that is, who turn from evil. Proverbs 16:6 reads: "By the fear of the Lord people depart from evil." *Who dread his face*, and out of reverence for God do not dare to sin, according to what Job says about himself in Job 32:23: "For I have always feared God as waves swelling over me, and his weight I was unable to bear." But this benefit of divine mercy and patience does not reach the wicked, and so it is more useful for them to die than to live.

21. So he says: *But let it not be well with the wicked*. He does not say this as a wish, but as a prophecy, just like the

---

[35]On p. 68 n. 3 QuarEd correctly indicate that the Vulgate reads *aliquos* ("some") while Bonaventure has *aliquem* ("any").

[36]Hugh of St. Cher, 93v, d alludes to Romans 2.

Psalmist does in Psalm 9:18: "The wicked will be turned into hell." *Let it not be well,* that is, for glory. Isaiah 26:10 reads: "The wicked is taken away, lest he see the glory of God."[37] Nor do the wicked have good in the present life. So he adds: *Neither let their days be prolonged,* that is, they will not be prolonged. We read in Proverbs 10:27: "The years of the wicked will be shortened." And Psalm 54:24 says: "Bloody and deceitful men will not live out half their days." *But as a shadow let those pass away who fear not the face of the Lord.* And in fact they do pass away like a shadow, for Psalm 36:35-36 states: "I have seen the wicked highly exalted. . . .I passed by, and lo, he was not." Thus, in the person of the wicked Wisdom 5:9-10 says: "All these things have passed away like a shadow, and like a messenger who runs ahead, and like a ship that passes through the waves."

QUESTIONS 26

I. It is asked what he means by the words: *Sometimes one person rules over another:*[38] whether one person can in justice rule over another. That this is true is seen from the following:

1. Romans 13:1 says: *There is no power but from God.* The Apostle also says that one must obey masters, not only out of fear, *but also for conscience's sake.*[39] Therefore, if everything from God is right and one person has power from God, then this too is right.

2. Moreover, if conscience only commands what is just because it is right. And conscience binds us to obey, as the

---

[37]On p. 68 n. 7 QuarEd rightly mention that the Vulgate differs. Isaiah 26:10b reads: "In the land of the saints he has done wicked things, and he will not see the glory of the Lord."

[38]See Ecclesiastes 8:9.

[39]Romans 13:5.

Apostle says.[40] Therefore, it must be right for one person to be subject to another.

3. The Apostle also says in Ephesians 6:5: *Servants, be obedient to those who are your lords according to the flesh.* But the Apostle only commands what is right. Therefore, etc.

Contra: 1. By nature men and women are equal.[41] Therefore, if one person rules over another, that is against nature. But everything against nature is a sin. Therefore, etc.

2. Also, all people by nature are free. Therefore, when one person is made a servant of another, this is by an unlawful seizure.[42] But every unlawful seizure is a sin. Therefore, it is a sin to rule over another person.

I reply by saying that one person can rule over another in justice, as is clear because Noah by divine authority made his son Canaan a servant of his brothers.[43] Isaac did similarly with Esau and Jacob.[44]

---

[40]Romans 13:5.

[41]On p. 69 n. 1 QuarEd quote Book XXI, chapter 15 n. 22 of Gregory the Great's *Moralia in Iob*. See *S. Gregorii Magni, Moralia in Iob Libri XI-XXII*, ed. Marcus Adriaen, CCSL cxliiia (Turnhout: Brepols, 1979), 1082: "For all of us men and women are equal by nature."

[42]On p. 69 n. 2 QuarEd quote Book I, Title 3 ("The Law of Persons"), laws 1-2 of Justinian's *Institutes*. See *Justinian's Institutes*, trans. Peter Birks and Grant McLeod with the Latin text of Paul Krueger (Ithaca: Cornell University Press, 1987), 39: "1. Liberty – the Latin 'libertas' gives us 'liberi', free men – denotes a man's natural ability to do what he wants as long as the law or some other force does not prevent him. 2. Slavery on the other hand is an institution of the law of all peoples; it makes a man the property of another, contrary to the law of nature."

[43]See Genesis 9:25.

[44]See Genesis 27:29 where Isaac blesses Jacob: "Be master of your brothers."

1.2 Against the objection that it is against nature and that every person is free, it has to be understood that there is a double status, namely, of nature *after* and nature *before* the fall. In their nature before the fall all were free and equal, and they were told only to rule over the animals.[45] However, it is another matter with the state of fallen nature. – Since some are worse and more evil than others, it is by a just decree of God that there be servants among them and their posterity. – Another reason for ruling over someone is to restrain the wicked. For if there were no temporal power, each person could do what each thought was right. And so there would be a disruption caused by wickedness, and each one could sin as he or she wished. For this reason it is right that there can be dominion and servitude among men and women.[46] – But whether the wicked can rule over good people is discussed later.[47]

II. It is asked what he means by: *The wicked sins a hundred times and is tolerated.*[48] Is this a matter of *kindness* or *severity*? That it is a matter of *kindness* is clear because Lamentations 3:22 reads: *It is the mercy of the Lord that we are not consumed.* Moreover, the Apostle says in Romans 2:4: *Know you not that the kindness of God is leading you to repentance?*

But contra: The longer a wicked person lives, the more evil he or she does. And the more evil that is done, the more severely will the person be tortured. Therefore, if the wicked person dies sooner, it is better for that person,

---

[45]See Genesis 1:26: "And he said: Let us make man to our image and likeness and let him have dominion over the fish of the sea, etc."

[46]On p. 69 n. 5 QuarEd refer to Book II, d. 44, a. 2, q. 1 and 2 of Bonaventure's *Sentence Commentary*. See Opera Omnia 2:1005-1009.

[47]See *Quaestio* #32 after Bonaventure's exegesis of Ecclesiastes 10:4-7.

[48]This seems to be Bonaventure's summary of Ecclesiastes 8:12: "But though a sinner do evil a hundred times, and by patience be borne with."

because if the person's days are lengthened, this would be bad rather than good for the person. Therefore, it is of *severity*.

I reply by saying that there are certain wicked people whom God foresees will return to God. To such people a lengthening of life is a great mercy whether the mercy be perceived or hidden. There are others whom God foresees will multiply their sins and will die in them. To prolong life for such is an act of *justice* and of *mercy*. Of *mercy*, because a cruel punishment is delayed. But of *hidden justice*, because it is allowed that the person *who is filthy is still filthy*.[49] For this person merits a lengthening of life from a decree of hidden severity.

ECCLESIASTES 8:14-15   HOW THE VANITY OF SECURITY ARISES FROM SEEING THE PLIGHT OF THE GOOD

22. *There is also another vanity*, etc. He showed above how security arises from the sight of the exaltation of the wicked. Here he shows in a second point how it arises from the sight of *the misfortune of the good*. And he does this in the following order. First, he set out *the misfortune of the good*. Second, *the security of the wicked* because of this. Third, he arrives at the conclusion that this is *vanity*. Finally, he commends *pleasure*.

23. (Verse 14). So he treats *the misfortune of good people*, from which arises vanity and says: *There is also another vanity, which is done upon the earth*, namely, different from the aforementioned one because it has a different cause. The preceding vanity came from *the exaltation of the wicked*, while this comes from *the misfortune of the good*.

---

[49]See Revelation 22:11: "And the person who is filthy, let him be filthy still."

So he continues: *There are just people to whom evils happen*, that is, misfortunes; *as though they had done the works of the wicked*, according to what Hebrews 11:36-37 says: "Holy people[50] experienced the trial of mockeries and stripes, moreover also of chains and prisons. They were stoned; they were cut asunder; they were tried." The story of Tobit's blindness in Tobit 2:11 is an example. In Job 1:13-22 there is also the example of Job, who suffered greatly.[51] And the reason for this is given in Judith 8:23: "All who have pleased God have passed through many tribulations and remained faithful."

24. *And there are wicked people.* Here he notes the second point, namely, *the security of the wicked.* Since the wicked see bad things happening to good people and good things to themselves, they feel secure. Therefore, he says: *And there are wicked people, who are as secure as though they had done the deeds of the just*, and this because they are free from misfortune. An example of this is the rich man who loved feasting, for to him it was said in Luke 16:25: "Remember that you received good things in your lifetime, and likewise Lazarus evil things."[52] And so the wicked are made to feel secure, because they prosper. Thus, Jeremiah 12:1 asks: "Why does the way of the wicked prosper? Why is it well with all who transgress," etc.?

25. *But this also I judge most vain.* Third, he *draws the conclusion* that the security of the wicked is a vanity. So he says: *But this also I judge most vain.* For it is vain when *good things* come to the good and to the wicked, because the wicked have no right to this. It is more vain when *bad*

---

[50]The Vulgate reads *Alii* ("Others") while Bonaventure has *Sancti* ("Holy people").

[51]Hugh of St. Cher, 94s mentions Job and Lazarus (Luke 16:19-31).

[52]Hugh of St. Cher, 94x also mentions the rich man who loved to feast, but from the aspect that he wore purple and fine linen.

things happen to the good and to the wicked, because the good do not deserve this. It is most vain when bad things happen to *the good,* and good things happen to *the wicked,* because this is both unjust and undeserving. So a person becomes indignant, as though wanting to argue with God over this situation. Habakkuk 1:13 queries: "Why do you not look upon those who do unjust things and hold your peace, when the wicked devour the person who is more just than they are?"

26. (Verse 15). *Therefore, I commended mirth.* Fourth, *he commends pleasure* from his detestation of the vanity by which good things come to the wicked and bad things to the good. And this is a word of praise from a person who is upset. So he says: *Therefore, I commended mirth,* namely, pleasure of the flesh, as if this were the only good. So he continues: *Because there was no good for people under the sun, but to eat and drink*[53] according to what Isaiah 22:13 states: "Behold, joy and gladness ... to slaughter rams, to eat flesh and drink wine,"[54] as if there were no other life or reward. So he adds: *And that they should take nothing else with them of their labors,* as if nothing else is to be expected other than to rejoice *in the days of their lives, which God has given them under the sun.* We read in Wisdom 2:9: "Let us everywhere leave tokens of joy, for this is our portion."

Questions 27

It can be asked here: Which status is better and more useful, namely, the condition of prosperity or adversity.[55] That *adversity* is better is seen from the following:

---

[53]The Vulgate reads *comederet et biberet atque gauderet* ("might eat and drink and be merry").

[54]Hugh of St. Cher, 94z quotes Isaiah 22:13 in its entirety.

[55]See Ecclesiastes 8:14-15.

1. For it is said in Revelation 3:19: *I rebuke and chastise those whom I love*. Therefore, tribulation is a sign of divine love.

2. It is also said in Hebrews 12:6: *Now God scourges every son that he receives*. Therefore, *to be scourged* is a sign of being a child of God.

3. Also, Tobit 12:13 says: *Because you were acceptable to God, it was necessary that temptation should prove you*. Therefore, etc.

4. Furthermore, Judith 8:23 reads: *All, however many there are to please God,*[56] *have passed through many tribulations and remained faithful*. Therefore, this condition is better.

Contra: 1.The Church asks for peace: "Lord, give peace in our days."[57] Therefore, if the Church asks for what is better, the condition of prosperity is better.

2. Also, the Apostle in 1 Timothy 2:2 would have us pray those *who are in high positions that we may lead a quiet and peaceable life in all piety and chastity*. Therefore, a condition of tranquility is better.

3. Moreover, if there were no sin, there would not be adversity, but total tranquility and prosperity. Therefore, a condition of prosperity is more in accord with the state of

---

[56]On p. 70 n. 6 QuarEd accurately intimate that the Vulgate reads *qui placuerunt Deo* ("who have pleased God") whereas Bonaventure has *quotquot placuere Deo* ("however many there are to please God").

[57]On p. 70 n. 7 QuarEd give this generic reference: "In an antiphon of the Roman Breviary for peace." Diligent searches through the Roman Breviary and books of Gregorian Chant have failed to uncover the exact source for this prayer. See, however, Sirach 50:25: "May God grant us joy of heart and that there be peace in our days in Israel forever."

innocence and glory. But "what is more similar to what is better is itself better."[58] Therefore, etc.

I reply by saying that the conditions of prosperity and adversity can be examined in relation to *good* and *wicked* people. If examined in relation to *wicked* people, who are happy when prosperous and cast down when afflicted, neither condition is useful unless divine grace helps, so that when they are afflicted externally they are enlightened inwardly. In this way when affliction is accompanied by inspiration, something that often happens, a condition of adversity is more useful.

However, if we speak of the relation to *good* people, it has to be said that some good people are *perfect*. About these it is said in Proverbs 12:21: *Whatever shall befall the just person, it shall not make him sad.* In view of this it is better and more useful for the perfect to be in a condition of adversity, for in adversity they are tested as gold is tested in fire.[59] The condition of prosperity is not useful to them, because they do not make progress or they become lukewarm or because their spirit fails them, as happened to David, who was strong in war, but fell at the sight of a woman.[60]

Other good people are *imperfect*. They love God and are led by temporal advantages. Since they do not have

---

[58]On p. 70 n. 9 QuarEd refer to Book III, n. 2 of Aristotle's *Topica*. See WAE, vol. 1, 117b: "Another commonplace rule is that which is nearer to the good is better and more desirable, i.e. what more nearly resembles the good: thus justice is better than a just man. Also, that which is more like than another thing to something better than itself. . . ."

[59]On p. 70 n. 11 QuarEd helpfully cite 1 Peter 1:6-7: "Over this you rejoice. Though now for a little while, if need be, you are made sorrowful by various trials, that the temper of your faith – more precious by far than gold which is tried by fire – may be found unto praise and glory and honor at the revelation of Jesus Christ."

[60]See 2 Samuel 11:1-27.

perfect charity, they fall easily and for such people prosperity is more useful. Since the Church has more delicate and weak than strong children, the Church is forced to pray for peace. Therefore, it is a gift of God that bad things happen to *good* people in the present, according to what Philippians 1:29 states: *Unto you it is given, not only to believe in him, but also to suffer for him.*[61]

ECCLESIASTES **8:16-9:10**   SECURITY ARISES FROM CONFUSION BETWEEN THE GOOD AND THE WICKED AND BECOMES A PRINCIPLE OF PLEASURE

27. *And I applied my heart*, etc. It has been seen how the vanity of security arises from *the exaltation of the evil* and also from *the repression of the good*. Third, he shows how it arises from *confusion between the good and the wicked*. Since the wicked cannot be discerned from the good, the wicked feel secure. And since this security arises from the confusion between the good and the wicked and also becomes a principle for pleasure, he divides this material into two parts. He shows, first, how *security* arises from the confusion. Second, how *pleasure* comes from the security where Ecclesiastes 9:4 reads: *There is no one who always lives*, etc.

ECCLESIASTES **8:16-9:3**   HOW SECURITY ARISES FROM THE CONFUSION BETWEEN THE GOOD AND THE WICKED

28. The first point is described in this order. First, he notes *the vain effort* of discernment. Second, *the uncertainty of the inquiry*. Third, *the reason for the uncertainty*. Fourth,

---

[61]On p. 70 n. 12 QuarEd rightly mention that the Vulgate's text is different. Philippians 1:29 goes: "For it has been granted to you for Christ, not only so that you may believe in him, but so that you also may suffer for him."

from this he draws the conclusion about *the origin of the vain security*.

29. (Verses 16-17). First, he treats *the vain effort* of discernment, an effort that was *diligent*. So he says: *And I applied my heart*, that is, I applied my mind, *to know wisdom* concerning what is invisible *and to understand the spread of things that are upon the earth*, concerning what is visible, for Romans 1:20 says: "The invisible things of God, from the creation of the world, are clearly seen, being understood by the things that have been made." And this effort is *vain*, because no matter how much one works it cannot be found. So he adds: *For there are some who day and night take no sleep with their eyes*, but work ceaselessly at their search. Ecclesiastes 3:10-11 above reads: "I have seen the trouble, which God has given to the children of men and women to be exercised in it. . . .He has made all things good in their time and has delivered the world to their consideration." And even though they work so much, they make no progress.

30. So he continues: *And I understood that a human being can find no reason for all those works of God that have been done under the sun*. We read in Sirach 43:34: "Do not be weary, for you can never go far enough." *And the more human beings shall labor to seek, so much the less will they find*. For Psalm 63:7-8 says: "A human being comes to a high heart,[62] and God will be exalted," that is, he will be turned aside. Augustine comments: "God is on high. If you raise yourself, God flees from you. If you humiliate your-

---

[62]The Vulgate reads *Accedet homo et cor altum* ("A human being and a high heart come") while Bonaventure has *Accedet homo ad cor altum* ("A human being comes to a high heart").

self, God comes to you."[63] *Yea, though the wise shall say that they know it, they will not be able to find it,* that is, if people think they know, the less they understand, because it is said in Romans 1:22: "Professing themselves to be wise, they became fools." Ecclesiastes 7:24 above says: "I have said: I will be wise, and it departed further from me." And he repeats his effort, adding that it was an effort born of curiosity, for to be solicitous in matters that are not useful is curiosity.[64]

31. So he says: *All these things I considered in my heart, that I might carefully understand them.*[65] And this is condemned in Sirach 3:24: "In unnecessary matters be not over[66] curious, and in many of his works you shall not be[67] inquisitive." And this makes clear the distinction between effort that is *diligent* and *vain*, and therefore, *curious*.

---

[63]On p. 71 n. 2 QuarEd refer to six places in Augustine where such a quotation occurs. See, e.g., his Sermon 177 n. 2 in PL 39:2083: "God is on high. You lift yourself up, and God flees from you. You humiliate yourself, and God descends to you." See also PL 36:598; PL 37:1082; PL 37:1779.

[64]For Hugh of St. Victor's definition of curiosity, see the commentary on Ecclesiastes 1:13 (#13) note 82 above: "Curiosity is an eagerness to examine things it is useless to know."

[65]On p. 71 n. 5 QuarEd say: "With all the codices, Hugh of St. Cher, and Lyranus we make these words verse 17 of Ecclesiastes 8, but the Vulgate commences Ecclesiastes 9 with them."

[66]On p. 71 n. 6 QuarEd rightly indicate that the Vulgate reads *multipliciter* ("over") while Bonaventure has *multum* ("over").

[67]On p. 71 n. 6 QuarEd correctly mention that the Vulgate has *non eris* ("you shall not be") whereas Bonaventure reads *ne fueris* ("you shall not be").

CHAPTER 9

1. (Verse 1) *There are just and wise people*, etc. Second, he treats of *the uncertainty of discernment*. Individuals do not know whether they are good or evil, even though they are good. So he says: *There are just and wise men and women*, and thus good. *And their works are in the hand of God*, that is, in God's power of knowing, accepting, and rewarding. In God's hands are *merits* and *rewards*. There are merits for good *thoughts*. Proverbs 21:1 reads: "As the divisions of waters, so the heart of the king is in the hand of the Lord." There are merits for good *affections*. Psalm 94:4 says: "In his hand are all the ends of the earth." There are merits for good *speeches*. Wisdom 7:16 states: "In his hand are both we and our words." There are also merits for good *works* as in this very verse. *Rewards* are also in God's hands. Wisdom 3:1 has: "The souls of the just are in the hand of God." And since they are in the hand of God, they should be known. *And yet men and women do not know whether they be worthy of love or hatred*, and so a person does not know how to discern. We read in 1 Corinthians 4:4: "I have nothing on my conscience. Yet I am not thereby justified," etc.[1]

---

[1]1 Corinthians 4:4 concludes with: ". . . but the one that judges me is the Lord."

2. (Verse 2). *But all things are kept uncertain for the time to come.* Third, he notes *the reason for the uncertainty.* The uncertainty comes from the fact that merits are not rewarded at the present time, but the reward is kept for the future. And so he says: *Men and women do not know. . . .But all things are kept uncertain for the time to come,* namely, so that they can be made evident. 1 Corinthians 4:5 reads: "Do not judge before the time, until the Lord comes, who will bring to light the hidden things of darkness and will manifest the counsels of hearts." God does not do this now, but holds back according to what Job 14:17 says: "You have sealed up my offences, as it were, in a bag." So all things are hidden for the present moment.

3. Ecclesiastes continues: *Because all things equally happen to the just and to the wicked,* etc. *All things,* good and evil, *happen equally* to the just and to the sinner, whom he describes under six differences. *To the just and to the wicked* with regard to *steadfast faith,* because faith justifies a wicked person.[2] Habakkuk 2:4 says: "The just person lives by his faith."[3] – *To the good and to the evil,* with respect to *the purity of love,* because holy love makes a person good. Matthew 7:18 states: "A good tree cannot bring forth evil fruit." – *To the clean and to the unclean* relative to *goodness of speech.* For this is concerned with external things as Tobit 4 testifies.[4] – *To persons who offer holocausts and victims and to those who despise sacrifices* with respect to *right worship.* We read in Exodus 12:43: "This is the service of the Passover. No foreigner shall eat of it."

---

[2]Bonaventure is alluding to Romans 4:5: "But to the person who does no work, but believes in God who justifies the wicked, his faith is credited to him as righteousness."

[3]The Vulgate reads *vivet* ("will live") while Bonaventure has *vivit* ("lives").

[4]For example, care of parents (4:3-5) and alms to the poor (4:8-12).

4. *As the good is, so also the sinner*, with regard to *observation of the commandments*, for to observe them makes a person good and to disobey them makes a person evil. Daniel 9:5 reads: "We have sinned. We have committed iniquity and have revolted. We have gone aside from your commandments and your judgments." *– As the perjurer, so he also who swears truth*, with respect to *truthful speech*. Here the prefix of the verb augments the verb's force rather than decreasing it.[5] *He swears*, that is, he really swears according to the meaning accepted in 1 Samuel 20:17: "And Jonathan swore again to David, because he loved him."[6] To all these people the same things happen according to the condition of *nature*, as Wisdom 7:6 states: "For all people have one entrance into life and a similar exit." It also stems from the condition of *sin*. Romans 3:23 reads: "All have sinned and have need of the glory of God." It also comes from the condition of *punishment*. Sirach 8:6 has: "Remember that we are all worthy of corruption."[7]

5. (*Verse 3*). *This is a very great evil*, etc. Fourth, he treats of *the origin of vain security*, because great security comes from this confusion that is the occasion of many sins. So he says: *This is a very great evil among all things that are done under the sun, that the same things happen to all people*. It is *very great*, because it is the occasion of many sins, for it seems that God is not concerned with us. This gives rise to the opinion found in Job 22:14: "The clouds are his hiding place, and he does not consider our things."

---

[5]Bonaventure is referring to the prefix *de* of the verb *dejerare* ("to swear") which is also spelled *dejurare*. Hugh of St. Cher, 94v, a also enters into this discussion of grammar and uses the terminology of *de privativum* and *de intensivum*.

[6]Hugh of St. Cher, 94v, a also cites 1 Samuel 20:17.

[7]On p. 72 n. 2 QuarEd accurately notice that the Vulgate reads *correptione* ("worthy of correction") while Bonaventure has *corruptione* ("worthy of corruption"). The editors also state that Hugh of St. Cher and Lyranus also have Bonaventure's reading.

That evils come from this is clear, because it gives rise to a security by which a person falls into malice and contempt. So he says: *Whereby also the hearts of men and women*, that is, of evil and carnal people *are filled with evil and with contempt*. The word *filled* indicates a multitude of sins, for *evil* is in the *concupiscible* part of the heart and *contempt* is in the irascible part of the heart. These are the two roots of sin. Genesis 6:11 reads: "The earth was corrupted before God and was filled with iniquity." This happens *while they live*, while they have the opportunity to merit. 1 Thessalonians 2:16 states: "So that they might fill up their sins always." And since such people fall into punishment, the text continues: *And afterwards they will be brought down to hell*. We read in Psalm 54:24: "But you, O God, will bring them down into the pit of destruction." And Job 21:13 has: "They spend their days in good things, and in a moment they go down into hell."[8]

Questions 28

I. A question arises from what he says: *I understood that a human being can find no reason for the works of God*.[9]

1. Therefore, if we should know the reason for what we understand and we can find no reason, then we understand nothing.[10]

2. Also, the purpose of rational nature is to understand and see reasons. So if we cannot find the reasons, we possess our rational power in vain.

---

[8]Hugh of St. Cher, 95v, x also cites Job 21:13.

[9]On p. 72 n. 5 QuarEd correctly intimate that the Vulgate of Ecclesiastes 8:17 reads *omnium operum* ("all the works") while Bonaventure has *operum* ("the works").

[10]On p. 72 n. 6 QuarEd provide a useful parallel in chapter 11 n. 25 of Augustine's *The Advantage of Believing*. See Saint Augustine, *The Advantage of Believing*, trans. Luanne Meagher, FC 4 (New York: CIMA Publishing Co., 1947), 425: "What we understand, accordingly, we owe

I reply that "words are to be understood with reference to the topic."[11] But he is not speaking about the works of God in general, but of divine judgments which are the works of God according to what Psalm 110:2 says: *Great are the works of the Lord*, etc. As Gregory says: "These judgments are not to be discussed, but venerated in an awesome silence."[12] While they have a reason, it is a hidden reason that is beyond us. If we do understand, it is by an inspiration of the Holy Spirit, who *searches the depths of God*,[13] not by human effort. With other works, for example, those of creatures, many reasons are worked out through many fields of knowledge, but Ecclesiastes is not talking about these works here.

II. Likewise, there is a doubt about the words: *Men and women do not know whether they be worthy of love or hatred.*[14]

This seems to be false. 1.For Romans 8:35-36 states: *Who will separate us from the love of Christ? . . . I am certain*, etc. So this text is an example of knowing whether a person is loved or not. – *You will say* that the Apostle knew this by revelation, but *the objection* presumes possible human knowledge on its own terms. For the dignity of divine love puts within us a grace that makes us pleasing to

---

to reason; what we believe, to authority; and what we have an opinion on, to error."

[11]On p. 72 n. 7 QuarEd refer to Book II, n. 2 of Aristotle's *Ethica nicomachea*. See WAE, vol. 9, 1104a: ". . . the accounts we demand must be in accordance with the subject matter."

[12]On p. 72 n. 8 QuarEd cite Book XXXII, chapter 1 n. 1 of Gregory's *Moralia in Iob*. See *S. Gregorii Magni, Moralia in Iob Libri XXIII-XXXV*, ed. Marcus Adriaen, CCSL cxliii b (Turnhout: Brepols, 1985), 1626: "Divine judgments, when they are not known, are not to be discussed in bold speech, but venerated in an awesome silence."

[13]On p. 72 n. 9 QuarEd helpfully refer to 1 Corinthians 2:10: "For the Spirit searches all things, even the depths of God."

[14]Ecclesiastes 9:1.

God. But Augustine says that things in the soul by reason of their *essence* are better known than things in the soul according to *an image*.[15] Therefore, if we are certain of things about which we know according to their *image*, for example, something sweet placed on the tongue, we should be more certain of grace.

2. Furthermore, Augustine says that whoever has faith is certain about having faith.[16] Therefore, whoever has love or charity is sure about having it. And so whoever has grace is sure about having it and, therefore, is certain whether he or she is pleasing to God.

3. Also, people can be certain about hatred, just as people who have sinned or want to sin are sure that they are worthy of hatred.

Contra: 1.1 Corinthians 4:4 reads: *I have nothing on my conscience, yet I am not hereby justified*, etc.

2. Moreover, Job 9:11 states: *If he comes to me, I will not see him. If he departs, I will not understand.* Again Job 9:21 says: *Although I should be without dissimulation, even this my soul will not know about.*

3. Furthermore, Sirach 5:5 has: *Concerning sin that has been forgiven, do not be without fear.* Wherefore, nothing is certain.

---

[15]On p. 72 n. 11 QuarEd refer to four passages in Augustine. See, for example, Book XII, chapter 6 n. 15 of *De Genesi ad litteram*. See *On Genesis*, 470-471: "Now anything that is seen not in images, but as it properly is in itself, and is not seen through the body, is seen with a kind of vision that surpasses all the other kinds. . . .But the third kind, by which love is understood and looked at, touches on things which do not have any images that are like them without actually being what they are."

[16]On p. 72 n. 12 QuarEd cite Book XIII, chapter 1 n. 3 of Augustine's *The Trinity*. See *Saint Augustine, The Trinity*, trans. Stephen McKenna, FC 45 (Washington: Catholic University of America, 1963), 371: "Faith

Some answer this by saying that the text is to be understood of the hatred of predestination and of condemnation, about which no one is certain. And so it does not apply since predestination makes no effect in us by which it can be known. – Another response is that the previous answer does not correspond to the text. For the text states: *Men and women do not know whether they be worthy of love*, but no one is worthy of nor merits predestination. So the text is to be understood of present justice.[17]

For this reason others reply that there is a double knowledge. The first one is *necessary* and infallible. We cannot have this kind of knowledge, because no one can know with certitude whether he or she has grace, other than by a revelation as in the case of the Apostle. The second knowledge is *probable* and comes through signs. And this, indeed, can be possessed and is possessed, because many know from probable signs that they are in grace.

1-2. So to the objection that a person sees into the *essence* of the soul, I say that habits of the soul are known only by the soul seeing itself capable of some action. And since acts of *unformed* and *formed* faith and acts of love due to *grace* and to *nature* are so similar, so that a person can hardly or never distinguish between them, a person does not know whether the habit comes from grace or not.

3. To the objection about hatred, I say that Ecclesiastes is speaking about *the just*, because they do not know whether

---

is not so seen (through images) in the heart in which it is, by him whose it is; but we know most certainly that it is there, and our conscience proclaims its existence."

[17]On p. 73 n. 4 QuarEd refer to Book I, d. 40, a. 2, q. 2 and d. 41, a. 1, q. 1-2 of Bonaventure's *Sentence Commentary*. See Omnia Opera 1:711 and 1:728-736 respectively.

they are worthy of love or of hate. He is not speaking of people who *openly do evil*.

However, whatever men and women know or do not know, namely, whether they have love and faith, they do not know whether they are worthy of God's love or hatred. For we can believe, but how do we know that God hates evil people and loves good people when so many and such great good things happen to the evil as well as to the good? So Ecclesiastes did not say that they did not know whether they are *just*, but that they do not know whether God *loves* them.[18]

III. One can also doubt the following words: *This is a very great evil ... under the sun, that*[19] *the same things may happen*[20] *to all people.*[21]

Contra: 1. It is worse when good things happen to evil people and bad things happen to good people than when the same things happen to both. For, as was said above on Ecclesiastes 8:4, that is not merited nor fitting.

2. Also, it was said above in Ecclesiastes 8:14: *This also I judge most vain*, namely, about this that the evil are secure, and evil things happen to the just. But "what is said as an exaggeration applies only to one thing."[22] Therefore, etc.

---

[18]On p. 73 n. 5 QuarEd refer to Book I, d. 17, p. 1, q. 3 of Bonaventure's *Sentence Commentary*. See Omnia Opera 1:298.

[19]The Vulgate has *quia* ("that") and Bonaventure reads *quod* ("that").

[20]The Vulgate reads *eveniunt* ("happen") whereas Bonaventure has *eveniant* ("may happen").

[21]Ecclesiastes 9:3.

[22]On p. 73 n. 7 QuarEd refer to Book V, n. 5 of Aristotle's *Topica*. See WAE, vol. 1, 134b: "So he errs if he has not expressly distinguished the property that belongs specifically, because then it will belong only to one of the things that fall under the term of which he states the property: for the superlative belongs only to one of them, e.g. 'lightest' as applied to 'fire'." See also Book VII, n. 1 and WAE, vol. 1, 151a.

I reply by saying that intensifying and lessening in vanity and evil can be taken *in a proper sense.* An example of *intensification* is found in the saying that a pearl is whiter than a horse. And so in terms of intensification, vanity is greater when evil people are exalted and the good are put down. The degrees of more and less can be understood further in an *extensive* sense, because this situation is the cause or occasion of sin in many or for many. In this sense confusion between good and evil people is a greater vanity, because it is a source of many evils. For if bad things were to happen to good people and good things to evil people, good and evil people could be distinguished. But when the same things happen to both, no discernment is possible.

ECCLESIASTES 9:4-10   PLEASURE ARISES FROM THE FEELING OF SECURITY

6. *There is no one who lives always.* Ecclesiastes has already shown how the vanity of security stems from this confusion. He now in a second point shows how *pleasure* arises from this security, and he does this in the following order. First, he notes *the certitude of death.* Second, *the deterioration of one's condition* by death. Third, *an approval of pleasure.* Fourth, *a confirmation of this approval.*

7. (Verse 4). First, he notes *the certitude of death* from the fact that no one can avoid its decree. So he says: *There is no one who lives always.* Psalm 88:49 reads: "Who is the person who will live and not see death?" And into this condemnation Adam and his posterity fell. To him it was said in Genesis 3:19: "You are dust, and unto dust you will return." – *Or who hopes for this thing.* Supply: there is no one. *For this thing,* that is, the hope of living forever. Job 7:6-7 states: "My days have passed more swiftly than the web is cut by the weaver and are consumed without any hope. . . . For my life is a wind, and will not return," etc.[23]

8. *A living dog is better than a dead lion.* Second, he shows
that a *condition of deterioration* follows death and states
this by means of a metaphor: *A living dog is better than a
dead lion.* Although a lion surpasses a dog, death makes it
inferior, because a live dog can do something while a dead
lion can do nothing, even though while the lion was alive
it was more powerful than a dog. Proverbs 30:30 says: "A
lion, the strongest of animals,[24] has no fear of anything it
meets." So he wants to say metaphorically that any living
thing, no matter how lowly, is better than something dead,
no matter how good.

9. (Verses 5-6). He proves the previous point, first, by the
act of *knowing. For the living know that they will die.* At
least they are sure of this. 2 Samuel 14:14 reads: "We all
die, and like waters that return no more, we fall down into
the earth." Or: *We will die,* that is, we are subject to the
necessity of death. Romans 8:10 says: "The body is dead
because of sin."[25] – *For[26] the dead know nothing more,* because knowledge presupposes life. And so the living sur-
pass the dead in the act of knowledge, for the dead can
neither move nor feel. With regard to the act of *remembering* he continues: *Neither have they a reward anymore,*
namely, of fame remembered by others, *for the memory of
them is forgotten.* Ecclesiastes 2:16 says: "There will be no
remembrance of the wise no more than of the fool forever
and the times to come," etc. Or: Because no memory of
them is recalled. Job 7:9-10 states: "The person who goes

---

[23]Job 7:7 concludes with: ". . . and my eye will not return to see good
things."

[24]On p. 73 n. 9 QuarEd correctly mention that the Vulgate has
bestiarum ("beasts") while Bonaventure reads *animalium* ("animals").

[25]Hugh of St. Cher, 95q also cites Romans 8:10.

[26]The Vulgate reads *vero* ("but") whereas Bonaventure has *enim*
("for").

down[27] to hell will not come up, nor will he return anymore into his house, nor will his locale know him anymore."

10. With respect to the act of *affection* the text says: *Their love also, and their hatred, and their envy have all perished*, because they are no longer honored as they were when alive. - Relative to the act of *external deeds* he says: *Neither have they a part in this world*. And then he explains what he means: *And in the work that is done under the sun*, because they cannot work anymore, according to what John 9:4 says: "The night comes, when no one can work."[28]

11. (Verses 7-9a). *Go, then, and eat*, etc. Third, he treats of *the approval of present pleasure*. He exhorts his readers to embrace this pleasure, first, with regard to *taste*. So he says: *Go, then, and eat your bread with joy*. By *bread* he includes all things connected with food. – *And drink your wine with gladness*. By *wine* he includes all things connected with drink. – *Because your works please God*, as if to say, you are not sure whether they are displeasing, so presume that they are pleasing and eat and drink securely according to what Isaiah 22:13 says: "Behold, joy and gladness . . . to eat flesh and to drink wine. Let us eat and drink, for tomorrow we will die."

12. Then regarding *sight*, he says: *At all times let your garments be white*, so as to appear neat in clothing. *And let not oil depart from your head*, so as to appear neat in appearance. All who adorn themselves to appear pleasing in

---

[27]On p. 74 n. 2 QuarEd accurately indicate that the Vulgate reads *descenderit* ("will do down") while Bonaventure has *descendet* ("goes down").

[28]Hugh of St. Cher, 95v, q cites all of John 9:4.

the sight of others act in this way. For example, Judith adorned herself when she wanted to be pleasing to the eyes of Holofernes, according to what is said in Judith 10:2-4. But Judith did this for a good reason, for otherwise it would be blameworthy. Sirach 11:4 counsels: "Glory not in apparel at any time."

13. Next concerning *touch*, he says: *Live joyfully with the wife whom you love.* Such enjoyment is described in Proverbs 7:18: "Come, let us be inebriated with the breasts, and let us enjoy the desired embraces, till the day appears." And this is to be done not just once, but *all the days of your unsteady life, which are given to you under the sun.* Our life is truly unsteady, according to what Job 14:2 has: "And never continues in the same state."[29] To add more emphasis he says: *All the time of your vanity.* Our life is a time of vanity. For Psalm 143:4 states: "Human beings are similar to vanity. Their days pass away like a shadow."

14. (Verses 9b-10). *For this is your portion in life*, etc. Fourth, he treats of *the confirmation of this approval.* And the confirmation consists in this that a person expects no other reward or receives any other benefit. Therefore, people must take what they can. So he continues: *For this is your portion in life and in your labor wherewith you labor under the sun*, namely, to take pleasure in the present moment. Wisdom 2:9 reads: "Let us everywhere leave tokens of our[30] joy, for this is our portion and this our lot."

15. And since there is nothing else to be expected, a person should take this as much as possible. So he says: *What-*

---

[29]Job 14:1-2 reads: "Human beings, born of women, living for a short time, are filled with many miseries. Who come forth like a flower and are destroyed, and flee like a shadow and never continue in the same state."

[30]On p. 74 n. 8 QuarEd rightly note that the Vulgate does not have *nostrae* ("our").

soever your hand is able to do, do it earnestly, that is, while there is time and do not wait for the future. And so he adds: *For neither work*, in things to be done, *nor reason*, in things to be decided; nor *knowledge*, in things to be known; nor *wisdom*, in things to be loved, *will be in hell, whither you are hastening*. Such things are not in hell, because, as it is said in Job 10:21-22: "That land is dark and covered with the mist of death . . . where . . . no order, but everlasting horror dwells."[31] Sinners *are hastening* thither, and all, before the coming of Christ, went as far as Limbo. Job 17:16 says: "All that I have will go down to the deepest pit." Thither sinners *are hastening*, as one day follows another. Deuteronomy 32:35 states: "The day of destruc-tion is at hand."

16. Now this can be expounded in *a spiritual sense*, as, first, an exhortation to *the joy of contemplation*, and second, to *urgent action*. Now the following are necessary for *contemplative men*: *to meditate on Sacred Scripture, to have a pure conscience, to embrace interior devotion*. – With respect to *meditation on Sacred Scripture* he says: *Go, then, and eat your bread with joy, and drink your wine with gladness*: *bread* concerning what is difficult and *wine* concerning what is easy. Wisdom says in Proverbs 9:5:[32] "Come, eat my bread and drink the wine that I have mingled for you."[33]

---

[31]On p. 74 n. 9 QuarEd correctly point to Bonaventure's adaptation of this citation for his purposes. Job 10:21-22 reads: "Before I go and return no more, to a land that is dark and covered with the mist of death: a land of misery and darkness, where the shadow of death, and no order, but everlasting horror dwell."

[32]Hugh of St. Cher, 95v, b also cites Proverbs 9:5.

[33]On p. 74 n. 10 QuarEd cite Book I, chapter 21 n. 29 of Gregory the Great's *Moralia in Iob*. See CCSL cxliii, 40: "Sacred Scripture is sometimes food for us, sometimes drink. It is food in the more obscure passages, because as it is expounded, it is broken and is swallowed after it is chewed. It is drink in the clearer passages, because it is drunk

17. With reference to *purity of conscience* he says: *At all times let your garments be white*, that is, with a clean conscience. Revelation 3:4 reads: "They have not defiled their garments, and they will walk with me in white garments." On the other hand, we read in Isaiah 9:5: "A garment mingled with blood will be burnt and be fuel for the fire." And since inner joy comes from a clean conscience, he says: *And let not oil depart from your head*. For Psalm 103:15 states: "That he may make the face cheerful with oil." Matthew 6:17 reads: "But you, when you fast, anoint your head," etc.[34]

18. Concerning *an embrace of inner devotion* he says: *Live joyfully with the wife whom you love*. This *wife* is the religious institute, in which time must be given to contemplation. Proverbs 5:18-19 states: "Rejoice with the wife of your youth. Let her be your dearest hind," etc. Such a beloved wife is prefigured in Rachel, for whom *Jacob served seven years*, according to Genesis 29:20.[35]

19. With regard to *an active life* he says: *Whatsoever your hand is able to do, do it earnestly*. To do something ear-

---

as it is found." See also Homily 10 n. 3 of Book I in *Sancti Gregorii Magni Homiliae in Ezechielem Prophetam*, ed. Marcus Adriaen, CCSL xclii (Turnhout: Brepols, 19710, 145: "But it is to be noted that [Sacred Scripture] is sometimes food, sometimes drink. For in the more obscure passages which cannot be understood without exposition, Sacred Scripture is food, for whatever is expounded so that it may be understood is like food that is chewed before it is swallowed. But in the clearer passages it is drink. For we swallow a drink without chewing it. So we drink the more clear commandments, since we can understand them without any exposition."

[34]Hugh of St. Cher, 95v, g also cites Matthew 6:17.

[35]See Bonaventure's commentary on Luke 10:42 (#75) in *St. Bonaventrue's Commentary on the Gospel of Luke Chapters 9-16*, trans. Robert J. Karris, Works of St. Bonaventure VIII/2 (St. Bonaventure, NY: Franciscan Institute Publications, 2003), 1006: "And this was well designated in Jacob's two wives, namely, Rachel and Leah, one of whom designates the active life and the other contemplative life."

nestly means to do it *quickly*, and this is against negligence. Sirach 31:27 reads: "In all your works be quick, and no infirmity will come to you." To do it *enthusiastically*. Proverbs 18:9 says: "The person who is loose and slack in his work is the brother of the person who wastes his own work. To do it *continually*. Sirach 27:4 has: "Unless you hold yourself diligently in the fear of the Lord, your house will be quickly overthrown." To do it *with perseverance*. We read in 2 Timothy 2:5: "The person who strives in the contest is not crowned, unless he strives lawfully," that is, with perseverance.

20. He adds the reason why one should act earnestly in doing good at the present time, namely, because the time for gaining merit is brief. Therefore, he says: *There is no work in hell*, for the exercises of piety. We read in John 9:4: "I must work ... while it is day." And therefore, it is said in Galatians 6:10: "While we have time, let us do good to all, but especially to those who are of the household of the faith."[36] *There is no reason* for searching and discerning what is good and what is evil. Job 12:25 reads: "They will grope as in the dark and not in the light,[37] and he will make them stagger like people who are drunk." Isaiah 19:14 states: "And the Lord has mingled in the midst thereof a spirit of vertigo." *There are no wisdom and knowledge*. *Knowledge* to contemplate God in God's works. *Wisdom* to contemplate God as God. About these Isaiah 33:6 says: "Riches of salvation, wisdom and knowledge: the very fear of the Lord is the treasure."[38]

---

[36] Hugh of St. Cher, 95v, q also quotes Galatians 6:10.

[37] On p. 75 n. 6 QuarEd rightly indicate that the Vulgate reads *non in luce* ("not in the light") while Bonaventure has *non in lumine* ("not in the light").

[38] On p. 75 n. 6 QuarEd accurately mention that the Vulgate has *eius* ("his") after *thesaurus* ("treasure").

Questions 29

I. It can be asked what he means by the words: *The dead know nothing more.*[39] This seems to be false, because a soul separated from the body is freer and the freer a substance is from the body, the more capable it is of knowledge.[40] Therefore, the dead are better able to know, for either the soul perishes or it knows.

II. There is also a doubt about the words: *Neither have they a reward anymore.*[41] – This is clearly heretical, because it takes away divine justice.

III. Moreover, there is doubt about the words: *Love and hate have perished at the same time.*[42]

Contra: Bad will always remains. Therefore, if bad will comes from love and hatred, therefore, etc.[43]

IV. Furthermore, there is doubt about the words: *Go, then, and eat your bread with joy and drink your wine*, etc.[44]

If we want to respond to points I-III by saying that Ecclesiastes is speaking in the person of Epicurus, then the answer is clear. But if we want to hold that he is speak

---

[39]See Ecclesiastes 9:5.

[40]See the second question of *Quaestio* #12, after Bonaventure's commentary on Ecclesiastes 3:22 (#24) above.

[41]See Ecclesiastes 9:5.

[42]See Ecclesiastes 9:6.

[43]On p. 75 n. 8 QuarEd refer to Augustine. See Book XIV, chapter 6 in *Saint Augustine, The City of God*, Books VIII-XVI, trans. Gerald G. Walsh and Grace Monahan, FC 14 (New York: Fathers of the Church, 1952), 358: "Man's will, then, is all-important. If it is badly directed, the emotions will be perverse; if it is rightly directed, the emotions will be not merely blameless but even praiseworthy. The will is in all of these affections; indeed, they are nothing else but inclinations of the will."

[44]See Ecclesiastes 9:7.

ing in his own name, it has to be said that the words *the dead know nothing more* are to be understood of things in this world. They know nothing more of things in this world. They are not remembered by people still in the world nor do they feel affection for the things of this world. This is clear from the words: *They do not have a part in this world.*[45]

To the fourth point, I say that the exhortation is not stated absolutely, but the conclusion is drawn from the aforementioned vanity. So he says: *Go, then.* These words are directed to persons who cannot discern that they must please God in the present and be rewarded in the future. I say, if a person cannot know this, neither can such a person live always. Then such a person can seek pleasure with confidence. But Ecclesiastes does not hold this unless it is presumed that the Lord will not reward in the future in a way different from now. This is the previously mentioned vanity which he will destroy as Ecclesiastes 11:1-2 states below.[46]

ECCLESIASTES 9:11-10:7   A SENSE OF SECURITY ARISES FROM WHAT SEEMS TO BE A LACK OF GUIDANCE BY PROVIDENCE

21. *I turned myself to another thing*, etc. As was said above, those who do evil feel secure for two reasons: first, because there seems to be a lack of an application of justice, and second, because the guidance of providence seems to be lacking. Consideration has already been given to the lack that appears to be present in the application of justice. Here in a second point Ecclesiastes deals with the lack

---

[45]See Ecclesiastes 9:6.

[46]On p. 75 n. 9 QuarEd refer to Book IV, d. 50, p. II. a. 1, q. 2 of Bonaventure's *Sentence Commentary*. See Omnia Opera 4:1047.

which appears to be present in *rule of providence*. For in these two areas control does not seem to be *ordered*, but by chance. This section has two parts, as he shows, first, the lack of order in general, and second, the lack of order in particular where verse 13 reads: *This wisdom I have also seen*, etc., concerning disorderly rule.

ECCLESIASTES 9:11-13   THE LACK OF ORDER IN GENERAL

22. He deals with the first point as follows. First, he shows the disorder and chance which seem to be present in *the course of a life*. Second, he shows the order and chance that seem to be present in *the ending of life in death* where verse 12 says: *A human being does not know his own end*.

23. (Verse 11). So he shows the disorder in *the course of a life*, because things are not adjusted to what is suitable. So he says: *I turned myself to another thing*, for he had already considered *the application of justice* and now wants to reflect here on *order*. *And I saw that under the sun*, and he lists five gratuitous gifts that are frustrated in their very use. *The race is not to the swift*, even though people are fit to run. Amos 2:14 reads: "Flight will perish from the swift." – *Nor the battle to the strong*, even though people are capable of fighting. 2 Samuel 1:27 states: "The valiant have fallen and the weapons of war perished." – *Nor bread to the wise*, even though people are able to distribute food. Isaiah 3:7 has: "I am no healer, and in my house there is no bread." – *Nor riches to the learned*, even though people are capable of owning everything. Later in this very book Ecclesiastes 9:15 says: "Now there was found in it a poor man." – *Nor favor to the skillful*, even though people are capable of fashioning pleasing objects. We read in Isaiah 20: "All who have worked well have been confounded."[47]

---

[47]On p. 76 n. 2 QuarEd discuss the manuscript tradition and rightly indicate that Bonaventure's quotation is not found anywhere in Isaiah

24. *But time and chance in all*, as if everything happens by chance, and temporal things are changed. Ecclesiastes 3:1 above states: "All things have their season, and in their times pass under heaven." And the aforementioned gifts are distinguished in this way: the first two apply to *the body*: speed in obtaining what is desired and strength in resisting a threatening evil. The next three concern *the soul*, namely, wisdom in the heart, teaching in the mouth, and skill in work.

25. (Verse 12). *No one knows his own end*, etc. Second, he treats of the defect in government concerning *the ending of death*, because no one decides when or how they are to die. And it seems that death comes by chance in one way or another. And so he says: *No one knows his own end*, that is, the day of death. Matthew 24:42 reads: "Watch therefore, because you know not at what hour your Lord will come."[48] And he gives an example of disorder and uncertainty by saying: *But as fish are taken with the hook*, namely, in ignorance, *and as birds are caught with a snare*, that is, by deceit. Sirach 11:32 states: "As the partridge is brought into the cage and as the roe into the snare, so also is the heart of the proud." *So men and women are taken in the evil time.* We read in 1 Thessalonians 5:3: "When they will say: Peace and security, . . . sudden destruction will come. . . ." *When it will suddenly come upon them*, that is, unexpectedly. Isaiah 30:13-14 reads: "Its destruction will come suddenly, when it is not looked for. And it will be . . . broken all to pieces like the potter's vessel."

26. In a *spiritual sense* Ecclesiastes indicates here *the heavenly election of the good*, and afterwards *the hidden damnation of the wicked*. Therefore, so that all the efforts of

---

20, but may have a basis in Isaiah 19:9: "They who worked with linen will be confounded."

[48]Hugh of St. Cher, 96f also cites Matthew 24:12.

the good will be attributed to God, he says first: *The race is not to the swift*, because their running is not from themselves, but from God. Romans 9:16 states: "It is not of him who wills nor him who runs, but of God who shows mercy."[49] – *Nor the battle to the strong*, because we read in Psalm 32:16: "The king is not saved by a great army." – *Nor bread to the wise*, from themselves, but from God. John 6:32 says: "My Father gives you the true bread from heaven." – *Nor riches to the learned*, for wisdom and knowledge come from God, not from oneself. 1 Corinthians 1:5 has: "In all things you have been made rich in him," namely, in Christ. – *Nor favor to the skillful*, from themselves, but from God. Psalm 83:12 confesses: "God loves mercy and truth. The Lord will give grace and glory."

27. Now concerning *the hidden damnation of the wicked*, he says: *No one knows his own end*, for "the way of the wicked is dark," etc.[50] *As fish are taken with the hook*, that is, pleasure seekers who are taken with the hook of pleasure. Habakkuk 1:15 reads: "He lifted them all up with his hook." *As birds are caught in the snare*, that is, ambitious people with the snare of honor. 1 Timothy 3:6 says: "Not a neophyte, lest being puffed up with pride, he fall into the judgment of the devil." *Thus human beings are taken*, that is, the avaricious *in the evil time*. Job 27:19 reads: "The rich person, when he shall fall asleep, will take nothing with him."[51]

---

[49]Hugh of St. Cher, 95v, c also quotes Romans 9:16.

[50]See Proverbs 4:19: "The way of the wicked is dark; they know not where they fall."

[51]On p. 76 n. 5 QuarEd refer to Jerome's commentary on Ecclesiastes 9:11-12 in his *Commentarius in Ecclesiasten*. See CCSL lxxii, 328-330 for some general parallels, e.g., the quotation from Romans 9:16.

QUESTIONS 30

I. There is a doubt about what he means when he says that *he saw time and chance in all*.[52] According to this it would seem that everything happens by chance.

But contra: It seems that not everything happens by chance:

1. For when things happen as a result of a decision, they do not happen by chance. And many things are a result of a decision. Therefore, not everything happens by chance.

2. Moreover, it seems that nothing happens by chance, because, as Plato says: "With the exception of the first cause there is nothing whose origin is not preceded by a legitimate cause."[53] Therefore, according to this nothing happens by chance, but all things come from a definite cause.

3. Furthermore, in every work God is the principal agent.[54] But whatever God does as the principal agent, God does knowingly and on purpose, and nothing comes about by chance. Therefore, nothing entirely happens by chance.

I reply that *chance* and *luck* are *incidental causes*, not because other causes are causes *through themselves*,[55] but because when nature and knowledge fashion something

---

[52]Ecclesiastes 9:11.

[53]On p. 77 n. 1 QuarEd quote from p. 23 of the 1876 Wrobel edition of Plato's *Timaeus*: "Now everything generated from some cause is necessarily generated. For nothing comes to be, whose origin is not preceded by a legitimate cause and reason." See *Plato VII, Timaeus, Cleitophon, Critias, Menexenus, Epistles*, trans. R.G. Bury, LCL (London: Heinemann, 1929), 49-51: "Again, everything which becomes must of necessity become owing to some Cause; for without a cause it is impossible for anything to attain becoming."

[54]On p. 77 n. 2 QuarEd refer to Book II, d. 37, a. 1, q. 1 of Bonaventure's *Sentence Commentary*. See Omnia Opera 2:861.

[55]The Latin is *per se* and is in contrast to *per accidens*.

that is their proper object, they do this *through themselves* and not by chance.[56] But when something happens from their efforts concerning something that is not their proper object and another cause is involved, this is by chance. Take the examples of finding a creditor in the market place and of a stone falling on a person's head.[57] I say, therefore, that if a succession of events is referred to the *first cause*, namely, to God, and since God foresees everything, nothing happens by chance in the order of divine foreknowledge. But if we speak of a comparison with *created causes*, this can be about something *unchangeable* such as the movement of the heavenly bodies or about something *changeable* such as inferior causes under the sun. In the succession of such *changeable* factors, it can hardly happen that an unforeseen and unintended factor does not intervene. In this way there is chance in everything, not because all things happen by chance, but because some element of chance is present in every changeable creature.

3. The objection about divine foreknowledge is already resolved. For one does not speak of chance in reference to divine foreknowledge.

---

[56]On p. 77 n. 3 QuarEd refer to Book II, n. 4-5 of Aristotle's *Physica*. See WAE, vol. 2, 198b: "We have now explained what chance is and what spontaneity is, and in what they differ from each other. Both belong to the mode of causation 'source of change', for either some natural or some intelligent agent is always the cause; but in this sort of causation the number of possible causes is infinite. Spontaneity and chance are causes of effects which, though they might result from intelligence or nature, have in fact been caused by something *incidentally*. Now since nothing which is incidental is prior to what is *per se*, it is clear that no incidental cause can be prior to a cause *per se*. Spontaneity and chance, therefore, are posterior to intelligence and nature. Hence, however true it may be that the heavens are due to spontaneity, it will still be true that intelligence and nature will be prior causes of the All and of many things in it besides."

[57]Both these examples are found in Aristotle's *Physica*. See WAE, vol. 2, 196b-197b.

2. To the second objection that all things have a cause, it has to be said that it is true that everything has a legitimate cause, namely, *nature* or *knowledge*.[58] But this does not exclude that they could do something or actually do something outside a set order, God excepted.

II. It is asked what he means by the words: *As fish are taken by the hook*.[59] Is the capture of fish by chance or not? That it is by chance would seem to be so:

1. Because, that one fish rather than another is caught does not come from nature or knowledge, and therefore it comes from chance.

2. Also, that one person catches a fish while another does not, is not due to nature or skill, and therefore it happens by chance.

But contra: If someone digs with the intention of finding gold, this is not done by chance.[60] Therefore, when a person fishes with the intention of catching fish, this is not chance.

---

[58]On p. 77 n. 4 QuarEd cite Book II, n. 5 of Aristotle's *Physica*. See WAE, vol. 2, 198b, to which reference is made in footnote 54 above. The editors also cite Book X, n. 8 of Aristotle's *Metaphysica*. See WAE, vol. 8, 1065b: "Since nothing accidental is prior to the essential, neither are accidental causes prior. If, then, luck or spontaneity is a cause of the material universe, reason and nature are causes before it." In addition, the editors refer to Book II, d. 37, a. 2, q. 2 of Bonaventure's *Sentence Commentary*. See Omnia Opera 2:871.

[59]Ecclesiastes 9:12.

[60]On p. 77 n. 5 QuarEd quote Book V, prosa 1 from Boethius' *Consolation of Philosophy*. See LCL, 387-389: "Whenever, she said, something is done for the sake of some given end, and another thing occurs, for some reason or other, different from what was intended, it is called chance: as, for example, if a man digging in the ground in order to till his field were to find he had dug up a quantity of gold. Now this is indeed believed to have happened by chance, but it does not come from nothing; for it has its proper causes, and their unforeseen and unexpected coming together appears to have produced a chance event.

I reply that the text speaks about the capture of fish, not about *those capturing* fish. And so is not talking about chance. The text refers to fish that take the hook, and they go to the hook for food. And if something else happens, then it is chance.

Ecclesiastes 9:13-10:7   The lack of order in particular

28. *This wisdom I have also seen under the sun.* He has just spoken of a defect in the rule of providence in general. Here he intends to show this *in particular*, namely, about the rule whereby the wise are despised and the stupid promoted. There are three parts to this section. He first shows *the putting down of the wise.* In the second he adds *the approval of this putting down* where verse 16 reads: *And I said that wisdom is better than strength.* In the third he notes *the advancement of the stupid* where Ecclesiastes 10:4 states: *If the spirit of the person who has power*, etc.

Ecclesiastes 9:13-15   The putting down of the wise

29. So he describes *the putting down of the wise* as follows. First, he *praises wisdom.* Second, he states a case in which there is a *lack of power.* Third, he notes *the help of wisdom.* Fourth, he expresses *the contempt of the wise.*

30. (Verse 13). So he begins with *the praise of wisdom* as he says: *This wisdom I have also seen*, that is, I learnt from its effect in earthly matters. *And it seemed to me to be very great*, that is, I approved and praised it as something very great. For it is great wisdom to overcome a lesser enemy. It is greater wisdom to conquer an equal. It is very

---

For if the man tilling his field were not digging the ground, and if the man who put it there had not hidden his money in that particular spot, the gold would not have been found."

great wisdom to overcome the strongest. So it is said in Job 26:12: "His wisdom struck the proud person.

31. (Verse 14). *A little city*, etc. He notes here *the lack of power* to resist an attack. So he says: *A little city, and few men in it*. One must supply here the verb *was*, that is, *there was a little city*. Or the verb is to be construed from the following words: *The siege was perfect*. Since it was a small town with few men, it was weak in self-defense. Thus, Jehoshaphat says in 2 Chronicles 20:12: "We have not strength enough to be able to resist this multitude," which is great. For they were few. They are least able to do this when the opponent is strong. So he continues: *There came against it a great king*, namely, in power, *and built a trench around it*, with great malice. The king *built bulwarks round about it*, for war. *And the siege was perfect*, because of the lack of power to resist. An example of this is seen in Judith 7:1-22 when Holofernes besieged Bethulia. The Lord also prophesied this about Jerusalem in Luke 19:43: "Your enemies will built a trench about you . . . and hem you in on every side."

32. (Verse 15). *Now there was found in it*, etc. Third, he notes *the help of wisdom* when power was weak. So he says: *Now there was found in it a man poor*, and therefore weak. *And wise, and he delivered the city by his wisdom*. An example of how a wise person delivered a city is found in the person of Judith. In her book the story is told of how she, although weak, freed Bethulia from Holofernes by her wisdom.[61] Another example is found in 2 Samuel 20:16-22 where the story is told of how a wise woman freed the city of Abel from the attack of Joab.[62] On the other hand, we

---

[61]See Judith 8-15. Hugh of St. Cher, 96v, e also refers to this story.

[62]Hugh of St. Cher, 96v, e also refers to this story. In Hugh of St. Cher the story of the wise woman of Abel precedes the story of Judith.

read in Baruch 3:28: "And since they did not have wisdom, they perished through their folly." This is said of the strong.

33. *And no one afterward*, etc. Fourth, he treats of *the contempt for the wise man who freed them*. For forgetting is a sign of contempt. So he says: *And no one afterward remembered that poor person*. Behold, contempt and ingratitude. For a contrary view, it is said in Sirach 29:19: "Forget not the kindness of the person who provided surety for you, for he has given his life for you."

34. There are four questions to be taken into consideration relative to *the spiritual sense*, namely, What is the city? Who is the great king? Who is the poor, wise man? Why is it that no one remembers him?

35. The city is *the church*. Psalm 86:3 reads: "Glorious things are said of you, O city of God." This city is *small* because of her humility, for only the Lord lives in it. Isaiah 66:2 states: "But for whom will I have respect, but to him that is poor and little, and of a contrite spirit, and who trembles at my words?" *And few men in it*, in comparison to the number of the wicked, as Matthew 20:16 says: "Many are called, but few are chosen."[63]

36. The *great king* is the devil, of whom it is said in Job 41:25: "He is king over all the children of pride."[64] He is also *great*, according to what Job 41:24 states: "There is

---

[63]Hugh of St. Cher, 96q-r comments: "q The small city] is the humble Church. About it Psalm 121: Glorious things are said of you, city of God. . . .r And there are few men in it] that is, strong and robust people, in comparison to the wicked, or those called by God. For many are called, but few are chosen. Matthew 20 & 22."

[64]Hugh of St. Cher, 96s has a similar interpretive beginning: "A great king came against him] that is, the price of this world, the devil. Job 41. Who is king over all the children of pride." Hugh of St. Cher's interpretation of "the great king" offers few other parallels to that of Bonaventure.

no power upon earth that can be compared with him." This king *comes against the city*, by his suggestions. He *digs a trench* by offering multiple delights. He *builds bulwarks* by creating occasions for sins. *And the siege is perfect*, when the devil involves people in transgressions of the commandments. About these Luke 19:43-44 reads: "Your enemies will dig a trench about you . . . hem you in . . . and beat you flat to the ground . . . and not leave . . . a stone upon a stone."

37. *The poor and wise man* is Christ and is *a man* in the strength of his power. Jeremiah 31:22 reads: "A woman[65] will compass a man."[66] Christ is also *poor*. 2 Corinthians 8:9 reads: "Although he was rich in all things,[67] he became poor for your sakes." He was *wise*, in fact Wisdom itself. 1 Corinthians 1:24 states: "We say that Christ is the power and wisdom of God."[68] He *is found* by those who see him. Matthew 7:8 says: "For everyone who asks receives, and the person who seeks finds." He *delivered* the people. Isaiah 19:20 has: "They will cry to the Lord because of the oppressor, and he will send them a savior and a defender to deliver them." *He delivered by his wisdom*, when he could have done so by his power. We read in Job 26:12: "His wisdom struck the proud one."[69]

---

[65]On p. 78 n. 6 QuarEd accurately indicate that the Vulgate reads *femina* ("woman") while Bonaventure has *mulier* ("woman").

[66]On p. 78 n. 6 QuarEd refer to Isidore. See Book XI, chapter 2, n. 17 of *Isidori Hispalensis Episcopi Etymologiarum sive Originvm Libri XX*, Volume II, ed. W. M. Lindsay. (Oxford: Clarendon, 1911): "*Man* is so called, because a man has more strength than a woman. And so the word *vir*tus (strength) is used of a man. . . ." That is, "man" is *vir* in Latin, and strength is *virtus* in Latin. See Bonaventure's commentary on Ecclesiastes 7:28-29 (#40) with note 75 above.

[67]The Vulgate does not read *in omnibus* ("in all things").

[68]The Vulgate does not have *dicimus* ("we say"). Also the Vulgate reads *Dei* ("of God") both after "power" and "wisdom."

[69]Hugh of St. Cher, 96y offers this mystical interpretation: "Christ the Lord, who alone is the true and perfect man, having nothing of

38. *And no one afterward remembered him*, because poverty is despised. Proverbs 19:7 reads: "The brethren of the poor person hate him. Moreover, his friends have also departed from him." No one remembered and felt *compassion*, according to Lamentations 3:19: "Remember my poverty and transgression, the wormwood and the gall." But on the contrary as Amos 6:6 says: "They are not concerned for the affliction of Joseph."[70] *Giving thanks.* Luke 17:18 states: "And there is no one found to return and give glory to God, but this stranger." *Imitating his actions.* Isaiah 17:9-10 has: "You will be desolate because you have forgotten God your savior and have not remembered the strong helper."[71] *Proclaiming with the mouth.* Genesis 40:23 reads: "The butler,[72] when things prospered for him, forgot his interpreter."

ECCLESIASTES 9:16-10:3   THE APPROVAL OF THE PERSON SO DESPISED

39. *And I said*, etc. He has shown the contempt and forgetting of the wise person. Here in a second point he shows *the approval of the person so despised* and commends wisdom for its threefold pre-eminence. First, by preferring it to *the strength of power*. Second, by preferring it to *the bulwarks of armor*. Third, by preferring it to *the height of earthly glory*.

---

feminine softness. About this Jeremiah 31:[22] says: 'The Lord will make something new upon the earth: a woman will compass a man.' Furthermore, he was poor, because he neither had nor loved riches. Psalm 68:[30] says: 'I am poor and sorrowful.' Moreover, he was Wise, because in him are all the treasures of Wisdom and of the knowledge of the hidden God. . . ."

[70]Hugh of St. Cher, 96v, c also cites Amos 6:6.

[71]Hugh of St. Cher, 96v, e also quotes Isaiah 17:9-10.

[72]On p. 78 n. 7 QuarEd rightly indicate that the Vulgate reads *praepositus pincerarum* ("the chief butler") whereas Bonaventure has *pincerna* ("butler").

40. (Verses 16-17). First, in his judgment he prefers wisdom to *strength*. So he says: *And I said that wisdom is better than strength*. Wisdom 6:1 reads: "Wisdom is better than strength and a wise man is better than a strong man." And since it is better, it should not be despised, and yet it is despised. Wherefore, he says: *How then is the wisdom of the poor person slighted*, when he should not be despised, but yet he is made little of because of his poverty. For Sirach 13:27-28 says this of the poor person: "He has spoken wisely, and no room was given to him. The rich man spoke, and all held their peace. And they extol[73] to the very skies what he said." And he adds a sign of their contempt of wisdom: *And his words were not heard*. However, there is much to listen to. Proverbs 8:32 states: "Now therefore, children, hear me. Blessed are they who keep my ways."

41. He indicates that we should listen to the words of the wise when he says: *The words of the wise are heard in silence*, that is, are worthy to be heard in silence. Sirach 32:9 states: "Hear in silence, and for your reverence good grace will come to you." For this reason Sirach also adds: "In the company of the great do not presume to speak."[74] – *More than the cry of a prince among fools*, and his speech is louder, because no matter how much a person calls out, a fool does not listen. Sirach 22:8-9 has: "He speaks with one who is asleep who utters wisdom to a fool,[75] and at the

---

[73]On p. 79 n. 1 QuarEd correctly mention that the Vulgate reads *perducent* ("will extol") while Bonaventure has *perducunt* ("extol").

[74]See Sirach 32:13 which Bonaventure has adapted and which reads in full: "In the company of the great do not presume [to speak], and when the elders are present, speak not much."

[75]Hugh of St. Cher, 96v, k quotes this first part of Sirach 22:8-9 in the same words that Bonaventure uses. This citation occurs in the third of the thirteen reasons Hugh of St.Cher gives why the world does not listen to the words of the poor Wise Christ.

end of the discourse he says: Who is this?"[76] So the reason why wisdom is despised is found in the foolishness of the listeners. Matthew 7:6 reads: "Do not give what is holy to dogs."[77] The Apostle gives the reason for this in 1 Corinthians 2:14: "But the sensual person does not perceive the things that are of the Spirit of God."[78]

42. (Verse 18). *Better is wisdom*, etc. Second, he prefers wisdom to *bulwarks of armor*, saying: *Better is wisdom than weapons of war*, because weapons of war are for protection. But wisdom is also a *protection*. Proverbs 2:11-12 has: "Counsel will guard you, and prudence will preserve you that you may be delivered from the evil way and from the person who speaks perverse things." It is clear that wisdom is a *better* protection, because those who lose wisdom through sin cannot defend themselves by armor without losing many good things. So he says: *And the person who will sin in one*, by withdrawing from wisdom, according to what has been said above in Ecclesiastes 8:3: "Be not hasty to depart from his face, and do not continue in an evil way." *He will lose many good things*, for by sinning one loses wisdom, and in losing wisdom many good things are lost. Wisdom 7:11 reads: "Now all good things came to me together with her." And so with the loss of wisdom many good things are lost. Another interpretation is this: *The person who will sin in one*, against charity, *will lose many*

---

[76]Bonaventure has adapted Sirach 22:8-9 which reads in full: "Who speaks a word to the person who doesn't listen is like the person who rouses an individual from a deep sleep, who speaks to the foolish and in the end he says: who is this?"

[77]Hugh of St. Cher, 96v, h quotes all of Matthew 7:6.

[78]Hugh of St. Cher, 96v, h alludes to 1 Corinthians 2:[14] and then quotes Matthew 7:6 in full.

good things, according to James 2:10: "The person who will sin in one point has become guilty of all."[79] – And he makes this clear with a metaphor by saying that knowledge of sin is compared to a dying fly, because it brings about an abomination to the affections and to conscience.[80]

---

[79]On p. 79 n. 5 QuarEd point to Bonaventure's adaptation of James 2:10 which reads: "For whoever keeps the whole law, but sins in one point, has become guilty of all." Hugh of St. Cher, 97v, b quotes James 2:10 in its entirety.

[80]This metaphor occurs in Ecclesiastes 10:1.

CHAPTER 10

1. (Verse 1a). So he adds: *Dying flies*, that is, thoughts coming to sinners and inciting them to mortal sin,[1] *spoil the sweetness of the ointment*, that is, the thoughts lose their anointing and with it many good things, for 1 John 2:27 reads: "Anointing teaches you about all things."[2] Another interpretation is: *The sweetness of the ointment*, that is, inner devotion and the sweetness of wisdom. Proverbs 27:9 says: "A person is delighted by ointment and various perfumes."[3]

2. (Verses 1b-2). *Wisdom is more precious*. Third, he prefers wisdom to *the height of earthly glory* or to the foolishness desired by the stupid. Therefore, he says: *Wisdom is more precious and a little glory*,[4] that is, with a little glory.

---

[1]Hugh of St. Cher, 97v, bc comments: "Restless sinners, unclean like flies."

[2]1 John 2:27 reads: "And as for you, let the anointing that you received from him, dwell in you, and you have no need that anyone teach you. But as his anointing teaches you about all things, and is true and is no lie, even as it has taught you, abide in him." Hugh of St. Cher, 97v, bc also cites 1 John 2:27 and has the future tense: "The anointing will teach you about all things."

[3]Proverbs 27:9 states: "The heart delights in ointment and various perfumes, and the good counsels of a friend are sweet to the soul." Hugh of St. Cher, 97v, c quotes Proverbs 27:9 in its entirety.

[4]The Vulgate reads *et gloria parva* ("and a little glory") while Bonaventure has *parvaque gloria* ("and a little glory").

For a time, that is, while still on earth. It is better, I say, than *foolishness*, even with much glory. Ecclesiastes 4:13 above states: "Better a child who is poor and wise than a king who is old and foolish." Or the meaning can be that wisdom is better than foolishness, and even a little passing glory, that is, glory given at a fitting time, is better than foolishness.

3. And he adds the reason: *The heart of the wise are in their right hands, and the heart of the fools is in their left hands*, the *right* representing good things and the *left* bad things. Matthew 25:22 has: "He will set the sheep on his right hand, but the goats on his left."[5] So his intention is to say that the wise think on good things and the foolish on bad things. We read in Proverbs 10:32: "The lips of the just consider what is acceptable, and the mouth of the wicked utters perverse things." *The right hand* gives knowledge of eternal goods; *the left* of temporal goods. Thus, Proverbs 3:16 states: "Length of days is in her right hand, and in her left hand are riches and glory."[6] So his intent is to say that the wise think of and desire eternal good while the stupid think of and desire temporal goods. The Song of Songs 2:6 says: "His left hand is under my head, and his right hand will embrace me." The foolish think of what is vain and do not know how to discern either in themselves or in others what is more fitting.

4. (Verse 3). So he adds: *But, and the fool when he walks in the way*, that is, in that way which seems to him to be good. Proverbs 12:15 reads: "The way of the fool is right in his own eyes."[7] *Whereas he himself is a fool*, that is, he walks stupidly, because he is walking in the dark. Ecclesiastes 2:14 above says: "The fool walks in darkness."

---

[5]Hugh of St. Cher, 98e also quotes Matthew 25:22.
[6]Hugh of St. Cher, 98g also cites Proverbs 3:16.
[7]Hugh of St. Cher, 98l also cites Proverbs 12:15.

He esteems all people to be fools. For Proverbs 26:16 reads: "The sluggard is wiser in his own conceit than seven men who voice their opinions."

QUESTIONS 31

A question arises here on what he means by the words: *The person who will sin in one*, etc.[8]

1. For if God always punishes according to what is fitting,[9] then a person who sins in one matter should not be punished except for that one sin. Therefore, a person should not lose many, but only one thing.

2. Also, it seems from this that there is a connection between sins just as there is between virtues.[10] For, if sin is a lack of good and if many good things are lost by one sin, then a person incurs much harm from one sin. But this can only be if sins are connected, and so there is a connection between sins.

3. Moreover, that there is a connection between all sins seems to follow from James 2:10: *Whoever sins in one matter, has become guilty of all*. Therefore, it seems that a person who commits one sin is as guilty as if he had committed all sins.

But contra: 1. Some sins are contrary to one another. And if there is a connection between sins, then two contraries would be in the same thing at the same time, which is impossible.[11]

---

[8]See Ecclesiastes 9:18.

[9]On p. 80 n. 4 QuarEd quote Wisdom 11:27: "But you spare all, because they are yours, O Lord, who loves souls." They also refer to Book IV, d. 46, a. 2, q. 2 on Bonaventure's *Sentence Commentary*. See Omnia Opera 4:963.

[10]On p. 80 n. 5 QuarEd refer to Book III, d. 36, q. 1 and 3 of Bonaventure's *Sentence Commentary*. See Omnia Opera 3:791 and 796 respectively.

2. Also, sins are not from God, but acquired from what we do. But it is sure that by the same deed we do not acquire temperance and justice, since they are acquired by customary action.[12] It is the same with sins.

I reply that the word *sin* is to be seen from the point of view of *deformity* and from the perspective of *liability to punishment*. With respect to *deformity* three things may be involved, namely, *the loss of a good freely given; the loss of a natural good* or of a natural ability; and lastly, *an inclination to act in a disordered way*, which is also called a certain ability. Concerning the loss of a good freely given, there is indeed a connection between sins, because to commit one sin is to lose grace and all the virtues in so far as they are freely given. Concerning the loss of an ability there is no connection, but a distinction among them because each sin deprives one of its own ability. Relative to the third loss, namely, the inclination to act in a disordered way, there is no distinction or connection whatsoever, nor does one sin incline one to another sin. Sometimes, however, one sin may lead to another sin, as the sin of gluttony can lead to a sin of voluptuousness. Likewise in spiritual matters pride may lead to envy.

---

[11]On p. 80 n. 7 QuarEd cite Book II, n. 14 of Aristotle's *Categoriae*. See WAE, vol. 1, 11b: "Pairs of opposites which are contraries are not in any way interdependent, but are contrary the one to the other. . . .Those contraries which are such that the subjects in which they are naturally present, or of which they are predicated, must necessarily contain either the one or the other of them, have no intermediate. . . ."

[12]On p. 80 n. 8 QuarEd quote Book II, n. 1 of Aristotle's *Ethica nicomachea*. See WAE, vol. 9, 1103a: ". . . moral virtue comes about as a result of habit. . . .Neither by nature, then, nor contrary to nature do the virtues arise in us; rather we are adapted by nature to receive them, and are made perfect by habit." The editors refer to Book III, d. 36, q. 1 of Bonaventure's *Sentence Commentary* for a consideration of virtues bestowed by grace, that is, the infused virtues. See Omnia Opera 3:791.

Seen from the point of view of *liability to punishment*, sin puts one under a double punishment, namely, lack of vision and the pain of fire. With respect to the first there is a connection, because whoever commits one sin loses the glory due to all the virtues. Concerning the second there is no connection, but a distinction, because there is a pain corresponding to each sin. – Therefore, this text of Ecclesiastes and that of James the Blessed are to be understood relative to the loss of grace and glory.[13]

1. To the objection that a person is punished beyond what is fitting, I say that this is false. For whoever sins in one act sins against the grace of all the virtues, and so deserves to lose all.

ECCLESIASTES 10:4-6   THE PROMOTION OF THE FOOLISH

5. *If the spirit of the one who has power.* He has treated above of the despising of a wise person and of the just approval of such a person. Here in a third point he adds *the promotion of the foolish*. Since the rule of the stupid is burdensome, he recommends *the armor of patience*. Further, he describes *the disordered rule of the foolish* where verse 5 reads: *There is an evil that I have seen*, etc.

6. (Verse 4). He recommends *the armor of patience* by saying: *If the spirit of the person who has power*, that is, the fury of a prelate. For in Isaiah 2:22 *spirit* is said to be fury: "Get away from the person, whose spirit is in his nostrils."[14] 1 Kings 19:11 reads: "A great and strong spirit,[15] overthrowing the mountains and breaking rocks to pieces." *Ascend*

---

[13]On p. 80 n. 9 QuarEd refer to Book III, d. 36, q. 4 of Bonaventure's *Sentence Commentary*. See Omnia Opera 3:799.

[14]Bonaventure is referring to the snorting of the person filled with fury.

[15]The reference is to the wind.

upon you, namely, to oppress. Jeremiah 4:13 states: "Behold, he will ascend like a cloud, and his chariots like a tempest. . . .Woe unto us, for we have been laid waste." *Leave not your place*, that is, a place of patience and constancy, in which your soul is at rest, according to what Luke 21:19 says: "In your patience you will possess your souls." 1 Peter 2:18-19 has: "Servants, be subject to your masters in all fear, not only to the . . . gentle, but also to the severe. For this is a grace, if a person endures on account of conscience towards God," etc. He gives the reason why this is useful: *Because care will make the greatest sins to cease*. Here the distress of troubles is called the *care*,[16] by which a person is cured. Wisdom 6:19 says: "The care of discipline is love, and love is the keeping of her laws." The predicates of both parts of Wisdom 6:19 have a causal connection,[17] because, if love is reached through many troubles and the law is observed, then love puts an end to sin.

7. There is another exposition: *If the spirit of the person who has power*, that is, if the spirit of *ambition*, that is, the malice of the ambitious person, *ascend upon you*, that is, if it enters your mind, so that you want to be a prelate, *leave not your place*, namely, the place of subjection and service. About this Luke 14:8-9 says: "When you are invited to a wedding, recline in the lowest place. And Sirach 11:22 reads: "Trust in God and stay in your place." And Ecclesiastes gives the reason: *Because care will make the greatest sins to cease*. The translation of Symmachus reads: *Because purity* will make the greatest sins to cease.[18] For

---

[16]Douay translates *curatio* as "care." Its basic meaning, however, is "cure" or "healing." As Bonaventure's commentary will indicate, the meaning of Ecclesiastes 10:4b is not crystal clear. NAB translates Ecclesiastes 10:4b: "for mildness abates great offenses."

[17]On p. 81 n. 1 QuarEd refer to Omnia Opera 3:528 note 5 for more detail on causal predication.

[18]On p. 81 n. 3 QuarEd quote Jerome's commentary on this verse. See his *Commentarius in Ecclesiasten* in CCSL lxxii, 334-335.:

1 Corinthians 9:27 states: "I chastise my body and bring it into subjection, lest, perhaps, after I have preached[19] to others, I myself should become a castaway."

8. Others interpret the text about *the devil*: *If the spirit of the one who has power*, that is, the devil. Job 41:24 reads: "There is no power on earth that can be compared with him." *Ascend upon you*, that is, through temptation. Luke 11:24 states: "When the unclean spirit has gone out of a person, it walks through places without water, seeking rest, and finds none." *Leave not your place*, namely, the place of penance. Ephesians 4:27 says: "Give no place to the devil." *Because care will make the greatest sins to cease*. The text of Origen reads *healing*, which results from the medicine of penance.[20] Sirach 11:29 has: "The affliction of one[21] hour makes one forget the greatest[22] voluptuousness," that is, a short penance makes one forget a great sin.[23]

"Symmachus translated in a similar way the Hebrew *marphe*, which all had translated as *hiama*, which means *health* or *cure*, according to its sense and said: 'If the spirit of the prelate rushes upon you, do not abandon your place, because purity conquers great sins.' That is, if the devil titillates your mind and incites you to voluptuousness, do not follow the most wretched thought and the one tempting to voluptuousness, but be strong and rigid, and extinguish by the frigidity of chastity the flames of voluptuousness."

[19]On p. 81 n. 3 QuarEd rightly mention that the Vulgate reads *praedicaverim* ("I have preached") while Bonaventure has *praedicavero* ("I have preached").

[20]On p. 81 n. 5 QuarEd refer to Origen's *Hexapla*. See PG 13:1553-1554 where Origen quotes both the LXX and Theodotion as reading: *quia medela sedabit peccata magna* ("because healing will appease great sins"). Interestingly, Bonaventure does not use *medela* ("healing"), but *salvatio* ("healing" or possibly "salvation"). In PG 13:1551 Origen says that the Latin of the Hebrew is *sanitas* ("healing").

[21]On p. 81 n. 5 QuarEd correctly state that the Vulgate does not read *unius* ("one").

[22]On p. 81 n.5 QuarEd accurately indicate that the Vulgate reads *magnae* ("great") while Bonaventure has *maximae* ("greatest").

[23]Hugh of St. Cher, 98r comments: "Because the healing] of penitential medicine. sWill make the greatest sins to cease] that is, that evil actions

9. (Verse 5). *There is an evil that I have seen,* etc. Second, he considers *the disordered rule of the foolish.* It is disordered both because of lack of *knowledge* and because of a lack of *life,* because the foolish and the wicked are promoted, but the wise and those rich in good behavior are dismissed. So he continues: *There is an evil that I have seen under the sun,* that is, in the present human condition, *as it were by an error proceeding,* not from an error concerning the truth, but seemingly from an error, which follows after a just discussion. *From the face of the prince,* namely, of the one from whom comes all power, who by a just decision sometimes gives the office of prelate to the wicked. Hosea 13:11 reads: "I will give you a king in my wrath and will take him away in my indignation."[24]

10. (Verse 6). Ecclesiastes states that this is an evil with respect to a lack of *knowledge: A fool set in high dignity.* His expression *set* is a good one, because the fool occupies a false position. Psalm 72:18 reads: "You have set them up. When they were lifted up, you have cast them down."[25] Another interpretation: *Set* like a useless stone. For the foolish prelate is addressed in Zechariah 11:17: "O shepherd and idol, who forsakes the flock, the sword upon his arm and upon his right eye. His arm will wither away, and his right eye will be utterly blackened."[26] And therefore,

---

are not performed. And therefore, one should resist suggestions and the giving of one's consent lest these temptations turn into actions. Sirach 11:[29] says: The affliction of one hour makes one forget the greatest voluptuousness. Another interpretation of 'healing will make the greatest sins to cease' is: as if he were saying, penance heals all sins, namely, those of heart, mouth, and deed and heals the soul." The astute reader will note that Bonaventure and Hugh of St. Cher quote Sirach 11:29 in the same way.

[24]See Hugh of St. Cher, 98v, m who also quotes Hosea 13:11.

[25]Bonaventure implies the first part of Psalm 72:18, but doesn't quote it. Psalm 72:18 reads: "But indeed in deceit you have set them up. When they were lifted up, you have cast them down."

[26]Hugh of St. Cher, 98v, o quotes the first words of Zechariah 11:17.

Proverbs 26:8 states: "As the person who casts a stone into the pile of mercury, so is the person who gives honor to a fool." On the other hand, *the rich sit beneath. The rich,* that is, who are rich in good behavior, knowledge, and grace. About these 1 Corinthians 1:5-7 says: "In all things you have been made rich in him, . . . so that nothing is lacking to you in any grace." And Isaiah 33:6 has: "The riches of salvation are wisdom and knowledge."

11. (Verse 7). With regard to the lack of *life* he says: *I have seen servants upon horses. Servants* are to be understood as sinners, about whom we read in John 8:34: "The person who commits sin is a servant of sin."[27] *Upon horses,* put in the plural to express pomp. Deuteronomy 17:16 says: "When he has been established, he will not multiply horses for himself."[28] On the other hand, *princes walking as servants,*[29] namely, those princes, whose concern is to lead a good life. Seneca says: "If you rule yourself well, you will be a prince."[30] He saw them *like servants,* but in the future it will be different. Luke 14:11 has: "Everyone, who humbles himself, will be exalted, and the person who exalts himself will be humbled."

QUESTIONS 32

It is asked here whether it is just that the wicked are over the good.[31] That it is just would seem to be so:

---

[27]Hugh of St. Cher, 98v, k also cites John 8:34.

[28]The context indicates that "a king" is the person being established.

[29]The Vulgate reads *ambulantes quasi servos super terram* ("walking as servants on the ground").

[30]On p. 81, n. 9 QuarEd cite two of Seneca's letters. On Letter 37, see *Seneca ad Lucilium Epistulae Morales I,* trans. Richard M. Gummere, LCL (Cambridge: Harvard University Press, 1934), xxx: "If you would have all things under your control, put yourself under the control of reason. You will rule over many, if reason rules over you." On Letter 113, #31, see p. 299 in LCL: "Self-command is the greatest command of all."

[31]See Ecclesiastes 10:6-7.

1. Because it is said in Romans 13:1: *There is no power, but from God*. Therefore, wicked rulers have their power from no one else, but from God.

2. We also read in John 19:11 that Christ said to Pilate: *You would not have any power against me, unless it were given you from above*. Augustine explains the words *from above* to mean "from God."[32] Therefore, if Pilate was evil and used power wrongly, it is from God that evil people are rulers.

3. Moreover, 1 Peter 2:18-19 says: *Be subject . . . not only to the good and gentle, but also to the severe* and gives the reason: *on account of conscience*.[33] Therefore, if it is just to be subject to them, and since all justice is from God, then this also is from God.

4. Furthermore, Job 34:30 reads: *Who makes a hypocrite to reign on account of the sins of the people*, etc.[34] Therefore, etc.

Contra: 1. Hosea 8:4 reads: *They have reigned, but not from me. They have been princes, and I knew not*. Therefore, it seems that rule by the wicked is not from God.

---

[32]On p. 82 n. 2 QuarEd refer to three places where Augustine gives an exposition of John 19:11. See, for example, Augustine's third exposition of Psalm 32 in *Expositions of the Psalms 1-32*, trans. Maria Boulding, Works of Saint Augustine Part III/Volume 15 (Hyde Park, NY: New City Press, 2000), 413: "*There is no power, except from God* (Rom 13:1); this is the apostle's authoritative teaching. . . .The God-Man, standing before a man, said the same: *You would have no power over me, had it not been given you from above* (Jn 19:11). Pilate was judging; Christ was teaching. Even as he was being judged, Christ was teaching, so that he might later judge those whom he had taught." The editors also refer to Book II, d. 44, chapter 1 of Peter Lombard's *Sententiae in IV Libris Distinctae*, 577-579.

[33]Bonaventure has adapted 1 Peter 2:18-19 to his purposes.

[34]On p. 82 n. 4 QuarEd correctly mention that the Vulgate reads *hominem hypocritam* ("a person who is a hypocrite") while Bonaventure has *hypocritam* ("hypocrite").

2. Likewise, servitude is a punishment imposed because of sin.[35] Hence, it is imposed on no sinner wrongly or unjustly. On the other hand, power is only given justly to a just person. So, if power is given to a sinner and servitude to a just person, there is a lack of order and justice in this instance. Wherefore, it is not from God.

3. Moreover, if the power of the wicked is just and from God, because anything from God has to be just, and since no one should take away the right of another,[36] then no one should have to work at the whim of an evil ruler. Therefore, whoever works under these conditions is sinning against this regulation.

I reply that there are three kinds of evil or unjust rulers. There is one who is unjust as a person, but has become a ruler in a just manner and rules with justice. Such a ruler can rule with justice without sinning, and it is just to be subject to such a ruler. There is another ruler who acquires his office unjustly and rules without justice. Such a person can neither rule with justice nor should one be subject to this person. There is yet another ruler who is unjust, but obtained his office in a just manner. However, this individual rules without justice in putting down the good and promoting the wicked. It is lawful to be subject to such a person in those things concerning justice. But in things against God one should not be subject. "Because the person who abuses the power given merits to lose the

---

[35]On p. 82 n. 6 QuarEd cite Book II, chapter 11 n. 79 of Ambrose's *De Abraham*. See PL 14:519B: "Servitude is contracted by sin, and sin is remitted at a price." The editors also refer to Omnia Opera 2:168 note 3 and 2:1008 note 3 for quotations from Augustine's works.

[36]On p. 82 n. 7 QuarEd cite Book I, title 6: Those who are *sui juris* and those who are *alieni juris*, law 2 from Justinian's *Digest*: "There must be no derogation from any man's legal rights." This text is not found in the appropriate spot in *The Digest of Justinian*, Volume 1, ed. Alan Watson (Philadelphia: University of Pennsylvania Press, 1998).

privilege,"[37] even though lawfully in office. However, it is unjust to remove such a ruler.

To the objection in the first part, namely, whether it is just for the wicked to rule, it has to be said that when the wicked rule and hold the first place *well*, it is not harmful to the state. But the person who rules *badly* holds the office lawfully, not because of his own justice, but because of divine justice, for God *makes* him *the ruler on account of the sins of the people*.[38] – And in this way an answer is given to the first objections that the power of evil rulers is from God.

1. To the first objection I reply that this is to be understood of those who take power unlawfully and by their own authority, not by God's authority.

2. To the objection about order, I reply that the punishment due sin remains even without further sins. I say that is also the case concerning servitude among the good.

3. To the objection that if the power is from God it must be just for a person to have such power, I reply that in comparison with the individual's *own merits* it is not just, but rather wicked. In comparison with the *merits of wicked* subjects, it is just. And since it is lawful for us, for various reasons, to want things that are contrary when the divine

---

[37]On p. 82 n. 9 QuarEd state that this principle comes from Pope Innocent III. See Book V, titulus 33 ("On the privileges and on the excesses of those holding the privileges"), chapters 11 and 24 of *Decretales D. Gregorii Papae IX, suae integritati una cum glossis restitutae Ad exemplar Romanum diligenter recognitae*, Editio ultima (Tavrini: Apud Nicolaum Beuilaquam, 1621), 1810-1811 and 1827 respectively.

[38]On p. 82 n. 10 QuarEd helpfully refer to Job 34:30: "Who makes a person who is a hypocrite to reign on account of the sins of the people." The editors also refer to Book XXV, chapter 16, n. 34-41 of Gregory the Great's *Moralia in Iob*. See CCSL cxliii b, 1259-1265.

will is not clear, and we do not know which of these will please God more in the future, a person can work in a just way to have an unjust ruler removed. – Therefore, while the unjust ruler has power from God, it is the ruler who exercises the power. He possesses the power justly, but exercises it unjustly. And hence, in so far as the power is from God, the ruler is to be obeyed. But since he exercises this power unjustly, efforts should be made to have the ruler removed. This is the answer.[39]

ECCLESIASTES 10:8-11:10   THE REMEDY AGAINST THE VANITY OF SECURITY

12. *The person who digs a hole*, etc. He has already treated the vanity of security, and now in a second point he wants *to provide a remedy* against this vanity. Since security comes from what seems to be a lack of just retribution and of a rule by providence, he divides the material into two. First he gives a remedy against the lack of *the order of providence*. Second is his consideration of the lack of *just retribution* where Ecclesiastes 11:1 below reads: *Cast your bread*, etc.

ECCLESIASTES 10:8-20   THE REMEDY AGAINST SECURITY ARISING FROM A SEEMING LACK OF DIVINE PROVIDENCE

13. Now *disorder in government* comes from a triple cause: from the promotion of an *evil* ruler, or of a *foolish* ruler, or of a *useless and negligent* ruler. So he first provides a remedy against an *evil* ruler. Second, against a *foolish* ruler where verse 12 says: *The words of the mouth of a wise*

---

[39]On p. 82 n. 11 QuarEd refer to Book II, d. 44, a. 2 and 3 of Bonaventure's *Sentence Commentary*. See Omnia Opera 2:1005-1016. The editors refer to Book II, chapters 2-6 of Alanus de Insulis, *De fide catholica contra haereticos* where the author counters the opinion of the Waldensians and later heretics who taught that the authority of wicked rulers was null. See PL 210:380-384.

person are grace. Third, against a *carnal and negligent* ruler where verse 16 says: *Woe to you, O land, when your king is a child*.

Ecclesiastes 10:8-11   The defect in government when an evil ruler is promoted

14. On the first point he proceeds as follows. First, he states that a good ruler *is not to be removed*. Second, he says that a wicked ruler is not *to be tolerated* or promoted. Third, he states that when a wicked ruler is promoted, the ruler is to be corrected. Fourth, he says that a wicked ruler is not *to be disparaged* in secret.

15. (Verse 8). First, he states that a *good* ruler is not to be removed, neither by *deceit* or by *violence*. He warns against *deceit*: *The person who digs a hole*, namely, in preparing a trap for a good ruler, *will fall into it*. We read in Psalm 7:16: "The person who opened a pit and dug it has fallen into the hole he made."[40] The ruler is not to be removed by *force*. So he warns the person attempting this: *The person who breaks a hedge*, that is, the good ruler who guards his or her subjects like a hedge. Sirach 36:27 says: "Where there is no hedge, the property will be plundered."[41] *A serpent will bite him*, that is, the devil with demons who are serpents who bite.[42] Jeremiah 8:17 has: "Behold, I will send among you the worst[43] serpents, against which there is no incantation, and they will bite you."[44]

---

[40]Hugh of St. Cher, 99b also quotes Psalm 7:16, as he interprets Ecclesiastes 10:8 to deal with deception.

[41]Hugh of St. Cher, 99c also cites Sirach 36:27.

[42]Hugh of St. Cher, 99c also takes the serpent to be the devil.

[43]The Vulgate reads *serpentes regulos* ("basilisk serpents") while Bonaventure has *serpentes pessimos* ("the worst serpents").

[44]Hugh of St. Cher, 99v, h also quotes Jeremiah 8:17 and reads *serpentes pessimi* ("the worst serpents").

16. (Verse 9). *The person who removes stones*, etc. Second, he shows that a *harsh and useless* ruler is not to be promoted. He warns against promoting a *harsh* ruler by saying: *The person who removes stones*, that is, he promoted harsh and wicked people to a higher dignity. *Will be hurt by them*, that is, through them or because of them. Proverbs 26:8 states: "As the person who casts a stone into a pile of mercury, so is the person who gives honor to a fool." Later on Proverbs 26:27 says: "The person who rolls a stone, it will return to him." And Sirach 27:28 has: "If a person casts a stone on high, it will fall upon his own head." – Further, a *vain and useless* person is not to be promoted. Therefore, Ecclesiastes says: *The person who cuts trees.*[45] Another translation has: *Who trims.*[46] The person who trims is the person who wants to put a useless ruler in charge of a building. A useless ruler is compared to wood, because, just as unproductive wood is cut up and put into the fire, this, too, will happen to a useless ruler. Matthew 7:19 reads: "Every tree that does not bring forth good fruit, will be cut down and will be cast into the fire." The ruler *will be wounded by them*, because the ruler will be wounded in conscience. Sirach 27:28 states: "And the deceitful blow will wound the deceitful." About such wounds Isaiah 1:6 says: "Wounds and bruises and swelling sores, they are not bound up . . . nor soothed by oil."

17. (Verse 10). *If the iron be blunt*, etc. Third, he treats of a ruler who in some way has turned to evil and is *to be corrected*. The ruler may change, even though it will require much work. So he says: *If the iron be blunt*, that is, if the sharpness of good and wisdom have been changed by some

---

[45]Hugh of St. Cher, 99g comments: "That is, who cuts by the sword of excommunication or correction unfruitful men and women, that is, heretics and other evil people, from the body of the Church."

[46]On p. 93 n. 3 QuarEd confess that they are unable to find the source of this "other translation."

sin in the ruler. *And be not as before.* Supply: sharp. *But be made blunt*, by sin. *With much labor*, namely, of correction. *It will be sharpened*, that is, restored to its former right sharpness.[47] Proverbs 27:17 reads: "Iron sharpens iron, so a man sharpens the countenance of his friend."[48] From this example in material matters he draws a parallel in spiritual matters. *And after industry*, that is, industrious work, *wisdom will follow*, just as after the sharpening of iron a straight and a sharp cutting edge follows. We read in Proverbs 15:31: "The ear that hears the reproofs of life will abide in the midst of the wise." And Proverbs 2:4-5 states: "If you will seek her[49] as money and will dig for her as for a treasure, then you will understand the fear of the Lord and will find knowledge."[50]

18. (Verse 11). *If a serpent bites*, etc. Fourth, he shows that such a ruler is not *to be spoken against* in secret, and he shows the gravity of the sin of detraction by an example in material matters. So he says: *If a serpent bites in secret*, which is the way with serpents, because they inject their venom in secret. *The person who backbites in secret is no better*, because just as a serpent acts in a fraudulent way, so too does the person who is a backbiter, for his action *speaks evil of the deaf.* Leviticus 19:14 reads: "You shall not speak evil of the deaf, nor put a stumbling block before the blind." Just as one is deadly, so too is the other. Galatians 5:15 states: "If you bite and devour one another, take heed lest you be consumed by one another." Proverbs 26:22 says: "The words of a talebearer are as it were simple,

---

[47]The translation "right sharpness" attempts to capture Bonaventure's change of vocabulary from *acumen* ("sharpness") to *rectitudo* ("sharpness/rectitude").

[48]Hugh of St. Cher, 99v, d also cites Proverbs 27:17.

[49]That is, wisdom.

[50]On p. 83 n. 5 QuarEd correctly indicate that the Vulgate reads *scientiam Dei* ("knowledge of God") while Bonaventure has *scientiam* ("knowledge").

but they reach to the innards of the belly."[51] Just as in former times they were liberated by looking at Christ,[52] according to what is said in Wisdom 16:7: "The person who had turned[53] was not saved by what he or she saw, but by you, Lord,[54] Savior of all," so it is now. Therefore, he himself says in John 15:20: "If they have kept my word, they will also keep yours."

QUESTIONS 33

It is asked whether it is detraction and a sin to speak evil of a person secretly, when it is sure to the speaker that it is the truth.[55] That it is *not* a sin would seem to be the case from:

1. Because, just as a good person is worthy of praise, so an evil person is worthy of blame. Therefore, just as it is just to praise a good person, so it is just to blame the evil person. Therefore, just as one does not sin by praising a good person, so too one does not sin by speaking evil of the evil person.

2. Also, just as one should rejoice with the good, so one should sorrow over evil. Therefore, just as one can tell another person some good thing, and they can rejoice together without sin, so they can be sorry together over evil.

---

[51]On p. 83 n. 6 QuarEd accurately mention that the Vulgate has *ad intima ventris* ("to the innermost parts of the belly") while Bonaventure reads *usque ad interiora ventris* ("to the innards of the belly").

[52]The implicit reference is to the bronze serpent of Numbers 21:9 and the use of this sign to refer to Christ crucified in John 3:14.

[53]On p. 83 n. 7 QuarEd rightly point out that the Vulgate reads *conversus est* ("turned") whereas Bonaventure has *conversus erat* ("had turned").

[54]On p. 83 n. 7 QuarEd correctly indicate that the Vulgate does not read *Dominum* ("Lord").

[55]See Ecclesiastes 10:11.

Therefore, the person who shares his sorrow when speaking evil of another in secret does not sin.

3. Moreover, the Lord says in Matthew 18 that when a neighbor sins, the neighbor is to be corrected before one or two others.[56] If the neighbor does not listen, the matter must be told to the Church. Therefore, it seems that a person can at least speak evil of an individual who is incorrigible.

Contra: 1. *See that you never do to another what you would hate to have done to you by another.*[57] Therefore, what you do not want to be said about yourself, you should not say about another. You do not want some to speak evil of you in your absence, because it will do you no good. Therefore, etc.

2. Also, whoever speaks evil of another takes away the person's good name. Thus, since *a good name is better than many treasures,*[58] and since a person may not without sin take the riches of another, therefore, etc.

3. Moreover, it is said in Leviticus 19:14: *You shall not speak evil of the deaf.* But to speak evil behind someone's back, is to speak evil of the deaf. So this is against the precept of Leviticus.

---

[56]See Matthew 18:15-17.

[57]See Tobit 4:16: "See that you never do to another what you would hate to have done to you by another." See also Matthew 7:12: "Therefore, all that you wish men and women to do to you, even so do you also to them. For this is the Law and the prophets." Luke 6:31 reads: "And even as you wish men and women to do to you, so also do you to them."

[58]See Proverbs 22:1. On p. 84 n. 3 QuarEd accurately mention that the Vulgate has *divitiae multae* ("many riches") whereas Bonaventure reads *treasuri multi* ("many treasures").

4. Furthermore, a sin committed in public causes scandal. Wherefore, whoever makes public a sin that is not done in public causes scandal, and the one doing this makes known a sin that was hidden. In this way the person to whom the words are addressed is scandalized.

I reply that a person who speaks evil of another does so: either because the person is *driven by necessity*, or *drawn by its usefulness*, or *stirred by a desire to detract*. Thus, a person *is compelled by necessity* when bound by a *human* or *divine* precept to speak. A *human* precept when the individual, who can command and does command, tells a person to speak. A *divine* precept when conscience dictates that one is bound to accuse a neighbor for the sake of correction, in accord with the precept of the Lord about correcting one another.

One *is drawn by its usefulness* when telling evil to someone to whom it is of benefit and does no harm. Hearing the evil will be for the good and not for the harm of such people. For example, when one is speaking with a person who is loved, with whom one is in sympathy, and with the intention of correcting the person involved.

But when there is neither necessity nor usefulness, even if what is said is the truth, a person is not excused by *the passion of committing detraction*. Further, such a person commits the sin of detraction, even if he is speaking the truth.

So the reasons that prove that it is a sin to speak evil of an absent person are to be accepted except in the case of necessity or usefulness. For then it is clear what reasons are not valid.

1. To the objection about the contrary, that it is just to blame, etc., it has to be said that even if men and women

are worthy of blame, nonetheless we should not blame them. Blame is not the same as praise, for a good name promotes good, but evil promotes evil. And so evil is not to be made public, in the way good is. - Moreover, it is not for me to judge.

2. To the objection about compassion, it must be said that true compassion exists in the compassionate person who is suffering with another, not in the condemnation of an unfortunate person. And since in the objection the good name of the sinner is lessened, there should be no such accusation.

3. To the objection based on the precept of the Lord, it should be said that the Lord's intention is that those who are to be called are able to and want to benefit from the correction. And the word *Church* does not refer to a multitude of people, but the text is directed to the person who can benefit and to the person who should perform the correction. To such people this text is addressed.[59]

ECCLESIASTES 10:12-15   THE DEFECT IN GOVERNMENT WHEN A FOOLISH RULER IS PROMOTED

19. *The words of the mouth of a wise person*, etc. Ecclesiastes has given a remedy against the malice of a ruler. He now gives a remedy against *the foolishness* of a ruler, showing that a foolish ruler should not be promoted, but rather is worthy of dismissal. He is worthy of dismissal, first, for a lack of *discretion in speech*; second, for showing a lack of *provident care*; third, for a lack of *profitable work*.

20. (Verses 12-14a). On account of a lack of *discretion in words*, the foolish ruler casts himself down in contrast to

---

[59]On p. 84 n. 7 QuarEd refer to Part II, q. 130 of Alexander of Hales' *Summa*.

the wise who are exalted. So he says: *The words of the mouth of a wise person are grace*, because in them grace is acquired through their discretion. Sirach 20:13 reads: "A person wise in words[60] will make himself beloved." But on the contrary: *The lips[61] of a fool will throw him down headlong*, that is, words coming from the lips of a fool. Proverbs 18:7 says: "The mouth of a fool is destructive, and his lips are the ruin of his soul."[62]

21. The reason why the foolish ruler is thrown down is his indiscretion, because he *begins* indiscreetly. Thus, he continues: *The beginning of his words is folly*. The reason for this is that the foolish do not reflect. Wherefore, Proverbs 29:20 states: "Have you seen a person hasty to speak? Folly is rather to be looked for rather than his amendment." He also *finishes* indiscreetly. Hence, he says: *And the end of his talk is a mischievous error*, because foolishness in the end leads to erroneous opinions. We read in Proverbs 14:8: "The imprudence of fools errs,"[63] because, as said above in Ecclesiastes 2:14: "The eyes of a wise person are in his head. The fool walks in darkness."

22. Further, the foolish ruler *perseveres* in foolishness. So he adds: *A fool multiplies words*, and, by multiplying foolish words, the fool becomes obstinate in evil. Against this we read in Psalm 140:4: "Incline not your heart to make excuses for sins,"[64] for this is useless and vain, for as it is said in Proverbs 19:7: "The person who follows[65] after words

---

[60]On p. 84 n. 8 QuarEd accurately indicate that the Vulgate reads *in verbis* ("in words") whereas Bonaventure has *verbis* ("in words").

[61]The Vulgate reads *et labia* ("and the lips").

[62]Hugh of St. Cher, 99v, m also cites Proverbs 18:7.

[63]On p. 85 n. 1 QuarEd rightly mention that the Vulgate reads *errans* ("is in error") while Bonaventure has *errat* ("errs").

[64]Hugh of St. Cher, 100c also quotes Psalm 140:4.

[65]On p. 85 n. 1 QuarEd accurately indicate that the Vulgate reads *tantum* ("only") which Bonaventure does not have.

will have nothing." And Proverbs 14:23 states: "Where there are many words, there is often want."[66]

23. (Verse 14b). *People cannot tell*, etc. Second, the fool shows a lack of *provident care* when, ignorant of the past, the fool is unable to provide for the future. So he says: *People cannot tell what has been before them*, for they are foolish and unthinking persons. James 1:24 reads: "The person looked at himself and went his way and immediately forgot what manner of person he was." – *And what will be after them, who can tell them?*, as if to say: No one. Ecclesiastes 8:7 above states: "The person who is ignorant of past things cannot know future things[67] by any messenger." And this is very damaging, for Deuteronomy 32:29 has: "O that they would be wise and would understand and would provide for their last end."

24. (Verse 15). *The labor of fools*, etc. Third, he shows that in the fool there is a lack of *profitable work*, because in his work he is much troubled and gains little. So he says: *The labor of fools will afflict them*, because they do not work in what is good. Jeremiah 9:5 reads: "They have labored to commit iniquity." Thus, Wisdom 5:7 states: "We wearied ourselves in the way of iniquity and destruction and have walked through hard ways, but the way of the Lord we have not known." He gives the reason for this: *who do not know how to go to the city*, that is, they are ignorant of the true way for reaching that city about which we read in Isaiah 26:1: "Zion, the city of our strength, a savior, a wall and a bulwark will be set therein." The foolish do not know how to reach this city. For he said above in Ecclesiastes 6:8: "What more has the wise person than the fool? And what the poor person, except to go thither where there is life?"

---

[66]Hugh of St. Cher, 100c also cites Proverbs 14:23.

[67]The Vulgate reads *et ventura* ("and things to come") whereas Bonaventure has *futura* ("future things").

25. In a *spiritual interpretation* we understand the *wise person* to be Christ and the *foolish person* to be the Antichrist. *The words of the mouth of the wise person are grace*, because the words of Christ are pleasing. Psalm 44:3 reads: "Grace is poured abroad on your lips. Therefore, God has blessed you forever." And Luke 2:47 states: "All who heard him were astonished at his wisdom and his answers." And in John 7:46 others were saying: "Never did a person speak like this man."

26. On the other hand, *the foolish person* is the Antichrist, of whom we read in Psalm 13:1: "The fool has said in his heart: There is no God." *The lips of a fool will throw him down headlong*,[68] because on account of the evil of his teaching he is cast into the depths. Job 18:7 reads: "The step of his strength will be curtailed, and his own counsel will cast him down headlong." For his words are blasphemy and pride and so are foolish and wrong. For it is said in Daniel 11:36: "He will speak great things against the God of gods and will prosper, till the wrath be accomplished." And 2 Thessalonians 2:3-4 states: "The man of sin will be revealed, the son of perdition, who opposes, and will be exalted[69] above all that is called God," etc.[70]

27. This fool is not only indiscreet in speech, but also *lacks foresight*, because he will not consider the ruin to follow in his wake, according to what the Apostle says in 2 Thessalonians 2:8: "Whom the Lord Jesus will kill with the spirit of his mouth." Foolish people follow this fool and are afflicted, *who do not know how to go to the city*, in true

---

[68]Ecclesiastes 10:12.

[69]On p. 85 n. 5 QuarEd correctly notice that the Vulgate reads *revelatus fuerit* ("will be revealed") whereas Bonaventure has *revelabitur* ("will be revealed") and the Vulgate reads *extollitur* ("is lifted up") while Bonaventure has *exaltabitur* ("will be exalted").

[70]Hugh of St. Cher, 100c explains Ecclesiastes 10:13 as referring to the Antichrist and alludes to 2 Thessalonians 2.

faith and love. 2 Thessalonians 2:10-11 reads: "God will send the operation of error to those . . . who have not believed the truth, but have consented to iniquity," because they did not receive the love of truth. So Psalm 81:5 says: "They have not known nor understood. Therefore, they are walking in darkness."

ECCLESIASTES 10:16-20   THE DEFECT IN GOVERNMENT WHEN A USELESS AND CARELESS RULER IS PROMOTED

28. *Woe to you, O land*, etc. He has given a remedy against disorder coming from an evil and foolish ruler. Now in a third point he gives a remedy against disorder from a *useless and careless* ruler. So he shows that such a lazy and carnal person is neither to be promoted nor endured. There are two sections because, first, he detests such a ruler and shows him to be *unworthy to rule*, and second, he says that people should not *speak against him in secret* where verse 20 reads: *In your thought*, etc.

ECCLESIASTES 10:16-19   A USELESS AND CARELESS RULER IS UNWORTHY TO RULE

29. He shows that a carnal and lazy ruler is worthy to be a ruler. First, on account of *the disorder of gluttony*. Second, on account of weakness or *the laziness of sloth*. Third, on account of *inappropriate celebration*. Fourth, on account of *the subversion of justice* through a love of money.

30. (Verses 16-17). Because of *the disorder of gluttony* a carnal and careless ruler is unworthy, and woe to those over whom he rules. Therefore, he says: *Woe to you, O land, when your king is a child*, that is, pursues passions. For children are pursuers of passions. Isaiah 65:20 states: "A child will die a hundred years old." Hence, *woe*, because it is an occasion of eternal damnation and a sign of divine anger. Isaiah 3:4 reads: "I will give children to be their

princes, and the effeminate will rule over them." And since princes follow a leader, he says: *And whose princes eat in the morning,* quickly looking for delicacies.[71] And therefore, they are always foolish, because it is said in Proverbs 20:1: "Wine is a luxurious thing and drunkenness riotous. Whoever delights in these will not be wise."

31. And since "when opposites are placed together they become clearer,"[72] he praises one saying against its opposite: *Blessed is the land, whose king is noble,* namely, in nobility of character, for true nobility consists in having a soul adorned with virtues.[73] For this reason Proverbs 31:23 says: "Her husband is noble in the gates, when he sits among the leaders of the land." And since princes follow a leader, he adds: *And whose princes eat in due season for refreshment, and not for riotousness,* that is, at a proper time after finishing work, and then *for refreshment and not for riotousness.* An *interlinear Gloss* comments: "They eat only to live, not live to eat,"[74] like those about whom

---

[71]Hugh of St. Cher, 100v, c comments: "And so since he gives himself over to gluttony in the morning, there follow confusion in business deals, loss of subjects, subversion of judgments, and justice is at risk."

[72]On p. 86 n. 2 QuarEd quote Book I, n. 15 of Aristotle's *De sophisticis elenchis*. See WAE, vol. 1, 174b: "For the placing of their contraries close beside them makes things look big to men, both relatively and absolutely, and worse and better." The editors also cite Book II, n. 6 of Aristotle's *De mundo*. See WAE, vol. 3, 396b: "It may perhaps be that nature has a liking for contraries and evolves harmony out of them and not out of similarities. . . ."

[73]Hugh of St. Cher, 100v, e has virtually the same wording of this saying: "*Nobilitas animi sola est, quae moribus ornat* ("Nobility of soul consists solely in having it adorned with virtues"). Hugh's editor put these words in italics and set them off as a citation. It seems that Bonaventure has cited this saying from Hugh of St. Cher. A search on the internet revealed that the saying ultimately comes from number 40 of Avian's *Fables*.

[74]On p. 86 n. 3 QuarEd state that Lyranus has this interlinear Glossa in his commentary on Ecclesiastes 10:17. Hugh of St. Cher, 100v, h quotes this *Interlinear Glossa*: "That is, they eat more from necessity than from voluptuousness. For they should eat, so that they may live for God; not live to eat, the Interlinear says."

we read in 2 Peter 2:13: "They are spots and blemishes, abounding in delicacies, wantonly enjoying banquets."[75]

32. (Verse 18). *By slothfulness*, etc. Second, he shows that a careless ruler is unworthy because of *the laziness of sloth*, which brings about the downfall of a building. For this reason he says: *By slothfulness a building will be brought down*.[76] *A building* is said to be a joining of wood beams to cover a house.[77] This building *is brought down by sloth*, because when repairs are neglected, it collapses. In the same way a spiritual building is destroyed by sloth. Proverbs 18:9 reads: "A person who is loose and slack in his work is the brother of the person who wastes his own works." And since where the fear of God is not active sloth takes charge, it is said in Sirach 27:4: "Unless you hold yourself diligently in the fear of the Lord, your house will quickly be overthrown." – *And through the weakness of hands the house will leak*. These words say the same thing, but give a more complete explanation. *A house leaks*, when it is not protected in rainy weather from showers, and this is not good. We read in Proverbs 27:15: "Leaky roofs on a cold day and a contentious woman are alike." This house is collapsing, when hands are weak and careless. Therefore, Hebrews 12:12-13 states: "Lift up the hands that hang down and the feeble knees, and take straight steps with your feet."

---

[75]On p. 86 n. 3 QuarEd correctly indicate that the Vulgate reads *conviviis suis* ("in their banquets") while Bonaventure has *conviviis* ("banquets").

[76]The Vulgate has *contignatio*, which Douay translates by "building," but as the context shows, its primary meaning is "woodwork." In this instance it refers to a roof made of wood.

[77]On p. 86 n. 4 QuarEd refer, amidst matters about wooden houses, to Jerome's commentary on this passage in his *Commentarius in Ecclesiasten*. See CCSL lxxii, 342-343. Hugh of St. Cher, 100vi comments: "That is, a construction of wood beams. Wood beams are wood for buildings, which are called 'forelocks' in French, because they interlock with one another as they bind together."

33. (Verse 19a). *For the sake of laughter they make bread,* etc. Third, he shows the anger of the lazy and carnal ruler on account of *inappropriate celebration*, during which they always want to be carnal and everything they do is directed to this end. So he says: *For the sake of laughter they make bread.* A Gloss states: Rulers who laugh, that is, inappropriate rejoicing.[78] Luke 12:19 says: "My soul, you have many goods for very many years... Eat, drink, feast."[79] And therefore, he adds: *And wine that those drinking*[80] *may feast.* For they are doing this, so that they may eat, not so that they may break bread for a hungry person. James 5:5 states: "You have feasted upon earth, and in voluptuousness you have nourished your hearts."[81] This conduct is condemned in Isaiah 5:12: "The harp and lyre ... and wine are in your feasts, and the work of God[82] you regard not."

34. (Verse 19b). *And all things obey money*, etc. Fourth, he shows how such rulers are unworthy on account of a *subversion of justice*, done out of love for money. So he says: *And all things love money*, for all love money more than anything else. Isaiah 1:23 reads: "All love bribes. They run after rewards. Then there follows a subversion of justice. Isaiah 1:23 says: "They judge not for the fatherless, and the widow's cause does not come before them." And

---

[78]On p. 86 n. 7 QuarEd quote the *Glossa Interlinearis apud Lyranum*: "Since rulers or whoever are given over to delicacies and laughter." They also refer to Jerome's *Commentarius in Ecclesiasten*. See CCSL lxxcci, 342 where Jerome interprets this passage via the instructions to preachers in 1 Timothy and Titus: Do not preach to please human beings, but the Lord.

[79]On p. 86 n. 7 QuarEd accurately indicate Bonaventure's adaptation of Luke 12:19: "And I will say to my soul: Soul, you have many good things laid up for very many years. Take your ease, eat, drink, feast."

[80]The Vulgate has *viventes* ("the living") while Bonaventure reads *bibentes* ("those drinking").

[81]James 5:5 concludes with: "... in the day of slaughter."

[82]The Vulgate reads *Domini* ("of the Lord") while Bonaventure has *Dei* ("of God").

Jeremiah 6:13 states: "From the least of them even to the greatest, all are given to covetousness."

ECCLESIASTES 10:20   DO NOT SPEAK IN SECRET AGAINST THE CARNAL AND LAZY RULER

35. *In your thought*, etc. He has shown above that a carnal and lazy person is unworthy to be a ruler. Now *he restrains subjects from speaking ill of a ruler in private*, should an unworthy ruler be promoted. First, he *exhorts* and, second, gives *the reason* for his exhortation.

36. (Verse 20). So *he exhorts* us neither to speak evil so as to lessen a good name, nor to curse people and wish them misfortune. So he says: *Do not speak detraction against the king in your thought*, that is, in secret. Exodus 22:28 reads: "You shall not speak detraction against the gods, and the prince of your people you shall not curse." – *And in your private chamber*, that is, in your conscience,[83] *speak no evil of the rich person*, for this is to curse him. Romans 12:14 states: "Bless those who persecute you. Bless and do not curse." And 1 Peter 3:9 says: "Nor rendering curse for curse."

37. *Because even the birds of the air*, etc. He now gives *the reason* for the exhortation, namely, because what you have said in secret will be made public by the angels, for *the birds of the air will carry your voice*. He calls the birds of the air demons because of their speed as they move swiftly[84] or because of their rapacity.[85] Thus, Genesis 15:1

---

[83]Hugh of St. Cher, 101b also has this interpretation.

[84]Bonaventure links *volucres* ("birds") by means of *velocitas* ("swiftness").

[85]On p. 87 n. 1 QuarEd refer to Book II, d. 6, a. 2, q. 1,2 and dubia 1-2 of Bonaventure's *Sentence Commentary* for his treatment of demons. See Omnia Opera 2:164-166, 169.

says: "The birds came down upon the carcasses, and Abraham drove them off."[86] And Matthew 13:4 has: "Other seed fell[87] by the wayside, and the birds came and ate them."[88] *The air* refers here to a gloomy atmosphere in which demons live. The demons carry the voice, because they frequently make known what was secret. Matthew 10:26 reads: "Nothing is covered . . . that will not be known." *And the one who has wings will tell what you have said,* that is, the devil will announce your evil words, because the devil is an accuser. But the devil will finally be overthrown, for Revelation 12:10 says: "The accuser of our brothers and sisters has been cast forth, the one who accused them . . . day and night."

QUESTIONS 34

I. A doubt arises here because he says that the birds of the air, that is, demons announce detraction that is in a person's mind.[89] This would seem to be so, because the devil knows our will and thought.

But contra: 1. Because of God alone is it said that he *searches hearts and innards.*[90] Therefore, only God knows our thoughts and affections.

2. Also, Augustine says that had the demons known of the patience of Job, they would not have tempted him, because

---

[86]The Vulgate reads *Abram* ("Abram") while Bonaventure has *Abraham* ("Abraham").

[87]On p. 87 n. 1 QuarEd rightly notice that the Vulgate reads *Quaedam ceciderunt* ("Some fell") whereas Bonaventure has *Aliud cecidit* ("Other seed fell").

[88]Hugh of St. Cher, 101d comments: "Birds of the air] that is, the demons, who are called birds of the air, Matthew 13 & Luke 8. Birds because of their swiftness."

[89]See Ecclesiastes 10:20.

[90]See Psalm 7:10 and Revelation 2:23.

they do not tempt a person except to overcome the person, not to be overcome.[91]

I reply that neither the demons nor the good angels can know our hidden thoughts and affections except in the Word. The adjective *hidden* refers to what is not made clear through signs. But the demons apprehend and understand those thoughts and affections manifested through signs. And since there are few thoughts and affections that are not revealed by some sign, action, facial expression, word, or in some other way, he says that they *hear*.[92]

II. Furthermore, one can ask what the text means: *The birds of the air will carry* or announce.

I ask how will the birds carry? If one says that they carry it to the person being spoken about, this is false, because then everyone would know all the hidden evils spoken about them. Therefore, it means that they will carry it to God.

But contra: 1. God is more immediate and present to us than demons, since *God is not far from any one of us*.[93] If *to carry* or *to announce* means to bring it to a person who is distant, it is clear that this is not the same.

---

[91]On p. 87 n. 4 QuarEd cite Book XII, chapter 17 n. 34 of Augustine's *De Genesi ad litteram*. See *On Genesis*, 482: "There have, all the same, been the most definite and certain indications to establish that what people have been thinking has been made public by demons; and yet if these could observe in people the inner beauty of their virtues, they would not even try to tempt them. Thus if the devil had been able to observe in Job that wonderful, noble patience of his, he would undoubtedly have been most unwilling to be defeated in his effort to tempt him."

[92]On p. 87 n. 5 QuarEd refer to Book II, d. 7, p. II, q. 3 n. 4 and d. 8, p. II, q. 6 of Bonaventure's *Sentence Commentary*. See Omnia Opera 2:194 and 232 respectively.

[93]See Acts 17:27 in Paul's Areopagus speech: "that they should seek God, and perhaps grope after him and find him, though he is not far from any one of us."

2. Also, who is *to carry* the words? It must be either by *good* or by *bad* angels. They are not carried by the good angels, for good angels work for our salvation, not for our damnation. Therefore, they do not bear evil things. If you say by *the demons*, the following is contrary to that: The demons do not see God nor speak with God any more than evil men and women. Wherefore, if evil people do not bring the words to God, neither do the demons.

I reply that in the text *birds* stand for evil spirits or demons, who are said to carry bad and hidden merits to God, while the good angels carry our good merits. Now the word *to carry*, as far as the meaning of the word is concerned, does not mean to speak to God or to inform God, as if God were ignorant, but to recognize our malice and by such recognition to remember it and be a witness to it. On the other hand, the good angels add intercession to our knowledge, memory, and witness, while the bad angels add the will to accuse.[94]

1.2. This makes clear the answer to the first objection, because it does not refer to someone distant, but to a judge. The reply to the second objection is that evil beings by nature observe evil and work for damnation. This is their proper work.

---

[94]On p. 87 n. 7 QuarEd refer to three helpful passages. In Tobit 12:12 the angel Raphael tells Tobias: "When you did pray with tears and did bury the dead and did leave your dinner and hide the dead by day in your house and bury them by night, I offered your prayer to the Lord." Revelation 12:10b reads: "For the accuser of our brothers and sisters has been cast down, he who accused them before our God day and night." See Book II, chapter 8 n. 13-14 of Gregory the Great's *Moralia in Iob* in ccsl, pp. 68-69: "But when our ancient adversary has found no evil by which to accuse a person, he seeks to turn the good into evil. When he is conquered by deeds, he scrutinizes our words to find some accusation. When he finds no basis for accusation in words, he seeks to darken the intention of the heart."

CHAPTER 11

ECCLESIASTES 11:1-10   REMEDY AGAINST THE VANITY
                         OF SECURITY ARISING FROM A
                         LACK OF JUSTICE IN
                         PUNISHMENT

1. *Cast your bread*, etc. Earlier he has given a remedy
against an apparent lack of direction by providence during a disorder in government. Here in a second point he
gives a remedy against what is seen as lack of *just retribution*. Because of this lack a person grows active in evil
and slothful in doing good. Now the remedy consists in a
reflection on future retribution. And since God gives good
things to those who do good and bad things to those who
do evil things, he first *challenges to good* by a consideration of reward. Second, from a reflection on punishment
he *calls his readers back from evil* where verse 8 reads: *If
a person live many years*, etc.

ECCLESIASTES 11:1-7   CHALLENGE TO GOOD FROM A
                        CONSIDERATION OF REWARD

2. Now the good to which he challenges us is the good of
mercy, which *is profitable in all respects*,[1] and is the major

---

[1]See 1 Timothy 4:8. In 1 Timothy *pietas* has the meaning of "godliness."
Bonaventure, however, generally takes *pietas* to mean "mercy," as the
immediate context makes clear.

reason why the just are saved, as is clear in Matthew 25 where only the works of mercy are enumerated.[2] So he exhorts here to works of mercy and almsgiving for the sake of a reward. He exhorts us first to give alms *willingly*. Second, that our almsgiving be *in abundance* where verse two reads: *Give a portion to seven*. Third, that our almsgiving be *constant* where verse 4 states: *The person who observes the wind will not sow*. – Therefore, since he exhorts to give voluntarily and *willingly*, he begins with *the exhortation* and adds *the reason*.

3. (Verse 1). So he exhorts us to give alms *willingly* and says: *Cast your bread*, that is, willingly and generously, not from being pressured or forced. 2 Corinthians 9:7 reads: "Everyone as he has determined in his heart, not with sadness, or of necessity. For God loves a cheerful giver." *Your bread*, not someone else's.[3] Sirach 34:24 states: "The person that offers sacrifice from the goods of the poor is like a person that sacrifices the son in the presence of the father." *Upon the running waters*. The many *waters* are many people, as Revelation 17:15 says.[4] *The running waters* are people who move from one people to another and from one kingdom to another. Such are pilgrims and strangers to whom alms should be given. Isaiah 58:7 has: "Deal your bread to the hungry and bring the needy and the homeless into your house."[5] Another interpretation is: *The waters* are present troubles, according to what Psalm 68:2 reads: "The waters have come up even to my soul."

---

[2]See Matthew 25:35-36: "For I was hungry, and you gave me to eat. I was thirsty, and you gave me to drink. I was a stranger, and you took me in. Naked, and you covered me. Sick, and you visited me; I was in prison, and you came to me."

[3]Hugh of St. Cher, 101k makes the same point.

[4]Revelation 17:15 reads: "The waters that you saw, where the harlot sits, are peoples and nations and tongues." Hugh of St. Cher, 101l quotes Revelation 17:15 in its entirety.

[5]Hugh of St. Cher, p. 101n also cites Isaiah 58:7.

The running waters are the poor and afflicted, because they pass from troubles to rest. Alms are to be given to such people. Luke 14:13 states: "When you give alms,[6] invite the poor, the maimed, the lame, and the blind," etc.[7] And he gives the reason: *For after a long time you will find it again*, that is, a reward for your alms. Therefore, the reward is not lacking, but deferred. We read in Sirach 12:2: "Do good to the just, and you will find great recompense. And if not from him, assuredly from the Lord." Luke 16:9 says: "Make for yourselves friends from the mammon of iniquity," etc.

4. (Verses 2-3). *Give a portion to seven*, etc. Here in a second point he exhorts us to give *abundantly* and does so by giving *an exhortation* and then adding *the reason*. So *he encourages* us to give in abundance when he says: *Give a portion to seven, and also to eight*. This means to give in accord with the amount of alms you can afford, so that, whether you are poor or rich, you give a seventh or an eighth of your goods, that is, you give a goodly portion to the poor. 2 Corinthians 8:14 reads: "Let your abundance supply their want." And Luke 11:41 says: "Give alms from what remains."[8] So he says: *Give a portion to seven*. For by *seven* we understand the amount necessary for one's own needs and what is over after that is called *seven* and *eight*. This excess is to be given to the poor, not hoarded as earthly treasures, but as heavenly treasures. Matthew 6:20 states: "Lay up for yourselves treasures in heaven where neither

---

[6]On p. 88 n. 3 QuarEd rightly indicate that the Vulgate has *facis convivium* ("you give a banquet") while Bonaventure reads *facis eleemosynam* ("you give alms").

[7]Hugh of St. Cher, 1011 quotes Luke 14:12-14.

[8]On p. 88 n. 5 QuarEd accurately mention that the Vulgate reads *Verumtamen quod superset date elemosynam* ("But give as alms what remains") while Bonaventure has *Date eleemosynam de eo quod superset* ("Give alms from what remains").

rust nor moth consumes." And Tobit 4:9 has: "If you have much, give abundantly. If you have little, take care that it, too, is willingly given."[9] He gives *the reason* for this largess, when he makes the point: *For you do not know what evil*, etc. He adds a multiple reason, namely, *to guard against evil* and says: *For you do not know what evil will be upon the earth.* Therefore, since you do not know, you must provide for yourself and avoid falling into danger. The best safeguard against danger is abundant almsgiving. Sirach 29:15 states: "Shut up alms in the heart of the poor, and it will obtain help for you and will deliver[10] you from all evil."

5. *On account of the increase of merit* he says: *If the clouds be full.* Supply: from God. *They will pour rain upon the earth*, making the earth fertile. Hosea 6:3 reads: "He will come to us as the early and the late rain to the earth." The rain makes the earth fertile and multiplies the goods of the earth by the merit of almsgiving. Just as full clouds moisten the earth with rain, so abundant alms moisten the soul with grace. 2 Corinthians 9:10 states: "And the person who ministers seed to the sower will both give you to eat and will multiply your seed and increase the growth of the fruits of your justice." On account of *the stability of the reward*, which could not be changed or lost. So he says: *If the tree fall to the south.* This *tree* is a human being, about whom Job 14:7 states: "A tree has hope. If it be cut, it will grow green again."[11] The *south* represents the

---

[9]On p. 88 n. 6 QuarEd correctly notice that the Vulgate reads *si exiguum fuerit etiam exiguum libenter inpertire stude* (If you have very little, take care to give willingly even that little") whereas Bonaventure has *Si parum, etiam illud libenter impertiri stude* ("If you have a little, take care that it, too, is willingly given").

[10]On p. 88 n. 7 QuarEd rightly point out that the Vulgate does not read *et liberabit* ("and will deliver").

[11]On p. 88 n. 9 QuarEd correctly mention that the Vulgate reads *virescit* ("grows green") whereas Bonaventure has *virescet* ("will grow green").

warmth of love and the state of glory. The Song of Songs
4:16 has: "Arise, O north wind, and come. O south wind,
blow through my garden." Wood falling to the south indicates a person entering glory after death. The person *will
be there*, that is, could never be moved. Revelation 3:12
reads: "The person who will overcome, I will make him a
pillar in the temple of my God, and he will go out no more."
— If the tree fall to the north, there shall it be, that is, if it be
for infernal punishment. Jeremiah 1:14 says: "From the
north every evil will break forth."[12] The person who falls
into hell *will be there*, because there will never be any re-
lease from there. For it is said to the just person in Isaiah
66:24: "Their fire will not be quenched, and their worm
will not die."[13] *In whatever place it will fall, there will it be*,
either good or bad. Galatians 6:8 notes: "What things a
human being will sow, these also will he reap."[14]

6. (Verse 4). *The person who observes the wind*, etc. Here
he exhorts his readers to give *without ceasing*. First, he
teaches that *seasons* are not to be calculated. Second, *divine works* are not to be analyzed. Third, that *works of
mercy* are to be continued.

7. Concerning the first point he says: *The person who observes the wind will not sow*, because wind frequently comes
when it is not wanted and does not come when wanted.
And the person who considers the clouds will never reap.
And so one ought not wait, but one ought to sow and to
reap at their proper times. In the same way a person should
do good while there is time. Sirach 4:3 says: "Afflict not

---

[12]On p. 89 n. 1 QuarEd accurately indicate that the Vulgate has a
different reading. Douay translates: "From the north will an evil break
forth upon all the inhabitants of the land."

[13]On p. 89 n. 1 QuarEd rightly notice that the Vulgate has these
clauses in reverse order.

[14]Hugh of St. Cher, 103d also quotes Galatians 6:8.

the heart of the needy, and defer not to give to the person who is in distress." And Proverbs 4:28 reads: "Do not say to your friend: Go and come again, and tomorrow I will give to you, when you can give at the present time." And so one should not wait.

8. (Verse 5). *As you know not what is the way*, etc. He said above that seasons are not to be calculated, and now in a second point he teaches that *divine works are not to be analyzed* or scrutinized, because that is beyond us. So he continues: *As you know not what is the way of the spirit.* The Spirit, who is *God*, because we are ignorant of this way. For John 3:8 reads: "The Spirit breathes where he wills, and you hear his voice, but you do not know," etc.[15] And Job 9:11 states: "If he come to me, I will not see him. If he depart, I will not understand." We do not know *the way*, that is, the origin or end of *the spirit* that is *a soul* or spiritual creature. Earlier Ecclesiastes 3:21 said: "Who knows whether the spirit of the children of Adam ascends upward." We do not know *the way*, that is, the origin, of *the spirit* which is *wind*. For Psalm 134:7 reads: "Who brings forth winds out of his stores." Exodus 15:10 states: "Your wind blew, and the sea covered them." So he says: *As you know not what is the way of the spirit, nor how the bones are joined together in the womb of her who is with child*, that is, how they are joined together and yet distinct For even Avicenna himself says that the power joining limbs together is a divine power.[16] 2 Maccabees 7:22 has: "I know

---

[15]Hugh of St. Cher, 102m quotes John 3:4-8.

[16]On p. 89 n. 5 QuarEd quote from Book I, Fen 1, Doctrina 6, chapter 2 of Avicenna's *Liber Canonis*. See *Avicenna, Liber Canonis,* Reprografischer Nachdruck der Ausgabe Venedig, 1507 (Hildesheim: Georg Olms, 1964), 23v: "Now the forming and impressing power is the one from which, at the command of the Creator, the delineation and figuration of the members proceed." The editors also refer to Book III, Fen 21, Tractatus 1, chapter 2 where Avicenna teaches that the work of this power is "from the secrets of God." See *Liber Canonis*, 362v.

not how you were formed in my womb, for I neither gave you breath, nor soul, nor life, neither did I[17] frame the limbs of each of you." But God framed the limbs. To God Job 10:11 speaks: "You have framed me with bones and sinews." Why are you ignorant of these things that are carnal? *So you do not know the works of God who is the maker of all*. *Works*, that is, hidden judgments, of which we read in Psalm 110:2: "Great are the works of the Lord, exquisite in all their delights." We are ignorant of these works. Romans 11:33 says: "O the depth of the riches of the wisdom and of the knowledge of God! How incomprehensible are his judgments, and how inscrutable his ways."

9. (Verse 6). *In the morning, sow*, etc. Here in a third point he exhorts his readers *to do good without ceasing*. He begins with an *exhortation*. Then he adds *the reason for the exhortation*. And third, he adds *the reward*.

10. So he *exhorts* his readers to do works of mercy *without ceasing* by saying: *In the morning, sow your seed*, that is, while you are a youth,[18] because as Lamentations 3:27 states: "It is good for a man when he has borne the yoke from his youth."[19] *And in the evening let not your hand cease*, that is, in old age,[20] as if to say that in every season and age good works are to be done unceasingly. Galatians 6:9 reads: "And let us not fail to do good. For in the acceptable time[21] we will reap, if we do not fail."

---

[17]On p. 89 n. 5 QuarEd rightly mention that the Vulgate reads *ego ipsa* ("I myself") whereas Bonaventure has *ego* ("I").

[18]Hugh of St. Cher, 102n interprets morning as the time of a young child.

[19]Hugh of St. Cher, 102v, a also cites Lamentations 3:27.

[20]Hugh of St. Cher, 102q also interprets evening as the time of old age.

[21]On p. 89 n. 7 QuarEd correctly indicate that the Vulgate reads *tempore enim suo* ("for at the due time") while Bonaventure has *tempore enim accepto* ("for at the acceptable time").

11. *For you do not know*, etc. Here he notes *the reason* for the exhortation, namely, because a person does not know when or what works God accepts, just as the sower does not know which seed will bear fruit. So he says: *For you do not know which may rather spring up, this*, that is, the evening sowing, or *that*, that is, the morning sowing. He had said earlier in Ecclesiastes 9:1: "And yet a person does not know whether he be worthy of love or hatred." *And if both together, it will be the better*, because "many goods are to be chosen rather than a few."[22] Isaiah 32:20 reads: "Blessed are you that sow upon all waters."

12. (Verse 7). *The light is sweet*, etc. Third, he notes *the reward*, namely, the vision of light and of the eternal sun in which is the highest delight. Thus, it is a great reward. So he says: *The light is sweet*, that is, to look at. Of this sweetness Psalm 30:20 says: "O how great is the multitude of your sweetness, O Lord," etc. *And it is delightful for the eyes to see the sun*, that is, the sun about which Malachi 4:2 states: "The sun of justice will arise for you who fear God."[23] *It is delightful to see* this *sun*. For 1 Peter 1:12 reads: "On whom the angels desire to look." And since only those on the right will see this sun, Psalm 15:10 has: "At your right hand are delights even to the end."

13. These verses can also be briefly interpreted to apply to *spiritual almsgiving* that consists in instructing one's neighbor. As he did earlier, Ecclesiastes exhorts us to do this *willingly* or liberally, *abundantly*, and *without ceasing*, when he says: *Cast your bread*,[24] etc., that is, give freely.

---

[22]On p. 89 n. 8 QuarEd refer to Book III, n. 2 of Aristotle's *Topica*. See WAE, vol. 1, 117a: "Moreover, a greater number of good things is more desirable than a smaller, either absolutely or when the one is included in the other, viz. the smaller number in the greater."

[23]On p. 90 n. 1 QuarEd correctly mention that the Vulgate reads *nomen meum* ("my name") while Bonaventure has *Deum* ("God").

[24]See Ecclesiastes 11:1.

Matthew 10:8 reads: "Freely have you received, freely give." *Give bread*, that is, the bread of *teaching*,[25] about which Lamentations 4:4 says: "The little ones asked for bread, and there was none to break it for them." *Upon the running waters*, that is, those who despise temporal goods. To these alone should the bread of teaching be given. Matthew 7:6 states: "Do not give what is holy to dogs."[26] Another interpretation: *Upon* those, about whom Psalm 65:11 says: "We have passed through fire and water, and you have brought us out," etc.

14. Alms are also to be dispensed *abundantly*, and so he says: *Give a portion to seven*.[27] By *seven* we understand the teaching about Christ in the Old Testament, because there it was commanded to observe the seventh day.[28] By *eight* we understand the teaching of the New Testament, because there it is commanded to observe the eighth day.[29]

---

[25] Hugh of St. Cher, 101i also interprets the bread as "teaching."

[26] Hugh of St. Cher, 101m, in talking about spiritual bread, cites Matthew 7:6.

[27] See Ecclesiastes 11:2.

[28] Hugh of St. Cher, 101pq comments: "Give seven parts] observe the Old Testament, which is understood by sevens on account of the seventh day and seven times seven, and the seventh month, and the seventh year which must be observed as jubilee. And also eight] moreover, observe the New Testament, which is represented by eight, on account of the eighth day of the resurrection."

[29] On p. 90 n. 3 QuarEd quote the pertinent comments of Jerome on this verse. See his *Commentarius in Ecclesiasten* in CCSL lxxii, 345: "What is commanded in both Testaments, namely, the Old and the New, we are to believe with equal reverence. The Jews gave seven parts, believing in the Sabbath, but they did not give eight, since they denied the resurrection of the Lord's Day." The editors go on to say that Augustine explains the text in the same way. See his Letter 55, chapter 13 n. 23 in *Saint Augustine, Letters*, Volume I (1-82), trans. Wilfrid Parsons, FC 12 (New York: Fathers of the Church, Inc., 1951), 279: "In Ecclesiastes it is used to signify the two Testaments: 'Give a portion to seven and also to eight' . . . after such Resurrection had taken place in the Lord's Body, so that the head of the Church might foreshadow what the body of the Church hopes for at the end, then the Lord's day – that is the eighth, which is also the first – began to be observed."

And since a person cannot give teaching in abundance unless that person is filled, he says: *If the clouds be full, they will pour out rain upon the earth.*[30] The clouds are good preachers,[31] who fly to the heights through contemplation.[32] Isaiah 60:8 reads: "Who are these who fly as clouds and as doves to their windows?" These are filled with knowledge from the Lord. Isaiah 11:9 states: "The earth has been filled with your knowledge like the water of the covering sea."[33] This knowledge comes through the Holy Spirit. Wisdom 1:7 has: "The spirit of the Lord has filled the whole world." Such full clouds *pour out rain*, that is, the teaching of the divine word. Sirach 39:9 reads: "He will pour forth the words of his wisdom like showers."

---

[30]See Ecclesiastes 11:3.

[31]Hugh of St. Cher, 101v, b comments: "Mystically. The clouds are preachers, who should be raised up from the earth by contempt for earthly things and suspended on high through the desire for things eternal."

[32]On p. 90 n. 5 QuarEd quote Jerome's exposition. See his *Commentarius in Ecclesiasten* in CCSL lxxii, 345-346: "The clouds are prophets and every holy man, who, after developing many disciples in their hearts, will then be able to rain down precepts of teachings." The editors also state that Augustine maintains that the clouds refer to preachers. See, e.g., *Enarratio in Psalmum 35* n. 8 in *Expositions of the Psalms 33-50*, trans. Maria Boulding, Works of Saint Augustine III/16 (Hyde Park, NY: New City Press, 2000), 78-79: "Truly, brothers and sisters, these clouds are the preachers of the word of truth. When God utters threats through his preachers, he is thundering through his clouds. When he works miracles through his preachers, he is sending brilliant flashes of lightning through his clouds. He terrifies us through his clouds, and through them waters the earth with his clouds." Finally, the editors refer to Book XVII, chapter 31 n. 36 and XXVII, chapter 30 n. 54-55 of Gregory the Great's *Moralia in Iob*. See CCSL cxliii a, 871: "Now the word 'cloud' in this text is nothing other than the holy preachers, that is, apostles. . . ." See also CCSL, cxliii b, 1374: "Now the clouds that shine their light are holy preachers, who spread the examples of life both by speech and action."

[33]On p. 90 n. 4 QuarEd rightly indicate how Bonaventure's quotation differs from the Vulgate, whose text is translated: "The earth has been filled with the knowledge of the Lord like the covering waters of the sea."

Isaiah 55:10-11 states: "As the rain and the snow come down from heaven and . . . soak the earth and water it . . . so will my word be," on the earth of the heart to make it fruitful. We read in Hebrews 6:7: "The earth that drinks in the rain which . . . falls upon it and brings forth vegetation useful," etc.[34]

15. Alms are also to be distributed *without ceasing*. So he says: *The person who observes the wind will not sow*.[35] *To sow* is to preach the word of God. Matthew 13:3 reads: "The sower went forth to sow," and afterwards in 13:19 states: "The seed is the word of God."[36] This *wind* is the wind of detraction and slander, about which Job 1:19 says: "A . . . wind came . . . from the side of the desert and shook the four corners of the house." The person who observes this wind of detraction never sows, because the person who fears the words of people who detract does not preach fruitfully, but is rather shaking like a reed. Matthew 11:7 says: "What do you go out into the desert to see, a reed shaken by the wind?"[37] *And the person who considers the clouds will never sow*.[38] *Clouds*, according to a Gloss,[39] are the flattery of adulation. And if a person wants to have this, he or she will never sow eternal life, because, as Matthew

---

[34]Hebrews 6:7 concludes with: ". . . to those by whom it is tilled, receives blessing from God."

[35]See Ecclesiastes 11:4.

[36]On p. 90 n. 6 QuarEd are right when they indicate that Bonaventure is actually quoting Luke 8:5, 11 when he thinks he is quoting Matthew 13:3 ("Behold, the sower went out to sow") and Matthew 13:19 ("When anyone hears the word of the kingdom"). Luke 8:3 reads: "The sower went out to sow his seed." Luke 8:11 says: "Now the parable is this: the seed is the word of God."

[37]Jesus' rhetorical question refers to John the Baptist and his courageous preaching.

[38]See Ecclesiastes 11:4.

[39]On p. 90 n. 7 QuarEd cite the *Glossa Interlinearis apud Lyranum*: "*Clouds*, the adulations of flatterers."

6:5 says, *he has received his reward.*[40] Such a person is sowing in the flesh and will reap corruption, as Galatians 6:8 says: "The person who sows in the flesh," etc.[41] And wherefore, these things are to be condemned, when the preacher preaches morning and evening. 2 Timothy 4:2 states: "Preach the word. Be instant in season, out of season." Acts 20:31 reads: "For three years I did not cease day or night,[42] as I admonished everyone of you with tears."

ECCLESIASTES 11:8-10   ECCLESIASTES RECALLS US FROM EVIL BY A CONSIDERATION OF FUTURE PUNISHMENT

16. *If a person lives many years*, etc. Above he has exhorted us to do good by a reflection on the reward. Now he intends *to recall us from evil* by a consideration of *future punishment*. He does this in the following way. First, he says that *a person must remember the many days still to come.* Second, he censures *present joy.* Third, he exhorts us *to put aside all wrongdoing* and multiplication of evil.

17. (Verse 8). He exhorts and admonishes a person *to remember days still to come*, especially the person who abounds in present prosperity. So he says: *If people have*

---

[40]On p. 90 n. 7 QuarEd accurately mention that the Vulgate reads *receperunt* ("have received") while Bonaventure has *receipt* ("has received").

[41]Galatians 6:8 continues: ". . . from the flesh will also reap corruption." Hugh of St. Cher, 102v, e has three winds: persecution, temptation, and detraction. About the latter he writes: "Similarly the person who observes the wind of detraction, that is, the person who, because of the fear of detraction and slander, is extremely afraid of doing good or of teaching. Such a person will never reap, except perhaps the corruption that he has sown by living a slothful and carnal life. For Galatians 6 says: The things that a person sows, these, too, will he reap. For the person who sows in his flesh will also reap corruption from the flesh."

[42]On p. 90 n. 7 QuarEd rightly mention that the Vulgate reads *nocte et die* ("night and day") while Bonaventure has *die ac nocte* ("day and night").

lived many years, because in truth, even though the years seem to be many, they cannot be many according to what Sirach 18:8 states: "The number of the days of a human being at the most are a hundred years." *And have rejoiced in them all*, like those referred to in Job 21:12-13: "They take the timbrel . . . and rejoice at the sound of the organ. They spend their days in good things," etc. *They must remember the darksome time*, that is, the day of judgment. Zephaniah 1:15 reads: "That day is a day or wrath[43] . . . a day of darkness and dark clouds." He must also remember *the many days*. These are the days or years of eternity. Psalm 83:11 says: "Better is one day in your courts than thou-sands elsewhere." One should remember the day of *judgment*, so as to fear. One should remember the day of *glory*, so as to hope and rejoice, and this according to works done. For Sirach 11:27 states: "In the day of good things do not be unmindful of evils, and in the day of evils do no be unmindful of good things." He says: *The many days*,[44] *which, when they shall come, the things past will be accused of vanity*, that is, they will be clearly shown to have been vain.[45] Thus, Jerome comments: "When the reign of Christ shall come, all kingdoms will vanish."[46] *The things*

---

[43]On p. 91 n. 2 QuarEd accurately notice that the Vulgate reads *dies irae dies illa* ("that day is a day of wrath") while Bonaventure has *dies illa dies irae* ("that day is a day of wrath").

[44]The Vulgate reads *et dierum multorum* ("and many days").

[45]On p. 91 n. 3 QuarEd quote Jerome's twofold interpretation of Ecclesiastes 11:8. See CCSL lxxii, 348: "Indeed, if you live for many years and have all good things or have done good works and have known that you will die . . . you will despise all these present things as unstable, fragile, and earthly. . . .A person, who has understood (namely, the saving knowledge of both Testaments) will see light, will see Christ, the Sun of justice . . . ."

[46]On p. 91 n. 3 QuarEd state that Bonaventure's citation of Jerome stems from his *Commentariorum in Danielem Prophetam*, but do not provide an exact source for Bonaventure's actual words. They quote what Jerome has to say about Daniel 12:7. See PL 25:578A: "Daniel is

past will be accused of vanity, namely, of the vanity *of being subject to change.* Wisdom 5:8-9 reads: "What has pride
profited us or what advantage has the boasting of riches
brought us? All these things have passed like a shadow."
They are accused of the vanity of *iniquity.* Sirach 17:30
states: "What is more iniquitous than that which flesh and
blood have invented?" And these are accused. Ephesians
5:13 says: "For[47] the things that are accused are made
manifest by the light."

18. (Verse 9). *Rejoice, therefore, O youth*, etc. Second, he
censures present joy, stating that human beings will be
judged for this. Wherefore, he says ironically: *Rejoice, therefore, O youth, in your youth*, for that age is well suited to
joy. Thus, Wisdom 2:6 reads: "Come, let us speedily enjoy .
. . creatures as in youth." As if to say: Do not rejoice in
youth nor be sorrowful in old age. For Sirach 5:2 has: "Do
not follow in your strength the desires of your heart." And
he explains joy, so that it may be complete in *soul* and in
work and in *sign.* – Concerning the joy of delight in *soul*,
he says: *And let your heart be in that which is good.*[48] As if
to say: You will not rejoice in your heart, because
Ecclesiastes 7:5 above says: "The heart of a fool[49] is where
there is mirth." – Concerning joy in *work* he says: *And
walk in the ways of your heart*, that is, do externally in
actions what you desire in your heart. As if to say: May

---

clearly speaking of the coming of Christ and the saints, because the
kingdom referred to is a kingdom of such power and size as to exceed
all kingdoms under heaven. It is given to the saints of the Most High
whose reign will be forever, and all kings will serve and obey this
kingdom."

[47]On p. 91 n. 4 QuarEd rightly indicate that the Vulgate does not
have *enim* ("for").

[48]The Vulgate concludes with *in diebus iuventutis tuae* ("in the days
of your youth").

[49]On p. 91 n. 6 QuarEd correctly mention that the Vulgate reads
stultorum ("fools") whereas Bonaventure has *stulti* ("a fool").

you not walk. Sirach 18:30 has: "Son, do not go after your lusts, but turn away from your own will." – Concerning joy in *sign*, he says: *And in the sight of your eyes*, so that the eye sees those things that the heart desires and your hand does them, according to what is said in 2 Peter 2:14 about these matters: "Having eyes full of adultery and of sin that ceases not." As if to say: Do not walk in this way. We read in Isaiah 3:16: "Since the daughters of Zion are haughty and have walked with preening necks and wanton glances of their eyes," etc. It is clear that he is speaking here ironically, because he threatens evil for those who rejoice in this way.[50] So he adds: *And know that God will bring you into judgment.* And therefore, everything is to be shunned. Job 19:29 reads: "Flee from the face of the sword, for the sword is the revenger of iniquity.[51] And know that there is judgment."

19. (Verse 10). *Remove anger*, etc. Here in a third point there is *an exhortation to put away all wrongdoing*, namely, *malice of the heart* and *uncleanness of the flesh*. With respect to *sin in the heart* he says: *Remove anger from your heart*, so as not to get angry, because anger makes a person evil. Matthew 5:22 reads: "But I say to you that[52] ev-

---

[50]Hugh of St. Cher, 102v, l states that there are three ways of reading this verse: the way the Jews read it (obey God's commands, enjoy the goods of life while possible, knowing that judgment awaits for all things done); ironically; consultatively of the day of judgment. On p. 103 a-f Hugh of St. Cher comments: "Second, this verse is interpreted ironically. As if to say: since all past things are to be accused of vanity in the judgment. a Rejoice, therefore, O youth, in your youth] that is, do not rejoice, because such rejoicing is vain, and is accused of vanity. . . .e In the days of your youth], that is, let them not be joyful, but days of sorrow and fear. f And walk in the ways of your heart], that is, in your desires and concupiscences. As if to say: Do not walk."

[51]On p. 91 n. 9 QuarEd accurately notice that the Vulgate has *iniquitatum* ("iniquities") while Bonaventure reads *inquitatis* ("iniquity").

[52]On p. 91 n. 8 QuarEd rightly indicate that the Vulgate reads *quia* ("that") while Bonaventure has *quod* ("that").

eryone who is angry with his brother, will be liable to the judgment." And if a person gets angry, that anger should not continue. For Ephesians 4:26 states: "Do not let the sun go down on your anger." – With regard to *uncleanness of the flesh* he says: *And put away evil from your flesh,* and thus exclude all uncleanness of the flesh. James 1:21 says: "Casting away all uncleanness and abundance of malice, receive the ingrafted word with meekness." A person who mortifies the flesh removes evil from the flesh. We read in Colossians 3:5: "Mortify your members that are upon the earth." And Ecclesiastes adds the reason for this: *For youth and pleasure are vain,* since they pass away quickly. 1 John 2:17 says: "The world passes away and its concupiscence." And therefore, Wisdom 5:8-9 states: "What has pride profited us or what advantage has the boasting of riches brought us? All these things have passed away like a shadow," etc.

CHAPTER 12

ECCLESIASTES 12:1-8   THE SECOND SECTION
OF PART III: PUNISHMENT
WHICH IS UNMIXED AFFLICTION[1]

1. *Remember your Creator*, etc. Earlier he treated two aspects of the vanity of being subject to punishment, namely, punishment and the occasion of sin. Here he considers that aspect which is *unmixed* affliction, which recalls a person from evil and makes a person careful in doing good. This section has two components. First, he touches on punishments and troubles *in general*. Second, he deals with them *in particular* where verse 3 reads: *When the keepers of the house will tremble*, etc.

ECCLESIASTES 12:1-2   PUNISHMENT AS AFFLICTION
DESCRIBED IN A GENERAL WAY

2. So he describes being subject to punishment, *in a common way*, from three points of view. First, with regard to *the presence of harm*. Second, with respect to *the absence of joy*. Third, concerning *the lack of a remedy*. From these considerations he exhorts his readers to remember God.

3. (Verse 1). With regard to *the presence of harm* he says: *Remember your Creator*, by giving praise and acknowledg-

---

[1]The first section of Part III ran from Ecclesiastes 7:24-11:10.

ing the Creator. *In the days of your youth*, while you are young and healthy. Sirach 17:27 states: "Give thanks while you are living. While you are alive and in health, you shall give thanks and shall praise the Lord[2] and shall glory in his mercies." And the reason for this is not to wait for old age, in which is the presence of harm. So he says: *Before the time of affliction comes*. We read in Sirach 18:20: "Before sickness take medicine, and before judgment examine yourself."[3] *And the years draw nigh of which you will say: They please me not*. These are the years during which human nature is disturbed by many troubles that occur and draw nigh in old age, for Psalm 89:9 has: "Our years will be considered as a spider," etc.[4]

4. Verse 2). Concerning *the absence of joy* he says: *Before the sun . . . is darkened*, for the sight of the sun brings much joy. He said earlier in Ecclesiastes 11:7: "The light is sweet, and it is delightful for the eyes to see the sun." For Tobit 5:12 reads: "What manner of joy will be to me, who sit in darkness and do not see the light of heaven." To represent the complete absence he excludes every light of heaven. Thus, he says: *Before the sun . . . is darkened*, so that the turning of the sun is not seen. *And the light*, so that its power is not seen by day. *And the moon and the stars are darkened* at night. Isaiah 13:10 states: "The stars of heaven and their brightness will not display their light. The sun will be darkened in its rising, and the moon will not shine with her light."

---

[2] On p. 92 n. 2 QuarEd correctly indicate that the Vulgate has *Deum* ("God") while Bonaventure reads *Dominum* ("the Lord").

[3] Hugh of St. Cher, 103u also cites Sirach 18:20.

[4] Psalm 89:10 reads: "The days of our years in them are seventy years. But if in the strong they be eighty years: and what is more of them is labor and sorrow. For mildness is come upon us: and we will be corrected."

5. With respect to *the lack of a remedy* he says: *And the clouds return after the rain*. After a rain a clear sky usually follows. Therefore, when the twirling of the clouds comes after a rain, it is a sign that there is not to be a return of rejoicing and joy. Tobit 3:22 reads: "After a storm you make a calm, and after tears and weeping you pour in joyfulness." But those days are turned into darkness and will not return to light. Job 3:9 has: "Let us expect light and not see it, nor the rising of the dawning of the day."

6. In a *spiritual sense* he here exhorts each person to remember *the gifts* of God and God's *generosity*, before a person is handed over to a *reprobate sense*[5]and falls into the blindness of error. Therefore, they should remember God, because God is *Creator*.[6] First, God gave *the essence*. Isaiah 45:2 reads: "I made the earth and created human beings upon it." Wherefore, God should be remembered, but the opposite is recorded in Deuteronomy 32:18: "You have for-

---

[5]See Romans 1:28: "And as they have resolved against possessing the knowledge of God, God has given them up to a reprobate sense, so that they do what is not fitting."

[6]Hugh of St. Cher, 103a comments: "Remember your Creator] completely, that is, remember God's justice, so that you might fear; God's mercy, so that you may hope; God's kindness, so that you might be grateful; God's Wisdom, by which you might continually see with God's eyes, so that you might blush at stinking deeds; God's magnificence, so that you might have reverence and show reverence; God's goodness, so that you might love; God's sweetness, so that you might hunger and thirst for God; God's truth, so that you might believe. In order that human beings might truly and continually remember God, God has left many memorials of his presence. First is the sign of his likeness, by which he formed human beings in his image and likeness. Second is the sign of the sacraments, through which God reforms human beings. The third memorial is the university of creatures. The fourth is the truth of Scripture. The fifth is the multitude of benefactions. The sixth is the obvious correction by means of afflictions. About each of these memorials Psalm 101 says: But you, Lord, endure forever, and your memorial for generation unto generation."

gotten God,[7] your Creator." – God also gave *power*. Deuteronomy 8:18 states: "You shall remember the Lord your God, because he has given you strength, that he might fulfill his covenant."[8] – God gave *good works*. Philippians 2:13 reads: "It is God who works in us to will and to accomplish."[9] And Isaiah 26:12 has: "Lord, you have wrought all our works in us." So God should be remembered. Psalm 76:12 says: "I remembered the works of the Lord, for I will be mindful of your wonders from the beginning."

7. God is to be remembered, because God *became incarnate for us*. The Song of Songs 1:3 reads: "We will be glad and rejoice in you, remembering your breasts more than wine." – God should be remem-bered, for God is our *redeemer*, who has suffered for us. Lamentations 3:19 states: "Remember my poverty and transgression," etc., who has been given to us as food from heaven. Psalm 110:4-5 says: "He has made a remembrance of his wonderful works. Being a merciful and gracious Lord, he has given food to those who fear him."

8. God should be remembered as the one who *rewards* according to *merit*. Psalm 61:13 reads: "You will render to each person according to[10] his works." So it is said in another place in the Psalms: "I remembered, O Lord, your

---

[7]The Vulgate reads *Domini* ("the Lord") while Bonaventure has *Dei* ("God").

[8]On p. 92 n. 8 QuarEd correctly intimate that there are three variations between the Vulgate and Bonaventure's text. The Vulgate reads *recorderis* ("May you remember") while Bonaventure has *recordaberis* ("You shall remember"). The Vulgate reads *quod* ("that") whereas Bonaventure has *eo quod* ("because"). The Vulgate reads *praebuerit* ("has granted") while Bonaventure has *tribuit* ("has given").

[9]Bonaventure has adapted the text to his purposes. Philippians 2:13 reads: "For it is God who works in you both to will and to accomplish."

[10]On p. 92 n. 11 QuarEd accurately mention that the Vulgate reads *iuxta* ("according to") while Bonaventure has *secundum* ("according to").

judgments of old," etc.[11] – God is to be remembered by acts of *homage*. Isaiah 26:8 says: "Your name and your remembrance are the desire of my soul," etc. And then adds in verse 9: "My soul has desired you during the night." – God should be remembered as giving more than is *desired*. Isaiah 63:7 reads: "I will remember the mercies of the Lord . . . for all the things the Lord has bestowed upon us," etc.

9. So we should remember this Creator both by *giving thanks* and by *turning towards* God. *Before the sun is darkened*, namely, before the sun of justice, Christ, is darkened when a person loses faith. Amos 8:9 reads: "The sun will go down for them at midday."[12] And before *the light is darkened*, that is, the light of grace, when a person loses love and thereby loses grace. Wisdom 5:6 states: "We have erred from the way of truth, and the light of justice has not shown on us." And before *the moon is darkened*, namely, an understanding of Sacred Scripture that receives its light from Christ. Revelation 12:1 says: "A woman clothed with the sun, and the moon under her feet." *The woman clothed with the sun* is the Church of the Gentiles, to whom is given the full understanding of Sacred Scripture. And before *the stars are darkened*, that is, the example of the perfect. Baruch 3:34-35 reads: "The stars have given light in their watches," namely, during the night, "and have said: Here we are." And before *the clouds return after the rain*, that is, when the teaching of the preachers ceases.[13] Ezekiel 3:25-26 says: "Son of Man, I will make your tongue stick fast to the roof of your mouth."

---

[11]See Psalm 118:52, which concludes with: ". . . and I was consoled."

[12]The Vulgate does not read *eis* ("for them") nor does it read *in* before *meridie* ("at midday").

[13]Hugh of St. Cher, 103v, e interprets the clouds as preaching, especially the preaching of the prophets.

Ecclesiastes 12:3-7   Punishment as Affliction Described in Particular

10. *When the keepers of the house shall tremble*, etc. Above he has treated the punishableness that comes with and accompanies youth in general. Here he deals with it *in particular*. First, he considers the troubles that *precede* death. His second consideration focuses on those that *accompany* death where verse 5c reads: *Since a human being will go*, etc. Third, he deals with the troubles that *follow* after death where verse 6 says: *Before the silver cord is broken*.

Ecclesiastes 12:3-5b   Troubles that Precede Death

Ecclesiastes 12:3-4   The Weakening of the Members

11. The first part has two sections. First, he treats of being subject to the punishment that comes with *the weakening of the limbs*. Second, with *the signs of debility* where verse 5a states: *They will fear high things*.

12. (Verse 3). First, he shows the future *debility* in old age with regard to six types of members. First, in *the trembling of the bones* that are meant to protect the body. He says: *When the keepers of the house will tremble. The house* is the structure of the body, which is fragile and so needs to be guarded.[14] And therefore, the Philosopher says that nature made the bones firm to protect the softer parts, e.g., the ribs for the entrails and the skull for the head.[15] These bones *tremble* when their joints are weakened.[16]

---

[14] On p. 93 n. 4 QuarEd state that the interpretation of Ecclesiastes 12:3-4 as references to the six members of the human body goes back as far as Jerome. See his *Commentarius in Ecclesiasten* in CCSL lxxii, 352-354.

13. Also, with regard to *the weakening of the legs* to carry the weight of the body, he says: *And the strong men will stagger. The strong men* are the legs, because just as the strong carry the weight of war, so the legs carry the weight of the body.[17] These strong men *stagger* when the legs tremble and shake and do not hold a person up securely.[18]

14. Third, with respect to *the diminished power of the teeth* to chew food, he says: *And the grinders will be idle, in small number. The grinders* are the two jaws that chew food like two mills. These become idle when, with a smaller number of teeth, they are not able to chew food for eating.[19]

---

[15]On p. 93 n. 4 QuarEd cite Book II, n. 9 of Aristotle's *De partibus animalium*. See WAE, vol. 5, 654b: "Round about the bones, and attached to them by thin fibrous bands, grow the fleshy parts, for the sake of which the bones themselves exist. For just as an artist, when he is moulding an animal out of clay or other soft substance, takes first some solid body as a basis, and round this moulds the clay, so also has nature acted in fashioning the animal body out of flesh. Thus we find all the fleshy parts, with one exception, supported by bones, which serve, when the parts are organs of motion, to facilitate flexure, and, when the parts are motionless, act as a protection. The ribs, for example, which enclose the chest are intended to ensure the safety of the heart and neighboring viscera. The exception of which mention was made is the belly."

[16]Hugh of St. Cher, 103v, f interprets "the keepers of the house" in this wise: "The house is the body. The keepers of the body are the senses . . . the ribs and other bones . . . the powers of appetite and nutrition . . . the nerves. . . . All these keepers are removed, that is, totally moved in death."

[17]On p. 93 n. 5 QuarEd refer to Book IV, n. 9 of Aristotle's *De partibus animalium*. See WAE, vol. 5, 686a: "For of all animals man alone stands erect, in accordance with his godlike nature and essence. For it is the function of the godlike to think and to be wise; and no easy task were this under the burden of a heavy body, pressing down from above and obstructing by its weight the motions of the intellect and of the general sense."

[18]Hugh of St. Cher, 103v, g interprets "the strong men" as "the legs holding up the entire body."

[19]Hugh of St. Cher, 103v, h interprets "the grinders" as "the molar teeth which grind food." On p. 103vi Hugh of St. Cher interprets "the small number" as a reference to "teeth."

15. Fourth, concerning *the darkening of the eyes* to see, he continues: *And they that look through the holes will be darkened. They that look through the holes* are the eyes, because the eyes are like two holes for seeing.[20] These become darkened when the elderly are unable to see the light like Eli, who "could not see. Before the lamp of God went out," etc.[21] The same is true of Isaac, about whom Genesis 27:1 says: "Now Isaac was old, and his eyes had become dim," etc.[22]

16. (Verse 4). Fifth, about *the inability of the lips* to speak, he says: *And they will shut the doors in the street. The doors* are the lips, by which the door of the mouth is closed.[23] These doors *are shut in the street* when a person because of old age is unable to speak loudly and thus be heard by many. So he says: *When the grinder's voice will be low*, that is, speaking softly. *To grind* means *to speak*, because, just as people move their jaws to chew food, so too the jaws and lips are moved to utter clearly formed words.

17. Sixth, with regard to *deafness in the ears* to hear, he says: *They will rise up*[24] *at the voice of the bird*, that is, of the rooster, because the elderly are not able to hear high sounds.[25] The reason is that they are easily troubled, and

---

[20]Hugh of St. Cher, 103v, l interprets "the holes" as "the eyes."

[21]See 1 Samuel 3:2-3: "And it came to pass one day when Eli lay in his place, and his eyes had grown dim, that he could not see. Before the lamp of God went out, Samuel slept in the temple of the Lord, where the ark of God was."

[22]The first part of Genesis 27:1 concludes with: ". . . and he could not see."

[23]Hugh of St. Cher, 104a offers four interpretations, e.g., eyes and ears, but not the one Bonaventure has.

[24]The Vulgate reads *et consurgent* ("and they will rise up").

[25]Hugh of St. Cher, 104b-d does not present an exposition similar to that of Bonaventure in the many he offers, e.g., the elderly cannot sleep past the crowing of the rooster because of their low blood temperature and dry humors.

most easily excited. Further, they are unable to hear *notes and harmonies*. Hence, he says: *And all the daughters of music will grow deaf. The daughters of music* that hear harmonies are the ears.[26] These grow deaf in the elderly, because they cannot hear sonorous voices. In 2 Samuel 19:35 Barzillai said to David: "I am eighty years old. Are my senses quick to distinguish between sweet and bitter. . . .Or can I hear anymore the voices of singing men and women?" – So these are the six weaknesses which come after or accompany old age, because the elderly cannot *resist what is harmful*. They cannot *hold themselves up*. They cannot *eat*. They cannot *see*. They cannot *speak*. They cannot *hear*.

ECCLESIASTES 12:5AB   THE FOUR SIGNS OF THE DEBILITY OF THE BODY IN OLD AGE

18. *And they will fear high things*, etc. He has spoken above of the debilitation of the body in old age. Here he adds the four *signs of debility*: *trembling* of the body, *gray hair* on the head, *swelling* of the belly, and *cooling* of the passions.

19. (Verse 5ab). Now the first sign of weakness in old age is *a trembling of the body*. So he says: *And they will fear high things, and they will be afraid in the way*, that is, all the members of the body have become shaky. This shaking is a sign of a breakdown and weakness of the binding strength in the limbs that can no longer be held together. Because of this the body has to shake all the time. So the miserable elderly person can say with Psalm 54:6: "Fear and trembling have come upon me," etc.

---

[26]Hugh of St. Cher, 104e comments: "According to the Glossa: The daughters of the son are the ears, which delight in music. These will grow deaf in old age or in the calamity of captivity or in the times of the Antichrist."

20. The second sign is *gray hair on the head*. With respect to this he says: *The almond tree will flourish*, that is, the head and beard become gray. The almond tree, while in flower, is white, and this is a sign of a loss of strength. In an elderly person the binding force of the bodily fluids, and so the fluids themselves, decay and cool. The sign of this is that the coverings of the body become white, and so the person becomes gray.

21. The third sign of senile infirmity is *a swelling of the belly* or other members of the body. Concerning this he says: *The locust will be made fat*. The fattening of the locust also deals with old age and is a swelling more than genuine fat. This is the way the elderly become fat, and it is a sign of weakness in digestive warmth. Since there is a lack of digestive warmth, a humor of watery and undigested phlegm abounds, and it fills and seems to fatten the body of an elderly person.[27]

22. The fourth sign is *a cooling of passion*, and so he says: *The caper tree*[28] *will be destroyed*. The caper tree is a kind of plant that "helps the kidneys," as a Glossa says,[29] and strengthens the act of the generative power. And according to Jerome the word in Hebrew is a common one for a plant and for passionate love.[30] So in whatever sense the

---

[27]In these paragraphs Bonaventure is dependent upon ancient medicine's view of the four humors. Black bile is cold and dry while yellow bile is hot and dry. Blood is hot and moist whereas phlegm is cold and moist. When these humors went awry and out of balance, a person became sick or elderly.

[28]The Vulgate reads *et dissipabilitur capparis* ("and the caper tree will be destroyed").

[29]On p. 94 n. 2 QuarEd state that this is the *Glossa Ordinaria apud Strabum et Lyranum*. See PL 113:1126B.

[30]On p. 94 n. 2 QuarEd quote Jerome's interpretation of this verse in his *Commentarius in Ecclesiasten*. See CCSL lxxii, 355: "In truth where we have *caper tree*, the Hebrew reads *abiona*, which in itself is

word is taken, the meaning is correct: *the caper tree will be destroyed*, that is, the strength of passion is lessened. And this is a sign of debilitation in old age. For in the act of sexual intercourse heat is a moving force, and the digestive humor adds material. But since old age is cold and dry, heat and humor are lacking, and so the ardor of passion is lessened.

ECCLESIASTES 12:5c   THE TROUBLES ACCOMPANYING DEATH

23. (Verse 5c). *Because a human being will go into the house*, etc. He has described the troubles that precede death. Now he depicts *the misery of death itself* both in *the dying* and in *the mourners*. In *the dying person*, when he says: *Because a human being will go into the house of his eternity*, that is, when the individual dies. For the house after death is an eternal house, because he has already said in Ecclesiastes 11:3: "If the tree fall to the south or to the north, there will it be." And so the house after death is rightly called a house of eternity. Concerning trouble in *the mourners* he states: *And the mourners will go round about in the street. They go round about*, because their sorrow does not allow them to rest. Psalm 139:10 reads: "The head of those who compass me about, the labor of their lips will overwhelm them." And *they weep over* the dead person, as if not wanting to be consoled, but they must act in this manner. Sirach 22:13 says: "The mourning for the dead is seven days."

---

ambiguous and is interpreted as *love, desire, concupiscence* or *caper tree*. And it means, as we said above, that the passions of old people have cooled down, and the organs of sexual intercourse are spent."

Ecclesiastes 12:6-7   **The troubles that come after death**

24. *Before the silver cord is broken*, etc. He has touched on the troubles that precede and accompany death. Now he deals with *the troubles that come after death*. And these are *the corruption of the body* and *the journey of the spirit to God*, which he describes in that order.

25. (Verses 6-7). First, he notes *the dissolution of the sinews*, when he says: *Before the silver cord be broken*. A person should keep in mind the text: "Remember your Creator in the days of your youth."[31] The joining together of the sinews is rightly called *a cord*, because the sinews enclose and bind together the whole body. It is *silver*, because of its whiteness and its close weaving. Therefore, the silver cord *is broken* when the bond between the sinews is broken.

26. Second, he notes *the corruption of the veins* or arteries when he says: *And the golden fillet shrink back*.[32] The pattern of veins is rightly called *a fillet*, because just as a fillet is wrapped around to protect what is bound up, so the entire structure of the body is surrounded and protected by the veins and arteries. This pattern of veins and arteries is rightly called *golden*, because the red veins of this type are called "red gold" on account of the redness of

---

[31]Ecclesiastes 12:1. On p. 94 n. 5 QuarEd indicate that Jerome also interprets Ecclesiastes 12:6 by referring to Ecclesiastes 12:1. See his *Commentarius in Ecclesiasten* in CCSL lxxii, 356 where Jerome's reference back to Ecclesiastes 12:1 is more involved than Bonaventure's. Bonaventure may be referring to Jerome through Hugh of St. Cher. See Hugh of St. Cher, 104v, b: "Before the silver cord be broken]: Supply: Remember your Creator."

[32]The Latin word used here is *vitta*, which means a fillet in the sense of a band or strip and so applies to the band of veins in the body.

the blood they contain. Hence, *the golden fillet shrinks* when the union of veins and arteries does not endure.[33]

27. Third, he notes *the collapse of the bladder* when he says: *And the pitcher be crushed at the fountain. A pitcher* is a receptacle for water coming from a fountain, and *the bladder* is a receptacle for urine coming from the liver as from a fountain. For urine is a discharge of blood and other humors, that flow from the liver into the entire body as from a fountain. So *the pitcher is crushed at the fountain* when the bladder is broken and cannot receive the discharge of humors that flow from the liver.

28. Fourth, he notes *the destruction of the passage of impure excesses* when he continues: *And the wheel be broken upon the cistern. The wheel* is an instrument by which foul and dirty water is drawn from the cistern. *The cistern* contains an abundance of dirty water, and our belly is like that. So the meaning of *the wheel be broken upon the cistern* is this: the passage of impure excesses coming from the belly is broken in death.

29. Fifth, he notes that the whole body turns to dust when he says: *And the dust return into its earth, from whence it was,* that is, the body returns to dust, according to what Genesis 3:19 says: "You are dust, and unto dust will you return."[34] *Into its earth,* because the body comes from the earth. Sirach 40:11 reads: "All things that are of the earth will return to the earth again."

---

[33]Hugh of St. Cher, 104v, b comments: "Before the silver cord is broken]. Supply: Remember your Creator. . . .The silver cord is the cartilage that contains the spinal cord because it has a silver color after roasting. The golden fillet is the flank, which after roasting has a color similar to gold."

[34]Hugh of St. Cher, 104vi also cites Genesis 3:19.

30. Sixth, he touches on the return of *the spirit* or soul to God when he says: *And the spirit return to God who gave it.* The Lord himself *gives the spirit.* Wherefore, it is said in Psalm 32:15: "Who made the hearts of every one of them," etc. And *every spirit returns* to the Lord as judge. Romans 14:10 states: "We will all stand before the judgment seat of Christ," etc.

Ecclesiastes 12:3-7   Spiritual interpretations of these verses

31. *The spiritual interpretation* commences with Ecclesiastes 12:3: *When the keepers of the house will tremble.* This verse describes the final state of the Church. First, in what *precedes* judgment. Second, in what *accompanies* judgment where verse 5c reads: *Because a person will go into the house.* Third, in what *follows* judgment where verse 6 reads: *Before the silver cord be broken.*

Ecclesiastes 12:3-5b   The state of the Church before the judgment

32. The state *before the judgment* will be the coming of the Antichrist. And this is depicted from three points of view. First is *a lessening of faith.* Second is *the spread of error* where verse 4b reads: *And they will rise up at the voice of the bird,* etc. Third is *the way in which error is spread* where verse 5b states: *The almond tree will flourish,* etc.

Ecclesiastes 12:3-4a   The lessening of faith

33. First, he predicts that there will be *a lessening of faith* among four kinds of people, namely, *prelates, the perfect, the simple,* and *the wise.* So he predicts *a trembling among the prelates* when he says: *When the keepers of the house will tremble.*[35] This *house* is the Church, about which Psalm

---

[35]Ecclesiastes 12:3.

92:5 says: "Holiness befits your house," etc. *The keepers are the prelates*, to whom is committed the care of the Lord's flock. Isaiah 62:6 reads: "Upon your wall, O Jerusalem, I have appointed keepers."[36] So *the keepers will tremble* when prelates are shaken in faith, as will indeed happen in the coming of the Antichrist. For Judith 16:18 states: "The mountains will tremble from the foundations."[37]

34. Second, he predicts that *the perfect will doubt* when he says: *And the strong men will stagger.*[38] *The strongest men are the perfect in love and hope*, according to what Isaiah 40:31 says: "Those who hope in the Lord will renew their strength." These will stagger. Matthew 24:24 reads: "False prophets . . . will arise and will show . . . signs . . . in order to lead into error, if it were possible, even the elect." And Matthew 24:22 states: "And unless those days had been shortened, no flesh would have been saved. But for the sake of the elect they will be shortened . . . ."

35. Third, he predicts that *the simple will fall* when he adds: *The grinders will be idle in a small number.*[39] That is, *the simple will stop doing good works*, tired out from being greatly deceived. So he says: *In a small number*, because their number will be greatly reduced. Matthew 24:41 has: "Two . . . at the mill. One will be taken, and one will be left."[40]

---

[36]The ordinary translation of *custodes* here would be "watchmen," but Bonaventure's context demands the translation, "keepers."

[37]On p. 95 n. 3 QuarEd correctly mention that the Vulgate has *movebuntur* ("will be moved") while Bonaventure has *commovebuntur* ("will tremble").

[38]Ecclesiastes 12:3.

[39]Ecclesiastes 12:3.

[40]On p. 95 n. 5 QuarEd correctly notice that Bonaventure has turned Matthew's reference to two women grinding at the mill to two men grinding there.

36. Fourth, he predicts *the error of the wise* when he says: *And those who look through the holes will be darkened.*[41] That is, the wise who see in a subtle way will become ensnared in the darkness of error. Job 12:25 reads: "They will grope as in the dark, and not in the light, and he will make them stagger like people who are drunk." And since a person who falls from faith also falls from confessing the faith, he says: *And they will shut the doors in the street,*[42] that is, in public. *The grinder's voice will be low,*[43] that is, muttering to oneself. But a genuine confession of faith is made in public. For Matthew 10:27 states: "What you heard in your ear, preach upon the housetops."

Ecclesiastes 12:4b-5a   The spread of error

37. *And they will rise up at the voice,* etc. In a second point he notes *the spread of error* after the lessening of faith and does so from three perspectives. First, he says the falsity will be preached and heard. Second, truth will be silenced. Third, the power of the Antichrist will be exalted and feared.

38. First, *falsity will be preached by the Antichrist* when he says: *They will rise at the voice of the bird.* The voice of the bird singing in the night is the preaching of the Antichrist who preaches in the night of obscurity and infidelity. Now those who believe in his preaching are those who *will rise at his voice.* Wherefore, it is said in Matthew 24:26 that they should not put their faith in him: "So if they say to you: Behold, he is in the desert . . . do not believe it." But many will listen to them and believe them. It is said to the Jews in John 5:43: "If another comes in his own name, you will receive him."

---

[41]Ecclesiastes 12:3.
[42]Ecclesiastes 12:4.
[43]Ecclesiastes 12:4.

39. Second, he predicts that *truth will be silenced*, because no one will listen. Therefore, he says: *All daughters of music will grow deaf.*[44] *The daughters of music will grow deaf* when they are unable to hear the sound of the truth which is like a harmony. This will happen during the time of the Antichrist, as has been foretold. Isaiah 30:9 predicted this of the people who will join the Antichrist: "It is a people that provokes to wrath,[45] lying children, children who do not want to hear the law of God."

40. Third, he predicts that *the power of the Antichrist will be feared* when he continues: *And they will fear high things, and they will be afraid*, etc.[46] That is, all, both small and great, will be in awe of the power of the Antichrist and out of fear will adore him. For Revelation 13:3-4 reads: "All the earth was in admiration of the beast . . . saying: Who is like to this[47] beast, and who will be able to fight with him?" And afterwards Revelation 13:7-8 states: "And power was given him over every tribe, and people, and tongue. . . .And all who dwell upon the earth adored him, whose names are not written in the book of life."

ECCLESIASTES 12:5B   **THE WAY IN WHICH ERROR WILL BE MULTIPLIED**

41. *The almond tree will flourish.* Earlier he described the weakening of faith and the spread of error. Here in a third point he describes *the way in which error will be multiplied.* This will happen in three ways, namely, by *miracles, gifts*, and *torture*.

---

[44]Ecclesiastes 12:4.

[45]On p. 95 n. 8 QuarEd rightly indicate that the Vulgate reads *et* ("and") here, and Bonaventure does not.

[46]Ecclesiastes 12:5a.

[47]On p. 96 n. 1 QuarEd accurately mention that the Vulgate does not read *huic* ("this").

42. First, he predicts the way leading to error by *miracles* when he says: *The almond tree will flourish,* just as the rod of Aaron miraculously flowered and produced almonds, according to what is said in Numbers 17:8.[48] In the same way the Antichrist will make a rod to flourish into jealousy and to shed its blossoms and many other miracles, by which the stupid are turned to him. Revelation 13:13-14 reads: "And the beast did great signs . . . and led astray the inhabitants of the earth on account of the signs, which were given to him to perform in the sight of men and women."[49]

43. Second, he predicts the way of drawing into error by *gifts* when he says: *The locust will be made fat. The locust is made fat* when a greedy person is taken up with money and turns away from God. Deuteronomy 32:15 reads: "The beloved grew fat and kicked. He grew fat and thick and gross; he forsook God." In this way Antichrist will turn many away from faith, something prefigured in 2 Maccabees 7:24: "Antiochus . . . when the youngest was yet alive, did not only exhort him by words, but also promised[50] him by an oath that he would make him a rich and a happy man, and if he would turn away from the laws . . . would consider him dear[51] to him. . . ."

---

[48]Numbers 17:8 reads: "He (Moses) returned on the following day, and found that the rod of Aaron for the house of Levi, was budded and that the buds swelling it had bloomed blossoms, which spreading the leaves, were formed into almonds." In the Hebrew this text occurs in Numbers 17:23.

[49]On p. 96 n. 2 QuarEd rightly notice that the Vulgate reads *bestiae* ("of the beast") while Bonaventure has *hominum* ("men and women"). Revelation 13:11-15 describes two beasts.

[50]On p. 96 n. 3 QuarEd accurately mention that the Vulgate reads *affirmabat* ("assured") while Bonaventure has *promittebat* ("promised").

[51]The Vulgate reads *amicum* ("friend") while Bonaventure has *carum* ("dear to him").

44. Third, he predicts that some will be drawn into error by *torture* when he says: *The caper tree will be destroyed. The caper tree*, as has been said, is a plant that incites passion. This refers to *carnal people*, who *make provision for the flesh in its concupiscence.*[52] These *are destroyed* when they withdraw from faith out of fear of torture. For they belong to those about whom Luke 8:13 says: "They believe for a while, and in time of temptation they fall away." *The time of temptation* will be at the coming of the Antichrist. For Matthew 24:21 states: "There will be such[53] tribulation, the likes of which has not been from the beginning of the world until now."

ECCLESIASTES 12:5c   THE JUDGMENT ITSELF

45. *Since a person will go into the house of his eternity*, etc. He has dealt with the things preceding judgment, and now in a second consideration he treats *the judgment itself*, in which *the good will be rewarded* and *the wicked punished*. With regard to *the reward of the good* he says: *A person will go into the house of his eternity*, namely, when it will be said to them: "Come, you blessed of my Father, receive[54] the kingdom prepared for you from the foundation of the world."[55] And then they will go into the house of eternal joy. Isaiah 31:5 reads: "They will come into Zion with praise, and everlasting joy will be upon their heads. They will obtain joy and gladness."

---

[52]On p. 96 n. 4 QuarEd helpfully refer to Romans 13:14: "But put on the Lord Jesus Christ, and as for the flesh, take no thought for its lusts."

[53]On p. 96 n. 4 QuarEd rightly indicate that the Vulgate reads *magna* ("great") while Bonaventure has *talis* ("such").

[54]On p. 96 n. 5 QuarEd correctly mention that the Vulgate reads *possidete* ("possess") while Bonaventure has *percipite* ("receive").

[55]Matthew 25:34.

46. With respect to *the wicked* he says: *The mourners will go round about in the streets*, namely, the wicked. For Wisdom 5:3 states: "They will say among[56] themselves, repenting and groaning for anguish of spirit." And Matthew 24:31 says: "They will see the sign of the Son of Man in heaven. And then all the tribes of the earth will mourn, and they will see the Son of Man," etc.

ECCLESIASTES 12:6-7   WHAT FOLLOWS JUDGMENT

47. *Before the silver cord is broken*, etc. He has dealt with what precedes and accompanies the judgment, and now he deals with its *consequences*. Now he describes six consequences after the state of judgment. First, he notes a weakening in *the art of speaking* when he says: *Before the silver cord is broken*. Silver applies to sounds and represents the art of speaking. A silver cord is a beautiful weaving and putting together of words that bind a person as by a cord when he or she is being persuaded, according to what is said in Proverbs 7:21: "She entangled him with many words and drew him away with the flattery of her lips." Therefore, the silver cord is broken when after judgment day the earthly art of speaking becomes dumb. Matthew 22:12 reads: "Friend, how did you come in hither not having on a wedding garment? But he was silent."

48. Second, he notes the weakening of the office of *prelates* or of power when he says: *And the golden fillet shrinks back*. A *fillet* was placed on the head of a priest,[57] and it represents an order of power and of being a prelate to bind

---

[56]The Vulgate reads *inter* ("between") while Bonaventure has *intra* ("among").

[57]See Exodus 28:37-39: "You shall also make a plate of the purest gold. On this you shall engrave with engraver's work: Holy to the Lord. And you shall tie it with a violet fillet, and it shall be upon the miter, hanging over the forehead of the high priest."

the Church together. This fillet goes back to its source when Christ alone will rule, and all other power will be taken away. And this will happen after the judgment. 1 Corinthians 15:24 reads: "Afterwards the end, when he will have delivered up the kingdom to God and the Father, when he will have brought to naught all principality and domination and power."

49. Third, he notes the weakening of *earthly wisdom* when he says: *And the pitcher is crushed at the fountain.* This *pitcher* is curiosity of the heart that drains off wisdom. This was prefigured in John 4:7: "A Samaritan woman came with a pitcher to draw water."[58] *The Samaritan woman* represents the Gentiles who come with a pitcher, that is, with curiosity to draw off wisdom, as it is said in Acts 17:21: "The Athenians . . . em-ployed themselves in nothing else, except in saying or hearing something new." Now *the fountain* is earthly wisdom. For Psalm 73:15 says: "You have broken up the fountains and the torrents." Wherefore, *the pitcher is crushed at the fountain*, when there is no place for pondering earthly wisdom out of curiosity. Isaiah 30:14 states: "And it will be broken into small pieces, as[59] . . . the potter's wheel with a mighty breaking."

50. Fourth, he notes the taking away of *earthly wealth* when he adds: *And the wheel is broken upon the cistern. The cistern* that holds the waters represents the piling up of earthly wealth, according to what Jeremiah 2:13 says: "They have forsaken me, the fountain of living water, and

---

[58]On p. 97 n. 1 QuarEd rightly indicate the Vulgate does not have *cum hydria* ("with a pitcher"). But see John 4:28: "So the woman left her pitcher and went into the city and said to the men and women. . . ." Hugh of St. Cher, 104v, f also refers to the Samaritan woman and her pitcher.

[59]On p. 97 n. 2 QuarEd accurately intimate that the Vulgate reads *sicut* ("as") while Bonaventure has *velut* ("as").

have dug for themselves cisterns, broken cisterns," etc.[60]
The wheel represents the changing fortune and variability in ownership, and so these things are called *the goods of fortune*. Therefore, *the wheel is broken upon the cistern*, when all hope of possessing earthly goods is taken away. This is signified in Exodus 14:24-25: "The Lord, looking upon the Egyptian army . . . overthrew the wheels of the chariots," for Sirach 40:13 states: "The riches of the impious[61] will be dried up like a river."

51. Fifth, he notes how *punishment is inflicted* on the wicked when he says: *And the dust returns into its earth*. *Dust* rightly represents the impious and the sinner, according to what Psalm 1:4 states: "Not so the impious, not so, but like the dust, which the wind drives from the face of the earth." *The earth* is the depth of darkness, according to what Proverbs 25:3 has: "The heaven above, and the earth below." *The dust returns into its earth* when a sinner is put down into the depth of the infernal darkness. Revelation 20:15 reads: "Whoever was not found written in the book of life was cast into the pool of fire."

52. Sixth, he notes how *glory is given* to the just and to the spiritual when he says: *The spirit returns to God who gave it*. *The spirit* is a good and spiritual person, who is joined to God by grace. 1 Corinthians 6:17 says: "The person who is joined to the Lord is one spirit." This *spirit returns to God*, not because it had been with God first and then had gone away when it came to the body and returned again at death. This was the opinion of Origen.[62] But it is said *to*

---

[60]Hugh of St. Cher, 104v, g also cites Jeremiah 2:13.

[61]On p. 97 n. 4 QuarEd correctly mention that the Vulgate reads *iniustorum* ("the unjust") while Bonaventure has *impiorum* ("the impious").

[62]On p. 97 n. 6 QuarEd are content to refer to Omnia Opera 2:448 n. 6 and 2:449 n. 8 for articulations of Origen's opinion.

return, because it comes from and through God and is ordered finally towards God. And this will happen in glory after the judgment, according to what is said in Colossians 3:4: "When Christ, your life, appears, then you also will appear with him in glory."

ECCLESIASTES 12:8   THE CONCLUSION OF THE
TRIPLE PROOF[63]

53. (Verse 8). *Vanity of vanities*, etc. As stated at the beginning of the book, the whole work is directed towards proving the one proposition enunciated at the beginning, namely, *Vanity of vanities*, etc. Throughout the whole book he has proven this proposition and now he concludes by saying: *Vanity of vanities, said Ecclesiastes*. Above in Ecclesiastes 1:2 *he said* something similar,[64] that is, *he set forth his proposition*. But now the text reads: *Ecclesiastes said*, that is, *he has come to a conclusion*. So I say: *He has concluded to the vanity of vanities*. This statement is to be taken substantively, and the action of speaking refers back to the speaker and has the sense: *Ecclesiastes* made this statement. In the expression *vanity of vanities* the genitive indicates origin and has the sense: *Vanity from vanities*, that is, vanity arises from vanities. Ecclesiastes also said that *all things vanity*.[65] From customary use of language a verb has to be understood here, so that the meaning is: *All things are vanity*.

54. From the two phrases one draws the argument: If vanity comes from vanities and if all things are a vanity, then

---

[63]In Ecclesiastes 1:3-3:15 the author proved the vanity of being subject to change; in 3:16-7:23 the vanity of iniquity; in 7:24-12:7 the vanity of being subject to punishment.

[64]Ecclesiastes 1:2 says: "Vanity of vanities, said Ecclesiastes: vanity of vanities, and all is vanity."

[65]In Latin *omnia vanitas* ("all things vanity"), that is, there is no verb.

all that is created does not make the person who loves them happy. Rather they make such a person vain, according to what Jeremiah 2:5 says: "They have walked after vanity and have become vain." Therefore, if everyone should desire happiness and flee from vanity, then everyone should despise earthly goods. And this is the conclusion of this book.

Ecclesiastes 12:9-14   Epilogue

55. *And whereas Ecclesiastes was very wise*, etc. It was said above that this book has three principal parts, namely, a prologue, a treatise, and an epilogue.[66] Having dealt with the first two parts, he now begins the third part. Now in this epilogue he proceeds according to the following order. First, *he notes the skill of the writer*. Second, *he notes the authority of his words*. Third, *he gives a warning against curiosity in the hearers*. Fourth, *he lays bare the high point of his words*.

Ecclesiastes 12:9-10   The skill of the writer

56. He indicates *the skill of the writer* by showing first that, while he was wise, he did not hide his wisdom, but expounded it for others. So he says: *And whereas Ecclesiastes was very wise*. 1 Kings 4:30-31 reads: "The wisdom of Solomon surpassed the wisdom of all the Orientals . . . and he was wiser than all people." Although he was so wise, he was not negligent, but diligent. For *he taught the people*. Sirach 24:46-47 states: "I will still pour out doctrine like prophecy, and I will leave it to those who seek wisdom. . . .See that I have not labored for myself

---

[66]See Bonaventure's interpretation of Ecclesiastes 1:1 above. The prologue or heading is Ecclesiastes 1:1. The treatise runs from Ecclesiastes 1:2 to 12:8. The epilogue covers Ecclesiastes 12:9-14.

only, but for all who search for the truth."[67] He explains
his diligence by the number of writings and instructions.
Here he touches on the three works he composed. He refers first to the book *Ecclesiastes* when he says: *And he
declared the things that he had done.* Supply: In this book
entitled *Ecclesiastes*. In chapters one and two above he
related his spiritual and carnal deeds,[68] so that through
his evil deeds he might give an example to detest and
through his good deeds he might provide an example to
imitate.

57. Second, he refers to the book of Proverbs when he says:
*And seeking out, he set forth many parables, which are
profitable words,*[69] that is, in Proverbs. We read in the beginning of Proverbs: "The parables of Solomon, the son of
David, king of Israel, to know wisdom and instruction, to
understand the words of prudence."[70] Third, he refers to
the book of Canticles when he says: *And he wrote words
most right and full of truth.* He says this, because the words
in the Canticles seem to be *words of voluptuousness and
passion.* And so he says: *Most right words,* that is, correct
and good words. Proverbs 8:8 reads: "All my words are just.
There is nothing wicked or perverse in them." Further,
the words of the Canticles seem to be *false and humorous,*
as, for example, when he says: "Your nose is like a tower."[71]

---

[67]On p. 97 n. 10 QuarEd rightly intimate that Bonaventure's text of
Sirach 24:47 differs from the Vulgate in three ways. The Vulgate reads
Videte ("See") while Bonaventure has *Respicite* ("See"). The Vulgate
has *quoniam* ("that") while Bonaventure reads *quia* ("that"). The Vulgate
reads *exquaerentibus* ("search for") while Bonaventure has *quaerentibus*
("search for").

[68]See Ecclesiastes 1:12-2:25.

[69]The Vulgate reads *quaesivit verba utilia* ("he sought profitable
words") while Bonaventure has *parabolas, quae sunt verba utilia*
("parables which are profitable words").

[70]See Proverbs 1:1-3.

[71]See The Song of Songs 7:4.

So he says: *And full of truth*. For a thing is full when it contains something within itself and retains it. In this way the words of the Canticles inwardly hide and encompass truth. And this is necessary for every teaching. Sirach 37:20 reads: "In all your works let the true word go before you."

ECCLESIASTES 12:11   THE AUTHORITY OF THE WORDS OR TEACHINGS

58. (Verse 11). *The words of the wise*, etc. Second, he notes *the authority of the words* or teachings, because they are not given lightly. Rather they are uttered with forethought and inspired by God, and so are firm and stable. And wherefore, he says: *The words of the wise are as goads*, that is, penetrating to the interior. *And as nails deeply fastened in*, that is, deeply. These are fixed and so are not easily rejected by the heart, but endure and incline a person to good. For the word of God is compared to a sword in Ephesians 6:17: "The sword of the Spirit, which is the word of God." And so the word pierces the heart according to what is said in Acts 2:37: "When they had heard these words, they were stung in their hearts."[72] Therefore, the words of the wise are penetrating, because they are not spoken lightly. So he says: *Which by the counsel of the masters*, that is, a deliberate discussion and statement, *given by one shepherd*, that is, by Christ who is the shepherd, according to what is said in John 10:11: "I am the good shepherd."[73] Words of the wise are given to them by this shepherd because, according to Augustine: "He has the office of teacher in heaven who teaches us in our

---

[72]The more usual translation would be: ". . . they had compunction in their hearts."

[73]Hugh of St. Cher, 105q comments: "Given by one shepherd], that is, by Christ, who alone is the true shepherd of souls. For John 10 says: I am the good shepherd. And Matthew 23 states: One is your teacher, the Christ."

heart."[74] For Matthew 23:8 states: "One is your teacher, the Christ." However, they are given *by the counsel of teachers*, that is, teachers of that highest teacher who sent and taught them. Hence, it is said in 1 Peter 5:1-4: "Elders . . . feed the flock of God that is among you. And when the chief shepherd appears, you will receive a never fading crown of glory." He himself sent these. Matthew 28:19 has: "Therefore, go and teach all nations."

ECCLESIASTES 12:12   HE WARNS ABOUT CURIOSITY IN THE LISTENERS

59. (Verse 12). *More than these*, etc. Third, *he warns against curiosity in the listeners*, whom he addresses in the person of his son: *More than these, my son, require not*, so that you always want to hear new things. For it is enough to know what is necessary. Sirach 3:22 advises: "Think always on the things that God has commanded you, and in many of God's works be not curious."

60. He gives a double *reason* for this warning, because the quest of this curiosity is *unending* and *laborious*. It is *unending*, and so he says: *Of making many books, there is no end*, because the curious never have enough, but want to hear more, never wanting to hear what is old, but always what is new. Hence, Acts 17:21 states: "The Athenians employed themselves in nothing else, except in telling or hearing something new." Therefore, it is said in Daniel 12:4: "Many times[75] will pass over, and knowledge will be manifold," for knowledge is always renewed in some way. Not

---

[74]On p. 98 n. 5 QuarEd refer to Tractatus IV, chapter 13 of Augustine's commentary on 1 John. See *In Epistolam Joannis ad Parthos Tractatus Decem* in PL 35:2004. Augustine is interpreting 1 John 2:27: "You have no need that anyone teach you, because his anointing teaches you about all things."

[75]On p. 98 n. 8 QuarEd accurately indicate that the Vulgate reads *plurimi* ("many") while Bonaventure has *plurima tempora* ("many times").

only is the quest of curiosity unending, but it is also *laborious*. And so he adds: *And much study is an affliction of the flesh*. Sirach 31:1 states: "Watching for goodness will consume the flesh."[76] It is, I repeat, a great affliction and really offers little value according to what was said in Ecclesiastes 8:16-17 above: "There are some who day and night take no sleep with their eyes. And I understood that a human being can find no reason for all those works of God that have been done under the sun."

Ecclesiastes 12:13-14   The high point of his words

61. (Verse 13). *Let us all hear together the conclusion of the discourse*. Here in a fourth point he considers *the gist* of the things said by way of a certain epilogue which would incite a group of disciples to listen to and remember them. He says: Let us all together hear *the conclusion of the discourse*, that is, an end and conclusion of the discourse, as something useful and necessary for all.

62. The summary of all the sayings consists in this, namely, *to avoid evil* or *to do good*. All the teaching and eloquence of Solomon, indeed of all Scripture, is directed towards this. So he says, first, with regard to *avoiding evil*: *Fear God*. Proverbs 16:6 states: "Because of the fear of the Lord everyone avoids evil."[77] With regard to *doing good* he says: *And keep his commandments*. Deuteronomy 6:3 says: "Hear, O Israel, and observe so that you keep the things that the Lord has commanded."[78] *This is the whole per-*

---

[76]On p. 98 n. 9 QuarEd rightly notice that the Vulgate reads the plural *carnes* ("the flesh") while Bonaventure has the singular *carnem* ("flesh"). The editors, however, fail to note that the Vulgate reads *tabefacit* ("consumes") whereas Bonaventure has *tabefaciet* ("will consume").

[77]On p. 98 n. 10 QuarEd correctly mention that the Vulgate reads *declinatur a malo* ("a person avoids evil") while Bonaventure has *declinat omnis a malo* ("everyone avoids evil").

[78]The clause, "the things that the Lord has commanded," is a variant and is not found in the critical text of the Vulgate.

son,[79] that is, the total and perfect person. The person who does good, but does not avoid evil, is not a whole, but a half person. The person who avoids evil, but does not do good, is only a half person. But the person who avoids evil through fear and does good through the observance of the commandments, is already *the whole person*, that is, completely just. The Lord asks nothing more of us. Deuteronomy 10:12-13 states: "And now, Israel, what does the Lord require[80] of you, but that you fear the Lord your God, and walk in the Lord's ways. . . . You should serve the Lord[81] with all your heart and with all your soul and keep the commandments of the Lord your God."[82]

63. (Verse 14). And the reason why God is to be loved, and God's commandments obeyed is because God demands a reckoning of all people, be they good or evil. So he adds: *And all things that have been done, God will bring into judgment for every error.* Nothing will be passed over, whether it is an action done in malice or an action done in error. Matthew 12:36 states: "For every idle word which men and women shall speak, they will render an account."[83] An account will be rendered not only of evil, but also of good, and so he says: *Whether it is good or evil.* Thus, Psalm

---

[79]The Vulgate reads *Hoc est enim omnis homo* ("For this is the whole person").

[80]On p. 99 n. 1 QuarEd are correct in noting that the Vulgate reads *petit* ("ask") whereas Bonaventure has *requirit* ("require").

[81]On p. 99 n. 1 QuarEd rightly maintain that the Vulgate reads *Domino Deo tuo* ("the Lord your God") while Bonaventure has simply *Domino* ("the Lord").

[82]On p. 99 n. 1 QuarEd accurately indicate that the Vulgate does not read *Dei tui* ("your God").

[83]On p. 99 n. 2 QuarEd correctly state that the Vulgate has a different wording, which is translated: "But I tell you that every idle word that men and women speak, of them they will give an account on the day of judgment." Hugh of St. Cher, 105g also cites Matthew 12:36 and in a form similar to that of Bonaventure.

74:3 reads: "When I set aside a time, I will judge most justly." And furthermore, 2 Corinthians 5:10 says: "All of us must be manifested before the judgment seat of Christ." Therefore, Christ will judge everything, because Christ sees everything. And this is why he strongly exhorts us to fear God and to observe the commandments. In this way Ecclesiastes comes to the same conclusion as Boethius at the end of his *The Consolation of Philosophy*: "A great necessity of doing well is imposed on us, for we do all things in the sight of the judge who sees all things."[84]

THE END OF THE COMMENTARY ON ECCLESIASTES[85]

SCHOLION[86]

I. In writing this commentary, St. Bonaventure used the *Glossa Interlinearis* and *Glossa Ordinaria*, which are derived for the most part from Jerome's commentary on Ecclesiastes. He also used the actual commentary by Jerome and the commentary by Hugh of St. Victor, a work which, at least in the published editions, stops at Ecclesiastes 4:7. Bonaventure adopted Hugh of St. Victor's triple division of vanity as mutability, iniquity, and punishment. That Bonaventure also knew the *Expositio mystica in Ecclesiasten* by Salonius, Bishop of Vienna,[87] who flourished about 453, seems to be indicated by the reference cited by us, unless Bonaventure took his inter-

---

[84]See *Boethius, The Consolation of Philosophy*, trans. H. F. Stewart, LCL (London: Heinemann, 1918), 410-411. Bonaventure has adapted the text of Boethius to his purposes by eliminating the words *si dissimulare non uultis* ("if you will not dissemble"), by changing *vobis* ("upon you") to *nobis* ("upon us"), by adding a second cuncta ("all things"), and by changing *agitis* ("you do") to *agimus* ("we do").

[85]On p. 99 n. 4 QuarEd write: "At the end of E: This is the exposition of Ecclesiastes according to Brother Bonaventure. It is brilliantly done."

[86]On p. 99 QuarEd provide this commentary on Bonaventure's commentary on Ecclesiastes.

[87]See PL 53:993-1012.

pretation from other authors.[88] We have not found certain proof that Bonaventure used Alcuin and Rupert of Deutz, authors who in their expositions of Ecclesiastes closely followed Jerome.

In all other respects this work reflects the personal style of the Seraphic Doctor. Sometimes he uses other translations, especially those of Jerome and the Septuagint. He expounds the literal sense of the Vulgate by means of many parallel passages of Scripture, so that he might illustrate the meaning of the Scriptures by the Scriptures. After giving a rather long exposition of the literal sense, he often adds a brief explanation of the mystical or spiritual meaning. He also adds more than eighty questions arranged in a scholastic style in which he briefly and clearly resolves special difficulties concerning doctrine or the meaning of the more obscure passages.

II. The ingenious subtlety of the holy commentator is clear in the way he draws, distinguishes, and orders serious opinions from the words of Sacred Scripture. Many of the more recent commentators deny that a clear order and logical progression is to be found in this book. Whatever one may think of this interpretation, the true opinion of our author on the order he proposes for Ecclesiastes can be understood in the light of what he says in Collation 14 n. 5 of his *Collations on the Six Days*. There he discusses the organic, if I may use this term, order of Sacred Scripture or the difference that exists between the order of Sacred Scripture and the order of human books, for in human books the writer places one sentence after another sentence. He writes: "Some people believe that . . . these Scriptures were so composed that the person who wrote them merely placed one sentence after another. It is not

---

[88]The editors provide no cross-reference.

so, for Scripture is supremely orderly, and its order is similar to that of nature in the development of vegetation on earth."[89] – It is difficult to remember the large number of divisions and subdivisions within this text. Lest the reader become fatigued and confused, we have done our best to order the text by means of headings and subheadings as well as marginal notes.[90] We feel that it is neither superfluous nor distasteful to the reader that we have highlighted the large number of divisions and main arguments that are contained in the exposition of the literal sense. We have also provided four outlines.[91] Similar outlines are occasionally found in the margins of the codices of commentaries on Sacred Scripture.

---

[89]*Collations on the Six Days*, trans. José de Vinck, Works of Bonaventure V (Paterson, NJ: St. Anthony Guild Press, 1970), 201. See Opera Omnia 5:393.

[90]This annotated translation uses footnotes rather than marginal notes and has introduced additional headings and subheadings to ease the reader's passage through this wisdom text.

[91]On pp. 100-103 QuarEd provide their four outlines. This annotated translation does not reproduce these outlines, the last three of which are very detailed.

INDEX OF
SCRIPTURAL PASSAGES

This index reveals how well versed Bonaventure was in Sacred Writ. Attentive readers will discover that Bonaventure quotes most of the books of the Vulgate Bible.

Ecclesiastes

New Testament

Church Fathers,
Ecclesiastical Authors,
and Glossae

With few exceptions, this index is global and indicates the rich heritage upon which Bonaventure drew. The studious reader will need to explore each "source" of Bonaventure's exposition on its own terms.

Philosophers, Jurists, and Historians

This index points to non-ecclesiastical influences upon Bonaventure's thoughts. It is obvious that Aristotle was very influential in this commentary.